The Asbury Theological Seminary Series in World Christian Revitalization Movements

It is a rare opportunity for students of the Holiness and Pentecostal traditions in America to be presented with a study which fills a major gap in the life of Benjamin H Irwin, perhaps the key figure in the rise of the Fire Baptized Holiness and Pentecostal traditions. Its value as a research volume is enhanced by joining the engaging and now completed life narrative of Irwin provided by Vinson Synan with the anthology of sermons and addresses from Irwin, as collected and edited through the archival work of Daniel Woods. To them we are indebted for bringing this lost resource to light, and are pleased to be able to feature this in the context of studies in movements of Christian revitalization.

J. Steven O'Malley
General Editor
The Asbury Theological Seminary Studies in World Christian Revitalization

Sub-Series Foreword
Pentecostal and Charismatic Studies

Pentecostalism has, arguably, made the most significant impact on global Christianity of any movement to have emerged out of the renewal traditions. The beginning of the 20th century saw a theologically and spiritually distinctive tradition beginning to emerge in numerous centers around the world (India, Chile, and Korea, for example) but this revival erupted into an explosive movement as a result of the catalytic Azusa Street Revival in Los Angeles, California, in 1906. The Pentecostal movement became a global one from that time onward and within one hundred years it was widely acknowledged that Pentecostalism, including the related Charismatic and neo-Pentecostal movements, had become the fastest-growing movement within Christendom. It is now believed that there are an estimated 600 million adherents worldwide, representing 25% of all Christians. In North America, Europe, and especially in the majority world, Pentecostals are noted for their vibrant worship services, marked by lively music and preaching, charismatic manifestations, such as speaking in tongues (glossolalia) and prophetic speech, and for their belief in miracles, including healing.

Just prior to this 20th century explosion that we now know as Pentecostalism, a smaller-scale explosion took place in the Midwest and Southeastern United States. A seedbed for numerous radical and some not-so-radical new forms of Christianity, and even new religions, many religious leaders called for a restoration of New Testament forms of Christianity, seeing the nation's spirituality as bankrupt. But the 19th century America was also full of optimism and possibility; this was an age of progress and new scientific discovery. In an obscure small town in Nebraska, these two paradoxical arenas, primitive Christianity and science, came together in a radical form of Holiness, that is, Fire-Baptized Holiness, with its tales of multiple baptisms of fire, dynamite and beyond. The creative genius and evangelist behind this movement that spread like wildfire was a man the author of this volume calls a "sanctified rascal," Benjamin Hardin Irwin.

Until recently, little was known of Irwin other than the accounts of this brief period of revivalism that created in the hearts and minds of adherents the possibility of further works of the Spirit in the life of sanctified believers. Despite his very public moral failure, Irwin has been recognized as significant for this theological contribution: he set the stage for a new theological trajectory. Seminal Holiness-Pentecostal historian, Vinson Synan, first outlined this contribution in his ground-breaking *The Holiness-Pentecostal Movement*, published in 1971, revised as *The Holiness-Pentecostal Tradition* (1997). Now, in the first part of this new work, he has labored to fill in the gaps, before, during, and after Irwin's dynamic flash of influence, to produce the only full account of Irwin's life and ministry to date. Synan's former student, historian Dan Woods (Professor Emeritus, Ferrum College) has collected Irwin's own writings, now transcribed and edited as a collection for the second part of this volume. For students of the Holiness-Pentecostal movement, both its history and theological development, these two parts are a welcome addition to the ever-growing field of Pentecostal studies.

Both the biography written by Synan and the reader edited by Woods raise as many questions as they answer, however. As is revealed in this brief biography, in Irwin's own words, and especially in those of his second wife, Mary Jordan Irwin, whose letters are also included, this is the story of a troubled man, a man of extremes, whose legacy is, in the final analysis, a mixed bag. As difficult as it is to read and to try to make sense of, it is a necessary story and our struggling with it is essential. Salvation history is messy and not as straightforward and triumphant as popular stories of "Great Men" or "God's Generals" would sometimes have us believe. The renewing of global Christianity, the focus of this book series, is the story of the Spirit's work with, for, but sometimes in spite of the humans who lead and participate in it. This has always been the case and will likely always be so. But perhaps this account will serve to speak prophetically to this dynamic movement as it continues to explode around the world.

Kimberly Ervin Alexander, Sub-series Editor

Fire Baptized:
The Many Lives and Works of Benjamin Hardin Irwin

A Biography and a Reader

Written and Compiled by

Vinson Synan
and
Daniel Woods

The Asbury Theological Seminary Series in Pentecostal/Charismatic Studies

EMETH PRESS
www.emethpress.com

*Fire Baptized: The Many Lives and Works of Benjamin Hardin Irwin:
A Biography and a Reader*

Copyright © 2017
Printed in the United States of America on acid-free paper

All rights reserved. No part of this book may be reproduced, or stored in a retrieval system or transmitted in any form or by any means, electronic, mechanical, photocopying, recording, scanning or otherwise, except as permitted by the 1976 United States Copyright Act, or with the prior written permission of Emeth Press. Requests for permission should be addressed to: Emeth Press, P. O. Box 23961, Lexington, KY 40523-3961. http://www.emethpress.com.

Library of Congress Cataloging-in-Publication Data

Names: Synan, Vinson, 1934- author.
Title: Fire baptized : the many lives and works of Benjamin Hardin Irwin : a biography and a reader / written and compiled by Vinson Synan and Daniel Woods.
Description: Lexington : Emeth Press, 2017. | Series: Asbury theological seminary series in Pentecostal/Charismatic studies | Includes bibliographical references and index.
Identifiers: LCCN 2017031030 | ISBN 9781609471156 (alk. paper)
Subjects: LCSH: Irwin, Benjamin Hardin, b. 1854. | International Pentecostal Holiness Church--Biography. | International Pentecostal Holiness Church--History.
Classification: LCC BX8776.Z8 I79 2017 | DDC 289.9/4092 [B] --dc23
LC record available at https://lccn.loc.gov/2017031030

Front Cover Photo
Benjamin Hardin Irwin in 1906 with his son Vidalin

This book is lovingly dedicated to outstanding graduates of Emmanuel College who have become noted scholars and church leaders.

Daniel Woods
Jim Goff
Cheryl Bridges Johns
Doug Beacham
Tommy McGhee

Contents

Foreword xi
Preface xv

Section One by Vinson Synan

Chapter 1 Who Was Benjamin Hardin Irwin? 3
Chapter 2 Sanctified 15
Chapter 3 Fire Baptized 23
Chapter 4 A Whirlwind from the North 35
Chapter 5 A New Denomination 47
Chapter 6 Dynamite, Lyddite, and Oxidite 53
Chapter 7 Beniah, Tennessee 65
Chapter 8 Irwin Falls 77
Chapter 9 Irwin Becomes a Pentecostal 83
Chapter 10 Irwin as a Two Seed in the Spirit Predestinarian Baptist ... 91
Chapter 11 The Legacy of Benjamin Hardin Irwin 95
Bibliography 105

Section Two by Daniel Woods
Selected Irwin Reader

Before the Fire 115
The Fire Falls 131
Spreading the Fire 139
Organizing the Fire 161
Live Coals of Fire 167
After the Fire 233

Index 243

Foreword

For over a century Benjamin Hardin Irwin has been a shadowy figure in the history of late nineteenth century Holiness movements and early twentieth century Pentecostal movements in the United States. From writers such as J.H. King, we knew that in 1900 Irwin ignominiously left the movement he birthed, the Fire-Baptized Holiness Church. But beyond that, very little was known of the life of this enigmatic man. However, after years of research bolstered by the accessibility of numerous sources otherwise unknown and inaccessible, noted Pentecostal scholars Dr. Vinson Synan and Dr. Dan Woods have provided a rich study of Irwin and his writings.

Synan, who wrote the eleven-chapter biographical section of Irwin's life, rightfully titled this book, *Fire-Baptized: the Many Lives and Works of Benjamin Hardin Irwin*. And many lives it was! From small town lawyer to holiness preacher to denominational father, Synan, in his characteristic engaging writing, traces the steps of Irwin to when he publicly fell morally. Afterwards, Synan traces the sad and complicated life of Irwin as he worked his way through two marriages (at one time a bigamist), through an effort to regain spiritual restoration through the Azusa Street revival, to the sad account of a man whose grave is unknown, and to the tragic outcomes of the lives of his children.

Woods has provided an invaluable service to readers and scholars by collecting selected writings of Irwin from 1880 to the final entries of letters from his wife in 1925. Known as a poet and flowery writer, this collection is a great resource helping us better understand the complicated theological and personal journey of the oft-tormented Irwin.

Irwin's life is especially important to several Pentecostal denominations that continue serving Jesus Christ to this day. These include the Fire-Baptized Holiness Church of the Americas, the Church of God of Cleveland, Tennessee, and the International Pentecostal Holiness Church. For the Fire-Baptized Holiness Church of the Americas and the International Pentecostal Holiness Church, Irwin was particularly significant as we count him as one of our founding fathers. In spite of his moral failures, Irwin is recognized by these two groups as someone the Holy Spirit used in birthing our movements and certain understandings of Scripture.

In light of that truth, it is important to remember that in the publishing of this book in 2017, we are now in the five hundredth anniversary of the Protestant Reformation. As Martin Luther's reforms and later movement spread across Europe, and separation occurred between the Roman Catholic Church and reforming movements, Luther had to come to terms with the problem of ungodly leaders of the church and the efficacy of the ministries they performed. Related to Irwin, Dr. Synan addressed this in Chapter Eleven of this book. As part of this Foreword, Luther's words at one of his famous "Table Talks" in the summer or fall of 1532 are applicable to Irwin:

> One ought to think as follows about ministers. The office does not belong to Judas but to Christ alone. When Christ said to Judas, 'Go, baptize,' Christ was himself the baptizer and not Judas because the command comes from above even if it passes down through a stinking pipe. Nothing is taken from the office on account of the unworthiness of a minister.[1]

Thousands of people were impacted by the ministry of B.H. Irwin. They were truly saved, truly sanctified, truly baptized in the Holy Spirit and fire, truly healed, because God's Word is true. While our hearts break at the brokenness of Irwin's life, our confidence is not in men but in God alone. The Holy Spirit who inhabits and uses these earthen vessels, is still able to accomplish His salvific work through we flawed creatures. This is not an excuse for B.H. Irwin, or any of us. In fact, this important book about Irwin's life perfectly illustrates Paul's admonitions in 1 Corinthians 10:1-13, and 1 Timothy 5:20, 24. In many ways Synan and Woods have shown us the necessity of guarding our lives.

But not all is dark regarding Irwin. As you will discover, he was a well-read and gifted communicator, a man able to inspire, mobilize, and organize, a m an willing to reach over racial and geographical lines for the sake of the Gospel. He had a movement that covered much of the United States from Oklahoma east and northward into Canada. I've often thought that if he had remained a faithful servant of Christ, no doubt the history of my own movement would have been very different.

His theology, while having some ideas that were scripturally unsound, was nonetheless rooted in historic Christianity and provided a template for holiness denominations when the Azusa Street revival occurred. For nearly a century there were no known photographs of Benjamin Hardin Irwin. Only recently have photographs been discovered that are usable.

That is particularly important for the movement that Drs. Synan, Woods, and I represent, the International Pentecostal Holiness Church. On the wall of our denominational executive offices in Oklahoma City are photographs of each of our General Superintendents. Dr. Synan's father, the late Bishop J. A. Synan, is on that wall. We have decided to add Benjamin Hardin Irwin's photograph to that

---

[1] Luther's Works, *Table Talk*, Volume 54. Edited and Translated by Theodore G. Tappert. General Editor Helmut T. Lehmann (Philadelphia: Fortress Press, 1967) p. 47.

wall. We do so not without awareness of his flaws; but with greater awareness of our gratitude to God for what this man gave us. While we may be somewhat embarrassed or ashamed of Irwin's later life, we are, like the Apostle Paul, "not ashamed of the Gospel of Jesus Christ" because it is "by grace, we have been saved" (Romans 1:16; Ephesians 2:5). May Jesus Christ be praised!

Dr. A.D. Beacham, Jr.
General Superintendent and Presiding Bishop of the International Pentecostal Holiness Church

Preface

When I was a teenager I developed an interest in the history of the Holiness and Pentecostal Movements in America. Since my father, Joseph A. Synan, was the presiding Bishop of the Pentecostal Holiness Church, he had many books and documents in his library that I read through. To my great delight, he and I enjoyed many conversations on the histories of the different American Pentecostal movements. In the years that followed, to my surprise I learned that the Pentecostal churches were part of the fastest growing Christian movements in the world. I determined to learn as much as possible about Pentecostalism as I went on to college. History was my favorite subject from my grammar school days and all the way through college and graduate school. It was my joy to have such history professors as Dr. Cub Melton at Emmanuel College and Doctors Charles Wynes and Horace Montgomery at the University of Georgia. It was Montgomery, a Unitarian deacon, who encouraged me to write my dissertation on American Pentecostalism which was published in 1971 under the title, *The Holiness-Pentecostal Movement in the United States.*

While researching for that work, I first learned about Benjamin Hardin Irwin, founder of the Fire-Baptized Holiness Church, a group that became part of my own church through a merger in 1911. Through several sources, I was able to write a chapter in my dissertation titled, "The Fire-Baptized Way." Although I learned a great deal about the middle portion of Irwin's life, I never knew much about his early yearsand especially missing was any information about the latter part of his life. Much about Irwin remained a mystery to me for the next fifty years. I knew that he was a dynamic Holiness preacher and founder of the most radical Holiness denomination thatwent on to become an important precursor of the Pentecostal movement. I knew that he led his followers into what he called the "baptism of fire," followed by other "baptisms" he called "dynamite," "lyddite," and "oxidite." I also knew that during this time he led a double life and finally fell into "open and gross sin" as described by Joseph Campbell in his *History of the Pentecostal Holiness Church.* I also knew that in 1900 Irwin resigned from the leadership of the church he had founded. For decades this was all I knew.

I learned more when Dr. Charles Jones, the great bibliographer of the Holiness and Pentecostal Movements, handed me a full run copy of Irwin's paper called *Live Coals of Fire*. I also purchased a reprint copy of William Seymour's paper sent out from Azusa Street titled, *The Apostolic Faith*. To my surprise, Benjamin Irwin sent in a testimony in 1907 stating that he had spoken in tongues and was now a Pentecostal believer and preacher. For several years that was all I knew about him. I never saw a photo of him or learned when or where he died. He was a mystery and an enigma to me and to other researchers.

Then, to my utter amazement, in just two weeks in 2013, I learned the rest of Irwin's story from two men I had never met. They were Dr. John Crowley, a professor at Valdosta State University in Georgia and Joseph Gainey from Winthrop University in South Carolina. Crowley was an authority on the Primitive Baptist tradition as seen in his book *Primitive Baptists of the Wiregrass South: 1815 to the Present,* while Gainey was a learned member of the Wesleyan Methodist Church and a librarian at Winthrop University. From them I learned about Irwin's connection with the Wesleyan Methodist Church in the 1890s and his ultimate return to his Primitive Baptist roots. Crowley also documented his final membership in the Two-Seed-in-the-Spirit Predestinarian Baptist Church in the 1920s. Above all, they gave me three photographs of Irwin so I could see what he looked like for the first time. Sometime later I also learned through Charles Jones the date and place of his death in Palestine, Texas, in January of 1927. I am greatly indebted to Crowley, Gainey, and Jones for their help in completing this book.

After these discoveries, in 2014 I was invited by Karen Lucas to speak to a gathering of church archivists in the historic camp meeting town of Falcon, North Carolina. Lucas is the archivist for the North Carolina Conference of the Pentecostal Holiness Church. We agreed to make this a symposium on Irwin and to invite other scholars to participate. In addition to Crowley and Gainey, Dr. Dan Woods, pastor of the Falcon church, Dr. Stan York, and Dr. Danny Rollins contributed to the sessions. The paper I prepared for Falcon was later delivered to the Society for Pentecostal Studies at Southeastern University in Lakeland, Florida, in 2015. In planning the book, I became convinced that it should have two sections, the first a full length biography of Irwin that I would write, and the second, an anthology of Irwin's major articles and sermons that Dr. Woods had been collecting. So after much collaboration in research and writing the book now appears under the title: *The Many Lives of Benjamin Hardin Irwin*.

In many ways this has been the most difficult book that I have ever written due to the dissolute life that Irwin led while carrying on a dynamic and charismatic ministry as a Holiness evangelist. I even pondered naming the book, *B. H. Irwin: the Sanctified Rascal*, but my better nature prevailed and I decided not to do so. Yet Irwin posed a challenge that had to be faced in this book, i.e. how could a man living a secret sinful double life contrary to what he was preaching and what the Bible so clearly condemns be so successful in winning converts, healing the sick, and planting churches? This is a problem that has plagued Christianity from the days of Judas Iscariot to the present day. I have attempted to face this vexing problem in writing this book. The last chapter in which I refer to the Donatist controversy is my answer. It is not the minister, but the message that brings salvation and healing.

I give special honor and thanks to Dan Woods, my former student at Emmanuel College who is an able historian in his own right, for being my colleague on this project. He helped in more ways than I can number in producing his book. His son, Danny worked long hours to transcribe many of the documents in the "Select Irwin Reader" in Part Two of the book. My wife Carol Lee, as usual, did a masterful job of editing the manuscript. I also thank Dr. Kim Alexander of Regent University for her encouragement and success in having the book published under the auspices of Asbury University and Emeth Press. I also salute another of my Emmanuel students, Dr. Bishop Douglas Beacham, for writing the Introduction.

In the end my prayer is that I have been fair to Benjamin Hardin Irwin, a man with many spectacular gifts who accomplished much in life despite his many weaknesses and failures. May his life be a warning to others.

Vinson Synan (Ph.D. University of Georgia)
Dean Emeritus, Regent University School of Divinity
Interim Dean, Oral Roberts University School of Theology and Missions

My fascination with the subject of this book began in an Emmanuel College classroom during the Spring of 1973. The course, titled "The Holiness-Pentecostal Movement," made me want to be an academic and birthed in me a desire to uncover more of the history of the Pentecostal Holiness Church. Early in the course Professor Vinson Synan told us the story—as compelling as it was fragmented—of Rev. Benjamin Hardin Irwin: flashing on the scene as the charismatic promoter of a "third blessing" about 1895, founding the Fire-Baptized Holiness Association in 1898, falling mysteriously from grace in early 1900, briefly reappearing to embrace the Pentecostal message of the Azusa Revival in 1907, and then disappearing again almost immediately. So much fire, yet so little certainty. His influence on the emergence of the Pentecostal Movement was undeniable, yet only five or six years of his story were visible to us. No photographs. No date of death. No descendants to interview. A mystery laid in the very foundation of our church.

I still remember Dr. Synan looking across the classroom one afternoon and saying, "Maybe one of you will be the person to find out more about this mysterious man." That comment seeded my soul. I eventually decided to devote myself to finding out as much as I could about Irwin and many of the other people who played vital roles in the early Pentecostal Movement. Therefore, the first debt I need to acknowledge is to Dr. Vinson Synan, who told our movement's history in a way that excited me about the past and the future, and who persuaded me by his words and his example that I could enhance that story through research, writing, teaching and preaching. He has been the quintessential mentor to me.

Friends have also helped me along the way. Rev. Wade H. Phillips, Rev. Karen H. Lucas, and Dr. H. Stanley York, in particular, have been willing to share their research and listen at length to my often tortured musings on Irwin's genius and depravity, his insatiable spiritual passion and his unquenchable physical lust, the need to remember him and the need to forget him. I distinctly recall how Stan helped me come to terms with my ambivalence toward Irwin while I was trying to complete my section of this book: "Dan, you seem to be saying that most of what is good in our Pentecostal Holiness heritage has its beginnings in Irwin, and at the same time most of what is bad does too." Exactly. I am so thankful for friends who listen and bring clarity to my thinking.

Several colleagues have helped facilitate this work. Special thanks are due to Cheryl Hundley, Interlibrary Loan specialist at Ferrum College's Stanley Library, and George W. Loveland, formerly Director of the Stanley Library and now Director of Barton University's Hackney Library. Both have searched far and wide to secure rare books and periodicals for me. And when they found them, both Cheryl and George were as genuinely happy as I was.

My family has helped too. I want to thank my wife Gwendolyn Kestner Woods for living with my obsession with Irwin and so many others, for listening to my latest discovery or theory, and for taking our vacation in places like Wilmore, Kentucky, and Cleveland, Tennessee, when other couples were off to the beach. (Sometimes we even took a carload of children with us on these "research getaways.") I also want to thank our youngest child Danny for working countless hours helping to transcribe hundreds of sheets of third and fourth generation photocopies of unevenly photographed microfilm of newspapers and religious periodicals. He often strained his eyes and his back in pursuit of Irwin's words. And along the way, he developed his own uneasy relationship with the Fire-Baptized founder, leading to many long talks between us about ministry and marriage and morality. My hope is that reading B. H. Irwin's life story, and considering his words in light of his actions, will prove as fruitful for the readers of this volume.

Daniel Woods (Ph.D., University of Mississippi)
Pastor of Culbreth Memorial Pentecostal Holiness Church, Falcon NC
Professor Emeritus, Ferrum College, Ferrum VA

Benjamin Hardin Irwin in 1906 with his son Vidalin

Chapter One

Who Was Benjamin Hardin Irwin?

"I do not remember a time when I had no regard for the Old Baptists; my parents and grandparents were Baptists. From my earliest recollection I have been associated with Baptist people. I always delighted to go with father and mother to meetings. I looked upon the solemn worship of God with reverence and awe."

B. H. Irwin

One of the most elusive figures in recent American religious history is Benjamin Hardin Irwin, a major mover and shaker in the Holiness movement of the late Nineteenth Century. He is known mainly as the founder of the Fire-Baptized Holiness Church which taught a "third blessing" after sanctification which Irwin called the "baptism in the Holy Ghost and fire." His movement served as a major bridge between the American Holiness and Pentecostal movements. For some reason Irwin has not been given due recognition by general historians of American religion. His life and ministry have been of interest mainly to historians of the Holiness and Pentecostal movements, but he deserves more recognition in the larger academy than he has received in the past. A man of many gifts and weaknesses, Irwin was in one person a lawyer, a spellbinding preacher, a student of theology, a poet, a brilliant writer, a bigamist, and a church founder. Described as a tall and handsome man with a clarion voice, he possessed a charismatic personality that drew large crowds to hear him preach and was blessed with organizing skills that drew talented people to help him create his new denomination. At the same time he struggled throughout his life with character flaws that ultimately caused his downfall and prevented him from becoming one of the most striking leaders in American church history.

From the earliest days, Pentecostal historians have recognized Irwin's movement as an important step towards Pentecostalism. These include Klaud

Kendrick in his *The Promise Fulfilled*, Carl Brumback in his *Suddenly... from Heaven*, John Nichol in his *Pentecostalism*, and Joseph Campbell in his *The Pentecostal Holiness Church 1898-1948*. Most Pentecostal historians became aware of Irwin through reading Campbell's book[1] which was based on a series of articles by Joseph H. King and George Floyd Taylor in the *Pentecostal Holiness Advocate* in 1921 and 1930 as well as personal interviews Campbell conducted with people who knew Irwin personally.[2] Another source was J.H. King's autobiography *Yet Speaketh: Memoirs of the Late Bishop Joseph H. King* which told much of Irwin's story as recalled by a contemporary observer and colleague of Irwin.[3]

Brumback acknowledged the importance of Irwin's influence in the Holiness Movement when he said: "the great majority of the Pentecostal believers were firm adherents of the second definite work of grace, having adopted the position of the Fire-Baptized Holiness group, founded by B. H. Irwin, who taught that there were three definite experiences: the new birth, sanctification, and the "baptism of fire...."[4] Nichol said: "the Fire-Baptized Holiness Church was formed in the 1890s through the efforts of Benjamin Hardin Irwin, a lawyer turned Holiness preacher who popularized the teaching that there was a religious experience beyond salvation and sanctification, namely a 'baptism of fire'."[5] Perhaps the most important recognition was that of Kendrick who said of Irwin:

> Certain persons connected with the (Holiness) movement went even further and advocated three "experiences" instead of two. The Rev. B. H. Irwin, while in the Holiness ministry, made a careful study of Methodist theology. In the works of John Fletcher, an early Wesleyan writer, he discovered the teaching of some sort of experience beyond sanctification which was described as a "baptism of burning love." Eventually Irwin sought for and claimed to have received this "third blessing." Subsequently Holiness circles became familiar with the new doctrine of the "baptism of fire...." The tenets of the Pentecostals were very similar to those of (Irwin's) own group. Both taught that the baptism in the Holy Spirit occurred after the experience of sanctification, the only difference being in what they regarded as evidence of the experience–the Pentecostals believed that it was "tongues," the Fire-Baptized folk, physical demonstrations.[6]

The idea that the baptism in the Holy Ghost and fire is an experience separate from and subsequent to both regeneration and sanctification is the most important contribution of Irwin's movement. This later became the basic foundation of the worldwide Pentecostal movement with the single addition of glossolalia as the "initial evidence" of the third blessing. This means that Benjamin Hardin Irwin is a major figure in the history of both the Holiness and Pentecostal movements. Although ignored or denounced by most early Holiness historians, Irwin has been and continues to be of major interest to those interested in Holiness and Pentecostal history. For instance, Melvin Dieter in his *The Holiness Revival of the Nineteenth Century*, an examination of the teachings and contributions of prominent Holiness leaders, makes no mention of Irwin.[7] However, more recent Methodist and Holiness historians have begun to recognize the importance of Irwin in their own tradition. One of the first of these was the Methodist historian Henry H. Knight in his book *From Aldersgate to Azusa Street: Wesleyan,*

Holiness, and Pentecostal visions of the New Creation. In reference to Irwin, he wrote:

> There were those who spoke of receiving two blessings following conversion. The first was entire sanctification which conveyed holiness, and following that was the baptism of the Holy Spirit, or the "fire baptism," which was an enduement of power. The fire-baptized movement became a distinct and growing form of holiness radicalism. Although he was not the first to propose the doctrine, Benjamin H. Irwin, who was himself influenced by the theology of John Fletcher, institutionalized it in 1875 [sic] the Fire Baptized Holiness Church. Irwin ultimately developed a theology of six distinct blessings, but it was the three blessing theology that began to spread through parts of the holiness movement.[8]

Prominent Nazarene historian Randall Stephens gave more attention to Irwin than any other Holiness writer in his book *The Fire Spreads: Holiness and Pentecostalism in the American South.* In this work he saw in Irwin a seminal figure in the holiness movement trend towards Pentecostalism. He wrote: "the former Baptist itinerant preacher in the Midwest took the notions of spiritual gifts even further than his holiness predecessors. B. H. Irwin, born in Mercer County, Missouri, and based in Iowa, accepted the Wesleyan message in the early 1890s. Irwin received what he called his 'baptism of fire' at Enid in Oklahoma in October 1895. After which he convened a national meeting in Anderson, South Carolina, to establish a more structured denomination." He further summarized the importance of Irwin's Fire-Baptized Holiness movement when he said:

> The Fire-Baptized Holiness Association had gained its greatest following in the South. And though its influence waned after Irwin's professional demise, the radical sect's impact on the region was profound. Swept away by speculations about the latter days and entranced by the possibility further works of the Spirit, numbers of southern holiness people, even those who did not join the Fire-Baptized fold, were now more than ever predisposed to radicalism.... The movement at this time was a "pre-Pentecostal tinderbox awaiting the spark that would set it off." It certainly seemed an auspicious age to southern enthusiasts.[9]

The Holiness-Pentecostal Movement in the United States, published in 1971, introduced Irwin to the wider Christian world. In a chapter titled "The Fire Baptized Way" Irwin and his movement are portrayed as the most important transitional force leading to the beginning of Pentecostalism in the United States.[10]

Early Life

Benjamin Hardin Irwin was born on the American frontier in Mercer County, Missouri, on January 23, 1854. He came from a long line of Irwins who had their roots in Northern Ireland. About his family history, Irwin wrote:

> My great grandfather's name was James Irwin. He had a son whose name was John Irwin. This James Irwin was my great grandfather. He was born somewhere

in the north of Ireland and not far from the beginning of the Eighteenth Century. My father who was au fait in the matter of family history is my authority for these facts. My great grandfather, John Irwin, emigrated [sic] from the North of Ireland to Augusta County, Virginia in the year of our Lord 1740. He married Margaret McFarland by whom he had nine children. [11]

From these roots, it can be assumed that the Irwins were Protestant Scotch-Irish, probably Presbyterians, who joined in the great migration to America and settled on the Appalachian frontier before moving on to the more western frontiers of the new nation. In perusing the extensive genealogy that Benjamin Irwin wrote about his family in 1918, it seems that some of the Irwins moved on to Kentucky, Tennessee, and Indiana before his branch of the family migrated to Missouri in the 1850s. The family tree shows that the Irwins were generally middle class people with some who were lawyers, druggists, teachers, and preachers. When the Civil war raged, several of the Irwin men from Tennessee served in the Confederate army with two, John Sevier Irwin, and James W. Irwin serving at the rank of captain. Later two Irwins, Brown Irwin and James' son Rowan Irwin, served as District Attorneys in California.[12]

The Irwins were generally quite religious and joined several different Protestant denominations wherever they went. In his genealogy Benjamin carefully noted that his uncle Isaac Irwin was a Primitive Baptist minister as was his uncle Charles Irwin. A cousin Lewis Irwin was listed as a "Missionary Baptist preacher" while another cousin Hardin was listed as "a Holiness preacher living in Alberta, Canada." Finally, Benjamin lists himself as a "teacher, writer, and Holiness preacher." The Tennessee Irwins were prominent in the Southern Methodist Church while one, John Irwin, was listed as a "Blue Stocking" Presbyterian while James Irwin, "a prominent member of the Southern Methodist Church," was also a "Freemason and Knight Templar" who served as a "Grand Master of the Grand Lodge of the Masons of Tenneesee."[13]

Benjamin Hardin Irwin was one of eight children born to Hardin and Hetty Irwin who were first cousins. Of the eight, two, James Thompson and Joseph Lewis, were born in Putnam County, Indiana, where many Irwins had settled. It is not clear where the other siblings were born. However, in the early 1850s, the family moved to Missouri where Benjamin Hardin Irwin was born in Mercer County on January 22, 1854.[14] Benjamin Irwin's youth was spent in Tecumseh, Nebraska, where his family moved in 1863 in a covered wagon.

Tecumseh was a relatively new town that was founded in 1856. So it was still rather new when the Irwins moved there. And Tecumseh struggled greatly until the railroad came through in 1872. This would have expanded 18 year old Benjamin's horizons and hopes. The fact that Tecumseh (though small) was the county seat of Johnson County and the coming of the railroad may have influenced his choice in his late teens to read law (though it bored him). Other than physical labor and merchandizing, what else might he have done to make a living? His father was a farmer and it can be assumed that young Benjamin did chores around the farm in his younger years.[15]

Irwin as a Primitive Baptist

Benjamin was raised in an ultra-conservative "old hard shell Baptist Church."[16] Of his religious upbringing he remarked in 1880, "I do not remember a time when I had no regard for the Old Baptists; my parents and grandparents were Baptists. From my earliest recollection I have been associated with Baptist people. I always delighted to go with father and mother to meetings. I looked upon the solemn worship of God with reverence and awe." He often wept while listening to sermons. He said of his father "He is a firm believer in the doctrine and practice of the Predestinarian Baptists and has an experience going back over fifty years."[17]

These "Old Baptist Churches" were more widely known as "Primitive Baptist" churches. One of his uncles, Isaac, a Primitive Baptist minister, had a profound influence on young Irwin's life. This denomination separated from the "regular" and "separatist" Baptists from 1820 to 1845 over the question of sending missionaries through organized Baptist mission boards. Those who objected were motivated by their predestinarian belief that everyone was already elected to be saved or lost and therefore needed no missionaries to go out to evangelize the heathen since their fate was already sealed "before the foundation of the earth." Other new trends such as the organization of temperance societies and Bible societies, requiring co-operation between churches were anathema to Primitives who valued their sovereign congregational government. The mainstream Baptists, including the American Baptist Church and the Southern Baptist Church, were thenceforth called "Missionary Baptists."[18]

In time other issues were added that made the primitive Baptists quite distinct from mainstream Baptists. These included: plain church buildings, no musical instruments in worship, footwashing as an ordinance, no Sunday schools ("family worship" was encouraged), and no theological seminaries or trained pastors. In addition to these differences, Primitive Baptists held tightly to five-point Calvinism although they refused to call themselves Calvinists, claiming to be descended directly from the New Testament Church with no ties to the Protestant Reformation.[19]

The most extreme branch of the Primitive Baptists was a very small group known as the "Two-Seed-in-the-Spirit Predestinarian Baptists" founded by Daniel Parker who was one of the first to speak out against the missions movement among Baptists. In 1820, he published a booklet called *A Public Address to the Baptist Society* in which he denounced the Baptist Board of Foreign Missions in Philadelphia. He later formed his own "two-seed" Baptist church which became the most ultra-Calvinist denomination in history. Some said that he was more Calvinist than Calvin himself! In his church, the two seeds were the elect "Good seed" of God and the non-elect "Bad seed" of Satan. The Two-Seed-in–the-Spirit Predestinarian Baptist Church never grew beyond a few churches with most of them located in Texas.[20]

In contrast to the two seeders and most other Baptists stood the "Free Will Baptist" Church which rejected Calvinism outright and embraced Arminian theology. Free Will Baptists believed in free grace, free salvation, and free will.

Their earliest roots were with the Regular Baptists who had already rejected strict Calvinism and opted for a more basic Arminian theology. American Free Will Baptists began in North Carolina under Paul Palmer in 1727 and later in New Hampshire under the leadership of Benjamin Randall in 1780. Free Will Baptists subsequently spread around the nation and eventually found its largest reception in the South and Midwest.[21]

Out of these major Baptist streams, Benjamin Irwin was raised among one the strictest branches of the faith, the "Old Baptists" or the "Primitive Baptists" as they were more widely known. After years of sitting under the strict fire and brimstone preaching of his Primitive Baptist pastors, Benjamin spent years in spiritual despair. In an article sent to the Primitive Baptist periodical *Signs of the Times: Devoted to the Old School Baptist Cause* in 1880 he told of his desperate spiritual condition:

> But it was in February 1871, when I was in my eighteenth year that I hope I was made to know and feel that I was a sinner. It seemed to me that I was the vilest wretch on earth. My sins against God rose up against me in fearful magnitude and number; they bore me down and crushed me under their awful weight. I was then living with my father, three miles south of Tecumseh, Nebraska. Brother George and I had been to that place, and were going to a dance that night, about two miles east of father's. We came to the valley of the Nemeha, and as we walked upon the creaking snow, and the myriad stars that shone in splendor above us...I saw the awful depth of my wicked heart, and learned that...my heart was desperately wicked and deceitful above all things.[22]

Soon afterwards, he went through a period where he "determined to become an infidel." Reading the works of Byron, Moore and Shelly, he said "I formed association of friendship with the leading infidels of the country." During this time he also immersed himself in reading John S. Mill, Herbert Spencer, Darwin, House and Paine. Also during this period of infidelity he lived on his father's farm and did odd jobs, tending his father's cattle and for a time working in a stone quarry. Here he learned the power of dynamite from first-hand experience. He also and read widely, studied botany, learned shorthand, and began the study of law.[23]

He then decided to become a lawyer and devoted himself to reading for the bar exam. He said of this time, "nothing was so irksome to me as the dull pages of Blackstone." Yet he persevered, was admitted to the bar, and began to practice law in the town of Tecumseh.[24] Here he maintained a mediocre law practice for eight years. In 1876, he married Anna M. Stewart. Together they had one daughter named Maud Irwin who was born in April of 1876 and one son, Stewart Toombs Irwin, born in August 1877 who was to help him in ministry in later years.

In 1879 he experienced a vivid conversion after years of reckless living mainly due to excessive drunkenness. He said of this period in his life, "I was the most wicked man in all that country." He also added: "When I was reclaimed I had sinned against God in many ways. I had sinned against my family and my neighbors, had cheated and wronged men in many ways...I used to come home drunk and abuse my wife and children, and had to ask them to forgive me...I used to lie — seemed to be a born liar. I used to lie to my parents, my brothers and sisters and everybody. It used to be a habit."[25]

Irwin's Conversion

After a long period of depression and conviction for his sins, he was converted in a Primitive Baptist church. In his usual florid language, he described his conversion eight years later: "I know when I got converted. I was there...my conversion made me wonderfully happy." It happened on Friday the 21st of April, 1879. He reflected:

> I saw myself a vile, wicked, corrupt, loathsome, condemned worm of the dust. I had been stricken down upon the road of sin. The whole head was sick, and the whole heart was faint. There was no soundness in me, but wounds and bruises and putrefying sores; they had not been closed…The long years of conviction and bondage had all expired. The first born smitten, and the angel of God's presence was there. The blood of the Pascal lamb, that taketh away the sins of the world that had been sprinkled on the lintel and the door posts of the door, and the destroying angel had passed over! It is with rapture that I speak of this. I called to God in my affliction and he answered me. "He brought me to his banqueting house, and his banner over me was love. I sat down under his shadow with great delight, and his fruit was sweet to my taste." It was on Friday the 21 of April, 1879. I was riding alone on the wide prairie, meditating on the power and justice of God, and mourning on account of my sins against the light and knowledge. Oh the anguish of my soul! The heavy burden that I then bore pressed me down to the earth, and I implored the heavenly master to have mercy on me. And there, where no ear could hear and no eye could see, save the Almighty one, the holy spirit of truth came to me, and removed the dark cloud and the heavy burden that had hung over me so long, and carried my burden into a land not inhabited—into the wilderness of forgetfulness.[26]

Later he remembered that:

> I went home that night, but did not sleep much. I was relieved from a great burden, and felt like one who had been liberated from a long imprisonment. Everything seemed to smile approbation upon me. I was a new creature; old things had passed away, and all things had become new. Joy inexpressible was mine. No language can ever express that sweet salvation and ease of mind that I then enjoyed. But I told no one; I only intimated to my wife "that another great burden was removed," but she understood it to have reference to the past week of school.[27]

This peace of mind remained for several days, "and it was worth more to me than all my life had been. Joy inexpressible was mine." But he told no one, not even his wife. A short time later, he went back to the Primitive Baptist Church where he responded to an altar call with "tears and sobs." The next week he was baptized in water by immersion in a river by his uncle Isaac A. Irwin who was pastor of the church. After this experience, Irwin confessed his sins and made restitution to his family, to his friends that he had cheated, and paid his debts to the bar where he bought his liquor. When he apologized on the streets, one man cursed him, while another wept and forgave him.[28]

For the next several years Irwin practiced law in Tecumseh and moved his membership to the First Baptist Church of Tecumseh, a member of the American Baptist Convention. Thus, he left the Primitive "predestinarian" Baptists American Baptists "Missionary Baptists," therefore more "liberal" and acceptable to the good people of Tecumseh, especially his well-to-do clients. For over a decade Irwin was a faithful member of First Baptist while maintaining a mediocre law practice. In 1888 he was appointed as the "collector" of unpaid pledges by the church trustees.[29]

About this time, Irwin felt a call to preach and soon began studying for the ministry. On August 4, 1888 he applied for a license to preach in First Baptist, his home church. The process did not go well. After a motion was made "to grant Bro. B. H. Irwin a license to preach the Gospel," the motion was tabled, and was tabled again in November. There were definite reasons for the reservations and delays by the church members. The church minutes for January 5, 1889 explained: "Bro. B. Irwin made an acknowledgement of wrong doing [sic] asking forgiveness, which upon motion was freely granted." Although the nature of the "wrong doing" was not revealed, Irwin was denied his request for licensure, and although the church was without a pastor at the time, Irwin was not called on to preach.[30]

Subsequently, Irwin transferred his membership to the Mt. Zion Baptist Church north of town. He then applied for ordination to preach there which was granted on April 6, 1889. When the folks at First Baptist were invited to attend Irwin's ordination, the board demurred, adopting the following resolution: "Whereas, this church has been invited to send delegates to meet in council with the Mt. Zion Church, for the purpose of considering the expediency of ordaining Bro. B. H. Irwin to the work of the Gospel ministry, and Whereas the brethren chosen to represent this church upon this subject, be it therefore Resolved: That it is the sense of the church that the interest of all parties concerned, make such ordination inexpedient."[31] Evidently, the members of first Baptist knew the nature of Irwin's failures and felt that he was unqualified for ministry. Despite these reservations and objections, the record shows that "he was ordained a minister of the Baptist Church" at Mt Zion Baptist Church north of town probably on April 6, 1889.[32] Even after his vivid conversion and his ordination to the ministry, Irwin continued to have spiritual struggles that festered in his soul. This was expressed in a poem he published in *Signs of the Times,* while visiting relatives in Indiana:

Is There No Balm in Giliad?

The road I travel here below
Is lonesome, dark and drear; Bleak
wintry winds around me blow, And
darksome clouds appear.

Dull clouds of grief and sorrow fly
Across my aching breast

>   And fill my soul with agony,
>   With wild and weird unrest.
>
>   But through the clouds of earth I view
>   The distant stars that move
>   In silence and grandeur through
>   The shoreless realms above;
>
>   And read, on heaven's page sublime,
>   In characters of gold,
>   A truth that ne'er in prose nor rhyme
>   By mortal man was told
>
>   But still beyond the stars there lies
>   A land of joy and peace,
>   Where saints redeem'd from earth shall rise
>   When this vain world shall cease.
>
>   For that eternal world I mourn,
>   And long to be at rest;
>   But oh how cruel is the thorn
>   That fosters in my breast.
>
>   For my complaint there is no balm,
>   Until my change shall come;
>   And then, in heaven's eternal calm,
>   I'll be with Christ at home.

Ben H. Irwin
Lena, Ind., Nov 7, 1879 [33]

    This poem not only demonstrated Irwin's gifts as a writer and poet, but also indicated a depressed and even defeated state of his personal spirituality. He was "lonesome, dark and drear" with "clouds of grief and sorrow" coupled with a "wild and weird unrest." Although he saw some ultimate hope, he said "for my complaint there is no balm, until my change shall come."

    That "change" was just what the fast-growing Holiness movement offered to such defeated souls. It was only a matter of time before the restless Baptist preacher would discover the preachers of the Iowa Holiness Association who preached a message of victory over sin through the "second blessing" of entire sanctification as taught by John Wesley.

Notes

[1] Joseph H. Campbell, *the Pentecostal Holiness Church, 1898–1948* (Franklin Springs, GA: The Publishing House of the Pentecostal Holiness Church, 1951).

[2] Joseph H. King, "History of the Fire Baptized Holiness Church," *The Pentecostal Holiness Advocate*, March, 24, 1921, pp. 4–5; George Floyd Taylor, *The Pentecostal Holiness Advocate*, May 2, 1930, p. 8; Campbell, *The Pentecostal Holiness Church: 1898–1948*, pp. 193–215.

[3] Joseph H., and Blanch Leon King, *Yet Speaketh: Memoirs of the Late Bishop Joseph H. King* (Franklin Springs, GA: Publishing House of the Pentecostal Holiness Church, 1949), pp. 77–103. See following footnotes for bibliographical citations.

[4] Carl Brumback, *Suddenly...From Heaven* (Springfield, Missouri: Gospel Press, 1959), pp. 8, 99.

[5] John Nichol, *Pentecostalism* (New York: Harper and Row, 1966), pp. 55,104.

[6] Klaud Kendrick, *The Promise Fulfilled* (Springfield, MO: Gospel Press, 1959), pp. 33, 177–182.

[7] See Melvin Dieter, *The Holiness Revival of the Nineteenth Century* (Metuchen, NJ: Scarecrow Press, 1980).

[8] Henry H. Knight, *From Aldersgate to Azusa Street: Wesleyan, Holiness, and Pentecostal Visions of the New Creation* (Eugene, OR: Pickwick Publications, 2010), pp. 199–200; See Melvin Dieter, *The Holiness Revival of the Nineteenth Century*.

[9] Randall Stephens, *The Fire Spreads: Holiness and Pentecostalism in the American South* (Cambridge, MA: Harvard University Press, 2008), pp. 178–189.

[10] See Vinson Synan, *Holiness-Pentecostal Movement in the United States* (Grand Rapids, MI: Wm. E. Eerdmans Publishing Company, 1971), pp. 55–76.

[11] B. H. Irwin, "Some Facts, Dates, Etc. In Our Family History" in John Hugh McDowell, *History of the McDowells and Connection* (Memphis: C. B. Johnston, 1918), pp. 562–564. Irwin seemed to have several great grandfathers.

[12] Ibid, pp. 561–562.

[13] Ibid.

[14] Ibid, p. 563.

[15] Dan Woods, personal interview with the author on September 30, 2015.

[16] This was in Irwin's paper, *Live Coals of Fire*, June 1, 1900, p. 2.

[17] This appeared in the Primitive Baptist magazine *Signs of the Times: Devoted to the Old School Baptist Cause* (April 15, 1880): pp. 86–89.

[18] The best source on Primitive Baptists is John G. Crowley's *Primitive Baptists of the Wiregrass South: 1815 to the Present* (Gainesville: University of Florida Press, 1998), pp. 1–54.

[19] Ibid, pp. 55–85. Also see Bertram Wynn-Brown, "The Antimission Movement in the Jacksonian South: A Study in Regional Folk Culture." *Journal of Southern History* Vol. 36, No 4. (November, 1970), pp. 501–529.

[20] See Crowley, pp.118–121. Also see Elmer Clark, *The Small Sects in America* (Nashville, TN: Cokesbury Press, 1937), p. 249.

[21] William F. Davidson, *The Free Will Baptists in History*, 2nd edition (Albany, GA: Randall House, February 20, 2001). Also see chapter one in Howard Dorgan's *Giving Glory to God in Appalachia: Worship Practices of Six Baptist Subdenominations* (University of Tennessee Press, 1987). The chapter is titled "Baptists, Baptists, and More Baptists" and differentiates these six central Appalachian groups: Regular, Primitive, Old Regular, Union, Free Will, & Missionary Baptists.

[22] B. H. Irwin, "The Sword of the Lord and of Gideon," *Signs of the Times: Devoted to the Old School Baptist Cause* (April 15, 1880), pp. 86–89. For the full account see Dan Woods, *Document 1* in the "Irwin Reader" in Part II.

[23] Irwin, "Editorial Correspondence," *Live Coals of Fire*, January 20, 1899, p. 1; *Live Coals of Fire*, January 26, 1900, p. 2.

[24] John G. Crowley, *Primitive Baptists of the Wiregrass South*, pp. 1–54.

[25] Also see B. H. Irwin, "Repentance and Confession," *Live Coals of Fire*, June 15, 1900, p. 2. This was largely copied from his prior articles in *Signs of the Times*.

[26] Ibid.

[27] Ibid.

[28] Ibid.

[29] Jim Kerwin, "Isaiah Reid (1836–1911), His Life Leadership, and Influence in the American Holiness Movement" (Unpublished MA thesis, Regent University, 2006), p. 182. Also see Hugh and Geraldine Staver, compilers, *First Baptist Church, Tecumseh, Nebraska 125th; 1868–1993, Grounded and Growing* (Tecumseh, NE: First Baptist Church of Tecumseh, Nebraska. 1993), p. 65 which lists Irwin as a member.

[30] Ibid. p. 183.

[31] Ibid.

[32] Ibid. Perhaps the reason the church refused to ordain Irwin was that his marriage to Anna and the birth of Maud were both in 1876.

[33] *Signs of the Times*, December 1879, p. 1.

Chapter Two

Sanctified

I know when I got converted, I was there. And then I know when I got sanctified wholly, I was a Baptist preacher at the time. It took place about 11:00 o'clock one Saturday night, May 16, 1891. And I was there too. Hallelujah! God sanctified me wholly.

B. H. Irwin

After practicing law and serving as a layman in the First Baptist Church and the pastor of the Mt. Zion Baptist Church in Tecumseh for some eight years, Irwin was ready for something new. With a brilliant but restless mind he was probably bored with his life in small town Nebraska. The change began in 1891 when he invited a Holiness preacher related to the Iowa Holiness Association to preach in his Mt. Zion pulpit. That morning he heard about an experience called "entire sanctification" which had its roots in the preaching, teaching, and writings of John Wesley, the founder of Methodism.

Nearby Iowa had been a hotbed for Holiness ever since Isaiah Reid, a Presbyterian preacher, founded the "Iowa Holiness Association" in 1879. A convert to the Holiness Movement, Reid in the same year founded a small Holiness camp meeting in Jefferson, Iowa, which later drew multitudes every summer to hear sermons on Holiness and help others to enter into the experience. In 1888 the camp meeting was moved to Des Moines to a much larger Chautauqua camp facility. In time the older Methodist-related National Holiness Association merged its "National Camp Meeting" with the Iowa Holiness Association Camp Meeting making it the largest such camp in the nation. Beginning in 1875, Reid began publishing a weekly Holiness periodical called *The Highway* (later called *The Highway and Banner*). By the 1890s, the Iowa Holiness Association Camp Meeting became the most important Holiness center in the nation.[1]

It is not known if Irwin ever attended the Des Moines Camp Meeting, but it is certain that he joined the Iowa Holiness Association in 1892. His name appears on the list of new members although his name is not included in the list of approved evangelists. The Minutes entry simply lists "B. H. Irwin, Tecumseh, Johnson Co., Neb."[2]

Enthralled by the prospects of victory over the sin that had tormented him for most of his life, Irwin earnestly sought for the second blessing of sanctification which would bring to him Christian perfection and perfect love as taught by Wesley. Years later he spoke of this as an "epochal" experience in his life: "I know when I got converted, I was there. And then I know when I got sanctified wholly, I was a Baptist preacher at the time. It took place about 11:00 o'clock one Saturday night, May 16, 1891. And I was there too. Hallelujah! God sanctified me wholly..."[3]

Of this experience Irwin testified, "my heart was cleansed from all interior pollution by the precious blood of Christ." Twelve hours later he "received the witness of the Holy Spirit" while sitting behind the pulpit of the Mt. Zion Baptist Church waiting to preach his Sunday sermon. He was "melted to a flood of tears...the Holy Ghost in his fullness came into my soul. The floodgates of heaven were opened wide, and there came into my soul successive waves and mighty inundations of light, love joy and faith, and power and loyalty to God." Years later he said "I am so glad that since God sanctified my soul, over eight years ago, nothing, absolutely nothing has ever been able to reach or disturb the abiding peace that God put in my soul then." He later said that sin was "eradicated" from his life and that his sanctification experience was at one and the same time his "baptism in the Holy Spirit."[4]

When he told of his experiences and preached Holiness to his congregation at Mt. Zion Baptist, they were not convinced. In short order he resigned as pastor and found himself an unemployed Holiness preacher depending on invitations as an evangelist.

As a "John Wesley Methodist"

With his new sanctification experience, Irwin became a profound student of Wesleyan literature, especially the works of John Wesley and John Fletcher. He also delved deeply into the lives of Catholic and Protestant mystics and saints for inspiration. These included: Madame Guyon, the French Quietist and devotional writer who gained great popularity with American Holiness readers; Francois Fenelon, the celebrated French Bishop and writer of devotional literature; and Geir Vidalin, the Lutheran Bishop of Iceland and popular writer on the deeper Christian life. Irwin was so taken with Fenelon and Vidalin that he named two of his sons for these men, two of his theological heroes.[5]

The writer who exerted the most influence on Irwin, however, was John Fletcher, author of the massive work, *Checks to Antinomianism*. John Fletcher of Madely was an Anglican priest who was Wesley's most trusted theologian and designated successor as head of the Methodist societies. Fletcher's *Checks* was written to stop the tendency of some of Wesley's followers to fall into the error of "sinless perfection" thereby feeling that they could sin with impunity. Two things that Fletcher stressed relative to Wesley's teaching on second blessing instant sanctification was that it should more properly be called a "baptism in the Holy Spirit." Another was that one could receive many subsequent blessings after conversion, not just one "second blessing." Fletcher wrote: Should you ask how many baptisms or effusions of the sanctifying Spirit are necessary to cleanse a believer from all sin and to kindle his soul into perfect love, I should reply if one powerful baptism of the Spirit seals you to redemption and cleanses you from all moral filthiness, so much the better. If two or more are necessary, the Lord can repeat them." In other places Fletcher spoke of a "baptism of burning love," of entering into "the full dispensation of the Spirit," of "the Pentecostal glory of the Church baptized with the Holy Ghost," and those who were "baptized with fire" and "endued with power from on high."[6]

Irwin read all this with great interest, taking a mental note of the possibility of multiple baptisms after sanctification. After soaking himself in this literature, Irwin said: "I was born and raised a Baptist and I joined a Baptist church when I was converted; but when God sanctified me wholly He made a John Wesley Methodist out of me."[7] Because of Fletcher's influence, perhaps it would have been more accurate to say, "He also made a John Fletcher Methodist out of me."

As a Holiness Evangelist

For the next four years, Irwin preached as a Holiness evangelist wherever he could. In this period his sermons were completely orthodox second blessing Holiness as taught and widely accepted by the Holiness movement at large. Everywhere he urged his hearers to come to the altars and be "saved" or "sanctified." His eloquence and dynamic preaching soon drew many people to his meetings. His first meeting was in nearby Douglas, Nebraska, probably in 1892. Reporting on a second meeting in Kenesaw, Nebraska, he stated that he was preparing for "The fall and winter campaigns." In 1893 he published a slate of meetings which were to run from May to October mostly in small towns in Iowa and Nebraska. These included meetings in Freed, Nebraska; Des Moines, Iowa; Ashland, Illinois; Denison and Lineville, Iowa; and in Bennett, Geneva, and Lincoln, Nebraska. In 1894 he continued his meetings, usually under tents, but sometimes in churches. In Kiowa, Kansas, he reported that: "This river of God which is full of water, this Holy Ghost life in the soul fills me unutterably full of peace and glory. Holiness is sweeter to me today than it ever was." He said furthermore that "I see the need of radical, thorough work in preaching holiness as I never saw before."[8]

By 1894, Irwin was reaching out to other churches that were being touched by the Holiness movement. For instance, in that year he preached for the River Brethren in Iowa as well as in some Methodist and Wesleyan Methodist churches. At this time, he made no negative comments about other churches that would later characterized his sermons. He was essentially an unremarkable Holiness evangelist like hundreds of others who preached in the fields, in brush arbors, in school houses, and, occasionally, in churches brave enough to hear Irwin's "red hot Holiness" message that was becoming more radical all the time.

As was true for most of his ministry, Irwin suffered often from pain and various illnesses that interrupted his heavy preaching schedule. In February 1894 he told the readers of the *Christian Witness* about a terrible pain that left him bedridden in Lansing, Colorado. He said:

> Sanctified wholly, glory to God! The field is white unto the harvest, and the laborers are few and I am unable to carry on the work, being confined to my room this week. Racked with pain, but rejoicing with unspeakable joy. Sick and sorrowful and shut in, but shouting "Glory to God for holiness." Jesus, who is my sanctification, is all and in all to me. My God supplies all my needs according to his riches in glory by Christ Jesus (Phil. 4:19). Holiness is sweeter and more precious to my soul now than ever before; and if I ever get up from this sickness I shall preach and teach the doctrines of entire sanctification more definitely and more constantly than I have ever done. Glory! The blood of Jesus Christ is all my plea. It cleanses me now.[9]

It seemed that the tireless evangelist would go anywhere and endure any hardship to preach holiness. On a trip to a remote village in Oklahoma he travelled in a covered wagon on rutty roads:

> From Mulhall the writer came across the country, by the way of Waukomis, in a covered wagon, and, after two and one half days' hard traveling part of the time over hard "gumbo," and part of the time through deep sand and "black jacks." I found myself on the banks of Indian Creek, twenty two miles due west of Enid, in a rich and fertile land. I was delighted to find some old and tried friends living here in true contentment and really happy. ... These meetings were held in a log school house 16x20 feet in size, with a sod roof and a dirt floor.[10]

In another meeting in Oklahoma in 1896 Irwin found a town, Woodward, that was riddled with wickedness. He said: "It has about five hundred inhabitants, fourteen saloons, about one hundred prostitutes, and gamblers and libertines and all other classes of sinners. The congregations are fair, respectful, and rapidly increasing in size. District Court is in session, and prominent lawyers are here from other cities in the Territory. The people are getting interested in the meetings, and the outlook is exceedingly good for genuine revival. The people here have never been used to the 'altar,' and the idea of being 'saved from sin' is entirely new to them. But the truth is beginning to dawn upon them."[11]

In Methodist Episcopal Churches

Some of his more notable meetings in this period were held in Methodist Episcopal Churches. In Smith Centre, Kansas, he said that "the M.E. Church has been greatly built up; nearly all the members have been wholly sanctified. The pastor's wife has been sanctified, the pastor greatly blessed, and the members wonderfully strengthened. The entire community for miles around has been stirred on the question of holiness." Later in Oxford, Nebraska, he reported to the *Christian Witness* that:

> I came here on the 22d and began on the 23d, with the M.E. pastor, Rev J. F. McKay. The meetings had been in progress for one week, and the altar was full the evening before I came. Bro. McKay is true holiness man—a loyal Methodist, and he preaches holiness without apologizing for it. We have had uniform victory all the way. The walls of sin are tumbling and crumbling, holiness has the right of way, and this "great potential idea of Methodism" and the gospel prevails. Hardened sinners and lukewarm church members are being greatly stirred.[12]

The next year in Oklahoma he reported that "Quite a number of these M. E. preachers have gotten out into the experience and are going back to spread the fire of holiness on their charges. One preacher last night renounced the lodge devil and said to the writer that God had been calling upon him for some time to do this, and that he finally got to the place where he felt the Spirit was about to leave him, and had to give up these Christless institutions of darkness or backslide altogether." He also added that "there are M. E. preachers in this part of Oklahoma who have been and will be true to God and real, practical, Bible holiness."[13]

In addition to these, Irwin spoke highly of another Methodist pastor from Oklahoma, "J.D.M. Buckner, pastor of the First M. E. church, Guthrie, who is here, soul and body, and preaches ably and with no uncertain sound, the blessed doctrine of entire sanctification as a second work. He related with great power and telling effect, last night, his own personal experience and the altar was filled with seekers after the great salvation. I knew Brother Buckner when he resided in Nebraska, and was the President of our State Holiness Association, and am glad to find him true and loyal to the doctrine and experience of holiness.[14]

Beyond the Methodist churches, Irwin saw many getting sanctified from other denominations including Baptists, Presbyterians, and "Campbellites." In Lincoln, Nebraska, he saw many people come to his meetings who were far from being Methodists. He reported:

> For a week past I have not been idle or asleep. There never before was such an awakening in this city on the question of sanctification. My own pastor, Rev. C. L. Lemon, has been preaching the gospel of full salvation until a large per cent of our church are in the experience of holiness, and among these all the leading members. And in nearly every other church in the city there are those who are enquiring the way. Even Lutherans and Presbyterians and Baptists are awakened. One blessed Presbyterian Brother has a regular holiness prayer meeting at his house every Monday night, and there are enquirers at most of the weekly meetings.[15]

As a "John Wesley Methodist" Irwin began a search for a denomination that matched his theology and experience. By 1894, the bishops of the Methodist Episcopal Church, South had adopted a resolution that opposed the growing presence of the Holiness Movement. It stated:

> But there has sprung up among us a party with holiness as a watchword; they have holiness associations, holiness meetings, holiness preachers, holiness evangelists, and holiness property. Religious experience is represented as if it consists of only two steps, the first step out of condemnation into peace and the next step into Christian perfection. The effect is to disparage the new birth, and all stages of spiritual growth from the blade to the full corn in the ear...We do not question the sincerity and zeal of these brethren; we desire the church to profit by their earnest preaching and godly example; but we deplore their teaching and methods insofar as they claim a monopoly of the experience, practice, and advocacy of holiness, and separate themselves from the body of ministers and disciples.[16]

Although the Northern Methodist Episcopal Church sheltered and approved the holiness movement for many years to come, many Methodists, both North and South, saw the handwriting on the wall and became "comeouters" from Methodism and joined the ranks of the dozens of new Holiness denominations that were springing up around the nation after 1894. Although the Iowa Conference was in the Northern wing of Methodism, and more favorable to holiness preachers, Irwin decided not to join that church.

As a Wesleyan Methodist

By early 1896, Irwin found a home in another Methodist Church known as the Wesleyan Methodist Church, a thoroughly Holiness denomination which began in 1844 as a split from the Methodist Church in a dispute over slavery. The Wesleyan Methodists and their founder, Orange Scott, felt that slavery was a terrible sin, especially for people who claimed to be sanctified. The church spread over the United States before the Civil War including Iowa. Probably most of the area ministers were members of the Iowa Holiness Association. In time, Irwin spent more and more time with ministers of the church which gave him a warm welcome as a traveling evangelist.

The April, 1896 issue of the *Wesleyan Methodist*, the official organ of the church, carried a report of a revival in the Marengo Circuit of the Iowa Wesleyan Methodist Church Conference which stated: "For the last ten days we were greatly helped by the labors of Rev. B. H. Irwin, the evangelist who has recently joined this conference. His preaching was assuredly in the demonstration of the Spirit, and with power. He wields the Sword of the Spirit with unusual effect and sin was uncovered and located with vivid heart searchings."[17]

The church also opened the door for Irwin to contribute articles to the church paper as well as reports of his meetings. In one 1895 article he criticized the "shoddy holiness" of the "lodge devil" and, "holiness women who wear ear bobs, gold rings and flower gardens on their heads and dress exactly as the harlots of Chicago, rather than women professing godliness." He added "but we are told that we must not be fanatical on the dress question. No, indeed, but let us be scriptural and stick to the Discipline."[18]

His meetings as a Wesleyan Methodist were similar to his meetings as an independent Holiness evangelist. In a meeting in the Oklahoma Indian Territory he reported the following results:

> The day after I arrived there a married daughter of one of the brethren who came after me gave birth to a fine boy; she was sanctified in less than two hours after and named the child BENJAMIN HARDIN IRWIN MOORE.[19] The child is doing well, and will no doubt become a fire baptized holiness preacher. This is the land of horned toads, centipedes, Campbellites, tarantulas, "freegrass" outlaws, poison belladonna, murderous "white caps," and backslidden Baptists who deny that anyone can backslide. A band of eighty "white caps" [presumably the Ku Klux Klan] was recently organized in this community, whose business is to frighten intimidate and murder. I organized these sanctified brethren into a Wesleyan Methodist church, the first one ever organized in the Territory, I presume. [20]

So the fiery Irwin joined a church that sided with the most conservative holiness preachers who spent time on the "dress question." As this shows, he was moving more and more to the side of the most radical holiness preachers, a move that was fine with the Wesleyan Methodist leaders and readers of the church paper. For the next several years, Irwin won the hearts of several Wesleyan Methodist leaders who opened the doors for him to preach in many of their churches in the Midwest and as a platform for his later whirlwind ministry in the South. Some of these included Oliver Fluke, S.P. Sage, W.E. Stephenson, and Jesse Bathhurst who were to be his closest supporters in his early meetings.

Notes

[1] Jim Kerwin, "Isaiah Reid (1836–1911)," pp. 148–153.

[2] Ibid., p. 182.

[3] B. H. Irwin. "A Whirlwind from the North," Part I. *Live Coals of Fire,* no. 7 (December 1, 1899), p. 2.

[4] B. H. Irwin, "The Baptism of Fire," *Way of Faith,* Nov. 13, 1905, p. 2.

[5] See B. H. Irwin, "Editorial Correspondence," *Live Coals of Fire,* October 20, 1899, p. 1.

[6] John Fletcher, *The Works of the Reverend John Fletcher* (New York: Lane & Scott, 1851), Vol. 2. pp. 356–632, and Vol. 4, pp. 230–232.

[7] B. H. Irwin, "Warning to Backsliders," *Live Coals of Fire* May 4, 1900, p. 2. Records of the Tecumseh Methodist Church show no record of Irwin being a member. He may have associated himself with the Wesleyan Methodist Church which he later joined. See Martin H. Schrag, "The Spiritual Pilgrimage of the Reverend Benjamin Hardin Irwin," *Brethren in Christ History and Life* (Volume IV, Number 1) June, 1983, p. 7.

[8] Irwin, "Camp Meeting Calendar," *Christian Witness and Advocate of Bible Holiness,* May 4, 1893, p. 8. Also see Irwin "Kansas," *Christian Witness and Advocate of Bible Holiness,* April 26, 1894, p. 13.

[9] Irwin, "From the Field," *Christian Witness and Advocate of Bible Holiness* (February 8, 1894), 12. See Document 5 in the Selected Irwin Reader.

[10] Irwin, "From Holt, Oklahoma," *Christian Witness and Advocate of Bible Holiness* (October 15, 1895), p. 12. See Document 8 in the Selected Irwin Reader.

[11] Irwin, "Woodward, Okla.," *The Way of Faith and Neglected Themes* (June 17, 1896), 6. See Document 15 in the Selected Irwin Reader.

[12] Irwin, "Nebraska," *Christian Witness and Advocate of Bible Holiness* (February 8, 1894), p. 3.

[13] Irwin, "From Oklahoma," *Christian Witness and Advocate of Bible Holiness* (October 10, 1895), 12–13.

[14] Ibid.

[15] Irwin, "Report," *Christian Witness and Advocate of Bible Holiness* (November 14, 1895), p. 12. See Document 11, Irwin Reader, Part II.

[16] See Vinson Synan, *Holiness Pentecostal Tradition* (Grand Rapids: Eerdmans, 1971, 1978), p. 40.

[17] The *Wesleyan Methodist Guide to Holiness and Revival Miscellany,* April 8, 1896, p. 5.

[18] Ibid. November 13, 1895, p. 8.

[19] Irwin Moore, the grandchild of the Werhans, was born on May 25, 1896. He grew up to own an electrical appliance store in Inglewood, California. See *Fifteenth Census of the United States,* 1940, Los Angeles, California.

[20] Irwin, "Minco, Indian Territory," *The Way of Faith and Neglected Themes* (June 17, 1896), p. 2. See Document 11, Irwin Reader.

Chapter Three

Fire Baptized

> All at once I became conscious of the fact that I was literally on fire. This expression may seem a strong one, but I cannot express it in any other way. Everything about me seemed to be on fire—actually burning, blazing, glowing. I felt that I was in the midst of a fiery presence. At no time in my life have I known or felt such unutterable bliss. For five hours I felt that I should certainly be consumed – and there I entered into an infinitely deeper and more wonderful rest than I have ever known before.
>
> B. H. Irwin

As a Wesleyan Methodist evangelist preaching "red hot holiness," Irwin was more and more influenced by the radical elements of the Holiness movement. Without the moderating influence of the Methodist Episcopal Church, both North and South, the more independent Holiness preachers began to preach on several themes that had not previously been part of the classical holiness movement. These included divine healing "as in the atonement," the any moment rapture of the saints at the second coming of Christ, and an emphasis on Pentecostal language that became more pronounced in the last decade of the century.

Some of the roots of this emphasis lay in the influence of the Keswick Holiness movement that began in England in 1874 and washed back onto the North American scene. Keswick teachers, including Canon T. D. Harford-Battersby, Robert Pearsall Smith, and Hannah Whitall Smith, downplayed the Wesleyan emphasis on the cleansing aspect of the second blessing, and placed much emphasis on the baptism in the Holy Spirit as an empowering power for witnessing. They also taught that the sin nature was only "suppressed" and "controlled" rather than "eradicated." Although Irwin kept to "eradicationist" theology, he was impressed with the power aspects of Keswick theology.[1]

Pentecostal Language

As Donald Dayton has shown, the decade of the 1890s saw a tremendous use of Pentecostal language across the American holiness movement. The venerable mother of the Holiness movement, Phoebe Palmer in her *Guide to Holiness and Revival Miscellany* magazine, permeated her paper with Pentecostal themes. In fact, the masthead was later changed to *Guide to Holiness and Pentecostal Life.* This change was made, because of:

> The signs of the times, which indicate inquiry, research and ardent pursuit of the gifts, signs and power of the Holy Spirit. "The Pentecostal idea," is pervading Christian thought and aspiration more than ever before, and we hope this year to contribute something toward a better understanding of the fact – that this is, "THE DISPENSATION OF THE HOLY GHOST.[2]

According to Donald Dayton, "The magazine fairly reverberated with the Pentecostal theme. Sermons were published in a column entitled 'the Pentecostal Pulpit,' womens reports under 'Pentecostal Womanhood,' testimonies as 'Pentecostal Testimonies,'– everything from camp meetings to choirs were 'Pentecostal' while private devotions were held in 'Pentecostal Closets.'"[3] In Cincinnati, Martin Welles Knapp not only led "God's Bible School" but published a full line of holiness literature which he called called the "Pentecostal Holiness Library." In Los Angeles, Phineas Bresee named his new Holiness denomination the "Pentecostal Church of the Nazarene" in 1895. With the Pentecostal language taking the Holiness movement by storm, some even began to wonder if the baptism in the Holy Spirit was a "third blessing" after sanctification.[4]

The idea of a third blessing after the experience of entire sanctification was not entirely new. Phoebe Palmer in recounting her sanctification said: "Over thirty years ago I bound the sacrifice to the altar. A few hours after I felt the consuming energies of the Divine Spirit through my whole being. I trust that baptism of fire has never been lost."[5] Another influential leader who seemed to suggest a subsequent experience to sanctification was Asbury Lowrey, a member of the National Holiness Association who wrote in 1879 "Is the Baptism of the Holy Ghost a Third Blessing?" He explained "sanctification purges, refines, restores in the image of God and makes a saint" while the Holy Ghost fire "empowers, works outwardly touching society and makes a priest mighty in God.[6]

Early Third Blessing Teachers

There were also those within the Wesleyan Methodist Church (which Irwin later joined) who ventured to say that there was a third blessing after sanctification which they called the baptism with the Holy Spirit. For instance, W.H. Kennedy, who later served as General Missionary Secretary, "distinguished between entire sanctification on the one hand, and the baptism with the Holy Ghost on the other, saying that they were distinct experiences which might or might not occur at the same time." Also, in the Western Kansas Ministerial Association "some of its members thought that there were three works: regeneration, sanctification, and the baptism of the Spirit."[7]

Other less well known Holiness people reported multiple baptisms and vivid experiences of the fire decades before Irwin propagated his version of a third blessing. A case in point is that of a man who had no less than four experiences in 1881. In the *Christian Witness* of December 26, 1895, was published the remarkable experience of Frederick Walters: "in January, 1881, just 10 years after my justification, the Lord graciously restored me. Shortly after this I entered into a crucified state. Some days after this my wife and I both received the *baptism of the Holy Ghost*. The next morning we spoke with tongues…Thursday, February 24, 1881, I received *the baptism of fire*.[8]

All of this caused a deep desire in Irwin for a deeper experience that went beyond his colorful sanctification experience in 1891. At this time he said that he was "profoundly thirsting" for a "more intimate personal acquaintance with the living God." He was also suffering from what he described as "loss of property, declining health, disappointments, persecutions, betrayals, and the slander of many." This led him to dig deeper into Holiness literature looking for answers. This included reading Thomas Upham's *Life of Madame Guyon* and George D. Watson's *Live Coals.* He reviewed John Fletcher's *Checks to Antinominianism* especially where he said, "if one powerful baptism of the Holy Spirit seal you until the day of redemption and cleanse you from all moral filthiness, so much the better. If two or more be necessary, the Lord can repeat them."[9] Another Holiness classic that may have influenced Irwin was the British Methodist writer William Arthur's classic *The Tongue of Fire or the True Power of Christianity* first published in 1849 but republished in 1891 for the American audience.[10]

In addition to these works, Irwin studied the scriptures searching for an even more fiery experience than entire sanctification. His attention was riveted byJohn the Baptist's statement in Matthew 3:11: "I indeed baptize you with water unto repentance, but he who is coming after me is mightier than I, whose sandals I am not worthy to carry. He will baptize you with the Holy Ghost and with fire." Of this quest Irwin wrote,

> I had been reading Upham's "Life of Madame Guyon" and Dr. Watson's "Coalds [Coals] of Fire." I knew that some of my brethren in the ministry, and in the ranks of the laity as well, professed to have an experience of fire which I had never known. Moreover I had been praying for fire all summer in my camp meeting, and had seen the need of it in many places. And as I read the word alone on my knees, the Holy Ghost seemed to direct my mind to those passages where fire is spoken of, and especially to Matthew 3:11—"and with fire." And to that wonderful Scripture in Rev. 15:2, "A sea of glass mingled with fire."[11]

Irwin's Fire Baptism Experience

From these scriptures Irwin concluded that the "baptism of fire" was a separate blessing from second blessing sanctification. Since most Holiness people taught that the second blessing included both entire sanctification and the baptism in the

Holy Spirit in one experience, i.e. two sides of the same coin, he concluded that the fire baptism was a third experience. In discussions with fellow Holiness preachers, he discovered that some of them had experienced such a fiery baptism subsequent to their second blessing. These included Miller Willis, C.P. Carkuff, Jesse Bathurst, and George M. Henson, some of his friends in the Wesleyan Methodist Church. He then began to earnestly seek for the experience over several months stating that he was in "the very furnace of desire for the experience." [12] It finally happened on October 25, 1895, in Enid, Oklahoma. He described this experience thus:

> God had sent Bro C.P. Carkuff two hundred and fifty miles, all the way from Ness City, Kansas to tell me of his experience, and while he was relating it to me, about 12 o'clock in the night of the 23rd of October, 1895 as we lay together and alone, I saw in the room above me a cross of pure, transparent fire. It was all fire. I have been able to see that cross in the same place above me every moment from that time to this. No fire that was ever kindled on earth was half as pure, so beautiful, so divinely transparent as that. In a few moments, the whole room where we were lying seemed to be all luminous with a seven fold light (Isa. 30:26), and a little later still the heavens were all aglow with transparent flame. The very walls of the room seemed to be on fire. But as yet there was no sense of heat connected with it. As powerful as this experience was, however, Irwin "did not feel any inner feeling of fire."

However, on the night of Oct. 25th on a train from Enid to Lincoln he reported a further fire experience: "All at once I became conscious of the fact that I was literally on fire. This expression may seem a strong one, but I cannot express it in any other way. Everything about me seemed to be on fire—actually burning, blazing, glowing. I felt that I was in the midst of a fiery presence. At no time in my life have I known or felt such unutterable bliss. For five hours I felt that I should certainly be consumed and there I entered into an infinitely deeper and more wonderful rest than I have ever known before." [13]

An excited Irwin wanted to share his fire baptized experience with all his friends, especially those who read the reports in the *Christian Witness and Advocate of Bible Holiness*. In October of 1895 he wrote the following glowing report from Enid, Oklahoma: "Dear Witness, My experience this morning is one of fire and glory. I am living beneath a cross of immaculate fire, in the center of an infinite ocean of eternal glowing flame and dashes and flashes, and great waves of pure fire surround, and overwhelm, and rest upon me! All is holy conflagration. I have the burning bush experience, tongues of fire, waves of fire, vast inundations of living flame—Glory, glory, glory! Holy, holy, holy! Hallelujah!" [14]

Irwin's Fire-Baptized Theology

Irwin wasted little time in spreading the news of his newly discovered experience, preaching about it and encouraging others to seek the fire experience. As he studied and preached, Irwin roughed out his theology of the third blessing.

It was not the same as the baptism in the Holy Spirit, even though it was linked with it in the same verse in Matthew. To explain his new baptism, he used the illustration of a head of wheat. The chaff was necessary for the wheat to grow, but later it was released and burned with "unquenchable fire" in the words of John the Baptist in Matthew 3. This, according to Irwin, was the baptism of fire.[15] As for what the new baptism would do for one's spirituality, Irwin explained that the fire "burns up the unnecessary things" that remain in the hearts of the sanctified such as "ignorance and negligence." It also "intensifies every faculty of our soul" such as faith, love, courage, hope and "holy boldness."[16] With his low view of most churches, Irwin explained that the fire baptized saints did not need to belong to a "rotten, corrupt church" to enjoy the blessing, or to enjoy the approval of other "dead" Holiness people who disagreed with his theology.

Furthermore, the fire baptism gave one a new appreciation of the Trinity; "the baptism of fire is the bursting forth of the pent up Trinity," he said. Also, he added that the fire "gives you backbone," enables one to do the will of God "without fear and without compromise," makes one more Christ-like, and gives one a desire to go to the ends of the earth in evangelistic work.[17]

Finally, the fire "blows up the work of the devil" and "gets under things it scorches and gives to all the agents and emissaries of Satan. It puts fire to the foxes tails and sends them howling through the cornfields of the Philistines."[18] Perhaps drawing from his Primitive Baptist roots, he claimed that those with the fire were the "very elect." To Irwin, "The sanctified people are God's elect, but the fire baptized people are God's very elect. They occupy the inner circle, stand right next to the Throne, and have the ear and audience of Jesus."[19]

Irwin expected his new fire experience to follow him not only for life, but also into eternity. He wrote, "I feel at this very moment these blissful, burning, leaping, love waves of living fire." As for eternity he said, "I expect to live and die in the flame and spend eternity in a big flame." This was the "white fire" of heaven and not the "horrid fire of hell."[20]

Not only did Irwin talk about fire, he also had much to say about lightning, as did many others in the Holiness movement. He based his rhetoric on Ezekiel 1:13 which said: "As for the likeness of the living creatures, their appearance was like burning coals of fire, and like the appearance of lamps: it went up and down among the living creatures and the fire was bright, and out of the fire went forth lightning." As time went by, Irwin peppered his sermons with references to: "the penetrating power of slant lightning, holy lightning, and forked lightning." This lightning would be "able to strike at any time," and to "seek out the sinners and the backsliders."[21]

In addition to the fire-baptized saints experiencing fire and lightening on earth, they would be sifted and end up in a special place in heaven. In his developing eschatology, Irwin began to teach that only a few overcoming saints would be in the final rapture. In an article titled "Let the Sifting Continue," he said: "We are living in the formative period of the fire-baptized holiness movement. These are the times that try men's souls already we are too many we need to be reduced in number or improved in quality. We need to get rid of those fearful and afraid ones." Perhaps he was referring to Benjamin Young who departed in 1898 possibly over the issue of Irwin's new dynamite teaching. Irwin added:

> God is bringing the movement down to the water's edge, and preparing for Himself a Gideon's band that will go forth with torch and trumpet, burning and blazing for God, and blowing, with no uncertain sound the Old Pentecostal ram's horn. Already we are too many- we need to be reduced in number or improved in quality. We need to get rid of these "fearful and afraid ones" (Judges 7:4), who see nothing but, and blunders, and mistakes, and perils, and disaster...we want those, and those only, who see nothing but victory, and conquest, and glory ahead. And who have never learned the language of disaster and defeat. We want men and women with the definite experience of the fire, and literally surcharged with the diving dynamite from the upper skies, who can be trusted anywhere on the field of carnage.[22]

With his new experience and developing theology, Irwin began by winning his closest minister friends from the Wesleyan Methodist Church. The first of these were Oliver Fluke, C.P. Sage, and W.E. Stephenson who were to assist him greatly with the first two helping him when he later formed a new denomination.

The Fire Spreads

The first meetings where Irwin preached the fire experience were in late 1895 in Iowa, Oklahoma, and Kansas in small towns. His first fire baptized revival meeting was in Guthrie Center, Iowa, in November of 1895. His report of this meeting was as follows:

> I am here in a blessed meeting with the pastor of the Wesleyan Methodist Church, Rev. J. H. Meek. He is also president of the Iowa conference of the Wesleyan connection. Rev. C. P. Sage is also assisting and Brother O. Fluke is here in charge of the music. These brethren are filled with the Holy Ghost and have the divine fire.[23] The outlook is glorious. One brother was sanctified last night and got delivered from the tobacco habit. God is still able to save to the uttermost. Others are seeking the great salvation, and still others are earnestly inquiring about this blessed doctrine of entire sanctification. Several of the M. E. people are in the experience and are coming over to help in the meeting. The fire is kindling in many hearts. Blessed be to God for the living fire![24]

From January to June, 1896 he held meetings in Viola Center, Coon Rapids, Knoxville, Cloud, Des Moines, and Woodward, all in Iowa. In June and July, he was in Minco, Woodward, and Purcell, Oklahoma, followed by meetings in Healy and Hess City, Kansas. In October and November he held meetings in Brethren in Christ churches in Dickenson County, Kansas. By the end of the year he was in Manitoba, Canada, and Marion, South Carolina.[25]

During these early meetings, Irwin maintained the support of the *Wesleyan Methodist* paper, with reports of his meetings falling along traditional Holiness lines. For instance, at Woodward, Iowa, nine were sanctified and five saved. In

Coon Rapids, "a dozen were converted, reclaimed, sanctified or healed." By July, 1896, however, the first report of people receiving the "fire" experience showed up in another report from Guthrie Center, Iowa, where, he reported, "During the entire meeting about twenty five were converted or sanctified wholly. Some remarkable cases of divine healing 'through faith in His name,' and most of the sanctified received the baptism of fire."[26]

Not only did the *Wesleyan Methodist* publish these reports, in July an article was published titled, "The Baptism of Fire," by Rev. J. F. Packard which added editorial support for Irwin's fire baptism thus giving him an unofficial stamp of approval from his denomination.[27] Much of this positive favor was due to the influence of A. P. Sage and Oliver Fluke who served as ardent sponsors and supporters of Irwin. Both of them had received the "baptism of fire" and became ardent followers of the eloquent and intrepid preacher.

One of the first testimonies of the fire experience was in Chetopa, Kansas, in 1896 at a meeting of the Neosho Valley Holiness Association camp meeting led by Benjamin Wesley Young. The crowds were so large that "it was nearly impossible for over half of the people to get into the canvas tent." Young reported that "wave after wave of glory swept down upon us with altar calls that lasted until 2:00 A.M." Benjamin Young himself received the fire. He said "I felt led to pray for the God of fire. God got a hold of me and the mighty cyclone came and I was prostrated. All at once the mighty wave struck me I rolled in the flames and the flames in me, and the building was a solid mass of fire. It was brighter than five suns could make it. It was broad daylight, but I couldn't see my wife. I saw Jesus as plain as I see my family now, and as soon as I saw Him I melted in tenderness before Him. It was a sea of glass mingled with fire, and it settled into a white heat."[28]

In the next two years, Irwin came back to the Neosho Camp meeting and held large meetings resulting in the formation of the "Southeast Kansas Fire Baptized Holiness Association," in 1898 under the leadership of Benjamin J. Young. This was one of the earliest state associations organized by Irwin. However, when Irwin organized nationally in Anderson, South Carolina, in 1898, Young was not listed as representing Kansas.[29]

The Way of Faith

These reports spread across the Midwest and soon reached the South through the Holiness press. The major breakthrough for Irwin in the south came when J.M. Pike, editor of the *Way of Faith* in Columbia, South Carolina, endorsed his ministry and opened its pages to his reports and articles. Irwin was clearly a major figure who was gaining fame and support every day. The November 18, 1895 issue of the *Way of Faith* carried not only Irwin's testimony of his fire baptism on page 2, but also a ringing endorsement of his ministry by Pike on page 4 titled "the Baptism of Fire." Of Irwin's testimony he said "It is a marvelous experience that stirred me deeply and set us to serious thinking." He added "We are sometimes pained to meet with some whose souls were once aflame with holy love and who gave promise of being steadfast and true to the great work of holiness, who have lost the unction and sweetness of their experience, and are living on a cold, formal expression. We fear for them."[30]

In the very next issue, Pike gave an even more ringing endorsement including an announcement of his upcoming preaching trip to South Carolina:

> Bro. Irwin is a local elder in the Wesleyan Methodist Church, is thoroughly Wesleyan in his view of entire sanctification as a work of the Holy Spirit subsequent to regeneration and received instantaneously after complete consecration and faith. He also believes that the Holy Spirit will lead the soul that is loyal to His teachings on to a fuller, and richer, deeper baptism of the holy fire that will be illuminating, energizing, empowering, and filling the being with flaming zeal for God. Give him a patient prayerful unprejudiced hearing. If he uncovers new truth from the divine word and reveals privileges of a deeper union with God, and greater fullness of God than you've seen before, grasp the truth that is for you to act on. Let not Satan cheat you out of the feast, by diverting your attention to the manner in which it is served. Give him a patient, prayerful, unprejudiced hearing.[31]

Soon after, an anonymous writer from Minnesota wrote to the *Way of Faith* a striking description of Irwin as a fearless preacher who would go anywhere to spread the news of his fire baptized experience:

> I thank God for the help received by reading *The Way of Faith*, especially for the deep, sweet, humble, yet powerful and sublimely profound writings of Bro. [G. D.] Watson. And the living, glowing, flaming, consuming words of Bro. B. H. Irwin, who contribute to your columns. Bless God forever for such holy, fearless, fire-baptized men, who cater to nothing but the will of God, who can be found preaching the gospel of full salvation to all people under all circumstances—in the crowded halls, churches, tabernacles; in little school houses, homes, or in the slum districts; on the streets to poor fallen men and women of every color, and the inebriate and criminal in jail, or the poor soul by the wayside. Hallelujah to Jesus. And do so without any guarantee from anybody but God.[32]

This explains a great deal about the attraction of Irwin's message and exciting new experience. By 1895, the modern Holiness movement was now almost 30 years old if marking its origin with the Vineland Holiness Camp Meeting of 1867. Three decades later, many holiness partisans had lost their fire and had become passive in their sanctification experience and testimony. To Pike and many more holiness people, Irwin seemed like a new hope for the revival and renewal of the movement. In fact, Irwin unleashed a rash of new fiery movements and books that reflected fire language in the years following 1895.

Some new fiery holiness denominations were founded in the wake if Irwin's ministry. In Zarapeth, New Jersey, Alma White founded her Pillar of Fire Church in 1901.[33] The Chicago based "Burning Bush " organization not only published its paper in 1902, but organized churches.[34] Also books appeared with fiery titles such as Martin Wells Knapp's *Lightening Bolts From Pentecostal Skies* published in Cincinnati in 1898.

But this period of acceptance was not to last, as vivid reports of uproarious meetings with much shouting, leaping, and praises to God led by Irwin proliferated. And the very idea of a "third blessing" caused Holiness theologians and editors to look more closely and critically at Irwin and his meetings. Added to these concerns was Irwin's preaching on some themes that had not been part of the Holiness Movement before the 1890s. These included the instantaneous second coming and rapture of the church and divine healing as in the atonement. In fact, Irwin soon also became known as a healing evangelist who claimed that many miracles took place in his meetings. In spite of these misgivings, Irwin's ministry reached a peak of popularity in 1896 with more invitations coming in than he could possibly accept, especially in the midwest states of Kansas, Iowa, Oklahoma, and South Carolina.

At almost the same time a sister "third blessing" movement was beginning in Canada that was almost identical to Irwin's movement in doctrine and experience. In1897 a Canadian Holiness evangelist, Ralph Cecil Horner, formed the Holiness Movement Church (HMC) in Ottawa, Canada, teaching a definite "third work" after salvation and entire sanctification which he called "the baptism of fire." Although there seems to have been no connection with Irwin's movement, it is highly probable that Horner and Irwin knew about each other's work since their churches were so similar.[35] By 1899, Horner's church sent a missionary to Egypt by the name of Herbert Edward Randall who founded a fast-growing holiness movement that spread rapidly from its base in Assuit, Egypt. Randall later became a Pentecostal after visiting the Hebden Mission in Toronto in 1907. He then returned to Egypt to begin the Egyptian Pentecostal movement.[36]

With Irwin's movement in America and Canada and Horner's movement in Canada, it seemed that the fire baptism would engulf North America by the turn of the century. And it might be argued that it did, but Irwin was not to be a part of that spreading fire.

Notes

[1] On Irwin's positive view on eradication see "The Eradication of Sin," *Live Coals of Fire*, November 3, 1899, p. 5. Also see Herbert F. Stephenson, *Keswick's Authentic Voice* (Grand Rapids, MI, 1959), pp. 13–22 and Vinson Synan, *Holiness Pentecostal Tradition*, p. 144. An excellent detailed account of this period in Irwin's life is Craig Fankhauser's "The Heritage of Faith: An Historical Evaluation of the Holiness Movement in America." (Unpublished M.A. Thesis, Pittsburg State University, Pittsburg, Kansas, 1983).

[2] Donald Dayton, *Theological Roots of Pentecostalism* (Grand Rapids, MI, Francis Asbury Press, 1987), pp. 87–114.

[3] Ibid., p. 92

[4] Ibid.

[5] See George Hughes, "Baptism of Fire," *Guide to Holiness and Revival Miscellany* (New York), February, 1879, p. 20.

[6] Asbury Lowrey, "Is the Baptism of the Holy Ghost a Third Blessing?," *Divine Life and International Expositor of Scriptural Holiness*, September, 1879, pp. 46–47.

[7] Lee M. Haines, "The Grander, Nobler Work; Wesleyan Methodism's Transition, 1867–1901" in Wayne E Caldwell, Editor, *Reformers and Revivalists: The History of The Wesleyan Church* (Indianapolis: Wesley Press, 1992), p. 136.

[8] B. H. Irwin, "Pyrophobia," *Way of Faith*, October, 28, 1896 p. 2.

[9] Irwin, "Whirlwind from the North," *Live Coals of Fire*, Dec. 15, 1899, pp. 2–3.

[10] Asbury Lowrey, "Is the Baptism of the Holy Ghost a Third Blessing?," pp. 46, 47. Also see William Arthur, *The Tongue of Fire or the True Power of Christianity* (Columbia, SC: L.L. Pickett).

[11] B. H. Irwin, "The Baptism of Fire Experience," *The Way of Faith and Neglected Themes* (November 18, 1895), p. 2.

[12] William T. Purinton, "'Red Hot Holiness,' B. H. Irwin and the Fire-Baptized Holiness Tradition," unpublished paper, p. 3. B. H. Irwin, "The Baptism of Fire Experience," *The Way of Faith and Neglected Themes*, Nov. 13, 1895, p. 2.

[13] Irwin "Baptism of Fire," *Way of Faith*, November 13, 1895, p. 2. Schrag, "Spiritual Pilgrimage," p. 10. Also see Purinton, "Red Hot Holiness," p. 3.

[14] Irwin, "Report," *Christian Witness and Advocate of Bible Holiness* (November 7, 1895), 10. See document 10 in a Selected Irwin Reader.

[15] Irwin, "A Whirlwind from the North," *Live Coals,* December 15, 1899, pp. 2–3.

[16] Irwin, "The Blood Cleanses from Sin," *Live Coals*, April 30, 1900, p. 2.

[17] Irwin, "Pyrophobia," *The Way of Faith*, October 28, 1896, p. 2.

[18] Irwin, "A Whirlwind from the North," p.2.

[19] Ibid. Part 2, p. 3.

[20] Irwin, "The Pentecostal Church," *Live Coals*, June 1, 1900, p. 2; "Faith in God," *Live Coals,* Nov. 9, 1899, p. 2; Schrag, "Spiritual Pilgrimage," p. 12.

[21] Irwin, "Let the Sifting Continue," *Live Coals*, Dec. 1, 1899, p.1; "A Whirlwind from the North," *Live Coals*, Dec. 1, 1899, p. 2.

[22] Irwin, "Let the Sifting Continue," p. 1.

[23] Irwin's claim here that his colleagues Sage and Fluke "have the divine fire" does not mean that they had already passed through a definite experience of fire baptism comparable to what had happened to Irwin in Oklahoma. E.g., Oliver Fluke later testified that his fire baptism occurred on "the 19th of December 1895, in a meeting near Coon Rapids, Iowa, . . . and from that moment to this there has been a constant, burning in my soul. Real fire, fire, fire; living, blazing, glowing without a break" ("Olmitz, Iowa," *Way of Faith* [July 1, 1896], 5).

[24] B. H. Irwin, "Guthrie Center, Iowa, Nov. 18," *Christian Witness and Advocate of Bible Holiness* (November 28, 1895), 12.

[25] Schrag, "Spiritual Pilgrimage," pp. 14–15.

[26] See *The Wesleyan Methodist Guide to Holiness and Revival Miscellany*, January 15, 1896, p. 8; March 25, 1896, p. 4; July 29, 1896, p. 5.

[27] J. F. Packard, "The Baptism of Fire," *The Wesleyan Methodist Guide to Holiness and Revival Miscellany*, July 15, 1896, p. 6.

[28] *Seeking4truth.com*, "B. H. Irwin: The Fire Baptized Revolt, 1895–1911," p. 2.

[29] Later when Irwin introduced additional baptisms which he called dynamite, lyddite and oxidite, Young and the Neosho Valley people separated from Irwin to form the "Fire Baptized Holiness Church (Wesleyan)." See Samuel J. Phoebus, "The Fire Baptized Holiness Church: Its History and Practices" (Unpublished A. B. Thesis, Biblical Seminary in New York, 1949).

[30] B. H. Irwin, "The Baptism of Fire," and J.M. Pike, "The Baptism of Fire," *Way of Faith*, Nov. 13, 1895, pp. 2–4.

[31] *The Way of Faith* November 25, 1896, p. 4.

[32] W. J. D., "All Hail! From Minnesota," *The Way of Faith and Neglected Themes* (August 26, 1896), 2.

[33] Charles Jones, *A Guide to the Study of the Holiness Movement* (Metuchen, NJ: The Scarecrow Press, 1974), pp. 253–254.

[34] Ibid. p. 239.

[35] See Laurence Croswell and Mark Croswell, *Lift Up a Standard- The Lifo and Legacy of Ralph C. Homer* (Indianapolis, IN: Wesleyan Publication House, 2012).

[36] Tharwat Adley, "Blessed Be Egypt My People: The Neo-Charismatic Movement in Egypt," in Vinson Synan, Amos Yong and Kwabena Asamoah-Gyadu, *Global Renewal Christianity: Spirit-Empowered Movements Past, Present, and Future, Volume 3: Africa* (Lake Mary, FL: Charisma House, 2016), pp. 93-108.

Chapter Four

A Whirlwind from the North

My soul is floating out into the boundless fiery ocean of infinite love as never before, and I feel as if the Lord has just emptied into my soul a cedar bucket full of strained honey! Halleluia [sic]. I am in for fire, and dynamite, and chain lightning. I love to see the pillars of hell tremble, and the foundations of iniquity topple.

B. H. Irwin

In Irwin's 1896 barnstorming series of evangelistic meetings in Iowa, Kansas, and Nebraska, he set a new standard for radical "red hot Holiness." He stunned his listeners with his fiery sermonic oratory that led hundreds of his followers into receiving the baptism of fire and giving some of the most colorful testimonies in all of Holiness literature. Also there was much shouting, jumping, and dancing in his services. George Floyd Taylor of the Pentecostal Holiness Church described their experiences with "the fire"

> The testimonies on fire were very interesting. Some said they felt the fire in their souls, but others claimed it as burning in their bodies also. It was felt in the face, in the tongue, in the fingers, in the palm of the hand, in the feet, in the side, in the arms, and so on. Then the Bible itself often felt warm to those who had the fire in them. The church would seem to be lighted with fire, the trees of the wood would appear as flames of fire, the landscape would seem to be baptized in the glory of the fire. As some rode from one appointment to another, according to their testimonies, they seemed to be enveloped with the holy fire. The noise of the engine seemed to sound notes of praise to God, and the clatter of the wheels beneath the cars seemed to be saying *Glory to God, hallelujah*! The coaches themselves were fire lighted and the wheels beneath seemed to be wheels of fire. Fire! Fire! Holy Fire! Was the ring of their testimonies.[1]

For a few months Irwin enjoyed the approval of his own *Wesleyan Methodist* magazine edited by A. W. Hall. Irwin submitted long flowing accounts of protracted meetings from Des Moines, Coon Rapids, Guthrie Centre, Woodward, and Olmitz, Iowa. This, along with the favor of J. M. Pike's *Way of Faith* in South Carolina, spread news of his meetings far and wide.[2] But in May of 1896, Irwin began to attack the organized denominations. In the *Way of Faith* he said "I shall not be bound by churchly prejudices and dogmas of men," while in December he boldly charged his opponents with an "ecclesiastical spirit" that was "churchly and pharisaical" like the "inquisitional order and popish bulls of the middle ages."[3]

Rejection

Reports of Irwin's fire baptism experience and theology and the loud shouting, jumping, and falling in his meetings soon reached the leader of the Iowa Holiness Association, Isaiah Reid, who reacted with horror. Although Irwin was probably still on the rolls of the Association, Reid reacted with uncharacteristic wrath in his column in the influential *Christian Witness*: "In some quarters today a third blessing is held up, called the baptism of fire. Instead of being the baptism of fire, *it is wildfire*. Entire sanctification includes the baptism of fire."[4] Afterward he added:

> [An evangelist] is preaching a third experience, or as he puts it, the baptism of fire, as something apart from and subsequent to the baptism of the Holy Spirit. Surely we are in the days when Satan would deceive the very elect. A brother has just written us of the "fire third blessingism" advocated by a wild and unbalanced advocate who professes holiness. A wreckage follows in the wake, in which the church is fought, and ordinary holiness associations besmirched and true holiness left as a kind of fifth wheel to something substituted in its place. We wish those people who are giving aid and encouragement to parties who are bringing false doctrines into the church, contrary to both the Bible and doctrines of the church would ponder the words of St. John "For he that biddeth him God speed is partaker of his evil deeds."[5]

Another critic was M.L. Haney who wrote a severe denunciation in the Iowa based magazine *Sent of God,* a publication of the Hepzibah Faith Mission which was based in Tabor, Iowa. He said that the fire experience was "fanaticism" and a "delusion." He also charged that "This false teaching is marked at the beginning by unnatural petitions to the Holy Ghost and a peculiar phraseology concerning the third person of the trinity."[6] These caustic criticisms failed to dampen the spirits of the embattled evangelist. Invitations continued to pour in from all over the nation. He returned to his most favored places in Iowa to continue with even greater success. The opposition of the Holiness press failed to discourage the intrepid evangelist. In July he exulted, "The Lord bless the WAY OF FAITH for its brave, yet sweet and loving way of standing by the truth. My soul is floating out into the boundless fiery ocean of infinite love as never before, and I feel as if the Lord has just emptied into my soul a cedar bucket full of strained honey! Halleluia [sic]. I am in for fire, and dynamite, and chain lightning. I love to see the pillars of hell tremble, and the foundations of iniquity topple."[7] With successful meetings in Olmitz, Coalfield, and Ontarioville, Iowa, Irwin felt that he had enough support to form his own organization. At some point in 1896, he asked his friends to join him in merging his Iowa followers into a new association to promote his new teachings. About 100 persons were present for the event. As he described it: "While at the Olmitz camp meeting, it was clearly opened to us by the Spirit of God, that the Fire Baptized saints should unite in a definite organization and the outline of a constitution came to me like a divine revelation. The next morning I wrote the organizational constitution and submitted it to some of the brethren. It met with their hearty approval. A few days later the first Fire Baptized Holiness Association was in existence."[8] The organizing of a new Association, consisting mostly of preachers in the Wesleyan Methodist Church, was the last straw. The Wesleyan Methodist Church closed it columns to Irwin and his fire baptized friends. This led Irwin to gradually withdraw from his Wesleyan connection.[9] In the Wesleyan Methodist General Conference of 1899, the church renewed its commitment to standard Holiness teachings and condemned Irwin's movement and his teachings as a "damaging heresy" claiming that "it was impossible to divide the baptism into two separate acts by the Holy Spirit and by fire, and by declaring that the Bible must always take precedence over men's experience."[10] Also, the major Holiness periodicals, *The Christian Witness* and *The Christian Standard* banned reports of Irwin's meetings from their pages in 1896.[11]

Violence

As his meetings continued, Irwin met with actual physical violence in addition to his editorial opposition. In an uproarious revival in Iowa in the fall of 1896 the *Way of Faith* reported:

A Murderous Assault on Evangelist B. H. Irwin

Dear Bro. Pike: This is the fifth meeting brother Irwin has held in this country since last December. He has been used of God in the uncovering of Sin and exposing hypocrisy and fashionable iniquity, as no other man has ever been used in this part of Iowa. As a consequence angry and malicious threats and several murderous attempts have been made upon his person and life. He was notified before he came to this camp that an organized plot of Campbellites, Unitarians, and lodge men had been formed against him, and that his life would be in danger if he came. But he knew that God was calling on him to take charge of this camp and so he came. He said he was packed up and ready for glory, or anything else they God might call it to do or endure or without a moment's notice.

The meeting has been one of marvelous power, surpassing anything I've ever witnessed. Several times, however, I have heard the coarse growl of the enraged

Tiger; and last night after God and anointed brother Irwin in an unusual manner an attack was made.

I never heard anyone who could probe, and search, and bring to light, and portray sin in such awful colors as Brother Irwin can. It is because he is been saved from such depths of sin himself. He speaks as one having authority. Ungodly sinners cannot sit under the preaching without being brought to judgment. The last night of the meeting brother Irwin preached again of murderous threats, to a large congregation, when the mob was lying in wait in the grove nearby. But the tabernacle was guarded on every side by armed men who had volunteered to defend Brother Irwin at the cost of their own lives.

According to reports "C.P. Sage [was] pistol whipped; Brother Oliver Fluke, hit in the face with a chair; Brother Hammer, struck in the face and one sister knocked down – but not one blow was returned."[12]

Another violent attack took place in a largely attended tent revival in Coon Rapids, Iowa, in July of 1896. The report in *The Way of Faith* described the attack:

Dear Bro. Pike: The devil is enraged again. Last night he cut twelve of our tent ropes down. Tonight he came in an organized (or what seemed to be an organized body of "ungodly sinners,") and while the writer was preaching on Gal. 3:30, and delineating the character of Ishmael, an "ungodly sinner" got mad, came toward the preacher in a rage, made some "hard speeches" and loudly threatened to commit some "ungodly deeds." I said to him as he came near me, "if you lay hands on me, God will strike you dead on the spot," and I believe He would have done it. He was followed by several others who were urging him to go on with his "ungodly" work. They went out and made awful threats and used awful oaths and vile language, and awaited in the dark till the meeting was out, and attempted to do violence again, but the Lord protected us. All the holiness people stood like a wall of fire. The preacher finished his sermon in the regular way, and four came forward, two for the baptism of fire, one for pardon, and one for entire sanctification.[13]

Despite these attacks and in defense of his baptism of fire movement, Irwin wrote a tract with the title, *Pyrophobia (A Morbid Fear of Fire)* which he offered to the readers of *Way of Faith* for 2 cents per copy. As the Editor explained, "This work is in the nature of a reply to some recent criticisms on the *Baptism of Fire* by Bro. Irwin. It is a lively production and will interest and profit the reader." Excerpts from this tract can provide insight into Irwin's polemic:

Pyrophoba
(A Morbid Dread of Fire)
By B. H. Irwin

In November 1895, there appeared in *THE WAY OF FAITH* a brief account of a remarkable experience of the baptism of fire. That account was written under a powerful anointing of the Holy Ghost, and was immediately sent to an evangelist of world–wide reputation who sent it at once to the paper for publication. This is how it came to get into print. Since that time certain editors, and several evangelists, have been greatly exercised over the matter, and of taking it upon themselves to steady the ark; and much has been written and spoken against the baptism of fire as a definite experience. They have condemned it as wildfire, fanaticism, a third work, and third experience, and so on to the end of the chapter: but still the fire burns.

With all candor, I would inquire, who gave these dear brethren the right to sit in severe judgment upon the experiences of others? If one's faith definitely lays hold of God for the baptism of fire, claiming the Scripture promise, He shall baptize you with fire," who shall Hinder? Would these brethren limit the holy one of Israel, and set the boundaries to the possibilities of grace?"

The position of the *Christian Witness* in January, 1894, was impregnable when it said, "experience is the test," and in April 8, 1891, when it declared, "experience is not to be controverted." In opposing the baptism of fire these advocates of popular holiness resort to the same old arguments which have always been used against sanctification itself.[14]

In addition to this larger tract, Irwin wrote two smaller ones that were advertised in *Way of Faith.* J. M. Pike promoted them:

We are now publishing two tracts by B. H. Irwin, the fire-baptized evangelist of Lincoln, Nebraska, and we have seen nothing more striking for some time. One is titled "The New Man," a tract of eight pages and hews to the line as fully as John Wesley's "Character of a Methodist." The title of the other is "The Old Man," and contains sixteen pages. It is original, unique, radical, and merciless in its exposure of wrong being and wrong doing. We still have a good supply of "The Baptism of Fire," giving the experience of Brother Irwin...[15]

Despite all opposition, Irwin continued to expand his ministry into newer regions. In November 1896, he traveled to Winnipeg, Manitoba, in Canada for one of his most successful meetings. At the invitation of the Winnipeg "Interdenominational Holiness League," Irwin was warmly received. A leading member of the League was Mrs. Annie Douglas who firmly supported Irwin's ministry. She described the services as "seasons of uninterrupted victory" with Irwin "appearing as a man sent of God who had the two-fold baptism of Jesus upon him," as he uncovered "sin of every kind, in the church and out of it." However, most of the holiness people in Winnepeg opposed Irwin's movement as "the third blessing heresy" although Irwin won many ardent followers as a result of the meeting.[16]

Although Irwin was often accused of teaching what his opponents called the "third blessing," Irwin refused to call it that himself. In his "Pyrophobia" tract he and Pike denied the accusation saying:

> The baptism of fire has never been called a third work by any of its advocates. We call it what God calls it in his Word—"the baptism of fire"—though there is nothing in the Word of God, nor in the teachings of Methodism, forbidding the use of the expression, "third experience." We prefer, however, the scriptural term. In this connection I refer the reader to THE WAY OF FAITH of May 20th, 1896, where the editor, who is a member of the National Holiness Association, uses these words: "We are, however, fully in sympathy with Brother Irwin and believe he is on the right track. In all that has reached us from his pen he never refers to his richer experience as the third blessing," neither does it cause him to deprecate the 'second blessing.' Even if he called it a third or a fourth or fifth blessing, it would be neither un-Methodistic or unscriptural."[17]

A Whirlwind from the North

His last meetings in 1896 were in South Carolina where the reports in the *Way of Faith* stirred great interest in the Palmetto state as well as in the rest of the South. As he said, Irwin took the South "in cyclone fashion," often referring to himself as the "Whirlwind from the North." His first revival was in Piedmont, South Carolina, in the local Wesleyan Methodist Church. The pastor, Andrew K. Willis, not only received the fire baptism but broke out in the "holy dance," the first to do so in Irwin's meetings. Soon the dance spread throughout the Fire-Baptized Holiness movement. Joseph King said that "this manifestation caught [on] everywhere. And at times there would be a multitude of people dancing at one time in the services."[18] In the first meeting seven were sanctified in the second one twelve, and in the third eighteen received the second blessing, while others received "the fire" experience. As in other meetings in the west, people in Piedmont "jumped, shouted, screamed, and praised God for the 'fire baptism.'" Later Irwin preached in the Wesleyan Methodist strongholds of Columbia, Central, and Anderson, South Carolina.[19]

The Piedmont meeting attracted other ministers who came to investigate Irwin and his fiery baptism. They included future converts Richard B. Hayes, Samuel L. McElroy, a medical doctor, and many other ministers and laymen from the Wesleyan Methodist Church. After Irwin's departure, these men went south into nearby Georgia and carried the fire to Elberton, Royston, Canon, and other points.[20]

Divine Healing

Although teaching on divine healing was spreading far and wide in the Holiness Movement in the mid-1890s, for several years Irwin made no mention of healing in his ministry, centering his attention on sanctification and the baptism of fire. He remembered, "When I got sanctified wholly, did not think on this question. The matter did not come prominently before me at the time, and I fell in with a class of preachers who shut the truth of divine healing out of their ministry and work. Consequently, I never seriously considered the question."[21] But in 1897 he was confronted by the wife of a Methodist minister who said, "I want you and others (naming them) to anoint me with oil and lay your hands on me, according to the word of God, and pray for me that I may be healed." Irwin said:

> I had never had such a request and it struck me like a thunderbolt out of a clear sky. I never saw such an operation carried on. But instantly the Holy Ghost led me to say, I will go, and I got the victory right there…then one of the brethren took charge and told the sister to kneel down: and he took oil and anointed her, and called on me to pray. While I was praying she began to shout, and said, "I feel the power of the Holy Ghost going through my entire body." God instantly healed her, and she jumped and shouted and testified to the experience of divine healing. I was convinced.[22]

Not only was this woman instantly healed, but several months later she told Irwin, "I have not had a single symptom of disease or pain since I was anointed." Irwin himself later experienced a touch of divine healing, testifying: "In my own case, after I had been down with nervous prostration for five weeks, shut up in a dark room with the doors guarded, God instantly healed me one morning about 1:00 O'clock, in answer to the prayer of faith and I felt the disease going from my system and the strength and health of God going into my body. Instantly I became hungry and, and as soon as God took the shout off of me, I had a hearty meal, and went to sleep and slept all morning, something I had not done for five weeks."[23] One of the most amazing claims of divine healing under Irwin took place in Mound Valley, Kansas in 1897. Irwin described the scene in *The Way of Faith:*

> One case especially requires special notice. A destitute family of movers trying to make their way to Missouri was passing through the country from the Indian Territory. The mother had been sick and unable to walk, or even turn herself in the wagon a good part of the time, with six small children. A sanctified woman near Coffeeville heard of their destitution and sickness and at once became interested in them. Through her kindness they were cared for; and she induced them to stay and attend the camp-meeting at Mound Valley. They did so, and drove in the camp on Saturday, September, 25th, the poor woman still sick, and unable to walk, or turn herself in bed. She was also unsaved. Some of the "holy women" went to the wagon, and insisted upon having her carried to the meeting. She did not want to come, but they persisted. Four strong men lifted her from the wagon, and placed her upon a cot, and, like the case in the Bible, "brought her to Jesus." We prayed for her, and the writer preached, and then anointed her with oil in the name of the Lord. The brethren laid their hands upon her and she was not only converted right there but instantly healed of all her diseases. The writer took her by the hand, and said, "In the name of Jesus Christ, rise up and walk," and she did so, running back and forth *across* the platform, and testifying of what God had done for her soul. She testified then and there, "The Lord has healed me, both soul and body." Afterwards (toward the close of the service) she walked, unassisted, to the wagon seventy-five or a hundred yards away. The next day she was sanctified wholly and

the same night received the experience of the baptism of fire as a separate and definite experience. [24]

After these three healing experiences, Irwin added divine healing to his list of teachings and experiences and soon became as famous as a divine healer as he was for spreading the baptism of fire. After his healing he said; "I expect to live for years if Jesus tarries preaching the mighty truth of the baptism of fire, and divine healing, the pre-millennial coming of Jesus, and radical entire sanctification. Blessed be God." [25] Increasingly, healing became an attraction that drew hundreds of people to his meetings.

A Nationwide Movement

By May 1897, Irwin was back in the West where he broke new ground by preaching in Brethren in Christ churches (also known as River Brethren) in Bethel, Zion, and Bell Springs Chapel, all in the Abeline, Kansas, area. The official organ of the Church, *The Evangelical Visitor* was positive in its reports. Irwin was a man who "undoubtedly is fulfilling the call for which he has been anointed," i.e. "the exposing of sin in all its forms and hues resulting in the conviction and conversion of sinners, reclaiming of backsliders, and the sanctification and filling with fire of believers." While preaching for the River Brethren he saw many cases of entire sanctification and divine healing as well as many baptized in fire. Among his hearers was a minister named A. L. Eisenhower, possibly a relative of the future President. The following year, 1898, Irwin returned to the area and organized his followers there into a Fire-Baptized organization in Moonlight, Kansas. [26]

Sometime later in 1897 Irwin's fire baptism reached Texas and Louisiana where Holiness stalwart C.B. Jernigan became concerned about the mushrooming growth of Irwin's movement. He called it "another form of fanaticism" which was taught by "unlearned and misguided teachers." At the Greenville, Texas, Camp Meeting newly sanctified people were encouraged to go back to the altars to seek the fiery third blessing. This Jernigan hotly opposed influencing the leaders to forbid their teaching these doctrines on the camp grounds. He rejected not only their "third blessing" of fire but other teachings that included divine healing and the idea that sanctified Christians could be demon possessed in order to "chastise them." According to Jernigan they also taught that there were "demons of sickness, and various other kinds of demons that often tormented the sanctified."[27]

Irwin himself finally came to Texas later in 1897 when the leaders of the Poetry Holiness camp invited him to teach them his new doctrine. From the Poetry camp where he was well received, he travelled to Wills Point, Texas, where he was run out of town by angry mobs. From there, Irwin attended the Hughes Springs camp meeting in eastern Texas where he gathered many followers in spite of opposition from Jernigan and others. With Irwin was W.T. Curry from Louisiana who "would dance across the platform while preaching, shouting, I feel the fire all through me. Can't you feel it? Why I feel as if I were walking on live coals of fire. It burns me through my shoes." According to Jernigan, "this brought division in the camp and great persecution from the holiness fighters."[28]

By September 1897, Irwin returned to one of his favorite camp meetings, the annual camp of the Neosho Valley Holiness Association in Mound Valley, Kansas. Here the services were said to have been one "great and decisive victory after another" where some thirty persons experienced "sky blue conversions, fifty cases of sanctification, more than as many cases of divine healing, and twenty-five or thirty cases of the 'baptism of fire.'" The closing service was a street meeting where some 3,000 people heard Irwin preach an impassioned sermon "on the blood and fire line." To Irwin's delight, at the end of the meeting, the Neosho Valley Association accepted the constitution of the Fire Baptized Association of Southern Iowa, the second such group. Irwin estimated that some one hundred new members took part in the session.[29]

Not everyone in Mound Valley was happy with the Neosho meeting, however. The editor of the *Mound Valley Herald* newspaper wrote the following indignant and scathing editorial:

> The holy show at the city park is conducted by a people professing to be holy, but those who are at the head of the show do not conduct themselves in that manner. A Holiness that does not make a man Christ like is a farce and a hypocracy (*sic*). Christ said "follow me!" But we fail to find in his teachings where Christ jumped, screamed, or rooted in the dust, kicked up his heels and cavorted around like the men and women do at the park...We voice the sentiment of our best people when we say – God deliver Mound Valley from this demoralizing, desecrating outfit at an early date.[30]

Another less violent criticism came down on Irwin when a popular Holiness evangelist and writer of the time, Beverly Carradine, got wind of Irwin's third blessing and gave it a damaging review in his influential 1897 book *The Sanctified Life*. In a chapter titled "Sidetracks," he attacked the "third blessing" on theological grounds. "It is unscriptural" he stated adding "we cannot find anywhere in the Bible where people sought for and received the Baptism of Fire as a third blessing." If so then the hymn *Rock of Ages* would have to be amended to read "be of sin the triple cure" instead of "double cure."[31]

As Irwin's movement grew in numbers, it also grew in aggressiveness. At some point in 1898 one of Irwin's followers in North Carolina tried forcefully to get an older Methodist minister to seek the fire baptism on his sickbed. The *Charlotte Daily Observer* ran a story from the *North Carolina Advocate* (Methodist) about a very sick Methodist minister who reported that "a good man but a fanatic called on me. He paid me the honor of saying that he thought me a Christian, but I didn't have enough of the Holy Ghost...the fellow wanted me to rant, to jump out of bed and dance the Holy dance and then go onto a trance." Then he would be instantly healed. It did not work. The editor complained about those who claimed to be "converted, sanctified and baptized with fire...and filled with the Holy Ghost." The title of the article was "When is it going to end?"[32]

Such denunciations and pointed opposition did not slow down the momentum of Irwin and his followers. Soon after the Mound Valley meeting, Irwin and Oliver

Fluke travelled to the town of Thompson in the Oklahoma Territory. Here they organized the Oklahoma Fire-Baptized Holiness Association with G. B. Henson as the Overseer. From there they went to Texas where they organized a similar Association with A.R. Hodges as Overseer. On a later trip to Georgia in 1898, Irwin organized a Georgia Fire-Baptized Holiness Association in the town of Royston where he had just held a revival in "the old school meeting." Attending this meeting were future leaders in the movement that included R. B. Hayes, J. L. McElroy, W. B. Harris, A.C. Craft, I. A. Marley, and a young Methodist preacher, Joseph King. R.B. Hayes was appointed as the Overseer in Georgia. After this, Irwin travelled to Williston, Florida, where he organized a Fire-Baptized Association with N.G. Pulliam as "Ruling Elder." In a very short time, the energetic and charismatic Irwin had established state organizations in Iowa, Kansas, Oklahoma, Texas, Georgia, Florida, and North and South Carolina. North of the border, followers in Manitoba and Ontario were ripe for similar organizations.[33]

Now Irwin began to envision an international church organization with congregations in both the United States and Canada. To this point the movement was loosely organized around the personality of its dynamic leader. In choosing a place to call for a national conference, he looked to the town of Anderson, South Carolina. By now the south had become the most fertile ground for the growth of the Fire-Baptized Holiness movement. Georgia and South Carolina were particularly strong. Anderson was on the border of both states and was the most strategic place he could find.

Notes

[1] G. F. Taylor, *The Pentecostal Holiness Advocate*, May 2, 1930, p. 8. Also see Vinson Synan, *The Old Time Power, A Centennial History of the Pentecostal Holiness Church* (Franklin Springs, GA: Lifesprings Resources, 1998), pp. 44–63.

[2] Craig Fankhauser, "The Heritage of Faith," p. 123.

[3] B. H. Irwin "Des Moines, Iowa," *The Way of Faith and Neglected Themes*, May 20, 1896, p. 2; "The Abiding Fire," *The Way of Faith and Neglected Themes*, December 16, 1896, p. 1.

[4] *The Christian Witness and Advocate of Bible Holiness*, March 26, 1896, p. 1.

[5] Ibid., *The Christian Witness and Advocate of Bible Holiness*, April 23, 1896, p. 4. See Kerwin, "Isaiah Reid," p. 188.

[6] *Sent of God* (Tabor, Iowa), June 15, 1899, p. 2.

[7] B. H. Irwin, *The Way of Faith and Neglected Themes,* July 1, 1896, p. 3.

[8] B. H. Irwin, "The Central Idea," *Live Coals of Fire*, (Lincoln, Nebraska,) Nov. 10, 1899, p. 4. There is a problem with the date of this organization. Joseph Campbell in his *The Pentecostal Holiness Church, 1898–1948* dates it to 1895, but most later scholars believe that it must have been in 1896. See Kerwin, "Isaiah Reid," pp. 279–287.

[9] Fankhauser, "The Heritage of Faith," p. 124.

[10] Lee M. Haines, "The Grander, Nobler Work; Wesleyan Methodism's Transition, 1867–1901" in Wayne E Caldwell, Editor, *Reformers and Revivalists: The History of the Wesleyan Church* (Indianapolis: Wesley Press, 1992), p. 137.

[11] Craig Fankhauser, "The Heritage of Faith," p. 123.

[12] W. E. Stephenson, "A Murderous Assault on B. H. Irwin," *The Way of Faith and Neglected Themes*, August 12, 1896, p. 1.

[13] B. H. Irwin, "Coon Rapids, Iowa," *The Way of Faith and Neglected Themes* (July 29, 1896), 2.

[14] "Pyrophobia" in *Way of Faith*, November 4, 1896, p. 5. The entire text was published in *The Way of Faith and Neglected Themes*, on October 28, 1896, pp. 2–4. It is also in the selected reader Document 25.

[15] J. M. Pike, "Tracts! Tracts!" *The Way of Faith and Neglected Themes* (August 26, 1896), 4.

[16] B. H. Irwin, "Canada, Winnipeg, Manitoba" *The Way of Faith and Neglected Themes*, December 2, 1896, p. 5.

[17] *The Way of Faith and Neglected Themes*, on October 28, 1896, pp. 2–4.

[18] Joseph H. King and Blanch Leon King, *Yet Speaketh*, pp. 82–83.

[19] B. H. Irwin, "South Carolina, Piedmont," *Way of Faith*, December 30, 1896, p. 5. Also see Joseph H. King, "History of the Fire Baptized Holiness Church," *The Pentecostal Holiness Advocate*, March, 24, 1921, pp. 4–5.

[20] Craig Fankhouser, "Fire Baptized Revolt, p. 129.

[21] B. H. Irwin, "Divine Healing," *Live Coals of Fire*, October 23, 1899, p. 2.

[22] Ibid.

[23] Ibid.

[24] "Brother Irwin's Letter," *Way of Faith and Neglected Themes* (October 20, 1897), p. 2.

[25] Irwin, "Divine Healing," *Live Coals of Fire*, October 23, 1899, p. 2.

[26] Fankhouser, "Fire Baptized Revolt," p. 130.

[27] C. B. Jernigan, *Pioneer Days of the Holiness Movement in the Southwest* (Kansas City: Pentecostal Church of the Nazarene Publishing House, 1919), pp. 152–154.

[28] Ibid.

[29] Fankhouser, "Fire Baptized Revolt," p. 131. See *Way of Faith and Neglected Themes*, October 20, 1897, p. 2.

[30] Ibid, p. 131. "State Holiness Camp Meeting," *Mound Valley Herald*, September 17, 1897, p. 3.

[31] See Beverly Carradine, *The Sanctified Life* (Cincinnati: Office of the Revivalist, 1897), p 262.

[32] J. C. Troy, "Religious Department," *The Charlotte Daily Observer* March 27, 1898, p. 2.

[33] See Vinson Synan, *The Old Time Power*, p. 54.

Chapter Five

A New Denomination

Christ is our commander, we know no defeat, we've sounded the trumpet that ne'er calls retreat, then onward, right onward at His blest command, Clear the way, we are coming, the fire-baptized band.
                                                                    Thurmon A. Carey

As Irwin continued his barnstorming through the South and Midwest, many calls came to him to form a national organization. By early 1898, he began making plans to organize a new denomination for his fire-baptized followers. By the summer of that year a call went out for a "General Council" to be held in Anderson, South Carolina, now a veritable stronghold for the movement. The meeting convened in a tent and met from July 28-August 8, 1898. In addition to the 140 representatives and ministers who attended, there were hundreds more laypersons and well-wishers.

The local *Anderson Intelligencer* newspaper ran the following notice about the meeting: "The Fire Baptized Holiness Association is now holding a series of meetings in this city in a big tent, which is stretched in the grove of the Blue Ridge Railroad Yard. Delegates are present from Canada and nearly all the states. Services are held three times a day and are attended by large crowds."[1]

Prominent representatives who gathered for the Anderson Council were: J. F. Wolford, Kansas; G. M. Henson, Oklahoma; Allen Hodges, Texas; R. B. Hayes, Georgia; I. W. Ogle, Florida; W.S. Foxworth, South Carolina; Samuel D. Page, North Carolina; John H. Wine, Virginia; and Daniel Awrey, Tennessee. Joining the new denomination at this historic meeting was Joseph. H. King, from Georgia, and William E. Fuller, a black. man from South Carolina, both of whom would later become leading figures in the movement.[2]

Irwin designated the Anderson meeting as the "First General Council of the Fire-Baptized Association of America." Before he arrived he had written a complete constitution for his new church with a doctrinal statement and governmental system. But before the business convened, there were days of preaching, singing, dancing, shouting, and altar calls. A critic wrote an account of the meeting in the *Christian Witness*, quoting Irwin who said "we had music and dancing, shouts of victory, hot thunder bolts and slant lightnings, billows of white fire, and devil shaking dynamite."[3] Also there was "triumphant music" including the favorite anthem of the movement called "the Battle Hymn of the Fire Baptized Holiness Association" which was sung to the tune of the "Battle Hymn of the Republic." Some of the stirring words were:

> Mine eyes have seen the glory of the coming of the Lord,
> He is leading forth his people with his bright and flaming sword,
> He is sending forth the holy fire according to his word,
> Our God is marching on
>
> Glory, Glory, Hallelujah
> Glory, Glory, Hallelujah (etc.)

This song and others were included in a new hymnal issued by C. T. Stevens titled, *Blood and Fire Songs*.[4]

Of the meeting, J. H. King later commented:

> The services that were held during this convention at Anderson were characterized by great earnestness, fervency, boldness, and fanaticism. The spirit of religious extravagance dominated the majority of those present and that which was wild and foolish was preached, testified to and endorsed. The severest denunciation of all churches and religious bodies was delivered notwithstanding the extravagance and fanaticism that characterized the services of this meeting, God was present and worked mightily in the salvation of souls and the sanctification of believers.[5]

A New Constitution

Despite these misgivings, King joined the new church as a charter member. Another new member, William E. Fuller, who had ridden in a wagon forty miles to the meeting, broke away from his friends from the A.M.E. church and joined Irwin's new denomination.

In the business sessions, the delegates enthusiastically adopted Irwin's new *Constitution and General Rules of the Fire-Baptized Holiness Association of America* thus creating a new denomination. The government was a total autocracy with Irwin elected as "General Overseer" for life. Beyond this, he had absolute power to appoint all state "Ruling Elders" and appoint all pastors. He also had the power to expel from the church anyone he disliked, and deprive ministers of their credentials. Rather than being alarmed at vesting such absolute power in one man, the delegates seemed to "regard it as quite appropriate and fitting."[6] An interesting aspect of these sessions was that no minutes were kept for future generations to see. Joseph King later said, "No minutes were kept of these General Councils or State Associations for years. Why such were not made and published is strange and inexcusable."[7]

The title "General Overseer" seems to have been original with Irwin although Alexander Dowie bestowed the title on himself in 1903 as head of his "Christian Catholic Church." It was also later used by A. J. Tomlinson the leader of the Church of God in Cleveland, Tennessee, who may have gotten the idea from Irwin. "Overseer," a term used in the King James Version as the equivalent of the word "bishop," derives from the Latin *episcopos* meaning, literally, to "over see." The term was also notorious in during the slavery era, especially in the south when "overseer" referred to the task master who had direct charge of the slaves. They, like Irwin, wielded absolute power.

As to its doctrines, the new church was similar to most of the other Holiness churches in most respects. The major distinction was the statement on the fire baptism. The following three statements stated the unique doctrine:

> We believe that the baptism of the Holy Ghost is obtainable by an act of appropriating Faith on the part of the fully cleansed believer.
> We believe also that the baptism of fire is a definite, scriptural experience obtainable by faith on the part of the Spirit filled believer.
> We do not believe that the baptism with fire is an experience independent of or disassociated from the Holy Ghost.[8]

Later Irwin referred to these doctrinal statements as the "MAGNA CHARTA" of the Church.[9]

Other doctrinal statements placed the FBHA in the most radical wing of the Holiness movement. The section on entire sanctification stated "We believe that entire sanctification destroys and eradicates inbred sin." On healing, the Constitution stated "We believe in divine healing as in the atonement," while the article on the second coming stated "We believe in the imminent, personal, premillennial, second coming of our Lord Jesus Christ."[10] Quite unusual for the times was the statement on women in ministry. It stated:

> In view of the increasing number and efficiency of women who are evidently called of God into the evangelistic, missionary, and rescue, provision is hereby made for the appointing, ordaining, and sending forth of women thus called of God, exactly the same as men, thus placing fire-baptized women, called of God, upon the same footing with our brethren of the stronger sex.[11]

In the "general rules" and "questions for applicants for ministry," the fire-baptized members and ministers were forbidden to belong to "oath bound societies." All members who were to "cleanse ourselves from all filthiness of the flesh and spirit, such as the use of tobacco in every form, or of morphine, or intoxicants, filthiness of speech, foolish talking or jesting, to wear no outward adorning, such as jewelry, gold, feathers, flowers, costly apparel, or ornamentation of any kind."

In addition to these rules there were several "unwritten but binding rules" which included the observance of Old Testament dietary law (therefore the consumption of pork, catfish, and oysters was proscribed) and men were banned from wearing neckties. In later years the church became known to the public as the "no neckties, no hog meat church." Another unwritten but strongly observed rule on divine healing was that members would abandon doctors and medicines and "trust God for their bodies."[12]

An article was added to the "Basis of Union" to combat the spreading movement among some Holiness people called "Marital Purity" which held that there should be no sexual relations between sanctified husbands and wives except for procreation. Not surprisingly, this was causing havoc in some marriages and was perceived by Irwin as a threat to his movement. The article stated:

> The Lord says "marriage is honorable in all and the bed undefiled." And the Fire-Baptized Holiness Association of America firmly holds that there are certain relations between husband and wife which are strictly private according to the Word of God, and into this sacred privacy no one has any right to inquire.[13]

The *Constitution* also provided for the publication of an "official organ" for the church which would be edited by the General Overseer who would also have "general management of the same, and may appoint as many assistants as he shall deem necessary." In addition to this the Church envisioned becoming international in scope by authorizing a missions program which would also be "under the general supervision of the General Overseer, who shall have authority to appoint one or two Superintendents of Foreign Missions, as the exigencies of the times may demand."[14] In the elections, Irwin was elected as General Overseer with a board of trustees that included a General Secretary and a General Treasurer. Of monumental importance was the acceptance of W.E. Fuller to full ministerial membership. In the Jim Crow South of 1898, this was revolutionary indeed. Fuller was commissioned to go forth and organize Fire-Baptized Holiness churches among the "Colored people." In a short time he was the most effective evangelist and church planter after Irwin himself, organizing some fifty Fire-Baptized churches in several southern states in the following years.

Only two general leaders were elected to head the church in Anderson. They were B. H. Irwin, General Overseer and Estelle Gaines, General Secretary and Treasurer. The list of "Ruling Elders" was as follows:

> Alabama - Olive E. Stombaugh; Arkansas – C. T. Stevens; Florida - Isaac W. Ogle; Georgia - S.J. Mc Elroy; Iowa – Oliver Fluke; Kansas – Jesse Bathurst; Manitoba – Annie Douglas; Michigan – Mattie Ritter; Missouri – Belle Lowcock,; Nebraska – Hattie Lydie; North Carolina – Edward Kelly; Oklahoma Terr. – A. L. George; Ontario – Joseph H. King; Pennsylvania – Mrs. Victoria Tuttle; South Carolina – Estelle Gaines; Tennessee – Daniel Awrey; Texas – A. R. Hodges; Ruling Elders for the Colored Fire-Baptized Holiness Association of America. South Carolina - Alice M. McNeil; South Carolina – W. E. Fuller. [The attribution of both McNeil

and Fuller as Ruling Elders for South Carolina is likely a misprint. McNeil is later listed as Ruling Elder for NC.]

Eight of the twenty are notably female. Then followed a list of 137 "Ordained Evangelists" from many parts of the United States and Canada. Of these 91 were men and 45 were women while four were listed as "colored." These lists and an analysis of them, indicate the size, scope, and diversity of the movement when it organized in Anderson as a new denomination. The Association was international, interracial, and composed of many women who served in various capacities. It faced an uncertain future with many committed followers but with a much larger host of critics.

The drumbeat of criticism continued after the national organization of the Fire-Baptized Holiness Association. Not long after the conference an article in the *Christian Witness* was especially severe: "Today how many who call themselves Christians, hanker after noise, ocular demonstration, shouting, trances, and bodily healing, and what they call 'fire,' and see more in these things than they do in refining of the Holy Ghost and the human spirit sweetened by grace, softened by love, quieted by the peace of God, and sitting clothed and in its right mind." [15]

When they left Anderson, however, the faithful went out unfazed by criticism and determined to spread the fire all over the United States and Canada and also around the world through the foreign missions board that was created in the General council. The future looked bright indeed for the new church. The spirit of Anderson was given poetic expression by a Georgia member of the Church, Thurman Carey:

> Christ is our commander, we know no defeat,
> We've sounded the trumpet that ne'er calls retreat,
> Then onward, right onward at His blest command,
> Clear the way, we are coming, the fire-baptized band. [16]

Notes

[1] *The Anderson Intelligencer*, August 3, 1898.

[2] J. H. King, "History of the Fire Baptized Holiness Church," the *Pentecostal Holiness Advocate*, March 31, 1921, pp. 10-11.

[3] "Irwin's 'Fire Baptism' Movement," *The Christian Witness and Advocate of Bible Holiness*, September 22, 1898, p. 15.

[4] C. T. Stephens, comp., *Blood and Fire Songs* (Oklahoma City: Reprinted by Charles E. Jones, 2004).

[5] Joseph H. and Blanche Leon King, *Yet Speaketh: Memoirs of the Late Bishop J. H. King*, pp. 86-87.

[6] Joseph H. King, "History of the Fire Baptized Holiness Church," p. 11.

[7] Ibid.

[8] *Constitution and General Rules of the Fire-Baptized Holiness Association of America* (1900), p. 3. The 1898 *Constitution* has not been found, but the 1900 version is practically the same according to internal evidence.

⁹ B. H. Irwin, "The Central Idea," *Live Coals*, November 10, 1899, p. 4.
¹⁰ *Constitution and General Rules*, pp. 3–4.
¹¹ Ibid, p. 15.
¹² Vinson Synan, *The Old Time Power*, pp. 56–57; Joseph H. Campbell, *the Pentecostal Holiness Church, 1898–1948*, pp. 204–205.
¹³ *Constitution and General Rules*, p. 5. Some holiness churches forced members to publicly declare in church business meetings if they were living up to this teaching. This Irwin sternly opposed.
¹⁴ *Constitution and General Rules*, pp. 17, 19.
¹⁵ "Earthquakes, Cyclones, and Fires in Which the Lord is Not," *the Christian Witness*, October 13, 1898, p. 4.
¹⁶ See Vinson Synan, *Holiness Pentecostal Tradition*, p. 44.

Chapter Six

Dynamite, Lyddite and Oxidite

We are at this writing – shouting, and leaping, and praising God for the fire, and the dynamite, and the lyddite, and the unutterable glory which fill(s) our soul. We expect to fight until the war is over, and then shout the victorious shout of eternal triumph with our feet on the devil's neck.

B. H. Irwin

As he left Anderson, Irwin reached the pinnacle of his ministry career having founded and organized an international denomination with churches in eight states and Canada. In accomplishing this, he attracted several important followers who became prominent leaders in the coming years.

Early Leaders

Joining in Anderson was Joseph H. King who had been converted and sanctified in local Methodist churches in Georgia before joining the Methodist Episcopal Church, North and gaining his license to preach in the Georgia Conference. After serving as pastor of several Methodist charges, he attended the U.S. Grant Theological Seminary in Chattanooga, Tennessee, where he received the equivalent of a Master's Degree in theology in 1895. He then was admitted into full connection as an ordained Methodist Elder in 1896. In 1898 he attended a Fire-Baptized Holiness meeting in a Methodist Church in Georgia where he was attracted to the movement. He soon left the Methodist Church and became an independent evangelist working mainly with Fire-Baptized ministers such as A. K. Willis. As a result, he attended the Organizational meeting in Anderson, South

Carolina, in August of 1898 and joined forces with Irwin. Two years later he succeeded Irwin as General Overseer of the Church.[1]

Another leading member of the Church was Daniel Awrey of Beniah, Tennessee, who was well known in Holiness circles. An ardent evangelist, in 1895 he walked 1000 miles from East Tennessee to Texas in order to preach holiness in the Lone Star State. Attracted to Irwin's ministry, he received the fire baptism in 1895, joined the movement, was a delegate in Anderson, and was named Ruling Elder of Tennessee in 1898. His home was only nine miles from Cleveland, Tennessee, the future headquarters of the Church of God. Not only did Awrey claim the baptism of fire, he also claimed to have spoken in tongues in 1890 when he was sanctified and filled with the Holy Ghost. He had a great deal of influence on Irwin after inviting him to visit him in Tennessee in 1898.[2]

William E. Fuller, a licensed minister in the African Methodist Episcopal Church, was the only black minister to join the FBHA in Anderson in 1898. He was a native of Mountsville, South Carolina, who read about Irwin in the *Way of Faith* magazine. His curiosity led him to walk hundreds of miles from South Carolina to Kansas where he was well received even though he was an African American. In 1898 he rode a wagon the forty miles to Anderson to attend the organizational meeting. After connecting with Irwin, he was appointed as Ruling Elder for the "Colored" churches of the movement and later served on the Board of Trustees of the church. In 1908, he separated from the White churches to form a separate Colored Fire-Baptized Holiness Church.[3]

One of the leading women of the movement was Annie Douglas of Winnipeg, Manitoba, Canada. A leading Holiness minister in Winnipeg, she was well known across Canada as a woman of deep prayer and fasting. After inviting Irwin to preach in Winnipeg in 1896, she joined the Fire-Baptized movement and later became the Ruling Elder of Manitoba. She was said to have a "marvelous gift called the Tongue of Fire" that she said "remained upon her ever since the Holy Ghost filled her" and later a "Crown of Fire" after receiving the fire baptism.[4] A friend of Douglas who joined the Fire-Baptized Holiness Church in Oklahoma at this time, was Mrs. Mattie Mallory who founded the Oklahoma Orphanage in Bethany and for a short time placed it under the care of the Fire-Baptized Holiness Church. Her Orphanage later developed into the Bethany Children's Home. In 1898 she published the first Fire-Baptized paper which she named *The Guide*.[5]

Rapid Growth in the U.S. and Canada

With these very able leaders and with Irwin's dynamic leadership, the movement grew rapidly across the Middle West and the South. In many ways, the Fire-Baptized Holiness movement was a religious expression of the populist revolt that swept the same regions of the nation in the same years that Irwin's religious populism was growing. It is interesting that the very states represented in Irwin's movement; i.e. Iowa, Kansas, Texas, Oklahoma, Florida, Georgia, North Carolina, South Carolina, Tennessee, and Virginia were the same states that made up the Northwestern and Southern Farmers' Alliances that were the backbone of populism.[6]

Be that as it may, the two years after the Anderson convention saw Irwin continuing his barnstorming ministry in the United States and Canada while consolidating the work of the Fire-Baptized organization. In August 1898 he preached in Iowa while in September he was back in Mound Valley, Kansas, where he conducted the Southeastern Kansas Fire Baptized Holiness camp meeting. Here he denounced the anti-ordinance advocates who taught that no ordinances such as water baptism and the Lord's Supper were required of the sanctified. Irwin opposed them so strongly that many members separated from Irwin to form an entirely separate Fire-Baptized Association that would be free from ordinances.[7]

In the South, the Fire-Baptized cause expanded greatly after the Anderson convention in 1898. In Georgia, Ruling Elder R.B. Hayes reported that "the tide of interest was rising higher and higher and a great tidal wave of salvation was sweeping over the country." Although he preached mainly in tents, he said he would "go right on in schoolhouses, halls, and streets, preaching until Jesus comes." He soon acquired a "Gospel Wagon" to help him in his travels.[8] Hayes told of "several tents [that]were burned; about rotten eggs dripping from his coattail how he used a Bible for a pillow and a bench for a bed."[9] In Texas the evangelist E. M. Murrill not only received the "fire" but established a mission in Fort Worth where there were claims of instantaneous divine healing in his services.[10] By 1899 William Wisdom Newberry of Virginia temporarily joined the movement at Beniah, Tennessee. A well-educated and respected Methodist preacher, he introduced other southern Holiness leaders to Irwin helping to spread Irwin's movement in the South. He later wrote a book titled *Untangling Live Wires* warning against excesses in the Holiness movement.[11]

In South Carolina a convert to the movement who was to play a leading role in future years was Samuel D. Page a former saloon keeper and notorious sinner. After his conversion and sanctification experiences, he joined Irwin's movement and became one of his most effective evangelists and church planters. Even though he was criticized for his poor preaching style, he led hundreds of people into the movement. He was forever memorialized by the noted Holiness scholar, W. B. Godbey who wrote in 1896:

> I went to North Carolina [to preach]. At the opening I was introduced to my comrade in labor, Sam Page, a former notorious infidel and drunken saloon-keeper, whose profligacy and wickedness had been proverbial in all the land. Having been wonderfully converted and gloriously sanctified, responsive to his heavenly calling he was then a flaming evangelist, shaking that country with the Pentecostal power, which, in the mercy of God, characterized his ministry. The power descended on us [each night] and waves of salvation began to roll over the audience, revealing Him who is mighty to save. Simultaneously with the rolling billows, Sam would leap on a bench and shout aloud, "Look here, all ye drunkards, gamblers, blasphemers, thieves, murderers, and adulterers, and see me. Do you not know that I am Sam Page, the saloon-keeper, drunkard, blasphemer, gambler and infidel? See what God will do for you if you will repent of your sins and seek Him with all your heart as I did. Oh, He will wonderfully save and gloriously sanctify you!"

Inspired by the startling boldness of his tall, raw-boned preaching partner, the diminutive Godbey leapt on the bench, threw his arms around Sam Page, and shouted to the people: "Look at me, O ye good [church members] Methodists, Baptists, Presbyterians and Campbellites, who keep the moral law and walk irreproachably before the world, but have never been born from above, regenerated by the Holy Ghost, and know not what it is to receive a new heart, I was once where you are and as surely on my way to Hell as Sam Page in his saloon...." [12]

In Iowa the Quaker, John E. Dull preached in Coalfield where some "twenty persons sought and definitely received the fire." When told by a Quaker authority "to cease and desist from teaching the baptism of fire," he leaped and shouted and said "do what you think best. We bear this testimony that we please God." Later he accused his former Quaker friends of preaching a "moonshine holiness that does not get anybody sanctified, they fight the fire, eat hog, and belong to the Iowa State Holiness Association, an apostate institution that fights divine healing, and the premillennial second coming of Jesus and the baptism of fire." This opposition only intensified Dull's desire to work even harder for the Fire-baptized testimony. [13]

A Georgia preacher, N. G. Pulliam reported that in a meeting in Eastman, Georgia, "rowdies threw pine knots at the meeting house after his wife had preached 'under the power and demonstration of the blessed Holy Ghost.'" But nothing stopped the fearless evangelists. [14] The same kind of violent opposition occurred around the country as the preachers became more radical and denunciatory in their preaching.

The second national convention of the Church convened from April 1 through April 10, 1899 in the small town of Royston, Georgia, only a few miles south of Anderson, South Carolina. Here Irwin tightened his grip on the organization. Even after a sizable amount of business was transacted, very few changes were made to the *Constitution* and all the Ruling Elders were reappointed. From Royston, Irwin took the train to Fayetteville, North Carolina, where he preached to large and enthusiastic crowds. From there he went on to the nearby city of Dunn, North Carolina, where he held a tent meeting emphasizing the fire baptism and divine healing. In this meeting the wife of a leading sanctified Methodist layman, Julius A. Culbreth, was instantly healed. Culbreth later founded the town of Falcon where he established the Falcon Camp Meeting in 1900 which became one of the largest Holiness camp meetings in the nation. [15]

This meeting was also important because it was in the territory of where the Methodist holiness evangelist Abner B. Crumpler was forming another Holiness church known as the Pentecostal Holiness Church. It was organized in Fayettville in 1900. This church was destined to merge with the Fire-Baptized Holiness Church in the octagonal tabernacle in Falcon in 1911. It is not known if Crumpler and Irwin met at this time. [16] One thing is certain, the Fire-Baptized movement grew rapidly in this part of North Carolina. In April of 1899, the *Fayettville Weekly Observer* noted a new twist to the story telling about the same Fire-Baptized leaders' opposition to beards. It read, "Our old sanctification friends, Messrs. Brooks, Avant and Page, arrived this morning to join in the Fire-Baptized

Holiness meeting. Brother Harper is already with them. One of the peculiarities of the new sect is that they preach against the wearing of beards or mustaches. The preachers are supplied with scissors, and when a convert desires it, will clip his whiskers for him. Thus it is a frequent sight to see young and old men being shorn in public of every remnant of hair on their faces." [17] Although the wearing of beards and mustaches was not forbidden in the *Constitution* of the Church, it is noteworthy that photos of Irwin, King, and other leaders show them all as clean shaven.

Live Coals of Fire

Soon after this Irwin decided to fulfill the *Constitution* which authorized the publication of an "official organ" for the Church. Money was raised to buy a printing plant which was placed in Irwin's home in Lincoln, Nebraska. He appropriately named the paper *Live Coals of Fire*. Irwin edited the paper while his young Canadian assistant Albert E. Robinson served as his editorial assistant. Robinson also served as General Secretary of the denomination and Ruling Elder for Ontario. Also working with Irwin was Thomas Bickley, plant foreman, Miss Dovie Jordan,[18] his son Stewart Irwin, and his wife, Anna M. Irwin. The first issue appeared in October 1899 as a semi-monthly paper which consisted of eight pages. The subscription price was one dollar per year.[19]

In the fifth issue in December 1899, Irwin stated his editorial policy for the paper, especially for those who submitted articles and testimonies. He wrote: "We want no tame articles for LIVE COALS OF FIRE, and no old dry-leaf experiences. We want articles which have in them the chain and ball lightning of the tropics, and testimonies which burn like a furnace heated seven times. We must have letters and contributions which will strike the enemy like hot thunderbolts from the skies, and shake the underlying foundations of sin, and cause the stones in the walls to turn over and cry out in terror. Everything henceforth must have in it the earthquake element. WE ARE FOR WAR."[20]

Live Coals of Fire became the major journal of record for the church and the major recruiting tool for attracting new members and organizing new churches. It also carried detailed first-hand descriptions of Irwin's travels and meetings. With an eye for history, Irwin mailed a copy of each issue to the Library of Congress in Washington, D.C., making sure that future generations could know about his life and ministry.[21] King later observed that it was "the first paper in the United States that taught that the baptism of the Holy Ghost and fire was subsequent to sanctification."[22]

Under the masthead title *Live Coals of Fire* were three subheadings which read, "Fill thine hand with coals of fire and scatter them over the city." Ezek. 10:2; Then flew one of the seraphim unto me, having a live coal in his hand (Isa. 6:6); and out of the fire went forth lightening Ezek. 1:13. On the next line was the city of publication, Lincoln, Nebraska. In a sermon preached in 1898 and published in the first issue in 1899, Irwin explained that the idea for the title of his paper came from the story in Isaiah 6: 1 where the Lord touched the prophet's tongue with live coals from off the altar thus cleansing him from all his sins.

When *Live Coals of Fire* appeared on October 6, 1899, it carried both a travelogue and a long sermon by Irwin titled *Atheoi*. Also included were testimonies of people who had received the fire. A report from R.B. Hayes, a white man, who held a district meeting in a black church in Abbeville, South Carolina, with W.E. Fuller, told of Fuller's tent being cut to pieces before it got out of the depot. Despite this setback, the tent was repaired and 27 people were "converted and sanctified" while 19 "received the real fire." On the last night the people shouted the word "fire" so loudly that the fire department was called out because they "thought the whole town was on fire." Rowdies then cut down the tent and the meeting ended. Just how much opposition was due to the new fire doctrine and how much was due to the interracial worship is unknown, but was probably a mixture of both. In the end a strong African-American Fire Baptized Holiness congregation resulted from the meeting. In the same article, Hayes explained the effects of the baptism of fire as he experienced it. He said "Brethren, if the baptism of fire is anything, it is this, and this makes a man cry out in horror against all manner of sin...it makes you loathe it – hate it with a divine hatred. Sin becomes abominable, and you long to see people out from its deceptions and delusions."[23]

This first issue of *Live Coals of Fire* also contained the "Official List" of "Ruling Elders" and "Ordained Evangelists" revealing the widespread and rapid growth of Irwin's movement. At the top of the list was the "General Overseer" B. H. Irwin followed by the General Secretary and Treasurer Estelle Gaines from Central, SC.[24] Then followed the list of "Ruling Elders" as established at the first General Council.

The next list contained the names of the 137 "Ordained Evangelists" of the church. They were from across the United States and two provinces of Canada. In the order of their numbers by state, the list was as follows: South Carolina 24; Oklahoma 17; Kansas 17; North Carolina 15; Iowa 15; Georgia 11; Manitoba 5; Tennessee 5; Nebraska 5; Ontario 4; Florida 3; Texas 3; Michigan 2; Indiana 2; Ohio 1;Missouri 1; Mississippi 1; Alabama 1; Arkansas 1; Pennsylvania 1; New York 1; Louisiana 1; Virginia 1.[25]

From this list it is clear that the centers of Irwin's ministry and denomination were clustered around South Carolina, North Carolina, and Georgia, in the South and Kansas, Iowa, and Nebraska, in the Middle West. Two centers in Canada were located. around Winnepeg, Manitoba, and Toronto, Ontario.

This first issue also contained a lengthy travelogue of Irwin's most recent trips to Kansas with vivid descriptions of his meetings in Moonlight, Kansas, where the people not only received sanctification and the fire baptism, but there were "dynamite explosions which literally confounded and terrified the Devil." He continued, "nothing short of this devil arousing dynamite will do the work of us as his ministers and followers in these 'evil days.' Glory, glory glory."[26]

In future issues of *Live Coals of Fire* Irwin lashed out against gambling, stealing, drunkenness, adultery, and abortion which he called "child murder." He charged doctors with this crime. In a sermon preached in Kendall, New York,

Irwin wrote: "I believe in my soul that the work of God is hindered because of the child-murder and heart murder in the country. People's hearts and hands are stained with the blood of their unborn children, and until they confess it they will never be saved. I know from observation what this thing means, and when a man preaches on this line he arouses the lust devil and the murder devil all through the country. It means something for adulterers, thieves and robbers to get saved of God."[27]

The Fourth and Fifth Blessings

As early as 1895, Irwin referred to dynamite in a letter to the *Christian Witness* in a general sense as a heightened manifestation of God's power, but not to a specific spiritual experience. He also used the term in letters to the *Way of Faith* in 1896. Furthermore he used the words "slant lightening" and other phrases, but not as separate spiritual experiences. It seems 1898 was the year that dynamite was first presented as an experience following the "fire." In *Live Coals of Fire* a man from Oklahoma, E.D. Wells, wrote to *Live Coals* that "One year ago I sought for this experience (dynamite) and received it." That would be the fall of 1898.[28]

In the fourth issue of *Live Coals of Fire* Irwin wrote an article titled "The Dynamite" in which he explained his new theology on the "baptism of dynamite." This now became the fourth blessing after salvation, sanctification, and the baptism of fire. For this new "blessing" Irwin had two slivers of scripture, Acts 1:8 which stated "You shall receive power (*dunamis*) after that the Holy Ghost has come upon you," and Romans 1:16 where Paul stated "I am not ashamed of the Gospel of Christ: for it is the power (*dunamis*) of God unto salvation." In both cases Irwin used the modern English word "dynamite" to translate the Greek word for power. Irwin therefore began to preach that there was a baptism of "dynamite" after the baptism of fire and urged his followers to seek this "blessing."[29]

In the same issue, Jesse Bathurst of Ness City, Kansas, described in unforgettable language his reception of the fourth blessing: "All at once there appeared right in front of me something which looked like a little round ball about the size of a small bullet, and I happened to have the spiritual hiccoughs at the time...and my mouth flew open without any effort on my part, and in went the little ball of pure, irresistible dynamite. Some of you who get scared and howl about the third blessing, what will you do with the fourth?"[30]

In short order, Irwin concocted a new fifth blessing which he called "the Lyddite." This was an even more powerful explosive that was used in the Boer War in South Africa in 1898 and was discussed in the newspapers at the time. Now his hapless followers were required to come back to the altars to receive this new and mythical experience, which had no scriptural basis whatsoever. No less a follower than Joseph H. King in Toronto claimed to receive all these experiences. Of the dynamite he wrote, "There is no mistake about our reception of it. For we sought definitely, believed definitely, and received definitely. And God was just as definite in giving as we were in receiving." He also added, "we also sought and received the explosive lyddite and we know it is of God."[31]

Another Irwin follower, Sarah Payne, who worked in the *Live Coals* office, went even further than King by claiming to receive the experiences of "Oxydite" and "Selenite" after the dynamite.[32]

For Irwin's first four experiences he could cite some scriptures, however far-fetched they might be, but for the others, lyddite, oxydite, and selenite, he must have resorted to chemistry textbooks and the newspapers. In later years, George Floyd Taylor of the Pentecostal Holiness Church called these experiences "a religious rainbow's end."[33] A sad case of a woman who claimed to have received all these experiences appeared in *The Holiness Advocate* in 1903:

> August 1st, 1898, I was *pardoned* of my sins. On the following Sunday at eleven o'clock, God *sanctified me wholly*. A few days later I received the *Comforter*. Later on in October, God gave me the *Baptism of fire*. The devil and all the hosts of hell cannot make me doubt this. When my sister Mattie was married I fell into a trance, and saw a vision. During services a night or so afterwards, God showed me that I needed more power for service; so I made my wants known, and prayer being offered, my faith took hold of God's promises, and I received *the Dynamite*. A few nights after this I received the *definite experience of Lyddite*. This gives the devil trouble, and he wonders what is coming next. Well, I am in for all that God has for me.

The writer of the article, A.M. Hills, who described all this as "fanaticism," said that this poor soul should have sought and received one more blessing, "the baptism of common sense."[34] W.E. Fuller who headed the African American branch of the church fully accepted all the new experiences Irwin was teaching. In an unforgettable testimony Fuller wrote in 1904, "I am still on the blood, fire, and dynamite line. I praise God for the blood that cleans up, the Holy Ghost that fills up, the fire that burns up, and the dynamite that blows up."[35]

Despite all this, the church continued to grow and entered new territory as the Nineteenth Century came to a close. In the second issue of *Live Coals of Fire* Irwin published a long list of Ruling Elders and ordained evangelists. It showed the impressive growth of the movement as an international and interracial body with women serving in leading positions, even as ruling elders. Irwin was listed as General Overseer while Estelle Gaines from Central, South Carolina, was still listed as General Secretary and Treasurer. It must be noted that of the twenty-one Ruling Elders eight were women while the general Secretary-Treasurer was a womanThe list also showed that the church was interracial with two ruling elders listed as "colored." Following the list of Ruling Elders was a long list of 138 "Ordained Evangelists" from many parts of the United States and Canada. Of these, fifty four were women with four listed as "colored." This. list proved that the church was a leader in giving opportunity to women and minorities, even at the highest levels, and was therefore all but unique for the times. Irwin's church provided equal ministerial credentials for those who were usually ignored or rejected by most of American society, including the churches. This was part of the appeal of the church.

As his church grew, some groups looked to the future by building Fire-Baptized Holiness church buildings. By 1900 there were two church buildings with more in the plans. The first one was "Willis Chapel" in Montevideo, Georgia, (1898) which was the first church building deeded to the denomination. The chapel was near Royston, Georgia, site of the second National Convention in April of 1899. It was built by the Wesleyan Methodists in 1896, but when Irwin's movement hit north Georgia like a firestorm, the entire congregation was swept into the movement. The second building seems to have been built in Royston, Georgia, soon afterwards.[36]

By 1900 Irwin was at the height of his ministry. He was a powerful preacher. Huge crowds came to hear his riveting messages. Some were repelled by his preaching and the noisiness of the meetings, but many others with "unfulfilled desires" were attracted to his ministry. In April 1900 he went on a "desert place apart" retreat where he reflected on his successes. He noted that he had preached the gospel in "twenty-three states, territories and provinces, to our people (North American Whites) to negroes and North American Indians." He also claimed that he had more than "one hundred and twenty five active fire baptized workers in the field."[37]

With an international organization in place and a national paper spreading the influence of the church to faraway places, Irwin began looking for a national headquarters with facilities for a school for his fast-growing denomination. By late 1898 he envisioned a "school for the prophets" to train and send fire baptized workers to the four corners of the world.

Notes

[1] See Joseph H. King and Blanch Leon King, *Yet Speaketh,* pp. 11–87.

[2] Daniel Woods, "Daniel Awrey, The Fire-Baptized Movement, and the Origins of the Church of God: Toward a Chronology of Confluence and Influence," in *Cyberjournal for Pentecostal-Charismatic Research* #19. http://www.pctii.org/cyberj/cyberj19/woods.html.

[3] See the *Discipline of the Fire Baptized Holiness Church of God of the Americas,* 1994, p. 2.

[4] See her autobiography, *A Mother in Israel: The Life Story of Mrs. Annie Douglas* (Oklahoma City: Charles Jones reprint, 2002), p.13. Strangely enough, Douglas never mentions Irwin in her autobiography. Also see Annie Douglas, "A Crown of Fire," *Live Coals of Fire,* October 13, 1899, p. 7.

[5] See Charles E. Jones, *Miss Mallory's Children: The Oklahoma Orphanage and the Founding of Bethany* (Oklahoma City: ND), pp. 395–396. This was copied from an article published in the *Chronicles of Oklahoma* (Vol. 71, No. 4, Winter, 1993–1994), pp. 392–421. Copies of *The Guide* can be found in the Bethany Children's Home.

[6] See Vinson Synan, *Holiness Pentecostal Tradition,* pp. 42–43 for a discussion on populism and the American religious scene in the late1890s.

[7] See Fankhauser, "The Fire-Baptized Revolt," pp. 136–137. This group continued into the Twentieth Century as the Fire Baptized Holiness Association of Southeastern Kansas that later merged with the Wesleyan Church.

[8] R. B. Hayes, "Georgia, Carlton," *The Way of Faith and Neglected Themes*, October, 12, 1898, p. 5. Hayes' trailblazing meetings in Georgia and South Carolina are described in W. M. Hayes, *Memoirs of Richard Baxter Hayes* (Greer, SC: Dunlap Print, 1945).

[9] See Hayes, *Memoirs of Richard Baxter Hayes*, p. 129.

[10] E.M. Murrill, "What of the Fire," *Way of Faith and Neglected Themes*, October 26, 1898, p. 2.

[11] See W.W. Newberry, *Untangling Live Wires* (1914, republished by Voice of Deeper Truth in 1945).

[12] W. B. Godbey, *The Autobiography of William Baxter Godbey* (Cincinnati: God's Revivalist Press, 1909), pp. 12–13.

[13] John E. Dull, "Iowa, Coalfield," *Way of Faith*, October 26, 1898, p. 5.

[14] Craig Fankhauser, "The Fire-Baptized Revolt," p. 139.

[15] Joseph Campbell, *The Pentecostal Holiness Church: 1898–1948*, pp. 361–362. Also see A. E, Robinson. "My Friend: Joseph Hillery King" in *The Apologist* (June 1946), p. 1.

[16] See Vinson Synan, *The Old Time Power*, pp. 118–123.

[17] See "Reinforcements" the *Fayetteville Weekly Observer*, April 20, 1899, p.1. Of interest is the fact that the future Full Gospel Business Men set up a barber shop in a London hotel to cut the long hair of hippy converts. Thus their "airlift" became a "hairlift." See Vinson Synan, *Under His Banner: History of the Full Gospel Business Men International* (Costa Mesa, CA: Gift Publications, 1992), p. 76–77.

[18] It seems certain that this woman, "Dovie" Jordan from Texas, is the same Mary Lee Jordan from Texas that Irwin later took as his second wife.

[19] See "Our Working Force," *Live Coals of Fire* (October 20, 1899), p. 4.

[20] B. H. Irwin, "The Dynamite and its Effects," *Live Coals of Fire*, December 15, 1899, p. 1.

[21] See B. H. Irwin, "Editorial Correspondence," *Live Coals of Fire*, October 6, 1899, p. 1.

[22] J. H. King, "History of the Fire-Baptized Holiness Church," *The Pentecostal Holiness Advocate*, March 24, 1921, p. 11.

[23] R. B. Hayes Letter, *Live Coals of Fire*, Oct 6, 1899, p. 2.

[24] Although Gaines was listed as General Secretary and Treasurer and Ruling Elder for South Carolina in the first list, she is notably absent from the list in the January 12, 1899, issue and disappeared from the movement thereafter. Perhaps she saw something about the autocratic rule of Irwin that caused her to resign.

[25] See "Official List," *Live Coals of Fire*, October 6, 1899, p.8.

[26] B. H. Irwin, "Editorial Correspondence," *Live Coals of Fire*, October 6, 1899, p. 1.

[27] B. H. Irwin, "Sermon by the Editor: Repentance and Confession," *Live Coals of Fire*, (June 15, 1900), 2–3. See Document 35 in the *Irwin Reader*.

[28] See E. D. Wells, "The Dynamite," *Live Coals of Fire*, December 1, 1899, p. 7.

[29] B. H. Irwin, "Editorial Correspondence," *Live Coals of Fire*, November 10, 1899, p. 2. Irwin had worked in a rock quarry as a youth and saw the power of dynamite first hand.

[30] Ibid. p. 5.

[31] Joseph H. King, "Our Sojourn in Toronto," *Live Coals of Fire*, May 4, 1900, p. 1.

[32] J. H. King, "Sarah M. Payne," *Live Coals of Fire*, June 1, 1900, p. 4.

[33] Joseph H. Campbell, *The Pentecostal Holiness Church*, p. 204.

[34] A. M. Hills, "Fanaticism Among Holiness People," *The Holiness Advocate*, April 1, 1903, p. 5.

[35] *Live Coals* (Royston, GA.), January 11, 1904, p. 2. Also see Vinson Synan, *The Holiness Pentecostal Movement*, p. 58.

36 B. H. Irwin, "In the Southland," *Live Coals of Fire,* January 12, 1899, p. 4. The "Willis Chapel" was named for A.K. Willis who served as pastor of several Wesleyan Methodist Churches in Northeast Georgia. The church is now known as the Beulah Pentecostal Holiness Church. For more on Willis, see Joseph H. King and Blanch Leon King, *Yet Speaketh,* pp. 82-83, also see "Beulah Pentecostal Holiness Church: Reminiscing, 1896-1996."

37 B. H. Irwin, "A Desert Place Apart," *Live Coals of Fire,* April, 20, 1900, p. 4. Also see, Martin H. Schrag, *Spiritual Pilgrimage,* pp. 22-23.

Chapter 7

Beniah, Tennessee Headquarters

> We are praising God for what He is doing for us here in the little log cabin used as a house of worship by the fire-baptized people. The first meeting was a day of shouting and leaping and praising God. The Lord put the dance on me for the first time. Hallelujah! The work is still going on, eighteen have been saved, sixteen sanctified, and filled with the Holy Ghost, eight or ten have the baptism of fire and several have the dynamite.
>
> Sarah H. Smith

As Irwin's movement spread rapidly around the nation, his first strongholds were in Iowa, Kansas, and Nebraska. By 1896 a new center developed in South Carolina around the city of Piedmont which resulted in the organization of the national movement in Anderson, South Carolina, in 1898. Another stronghold was in and around Royston, Georgia, where the second national convention was held in 1899 and the location of the first FBHA church buildings. A further stronghold soon developed in 1899 in and around Cleveland, Tennessee, in the tiny town of Beniah, which Irwin hoped would become the FBHA national headquarters with a "School of the Prophets" which hopefully would send missionaries to the nations of the world.

When the FBHA was organized nationally in Anderson, South Carolina, in 1898, Tennessee was not listed as a state organization although Daniel Awrey, an outstanding evangelist from Beniah, Tennessee, was in attendance. The reason for this omission is unknown. For several years East Tennessee had been a hotbed for Holiness revivals through the East Tennessee Holiness Association which was organized among Methodists by F.W. Henke in 1888. Known as "Holy Henke" and the "Railroad Evangelist," he was a former Methodist preacher born in Baltimore and educated at Boston University. Leaving the Methodist Church in 1888, he spread holiness from his home in Bradley County after moving to

Tennessee. He died in 1893 at the age of thirty-seven the same year that Daniel Awrey arrived in the community.[1]

Daniel Awrey, who had been ordained in the Congregational Methodist Church in 1895, was a very capable Holiness preacher who spread the Holiness flame around the mountain areas near his home in Beniah, Tennessee. In 1895 he journeyed fifty miles "up into the mountains" to preach Holiness. Here, he reported that at least fifty people were "saved and sanctified" before he was "threatened with whips" and turned out of the schoolhouse where he was preaching. Although Awrey did not specify which mountains he went to, it could well be that future Fire-Baptized stalwarts, Billy Martin, Milton McNabb, and Joe Tipton, who had been members of local Methodist and Baptist Churches, were sanctified in these meetings. Sometime after this, these three were swept into the Fire-Baptized Holiness movement, possibly from reading Irwin's reports in the *Way of Faith* magazine.[2]

The Schearer School House Revival

Be that as it may, Martin, Tipton, and McNabb are credited with leading an important revival in Western North Carolina at the Schearer Schoolhouse in Cherokee County. Here, in addition to the many that were saved and sanctified, it was reported that some 100 persons spoke in tongues. One person who spoke in tongues was Sarah A. Smith, from Beniah, Tennessee, who spoke of the meeting as part of the "Fire Baptized Association" which was just reaching that part of North Carolina. She said that "members of the [Fire-Baptized] Association frequently went over from Tennessee (where they lived) to hold meetings for them." They were Tipton, Martin, and McNabb. She reported that "a woman began to pray and presently broke out speaking in another tongue." Soon afterward, Tipton himself spoke in tongues. According to Smith, tongues soon broke out in Beniah, Tennessee, where she and "about forty or fifty others were baptized in the Spirit."[3] Sometime later Sarah Smith received the fourth blessing, the baptism of dynamite. In a letter to *Live Coals* in 1899 she wrote:

> We are praising God for what He is doing for us here in the little log cabin used as a house of worship by the fire-baptized people...The first meeting was a day of shouting and leaping and praising God. The Lord put the dance on me for the first time. Hallelujah! The work is still going on, eighteen have been saved, sixteen sanctified, and filled with the Holy Ghost, eight or ten have the baptism of fire and several have the dynamite. Brother Awrey came over last Wednesday and was with us for four meetings, and Sister Awrey is still here, filled with the Spirit. Many are under awful conviction, and the shouts of the fire-baptized ring out all over the neighborhood. Yours, dynamited for God.[4]

In the Glorious Southland

Probably at the invitation of Awrey, now the Ruling Elder for Tennessee, Irwin decided to visit Tennessee in October of 1899 because of the "great amount of activity in the region."[5] Leaving from Denver for the "glorious Southland," he took many books to read on the way, and during a stopover in St. Louis visited a used bookstore to add to his reading resources. Traveling with him was John E. Dull and Mary Lenhert. When he arrived at the "Beniah Camp" he was met by Edward Kelly, William Martin, Robert Porter, and Joe Tipton who he said, "had done faithful work in this region." He also added, "the fire and dynamite are here to stay, and will continue to spread in spite of all the devil's devices."[6] He credited Martin and Porter for bringing the dynamite to Tennessee after "they came back from the west and north and preached the dynamite."[7] Irwin was so impressed with the growth of his movement that he envisioned taking the whole state for the Fire-Baptized cause. He wrote:

> Praise the Lord for a few young men with enough spiritual backbone and holy courage to act on their convictions and obey God rather than man. A score of such men filled with the Holy Ghost and baptized with fire and "dynamited with all dynamite" would spread the fire and dynamite throughout the entire state and Tennessee, and give great trouble to the backslidden preachers and the apostate churches. We are praying God to raise up men and women enough to carry this glorious gospel of fire and dynamite into every county and precinct of this beautiful state.[8]

School of the Prophets

One reason for Irwin's trip to Tennessee was to accept 75 acres of land for a "school of the Prophets" which was donated to the FBHA by Dolly Curry Lawson in the town of Beniah. The school was already open for children's classes taught by Emma De Friece. Irwin was so excited about the school that he made an appeal in *Live Coals of Fire* for $5,000 in donations from the FBHA faithful to build the school where pastors and missionaries could be trained. He said that he already had $1,000 "in hand" and another $1,000 "definitely promised." About the new school, he added:

> Many of our evangelists and workers are greatly in need of this school. Some of them need to learn the first principles of a common school education; they need to learn to spell and read and write. And they need to know the scriptural proofs of the foundational doctrines of the Bible, such as justification, regeneration, adoption, sanctification, divine healing, the coming of the Lord, and the baptism of fire and the dynamite. And it is necessary also that our workers become acquainted with the doctrines of men and devils, that they be not deceived by these subtle delusions. In short, it is highly important and even necessary, that our people and especially our workers and public teachers, be indoctrinated in the principles of the fire baptized holiness faith.[9]

Irwin also promised to hire no teachers who were "opposed to the teachings of our Association." Moreover "the trustees have decided that cottages may be erected on the premises by those who may want to make Beniah their home, provided they are in full sympathy with the Association and our methods and teachings." In fact one leader, W. B. Martin "has already erected a nice little cottage of five rooms for his family and another, and Brother Daniel Awrey has selected a lot for his family." Also, Irwin added, "We also selected one for ourselves where we hope to build a neat, cheap building in the not too distant future. Here we shall have our private library, and it shall be for us a retreat, where we can go when greatly in need of a rest and quiet and shut ourselves in from the noise and clamor of the wicked world, and where we can live for a few days or weeks in the society of the old masters."[10]

Irwin also let it be known that students would have to work hard in the new school, not only in the classroom, but also at many other jobs on campus. He said "we want no one here who will not plow corn, hoe cotton, dig potatoes, wash clothes, or milk the cows." He envisioned a school that would eventually number some 250 students who would work their way through the program.[11]

A Missionary Vision

Before leaving Tennessee, Irwin became excited about sending Fire-Baptized Holiness missionaries around the world, beginning in the "Dark Continent" of Africa. It was hoped that the school of the Prophets would train them to go to Africa and make that mission "the centre of fire baptized holiness in Africa from which shall radiate divine fire and glory and power into every part of the Dark Continent." He added, "We praise the Lord that in answer to prayer, He is calling some of the fire-baptized saints into distant lands. We confidently expect to go to Africa in the not too distant future."[12] Irwin's son Stewart Toombs Irwin was with his father in Tennessee and already making plans to go as a missionary to the "wilds of Africa." Shortly after this, the November 1999 issue of *Live Coals of Fire* announced that plans were being made to open "Our Cuban Work." John E. Dull felt "a special call to go to that island and preach the fire and dynamite and he expects to go within a month or six weeks. He was scheduled to leave on January 1, 1900.[13]

In December 1899, Irwin enthusiastically told his readers that: "God is sending missionaries to Africa. We have three, possibly five who are to go to South Africa, and they will plant the standard of the fire and spread this everlasting gospel of fire and dynamite throughout the whole of that wonderful continent. God will do it through them. Others are going to Manila and to Cuba. *Live Coals of Fire* is circulating in Manila tonight. Others are going to South America, India, and China."[14] Beyond Africa and Cuba, Irwin developed a worldwide vision where his missionaries would cover the globe for the Fire-Baptized saints. He exulted,

We have been asking the Lord for nearly two years now, to send forth fire-baptized missionaries into every part of the earth, and plant the standard of the **white** fire in every continent, and on every island of the sea; and we have the assurance that He will do it. "And when this gospel of the kingdom" (which is the **dynamite** of God unto salvation to everyone that believeth) is preached "in all the world as a witness unto all nations," then Jesus will come in the clouds of heaven and set up His kingdom upon the earth, and we shall reign with Him Glory, glory, glory! This dynamited gospel has not yet been preached in all the earth; it is the mission of the fire-baptized movement to deliver the nations, peoples, and kindreds, and tongues, of the earth, this glorious, manifold gospel.[15]

As is evident, Irwin's movement had adopted a clear missionary vision with the goal of spreading the Fire-Baptized message around the world. While he was in Beniah, Irwin described the manifestations that followed the Fire Baptized saints whenever they received the "fire" or "dynamite." They were probably manifested in the Beniah meetings and were similar to the "exercises" that occurred in Cane Ridge, Kentucky, a century earlier. Irwin described these: "Sometimes it is the holy dance, sometimes the holy scream, and sometimes the holy laugh; some leap and jump while others fall prostrate under the power of God. Some have the 'jerks,' while others have sudden and long continued attacks of the 'hot chills.' Glory to God for the diverse manifestations of the Spirit."[16]

When he left Beniah the Fire Baptized people spread over the region with great speed. With Irwin's dynamic preaching in and around Beniah and in nearby Cleveland, Tennessee, a few Fire-Baptized people in and around Cleveland later became leaders of the Church of God after 1902. After only two months, Irwin came back to the "glorious Southland" to "look after the interests of the School of the Prophets and make some arrangements in the matter of building." Although the school was in operation under the newly appointed principal, Emma de Freise, there was no space for students and classrooms. A building was desperately needed since "many have applied for admission" to come to Beniah in June 1900 when the school was scheduled to open. Little had changed since his trip in October. He still claimed to have $1,000 "in hand" and another $1,000 "definitely promised," but nothing more had come in since December.[17]

Despite the slowness of fund raising for the project, Irwin spent the better part of one day "looking over the ground, locating the site for the school building, and mapping out the sites for the cottages." As before, W. B. Martin had already erected a small cottage while Daniel Awrey and Irwin himself selected the sites for their own cottages. After his visit to Beniah, Irwin caught the train to Atlanta and went on to Royston, Georgia, where he experienced a "pitched battle with the powers of darkness." He also visited the newly deeded church building in Montevideo.[18]

Irwin Ministers in Interracial Services

After leaving Beniah, Irwin went by train to Abbeville, South Carolina, where he preached for Ruling Elder William Fuller in a Fire-Baptized Holiness church. Meetings were held in "a little despised, out of the way back alley building called Zion" where "such singing, such shouting, such dancing, such praying, it has never before been our privilege to hear." Irwin also observed that "the colored people dance before the Lord differently from our white people. They got to dancing all over the house and kept it up for over an hour." Irwin was so affected that he said "I shouted, and cried, and laughed, and jumped and praised God, and that is the kind of salvation I believe in."[19]

He also found that "some of the colored people fight the fire as bitterly as do some of the whites." He saw great prejudice from the "ungodly whites" who "look upon us with severe scorn and contempt because we hold meetings for the colored people." On the other hand, he pointed out that "the unholy hypocritical Negroes persecuted the sanctified amongst them because they allow white men to come and preach to them occasionally." On this trip Irwin found that the "glorious Southland" was filled with racial hatred and division which he was determined to overcome with the fire and dynamite gospel.[20]

From Abbeville, Irwin travelled to Kingstree, South Carolina, where he stayed in the "genuine old-time plantation home of James Epps. He was invited to come to Kingstree by Isaac Gamble," a black Fire-Baptized Holiness evangelist who suggested that the meeting be held "conjointly for the colored and white people." Still, the plan honored the segregated world of the South, "The colored brethren occupied one part of the tent and the whites the other part. One part of the altar was for the whites and the other for the colored. Everything went on harmoniously the Kingstree meeting was a wonderful meeting. In some respects it surpassed any meeting we have ever held."[21]

Back in Georgia

On the first day of the Twentieth Century, Irwin was back in Georgia where he saw the New Year arrive in the Willis Chapel Church near Royston. Here, he reported, "the Fire-Baptized saints were all aglow, and the work of the Lord went on triumphantly." But all was not well among his own Holiness people in that part of Georgia. In Royston, Canon, and Montevideo, he found "hog eating, nicotine professors of holiness, chewing, smoking, snuffing, and smelling like a hog on a dung hill, filthy, depraved and nasty. Yet they were in good standing in the 'church.'" Even the Wesleyan Church was "twice dead and utterly without the Spirit," because the "Conference has officially denounced the Baptism of fire, and we are informed, will not let their members or others testify to it." He added, "no wonder the people are deserting and turning against such a corrupt apostate body." Despite all this, Irwin was invited to preach in the "Opera House" in Royston to an "immense crowd." Here, he exulted "the pillars of hell were shaken and the foundation of sin and iniquity actually trembled."[22]

It was in Royston that Irwin heard his son Stewart Toombs Irwin preach for the first time. His sermon was on regeneration and was "from the throne." The proud father saw a bright future for his son, stating "we believe he is in apostolic succession, and we are unspeakably glad that God has raised him up to assist us in the battle against sin and the devil." It seems that Irwin saw his son as his possible successor in leading the church in the future.[23]

In Canada

After his trip to the "Southland," Irwin went north in February by way of Washington, D.C. He continued on to Iron City, near Pittsburgh, Pennsylvania, where he fell sick for a week, but after much prayer was "up and about again." While there, the ever creative evangelist promoted his new experience which he called the "heavenly Lyddite." This would follow the fourth blessing baptism of dynamite as a new fifth blessing. He explained, "we are against a strong and wily foe, and we have to meet him with the mightiest artillery of heaven."[24] From Pittsburgh, Irwin went on to his stronghold in Toronto, Canada, where Joseph King served as pastor of the church and Ruling Elder for Ontario. King had recently received the "dynamite" and was ripe for the new lyddite experience. In Toronto Irwin added the new experience to his report: "we are at this writing – shouting, and leaping, and praising God for the fire, and the dynamite, and the lyddite, and the unutterable glory which fill(s) our soul. We expect to fight until the war is over, and then shout the victorious shout of eternal triumph with our feet on the devil's neck."[25]

Not long after introducing the lyddite to his arsenal of spiritual baptisms, Irwin went on to promote the baptism of "oxidite" while his friend, the seminary educated pastor King, in Toronto advocated a new baptism of "selenite" to add to the growing list. Soon the faithful were testifying to at least six post-conversion experiences. They were entire sanctification, the baptism in the Holy Ghost and fire (sometimes separate experiences), the dynamite, the lyddite, the oxidite, and the selenite.[26]

The erudite .King attempted to theologize about these multiple baptisms in articles to *Live Coals of Fire*. In a letter titled, "The Twofold Aspect" he wrote, "Jesus' baptism is twofold: the conscious filling of the Holy Ghost, and the mighty, illuminating baptism of fire. The mighty destructive enduement, destructive in its outer manifestations is also twofold in its significance. There is the incoming of the omnipotent dynamite, and the explosive lyddite. And yet the double significance of these great events and experiences are simultaneous in their occurances. [sic] There is a distinctiveness and subsequency in their appearance that is noticeable."[27]

In another attempt to add theology on Irwin's multiple baptisms, King offered an article titled "Our Weapons of Warfare." It was a brave and intellectual argument which accented the fact that King was now becoming the prime theologian of the movement:

> If the combination of certain substances in nature constantly increases the power of destruction, is there not a corresponding higher destructive power in the divine kingdom which if obtained will enable us to be more and more powerful in our opposition to the devil's forces? All laws in nature were instituted by the Lord, in all their innumerable varieties and degrees of operation, and the laws of the natural and spiritual kingdoms are largely analogous, so what is found to exist in the lower has its counterpart in the higher. And upon this basis, as well as the word of God, many of the dynamited saints sought and received the addition of power to their souls called the heavenly lyddite.... Glory to God! As long as the devil opposes and severely denounces this new experience it is all the evidence we desire, and it is the only apology we have in testifying to and preaching it.[28]

After leaving Toronto, Irwin went back to Missouri and Nebraska where he met great opposition from local Methodist preachers. These he called "ungodly nicotine pastors who would not even give the hapless evangelist a 'Methodist bed' for one night." He added that they called us "wild and fanatical and beside ourselves because we preach the fire and dynamite: and when we throw a lyddite shell into their ranks, they say that we are crazy." Yet the same paper carried plans to build yet another Fire-Baptized Holiness church building to be called "Oliver Fluke's Chapel." [29] From Nebraska, Irwin travelled to Eddyville and Ottumwa, Iowa, where he confronted a new "teaching of Satan and his deluded followers," marital purity.

Irwin Again Rejects Marital Purity

This teaching held that for the sanctified there should be no sex in marriage except for procreation. Thousands of Holiness wives adopted this view and abandoned sexual relations with their husbands for the rest of their lives. Furthermore, sanctified members of the church were forced to affirm that they had had no sex with their spouses except for procreation at least every quarter. This doctrine was promoted by Mother Elizabeth Ryder Wheaton and a Mrs. Lawson, part of the Hephzebah Faith Mission, a tiny radical Holiness Church.[30] Although the teaching was never adopted as an official doctrine of any major Holiness church, many Holiness women not only adopted this view but put it into practice. In response, Irwin stated, "We do not want this detestable doctrine of the devil taught in our Association, and by the help of God, it shall not be. If any one of our evangelists are teaching it, we request of them to send us their credentials at once, and leave the Association."[31] In another article in *Live Coals of Fire* Irwin explained how this "doctrine of Devils" destroyed marriages and made life miserable for everyone:

> This doctrine is an assault upon the institution of marriage itself. They falsely assume that to be lust which God permits, and upon this assumption the advocates

of this doctrine proceed to build their unscriptural and pernicious argument against all intercourse between husband and wife, except as above stated. They assume as a fact the very thing in question, which requires to be proven; and because their position cannot be supported by the Word of God, they unhesitatingly denounce as lustful everyone who does not accept and teach their pernicious doctrine. This doctrine not only strikes a blow at the institution of marriage, but it is a calculated to lead men and women into the promiscuous practice of free love, fornication, and adultery. It produces alienation, unholy discord, and unwarrantable separations in the family, and leads to distrust, deceit, and domestic infelicity. It produces marital infidelity rather than marital purity. It ignores the sacred privileges of the married state, and places men and women on a level with brute creation. It disregards the inherent, God-given laws and propensities of our nature.[32]

Despite Irwin's dictum, the marital purity doctrine broke out in Hamlin, Kansas, necessitating that Irwin make a trip to combat it in March 1900. He reported that here "one man (is) teaching this damnable delusion of the devil, and loudly professing that he was 'delivered.'" He had induced his wife to accept "the same delusion" before running off with a "hired girl." After four days Irwin reported that he saw this "doctrine of devils blown to atoms." Later the man repented and was restored.[33] Another case occurred in Sanford, North Carolina, where "grievous wolves had entered in among the band" and caused the separation of one young married couple in the church. North Carolina Ruling Elder Edward Kelley was able to convince the wife of her "fearful mistake."[34]

Beyond marital purity, Irwin and his followers continued to attack the devil and all his minions. On at least one occasion one of his preachers, M.D. Sellers, confronted a demon possessed man in Lumberton, North Carolina, and performed the only known exorcism among the Fire-Baptized preachers. Sellers and another preacher R. B. Jackson noticed a businessman who "followed them at a discrete distance wherever they walked." Finally the man came up to them and said "men, I need help. I am in a bad fix." When Sellers tried to pray for him, the hapless preacher "lost consciousness and seemed to go into a trance." Then he saw the man's mouth open wide and "something like a tan colored frog came out of his mouth and leaped into the air." Then the businessman "sprang to his feet, slapped his hands together, and cried out 'he is gone.'"

The deliverance was not complete, however, because on a later visit to the man's house "a voice like that of a child began to cry piteously behind the bed." When the three men moved the bed, "no one was there." It turned out to be the voice of the woman with whom the man had been having an affair. Then the two preachers "laid hands on him demanding that the demon come out of him and depart forever." This time "he got free for good."[35]

On the Mountain Top

By the middle of 1900, Irwin was at the peak of his influence. He had spread the teachings of the Fire-Baptized movement far and wide. He was building church buildings under the Fire-Baptized Holiness banner, and was sending out copies of *Live Coals of Fire*, not only in the United States, but to other countries as well. He had founded a new headquarters location in Beniah, Tennessee, where he was raising money to build a "School of the Prophets" as well as a resort area for cottages for the leaders of the movement. His newly budding theologian, Joseph H. King, was attempting to create a theological apology for Irwin's multiple experiences while building a strong center for the denomination in Toronto, Canada. In all these years there had been only one schism in Irwin's movement. Late in 1898 in Kansas, some of his followers rejected Irwin's "Baptisms" of dynamite, and lyddite and created the "Southeast Kansas Fire- Baptized Holiness Association," led by Benjamin W. Young. In time it adopted the name Fire Baptized Holiness Church (Wesleyan).[36]

Despite this division, the church continued to grow. The "Official List" of the church in May, 1900 listed Ruling Elders in 16 states and one Canadian province. In addition, the list included 143 "Ordained Evangelists" who covered most of the nation. It was obvious that the Fire-Baptized Association was growing rapidly into a national denomination which threatened to outgrow the older Holiness Churches if things continued as they had over the past five years.[37]

As time went by, Irwin began more and more to use the word "Pentecostal" in his sermons. One such example is found in a sermon preached in Royston, Georgia, on April 5, 1899 titled, "The Pentecostal Church." In addition to serving open communion, contrary to his Primitive Baptist upbringing, Irwin now served the "real Holy Ghost communion." Further, he contended, that a true Pentecostal church would teach the multiple baptisms of fire, dynamite, and lyddite. He asserted, "If you were to talk about the fifth, sixth or seventh blessings you could not frighten me. I am in for all the blessings there are for me, no matter how many there may be."[38]

Although many holiness leaders were also adopting Pentecostal language at this time, there was an increasingly rising tide of opposition to the Fire-Baptized Holiness movement from many Holiness leaders and periodicals. Despite this crescendo of criticism, Irwin never wavered in preaching the gospel of fire, dynamite, and lyddite. He and his movement had built momentum that was challenging the Holiness movement and its mother, the Methodist Episcopal Church. Everything looked bright for the intrepid evangelist in the middle of the year 1900. And then, everything suddenly changed.

Notes

[1] See Daniel Woods, "Daniel Awrey, The Fire Baptized Movement," pp. 3–4. The best source on Henke is: John S. Keen, *Memoir of F.W. Henke With Notes and Comments,* (Highway, KY: Bible Advocate Print[ers]), 1899.

[2] Daniel Woods, "Daniel Awrey, The Fire Baptized Movement," p. 4.

³ See B. F. Lawrence, *The Apostolic Faith Restored* (St. Louis: The Gospel Publishing House, 1916), pp. 45–46. Also, see B. F. Lawrence, "Incidents of the Spirit's Work from 1890–1900, in *The Weekly Evangel*, January 29–February 5, 1916, p. 4. According to Church of God historian Charles R. Conn the Schearer School house revival was the beginning of the American Pentecostal movement thus making the Church of God the oldest Pentecostal church in the world. See Charles R. Conn, *Like a Mighty Army Moves the Church of God* (Cleveland, Tenn.: Church of God Publishing House, 1955), pp. 16–27. Conn moderates this position somewhat in the third and final edition of his history but never acknowledges the connection with Irwin's group or Beniah and in e.n. 5 (p. 55) clearly states that the names of those who brought in the "false teaching" are unknown.

This seems to be an understated objection to the claim that there was a Fire-Baptized Holiness connection. He goes on to acknowledge that there was wide-spread false teaching at the time, citing Pentecostal Holiness historian, Campbell, pp. 2–3, 205. See Charles R. Conn, *Like a Mighty Army: A History of the Church of God 1886–1995 Definitive Edition* (Cleveland, TN: Pathway Press, 1996), pp. 51–55. The evidence, however, clearly shows that the meetings were part of Irwin's Fire-Baptized Holiness movement.

⁴ "Sarah A. Smith's letter," *Live Coals of Fire,* December 4, 1899, p. 8. Also see, Daniel Woods, "Daniel Awrey, p. 1. It is interesting the speaking in tongues was not mentioned here although Smith had spoken in tongues three years earlier. Seemingly tongues were not as important as fire and dynamite, much less as the initial evidence of the baptism in the Holy Spirit.

⁵ See Nicholas Fugate, "The Ring of Fire, Church of God and the Fire-Baptized Holiness Movement" (NP. ND.). Also see, Wade Phillips, *Quest to Restore God's House: A Theological History of the Church of God (Cleveland, Tennessee)* (Cleveland, TN: CPT Press, 2014) pp. 119–136. More recent Church of God historians discount the claims that the modern Pentecostal movement originated in the Schearer School House meetings, and give more attention to the Fire-Baptized Holiness roots in the founding of the church.

⁶ B. H. Irwin, "Editorial Correspondence," *Live Coals of Fire,* October 20, 1899, p. 1.

⁷ Ibid.

⁸ Ibid., pp. 1, 3. See Document 38 in *Irwin Reader.*

⁹ *Live Coals of Fire,* October 12, 1899, p. 1.

¹⁰ Ibid. Also see "The School of the Prophets," *Live Coals of Fire*, November 3, 1899, p.6.

¹¹ Ibid. In fact only children were ever taught at the school. The school closed before any adults could enroll.

¹² "Editorial Correspondence," *Live Coals of Fire,* October 27, 1899, p. 1.

¹³ "Our Cuban Work," *Live Coals of Fire,* Nov. 3, 1899, p. 4. Also see *Live Coals of Fire,* "Our Foreign Missionaries," Ibid. December 15, 1899, p. 8; "Our Missionaries to Africa," Ibid. December 29, 1899, p. 4; "Our African Missionaries." Ibid. April 6, 1900, p. 5.

¹⁴ "A Whirlwind from the North," *Live Coals of Fire,* December 15, 1899, p. 2. Also see Irwin's "Our Foreign Missionaries," *Live Coals of Fire,* December 15, 1899, p. 8.

¹⁵ Irwin, "Editorial Correspondence," *Live Coals of Fire* (October 27, 1899), 1, 3. See the *Irwin Reader* Document 38.

¹⁶ Irwin, "A Whirlwind from the North," p. 2.

¹⁷ "Editorial Correspondence," *Live Coals of Fire,* January 12, 1900, p.1.

¹⁸ Ibid.

¹⁹ "A Whirlwind from the North," *Live Coals of Fire*, December 1, 1899, p.2.

²⁰ "Editorial Correspondence," *Live Coals of Fire,* November 3, 1899, p. 1.

²¹ Ibid.

[22] "Editorial Correspondence," *Live Coals of Fire,* January 26, 1900, p.1. Also see *Live Coals of Fire,* February 9, 1900, p.1.

[23] "Editorial Correspondence," *Live Coals of Fire,* February 9, 1900, p. 1.

[24] "Editorial Correspondence," *Live Coals of Fire,* February 23, 1900, p. 4.

[25] Ibid.

[26] Joseph H. King added a "selenite" baptism in *Live Coals of Fire* "The Superlative Profession," June 1, 1900, p. 1. He said that he hoped "that these new and definite experiences will spread throughout the ranks of the Association."

[27] J. H. King, "The Twofold Aspect," *Live Coals of Fire,* March 23, 1900, p. 6.

[28] J. H. King, "Our Weapons of Warfare," *Live Coals of Fire,* May 18, 1900, pp. 1, 8.

[29] B. H. Irwin "The Spirit of Compromise," *Live Coals of Fire,* April 6, 1900, p. 4.

[30] See Charles E. Jones, *Guide to the Study of the Holiness Movement* (Metuchen, NJ: The Scarecrow Press, 1974), p. 780.

[31] "Editorial Correspondence," *Live Coals of Fire,* April 20, 1900, p. 1. Mrs. Lawson also banned corsets for her female members. For further denunciations of marital purity see Irwin's "Doctrines of Devils," in *Live Coals of Fire,* February 9, 1900, p. 4. Also see Elder A. H. Kaufman, *Fanaticism Explained* (Published by the author, Grand Rapids Michigan, 1904), pp. 82–91. Among the "fanaticisms" Kaufman denounces is "social Purity" (Marital purity) and the Fire-Baptized "third experience."

[32] B. H. Irwin, "Doctrine of Devils," *Live Coals of Fire* (February 9, 1900,) p. 4. Also see *Irwin Reader* Document 43.

[33] B. H. Irwin "Editorial Correspondence," Ibid.

[34] Edward Kelley's letter to *Live Coals of Fire,* May 18, 1900, p. 7.

[35] M. D. Sellers in an unpublished manuscript in the possession of Dr. Dan Woods.

[36] Charles Edwin Jones, *A Guide to the Study of the Holiness Movement,* p. 222.

[37] The Ruling Elders were listed as follows: Alabama, Olive E. Stambaugh; Arkansas, C. T. Stephens; Georgia, R. B. Hayes, Iowa, Oliver Fluke; Kansas, Jesse Bathurst; Louisiana, Wm. T. Currie; Michigan, Mattie Ritter; Mississippi, J. C. Martin; Nebraska, Hattie Lydie; North Carolina, Edward Kelley, Alice, M. McNeill (Colored); Oklahoma, Ter., A. L. George; Ontario, Canada, J. H. King; Pennsylvania, Mrs. Victoria Tuttle; South Carolina, W. S. Foxworth, W. E. Fuller (Colored); Tennessee, Daniel Awrey; Texas, A. R. Hodgre; Virginia, John H. Wine "OFFICIAL LIST," *Live Coals of Fire,* May 18, 1900, p. 8.

[38] B. H. Irwin, "The Pentecostal Church," *Live Coals of Fire,* June 1, 1900, p. 2. This sermon was preached in Royston, Georgia, on April 5, 1899.

Chapter Eight

Irwin Falls

> In the spring of 1900 he was guilty of open and gross sin such as could not be further hidden or palliated. Confessions that he made afterwards revealed that he had been living a double life for many years.
>
> Joseph H. King

Irwin's move to Toronto in the spring of 1900 turned out to be a fateful one for the future of the Fire-Baptized Holiness movement. Back in April 1899 in the Royston General Council, Irwin had assigned King to move to Toronto and pastor the small church there and to serve as the Ruling Elder for Ontario. The trip had been a difficult one for King who, along with his traveling companion, Daniel Awrey, were forced to live for three days on only $1.50 cents ($1 for beds and $.25 cents for food). King became so hungry that he "could have eaten the banana peels that had been thrown in the streets." Yet he persevered and arrived to take up his ministry in Toronto.[1]

King Moves to Nebraska

In March 1900 King received a letter from Irwin asking him to be the Assistant Editor of *Live Coals of Fire*. Earlier, Irwin's Personal Secretary Albert E. Robinson, formally Ruling Elder for Ontario, had moved to Lincoln to help in the printing of the paper. King was prepared for this new appointment. He stated that "I knew nothing of that to which I should soon be called upon to assume in the way of added responsibilities in the Lord's work. But the Lord who foresaw this was preparing me for the work that He would soon give to me." That work was for him to move to Lincoln, Nebraska, live in Irwin's home, and work with Robinson in producing *Live Coals of Fire*. Soon afterward King moved to Lincoln where he found the work load heavy, "but I enjoyed it." Interestingly, King later said that during the months that he lived in the Irwin home, Irwin was "not at home but was sojourning elsewhere.[2]

In fact, Irwin often spent weeks "resting" from his heavy schedule while no one, not even his wife, knew where he was. In April 1900 Irwin announced that he would take an extended break away from his family and friends in Nebraska. Utilizing the "royal we," Irwin wrote:

> The Lord has graciously opened up the way, supplied the necessary means, and enabled us to go apart, for four or five months into some "quiet resting place," where we can take a much needed rest from all active evangelistic work. But we shall not be idle. We expect to be closely and constantly occupied in other directions. All our engagements for the future have been or will be provided for, and the work will continue the same as heretofore. Brother J. H. King, who for nearly a year has had charge of our work in Toronto, Canada, has kindly consented to assist on the paper during our absence. He is already in Lincoln and at his post of duty.[3]

Irwin's last editorial appeared in the April 20, 1900 issue of *Live Coals of Fire*. After this the major editorials and articles were written by Joseph King under the initials of J.H.K. Ominously, a small notice appeared in the April 20 edition of *Live Coals* that warned:

> **Read Carefully**
> All remittances must be sent by draft, bank check, express, or Postoffice [sic] money order and must be made payable to B. H. Irwin or to "Live Coals of Fire." Otherwise they will be refused. Canadian stamps will not be returned. Do not send money loosely in envelopes. We cannot be responsible for money sent this way.[4]

It is not known if King had found financial irregularities in the running of the paper, but the warning showed that money had been sent to B. H. Irwin personally for subscriptions to the paper. Perhaps King was a new broom that was sweeping clean. Although King now wrote the editorials, *Live Coals of Fire* continued to run sermons preached by Irwin in his travels.[5]

During the long absences of Irwin from his home, his family and his staff began to question what was going on. King, too had some misgivings. In an editorial titled "Impressions" he spoke of "human impressions" that were in error: "These could originate from a disordered state of the system. Ardent and incessant labor in revival work, overtaxing the body, and being deprived of the necessary amount of rest and sleep will produce an abnormal state of the nervous system and this furnishes the cause of many impressions." Could he have been referring to Irwin?[6]

The Thunderclap

Whatever this meant, news finally came to Lincoln, Nebraska, that had the effect of a thunderclap. In his months of absence, Irwin had returned to his old habits of drinking, smoking, and womanizing, even while preaching the strictest holiness code ever found in the Holiness movement. In June 1900, some of his acquaintances happened to see him coming out of a bar in Omaha, Nebraska, drunk and smoking a cigar. In a short time, H.C. Morrison, the highly respected editor of the *Pentecostal Herald* in Asbury, Kentucky, ran the following short expose:

A Sad Duty

Rev. B. H. Irwin, editor of *Live Coals of Fire,* the official organ of the Fire Baptized Holiness Association of America, was seen on the streets of Omaha, Neb., a short time ago drunk and smoking a cigar. When recognized he tried to hide his cigar, and at first denied being drunk, but afterward offered to give money to the party who found him drunk, if he would keep the matter quiet. I have these facts from the man he attempted to bribe, and the names of good witnesses who saw Irwin drunk. I regret to have to make this publication, and if it were the first time this man had been detected in sin I might refrain from doing so. I do not publish this matter as a punishment for him, but in order to protect others, who are being imposed upon by him. It is hoped this unfortunate man will confess, repent, and seek forgiveness of his many sins.[7]

This article was widely repeated in the Holiness Press, sometimes with an unheard sigh of relief, at the downfall of the evangelist that many felt to be a wild and dangerous man. An article in the respected *Christian Witness and Advocate of Bible Holiness* ran Morrison's article verbatim and added its own pithy title and editorial note:

Whisky Baptized

We have no desire to hear of, or see, the downfall of anyone, nor to repeat the same, unless there is a cause. Our reason for putting the following into our columns is mainly stated in what Brother Morrison says, and in the added fact that our association and its work and officers have been so misrepresented and hindered in places by this man and his work. The holiness work in a number of places in our State has been wrecked through him, and those he influenced to go with him. We have warned again and again, and can but sorrow with those who have been deceived. To prevent further work of the kind, and to give warning to those who persist in following such leadership, we insert the following from the Pentecostal Herald, written by brother H.C. Morrison, the editor.[8]

In Lincoln, Nebraska, in the Irwin home, J.H. King and Albert E. Robinson were dumbstruck as was Irwin's wife Anna. King said it came as "a tremendous shock, and yet I was not altogether surprised."[9] He added that "the news of his downfall was flashed over the wires, and many were made sad, while opponents of the gospel that he preached seemed to rejoice."[10] In later years, King recalled that there had long been signs that Irwin's behavior had not lived up to his lofty holiness preaching. In 1921 he wrote about his early suspicions about Irwin:

> At what point he did backslide cannot be definitely determined. Even at Anderson, S. C. when the state associations were concentrated into one organization he did that which caused misapprehension as to his uprightiousness and sincerity. During the year 1899 in various meetings he gave evidence of an apostate condition of heart, and those that possessed a degree of discernment could see in him a spirit that proved conclusively that he was far from possessing the experience of sanctification. In the spring of 1900 he was guilty of open and gross sin such as could not be further hidden or palliated. Confessions that he made afterwards revealed that he had been living a double life for many years.[11]

Some years later, King gave a more explicit account of Irwin's sins. He said, "How glad I am that the last vestige of Irwinism has been swept from the P.H. Church. His life for many years alternated between the pulpit and the harlot's house. He would go from the pulpit to wallow with prostitutes the rest of the night. During that time he was preaching fiercely against wearing neckties, eating pork, and drinking coffee."[12]

Evidence of Irwin's weakness for alcohol was revealed some years later by a relative who related what happened when he visited a cousin for rest and relaxation in Kansas: "Benjamin H. (Irwin) was my grandfather's 1st cousin. My grandfather was a wheat farmer in SE Kansas. I remember my mother mentioning a cousin of her Dad's who was an itinerant preacher who would come by ever so often when he wanted a place to stay for a while. It must have been Benj. H. Apparently, he wasn't well thought of. She said he went to the barn and drank liquor – my grandfather would not have it in the house." She didn't say anything about the rest of the story.[13]

King also recalled the "appointment" that he received before he left Toronto. He said: "Sometime before I left Toronto, I was suddenly and unexpectedly impressed that the Lord was going to give me a work that I had never done in many respects in all my life. It seemed to be in the way of an appointment to a position that I never thought that I should receive in this world. I kept this in my own mind, and did not reveal it to anyone for months to come."[14]

Now that Irwin had fallen into what King described as "open and gross sin," in time more evidence began to emerge about his financial indiscretions as well as his sexual escapades. His son Fenelon (Robert) told of his father once taking $900.00 that was given to him to build a church and spending it on liquor and prostitutes.[15] King now had some decisions to make. On the night of June 4, 1900, as he and Robinson were about to retire, they knelt in prayer. Then King said that the Lord revealed that "This organization was not of the devil, but He Himself had launched it. I was given to see that all the opposition that might arise would not overthrow it. He gave me the appointment as General Overseer of the church to which I belonged. I felt an authority conferred upon me by the Lord in connection with the appointment."[16]

King Elected General Overseer

In the meantime, Irwin resigned as Overseer of the Association and his assistant, Joseph H. King, announced the convening of a General Council of the denomination to meet in Olmitz, Iowa, on the first day of July "for the purpose of electing a General Overseer of the Church." In the meeting, after much debate and opposition, King was "unanimously elected." One of his first duties was to settle with Irwin on the purchase of the *Live Coals of Fire* printing plant. With that done, King faced the gargantuan task of holding the remnants of the church together since a majority of the pastors and evangelists of the Church had abandoned it when they heard of Irwin's downfall. [17] In short order, King abandoned the baptisms of dynamite, lyddite, oxidite, and selenite. However, although he harbored doubts, he maintained the "third blessing" of the "Holy Ghost and fire." There is some evidence that as late as 1903 he and some other leaders were still open to the possibility of a baptism of dynamite. [18]

The remnants of the church were strongest in Oklahoma, Georgia, South Carolina, and North Carolina. In the months following the Olmitz General Council, King concentrated on these areas in his attempts to save the church. The dream of a "school of the Prophets" in Beniah, Tennessee, went up in smoke after Irwin's fall. Most of Irwin's followers in Tennessee and Western North Carolina eventually joined the Church of God after its first congregation was formed as The Holiness Church at Camp Creek in 1902. [19]

King's first instinct was to organize what was left of the church. He explained "the government was in my power almost absolutely, but I did not want to exercise such authority, as it imposed too much a responsibility." As to the losses after the fall of Irwin, King wrote: "Everything west of the Mississippi River went to pieces in the course of a few years. South Carolina was divided. The upper portion put with the Georgia Convention and the lower part was put with the North Carolina Convention. The work in Florida, Tennessee, and Virginia was lost to the church, and so we were reduced in membership to such an extent that there were only two conventions, that of North Carolina and Georgia. These conventions under the superintendency of Irwin were but symbols of an organization."[20]

Little was left of the Fire-Baptized Holiness movement in America and Canada after 1900. Except for Georgia and the Carolinas the church collapsed in spite of King's efforts to hold it. together. The church grew in Georgia due to the influence of King who moved to the town of Royston after Irwin's fall. In South Carolina the church continued to grow exponentially under the leadership of W. E. Fuller. In 1908, Fuller requested that the then-called "colored" congregations become a separate denomination which was duly granted by King. In time, this church became the largest legacy carrying the name of Irwin's movement spreading throughout the United States under the name "Fire-Baptized Holiness Church of God of the Americas."

It is not clear what Irwin did immediately after his fall. What is known is that after leaving the movement he founded, Irwin moved on to Oregon leaving his wife behind in Lincoln. During some of these years Irwin returned to the practice of law to make a living. In these years of wandering, he eventually met and married Mary Lee Jordan, a well-bred young woman in Texas who came from a socially prominent family. They were married in Canada. He married her, however, without divorcing his first wife Anna. Thus he was guilty of bigamy. To this marriage was born three sons and one daughter. The boys were named for three of Irwin's theological heroes, Vidalin, Fenelon, and Pember.[21]

Notes

[1] Joseph H. King and Blanch Leon King, *Yet Speaketh*, pp. 98-101.
[2] Ibid., pp. 100-101.
[3] See B. H. Irwin, "A Desert Place Apart," *Live Coals of Fire*, April 20, 1900, p. 4.
[4] *Live Coals of Fire*, April 20, 1900, p. 1.
[5] See B. H. Irwin, "The Dynamite of God," *Live Coals of Fire*, May 18, 1900, p. 2.
[6] J. H. King "Impressions," *Live Coals of Fire*, June 15, 1899, p. 1.
[7] H. C. Morrison, "A Sad Duty," The *Pentecostal Herald*, XII, June 20, 1900, p. 8.
[8] See "Whisky Baptized," *Christian Witness and Advocate of Bible Holiness*, July 5, 1900, p. 5. This paper was published from both Chicago and Boston under the editorship of two men, George McLaughlin and Joshua Gill. From the pages of *Christian Witness*, word of Irwin's fall spread like wildfire throughout the Holiness movement.
[9] See Joseph H. King "History of the Fire Baptized Holiness Church," in *The Pentecostal Holiness Advocate*, April 7, 1921, p. 11.
[10] J. H. King, *Yet Speaketh*, p. 102.
[11] Joseph H. King, "History of the Fire-Baptized Holiness Church," *Pentecostal Holiness Advocate*, April 7, 1921, p. 10.
[12] Ibid.
[13] Judy Hunt in *Ancestry.com* reported by Dan Woods on May 17, 2014.
[14] Joseph H. King and Blanch Leon King, *Yet Speaketh*, p. 102.
[15] See "Robert Irwin's own Story," *New York Daily News*, April 12, 1937, p.3.
[16] Ibid., p. 103.
[17] Ibid., p. 105.
[18] Evidence for this is contained in an unpublished letter from S. Minerva Payne sent to S. D. Page on September 1, 1903. She counseled King and others to promote an ongoing quest for spiritual power without naming unscriptural experiences that would confuse sincere people.
[19] See Harold Hunter, "Beniah at the Apostolic Crossroads," *CyberJournal #1*, pp. 6-8. http://www.pctii.org/arc/beniah.html.
[20] Joseph H. King, "History of the Fire-Baptized Holiness Church," *The Pentecostal Holiness Advocate*, April 7, 1921, p. 11.
[21] Much of this information is from Harold Schechter's *The Mad Sculptor* (New York: New Harvest, 2014), pp. 53-99.

Chapter Nine

Irwin Becomes a Pentecostal

> I waited for God, the Holy Spirit, to speak through me. Then I felt my lips and tongue and lower jaw being used as they had never been used before. My vocal organs were in the hands and the control of another, and the Other was the Divine Paraclete within me. He was beginning to speak through me in other tongues. I lay there and listened to the voice of the Holy Ghost. For nearly an hour he continued to speak in different unknown tongues. He caused me to use words which I had never heard or conceived of before. I was enabled to speak with greater fluency than I had ever spoken in my native English.
>
> B. H. Irwin

Benjamin Irwin's marriage to Mary Lee Jordan in 1902 was to drastically change the direction of his life. Mary Lee came from a Texas family that boasted "a number of prominent businessmen, judges, and men of wealth." It was also a family that was known to have a "certain amount of mental instability." Mary herself was described as "easy going" but at the same time possessing a "nervous high-strung temperament." She was also very religious. As a child while walking at night she had seen "a ball of light" that caused her to "fall on her knees" and "pray all night until she was converted." [1] Later she became part of the Holiness movement where she probably met Irwin on one of his evangelistic forays into Texas. It seems certain that Mary Lee was the "Dovie" Jordon from Texas that had worked in the office of *Live Coals of Fire*. A possible reason that Irwin took her to Canada for the wedding was because, unknown to Mary, Irwin had not divorced his first wife Anna.

For the next four years Irwin became domesticated enough to settle down in Salem, Oregon, and father five children with Mary. They were: Vidalin and his twin Victor who died at under two weeks, a girl named Mary Louise who died of a "membrane cramp at three months." It was reported that the child died "because her father neglected her care when left alone with the baby." The other two sons were Fenelon and Pember. [2]

Irwin as a Husband and Father

The naming of his three sons showed that Irwin was still theologically minded even after his fall. His first son Vidalin Bathurst Irwin, was named for the famed Icelandic bishop Jon Vidalin, while his second name honored one of Irwin's early Fire-Baptized Holiness friends, Jesse Bathurst. His youngest son, Pember, was named in honor of G.H. Pember, the English evangelist and author of several books on prophecy. The second was named Fenelon Arroyo Seco Irwin in honor of the seventeenth century French theologian Francios Fenelon. The middle name was for the place where he was born near Pasadena, California, in a Pentecostal camp meeting called Arroyo Seco. Fenelon was born in a covered wagon without the help of a doctor.[3]

The fact that Irwin was at a Pentecostal camp meeting when his second son was born is another story. The Pentecostal movement had its beginnings in Topeka, Kansas, when a young lady, Agnes Ozman, spoke in tongues on the first day of the Twentieth Century. This came in the Bethel Bible School led by former Methodist Holiness preacher, Charles Fox Parham. After much Bible study, Parham and the students, concluded that there was a "third blessing" consisting of the baptism in the Holy Spirit with the "Bible evidence" of speaking in tongues. This was very close to Irwin's teaching on the "fire" as a third blessing.[4]

From Topeka, Parham moved his school to Houston, Texas, in 1905 where student, William Joseph Seymour, the son of former slaves, accepted Parham's Pentecostal teaching of "Bible evidence." In 1906, Seymour moved to Los Angeles where he was locked out of his Holiness church for his new Pentecostal teaching. After searching downtown Los Angeles, Seymour and his followers rented a former African Methodist Episcopal church on Azusa Street where he could freely teach his new experience. In April 1906, one of the greatest revivals in history broke out on Azusa Street where hundreds came from all over America and around the world to receive their "Pentecost" and speak in tongues. Soon Azusa Street saw a stream of "Pilgrims" flowing out from Los Angeles to spread the Pentecostal flame around the world.[5] One of these was Benjamin Hardin Irwin.

Irwin Speaks in Tongues

Irwin began to seek this experience in October of 1906. Part of his motivation was his deep grief at the death of his daughter Mary Louise. Out of curiosity or because of a renewed spiritual hunger, Irwin attended a Pentecostal service in Salem, Oregon, under the leadership of Florence Crawford who led a large Apostolic Faith congregation in Portland. While seeking for the tongues attested baptism, Irwin was careful to "do his first works over" by again praying through to salvation and the second blessing sanctification experience which he had evidently lost in his wanderings. "I repented in sackcloth and ashes, confessed backslidings, and made restitution" he said. In his usual colorful language Irwin described his experience as "My Pentecostal Baptism – A Christmas Gift:"

A supernatural tranquility and unearthly sweetness, a divine assurance that the Holy Ghost, the promised Comforter, had come into my soul to abide forever, was then and there vouchsafed to me, I knew that I was filled with the Holy Spirit. Then it was that my soul "waited in silence for God only" (Ps 62:1). I waited for God, the Holy Spirit, to speak through me. Then I felt my lips and tongue and lower jaw being used as they had never been used before. My vocal organs were in the hands and the control of another, and the Other was the Divine Paraclete within me. He was beginning to speak through me in other tongues. I lay there and listened to the voice of the Holy Ghost. For nearly an hour he continued to speak in different unknown tongues. He caused me to use words which I had never heard or conceived of before. I was enabled to speak with greater fluency than I had ever spoken in my native English. I tried to remember or to retain some of the words, but could not, and to this day I cannot recall a single word. I arose about midnight and went into the auditorium, where Mrs. Irwin, Sister Crawford, and one or two others still lingered, and testified to the baptism of the Holy Ghost and fire. But I did not speak in tongues to them. I could not do it of myself. I have never put forth the least effort to speak in unknown tongues. I can speak only "as the Spirit gives me utterance." Since that time, I have been used of God in speaking many times in Chinese, Hindoostani, Bengali, Arabic, and other languages unknown to me.[6]

In another account of his Pentecostal experience, Irwin added more details about his experience. This was included in a letter he wrote to Thomas Ball Barratt at the request of the Azusa Street leadership. Barratt was a Norwegian Methodist leader who was in the United States trying to raise funds for an orphanage in Oslo, Norway (then called Christiana). After hearing of tongues at Azusa Street, Barratt wanted to know more about the experience. A strong second blessing sanctificationist, he had visited many Holiness centers in America including the famous Iowa Holiness Association Camp Meeting in Oskalooska, Iowa, the place where Irwin learned about the Holiness movement. In fact, Barratt said that he was seeking a "fuller baptism of fire" in a letter to Evan Roberts in Wales. Could it be that he knew of Irwin's idea of a baptism of fire as a "third blessing?"

In this letter to Barratt dated November 28, 1906, Irwin said, "I received my personal Pentecost last Saturday night and such glory as God manifested in my soul no words can describe." He went on to say that the next evening he spoke "one sentence in Portuguese followed by one single sentence in three other tongues." He then asked of Barratt, "will you pray for me that I may speak fluently to preach in other tongues?" Then followed a remarkable vision Irwin experienced of the Pentecostal work in many countries:

God showed me Iceland, Norway and Sweden – I could see the multitudes of souls weeping their way to Jesus in those countries. He showed me West Africa the Gold Coast and the Congo country where hundreds of thousands of souls were crying for this glorious gospel. I could see large cities in West Africa where thousands of *black faces* were turned before God eagerly drinking in the blessed truth; then he took me to Brazil in South America, all I could see were multitudes of souls who were on their way to the cross. Then the West Coast of South America came before me I believe I should know the faces of the people I saw in Brazil and Sweden and Iceland. Then he showed me the devil worship in South India and the poor souls in China accepting the full gospel. In Japan I saw three large cities all of which I am sure I would recognize should I ever see it. Oh it was wonderful.[7]

After speaking in tongues, Irwin rejected his former fire, dynamite, lyddite, and oxidite "baptisms" and accepted the theology of Parham and Seymour. He wrote, "My conception of the Pentecostal baptism not only implied the experience of justification and entire sanctification as essential prerequisites, but the baptism itself includes the fullness of the Spirit AND speaking with other tongues. The speaking in tongues is not simply the sign or evidence of the baptism, but a part of the divine baptism itself."[8] Thus Irwin continued to teach a "third blessing" although it was now the baptism in the Holy Ghost and tongues, rather than the baptism in the Holy Ghost and fire.

To let his thousands of friends from his Fire-Baptized Holiness days know about his new experience, he sent a letter to Seymour's Azusa Street paper *The Apostolic Faith* telling of his restoration and his new Pentecostal experience. He wrote in November 1906 from Salem, Oregon:

> The work here is progressing gloriously, although the opposition is deep and bitter. Two days ago in the preliminary service in the prayer tower, the "upper room," Sister Ryan received her personal Pentecost. She spoke in tongues for nearly three quarters of an hour without intermission, it is the most astonishing case we have had yet in this city. Everyone that saw it was amazed and strengthened in their faith. She spoke in at least seven languages. Glory to Jesus. The whole city and country round about are being shaken. There are those here from Portland, the Dalles, and from near Astoria seeking their Pentecost, Sister Glasco among the rest. Myself and wife have received our Pentecost and speak in tongues.[9]

Years later, Irwin met Charles Fox Parham and discussed his new Pentecostal experience. He made it clear that the tongues attested baptism was in reality what he had been seeking all along. Irwin told Parham with some regret that the Fire-Baptized Holiness saints would scream "until you could hear them for three miles on a clear night, and until the blood vessels stood out like whipcords." He also said that when the fire fell "a tremendous power took hold of us until we nearly screamed our heads off."[10] As a newly minted Pentecostal, Irwin would now employ his oratorical powers in the service of the new movement.

Irwin as a Pentecostal Evangelist

Irwin, ever the fiery evangelist, now began to conduct Pentecostal meetings up and down the West Coast. In an article titled "Pentecost in San Francisco," he reported "striking cases of conversion and sanctification" as well as "some remarkably clear cases of the divine baptism." These included a "Hawaiian brother," a "Catholic," and a "German lady." To his surprise William. J. Seymour from Azusa Street came in to preach one "blessed sermon" near the end of the meeting. Irwin reported that "all were pleased with the simplicity and power of his discourse." Furthermore, "it was all inspiration to me to see his beaming face and to hear him open up the scriptures to our hungry hearts."[11]

As much as possible, Irwin and his family often travelled to Portland, Oregon, where his wife could attend services at Florence Crawford's annual camp meeting. Soon Mary became an effective altar worker where she was gifted in leading seekers into the Pentecostal experience. While she became very active in the church, spending much time in services several times a week, her children suffered from the lack of attention. Added to this was the absence of Irwin who continued to travel and preach wherever he could get an invitation. In 1908 the family moved to Los Angeles so that they could attend services at the Azusa Street Mission, the epicenter of the Pentecostal revival. Her Mary volunteered to be an altar worker and to do many other tasks for the church. Here religion became the center of her life. "She awoke at five each morning to pray for an hour and then spent every available minute at the Azusa Street Mission, seeking respite from her troubles in the ecstatic transports of Pastor Seymour's revival."[12] In the meantime, her children were largely unattended and suffered from a neglect and a lack of discipline.

Irwin Falls Again

Mary's troubles began in early 1910 when Irwin suddenly abandoned her and her three young boys and ran off with a younger woman. At this time, she also found out that Irwin had never divorced his first wife and that she had been living in a bigamist marriage for eight years. She soon sued for a divorce. It is not known if she ever saw Irwin again. She now had to support her boys any way she could. She sometimes had to beg day old bread from local bakeries to avoid starvation. She moved from one place to another in Los Angeles, finally settling in a ramshackle cottage on Omaha Street in a run-down part of the city. Here she had no indoor plumbing or electricity and one of the boys had to sleep on the porch due to the lack of room in the tiny house she was forced to get odd jobs as a washerwoman and house cleaner to keep her family together.[13]

Mary seems to have been aware that, despite speaking in tongues, Irwin continued to womanize during their entire marriage. She said of him, "he was definitely immoral and a slave to his passions." Years later, Fenelon remembered a day in 1912 when, at five years of age, his father took him downtown to a house where two women lived. "These women were very nice to me and they put me in a room and my father went away with these women for an hour or two." It was years later that the son realized what was going on. Fenelon said of his father, "he tried to reform others, but he could not reform himself."[14]

Despite everything, Mary took her three boys to the Azusa Street church faithfully where they saw early Pentecostalism firsthand. Mary followed the early practice of "putting the love of Christ above all else." She was "increasingly neglectful of her children. Her religion was her consolation." In 1929 after she moved back to Portland, Oregon, all of their boys turned out to be petty criminals and were confined to the penitentiary for criminal behavior.[15] In the meantime

Irwin was not to be found. The story of the rest of his life turned out to be in total contrast to his twenty years as a holiness zealot and his four years as a Pentecostal evangelist.

Notes

[1] Harold Schechter, *The Mad Sculptor: The Maniac, the Model, and the Murder that Shook the Nation* (New York: New Harvest Haughton Mifflin Harcourt, 2014), p. 61. Although this book is about Irwin's son Robert who became famous as a sculptor in New York, murdered three people in 1937 and was sentenced for life in an insane asylum, it has much information about B. H. Irwin and his family.

[2] Ibid., p. 316.

[3] Ibid., pp. 60-61.

[4] Vinson Synan, *The Holiness Pentecostal Tradition*, pp. 95-103.

[5] Ibid. pp. 103-116. See Frank Bartleman, *How Pentecost Came to Los Angeles* (Los Angeles, 1925) for an eyewitness account of the Azusa Street meetings.

[6] B. H. Irwin, "My Pentecostal Baptism—A Christmas Gift," *Triumphs of Faith*, May 1907, pp. 114-117. Also see David Bundy, "Spiritual Advice to a Seeker: Letters to T. B. Barratt from Azusa Street, 1906," *Pneuma* 14:2 (Fall 1992), pp. 160-167.

[7] David Bundy, "Spiritual Advice to a Seeker," pp. 167-168. Indeed, these are the very countries where the Pentecostal movement was destined to grow greatly during the twentieth century.

[8] Also see Vinson Synan, *Voices of Pentecost: Testimonies of Lives Touched by the Holy Spirit* (Ann Arbor, Michigan, Servant Publications, 2003), pp. 88-90.

[9] B. H. Irwin, "In the Upper Room, Salem, Oregon," November 24," *Apostolic Faith*, December, 1906, p. 4. In the earlier copies of *Apostolic Faith* Irwin's name is barely legible. In later copies it is completely deleted. Also Irwin's testimony speaks of his Pentecostal experience as a "Christmas Blessing" on December 25, 1906. In his letter to Barratt he dates it to November 1906. There is a contradiction here.

[10] See Charles Parham's *Apostolic Faith* (Baxter Springs, Kansas), April 25, 1925, p. 3.

[11] B. H. Irwin, "Pentecost in San Francisco," *Apostolic Faith*, April, 1907, p. 4.

[12] Harold Schechter, *The Mad Sculptor*, p. 63.

[13] Ibid.

[14] Ibid.

[15] Ibid., pp. 64-65.

Irwin (second from the left) and three other Two Seeder leaders in Texas in 1923

BeN Ha.,r-dt'N IrwiN

Chapter Ten

Irwin as a Two Seed in the Spirit Predestinarian Baptist

By God I will preach!

B. H. Irwin

The paper trail on Benjamin Irwin grows thin after he left Mary for a younger woman in 1910. There is no extant record of the young woman's name. What is known is that in the 1910 Federal Census, Benjamin Hardin Irwin was listed as living in Greenfield Ward 2, Dade, Missouri, a village north of Springfield. He was 56 years of age. Possibly this was the home of his new girlfriend. He did not stay here long because California records in 1913 show him living back in Hanford, California, near Fresno, with his occupation listed as "attorney."[1] It is not known how many years he worked in California as a lawyer.

At some point after 1913, Irwin went back to his Primitive Baptist roots and joined the most radical one of all, the "Two-Seed-in-the-Spirit Predestinarian Baptist Church." Although they refused to call themselves "Calvinists," this very small group was the most extremely Calvinistic church in history, teaching double predestination, with the "Good seed" predested for heaven, and the "Evil seed" predestined for hell. The founder of the Church, Daniel Parker, saw no need for missionaries since everyone's fate had already been sealed "before the foundation of the world." Other Baptists who felt the call to evangelize and send missionaries to the nations of the world were dubbed "Missionary Baptists" which included the American Baptist Convention in which Irwin had previously been ordained. In Parker's view these Baptists were tainted with Arminianism, a cardinal sin. From Irwin's testimony of his conversion in 1871, his father had been a staunch believer in the teachings of this church. Irwin said of him "he is a firm believer in the doctrine and practice of the Predestinarian Baptists, and has an experience dating back over fifty years." So he now returned to the deepest roots of his childhood Christian experience as a Two-Seed-in-the-Spirit Predestinarian Baptist.

Irwin as a Parkerite

The 1920 Federal Census listed Ben. H. Irwin, as he was known for the rest of his life, as living in a boarding house in the village of Brickstore, Georgia, in Newton County near the town of Social Circle. The owner, Fannie Norris, rented space to six people including Irwin. At this time Irwin was sixty-five years old. He was listed in the Census as "single" and his occupation was listed as "preacher." The reason he chose to live in Bricktown is unknown and his relationship to the sixty-five year old Fannie is unknown. It is probable that Norris was a member of the Two Seeder church.[2]

What is known is that while living in the Norris boarding house, Irwin took on the task of typing new copies of three of Daniel Parker's books on the two seed doctrines which had first been published in 1826. The three were: *Views on the Two Seeds Taken from Genesis, 3rd chapter and part of the 15th Verse; A Supplement or Explanation to My Views on the Two Seeds;* and *The Second Dose of Doctrine on the Two Seeds.*[3] Irwin explained that no man in this country has been so misrepresented, abused, and slandered by the "Arminian element" which has crept into the Old School Baptist Church, as has been Daniel Parker. Another book he typed at this time was Parker's voluminous 417 page book, *A Brief Account of the Life, Experience, Labours, Privations, Struggles, Persecutions, Sufferings, Victories of Elder Daniel Parker* which was first published in 1831. Irwin added that it was "typewritten, *verbatim et literatum*....during the second week in February, 1923." Thus he spent the entire two months, of January and February 1923 typing these books.[4] This task included typing several hundred pages, a difficult task indeed. This work was done in the home of "Sister Kate Alston" who lived near Social Circle. It is not known if they were ever republished. An interesting side note on the title page is the fact that Parker published the *Brief Account* in 1831 "shortly before he left Illinois, with his faithful flock for Anderson County, State of Texas."[5]

During Irwin's last years, he seems to have divided his time between his boarding house in Georgia, and in Indiana and Texas where he was connected with the Otter Creek and Trinity River Two-Seed-in-the-Spirit-Predestinarian Baptist Associations. Records show that he applied for ordination in Texas 1917 and was rejected because he preached that "everything was predestined, both good and evil." After the refusal to ordain him, Irwin stalked out saying "By God I will preach." One lady said to him as he left "if you do preach it will be by God." After returning to Georgia, he was ordained by another group of Two-Seed-in-the-Spirit Predestinarian Baptists. Returning to Texas, he was welcomed back since he now preached "sound doctrine." A photo of him with three other Texas Two-Seed leaders in 1923 showed that he was then in good standing with the church. Another photo shows Irwin in Texas in 1924, smoking a pipe.[6]

To prove that he now preached "sound doctrine" Irwin wrote a long poem on the problem of the origin of evil. A small portion of the poem reads as follows:

> Is God the author of all wickedness?
> Doth He a part of His creation bless,
> And damn a portion to eternity?
> Is this consistent with the Deity?
> Tis false, and blasphemous, and I deny,
> That wickedness proceeded from on high.
> Sin issued from the dark abysmal pit
> And the truth bears full witness to it.
> The doctrine has a foul, sulphurious smell,
> And I have traced it to its native hell.
> Sweetness and bitterness do not proceed
> From the same fountain; so the scriptures read. [7]

The End

In the end, Irwin became the pastor of the small headquarters congregation of the denomination in Palestine, Texas, and was in good standing with the leadership of the church. In the long history of Christianity few people have made a more drastic theological change than Irwin did when he became a Two-Seed-in-the-Spirit Predestinarian Baptist preacher. He went full circle from the strictest and most radical Holiness perfectionist Arminianism to the most extremely radical Calvinism. He was never moderate in anything he did in life.

Little is certain about the end of Irwin's life. According to genealogical records, Irwin's many lives came to an end on January 22, 1926 in Palestine, Texas, the historic last stronghold of the Two-Seed church in America. It is interesting that this date shows that he died on his birthday at 72 years of age. Other less certain dates for his death, however, were given by his sons. One son, Pember, said that he died in Los Angeles in 1927, while another son Stewart, reported that he died in 1924. Since no death records for those dates have ever been found in Los Angeles or anywhere else, the Palestine, Texas, date in 1926 seems to be the most probable one. [8] It is possible that the sons lost all contact with their father and never knew exactly what happened to him.

A search of Anderson County, Texas, records make no mention of the death or burial of a Ben H. Irwin. It is possible that he was buried in an unmarked pauper's grave in or near Palestine, Texas. Thus this gifted man who cut such a broad swath across America as a Fire-Baptized Holiness preacher and helped to pave the way for the Pentecostal movement that swept the world in the Twentieth Century died in obscurity. One can only speculate what might have happened if he had lived up to the high standards of holiness that he preached with such passion. In the end, despite his many gifts and charismatic personality, Irwin's failure to control his baser passions led to his downfall. Like a meteor that flashes across the sky in amazing splendor and then disappears as suddenly as it appeared, Irwin flashed across the American religious skies for a brief time and then flamed out.

Notes

[1] He was listed on September 15, 1913 as "Ben Hardin Irwin, Occupation Attorney" in the "California, Occupational Licenses, Registers, and Directories, 1876-1969."

[2] Year: 1920, Census Place: Brickstore, Newton, Georgia; Roll: T625, p. 2A; Enumeration District: 109, Image: 440.

[3] See "Note By Elder Irwin," February, 1923.

[4] See Irwin's preface to the *Brief Account*.

[5] Ibid.

[6] This information was taken from the Minutes of the Otter Creek Two Seed Baptist Association in Indiana in 1924 and 1925 and the Trinity River Two Seed Baptist Association in Texas in 1923 and 1924 where Irwin was the featured preacher and Messenger from the Little Hope Church. These Minutes were supplied by Dr. John Crowley of Valdosta State University in Georgia.

[7] This is a fragment of some poetry that I discovered in my research. It has no title or date, but the internal evidence shows that he was attempting to correct the sermon on the origin of evil that doomed his ordination.

[8] See the *Sunday Oregonian*, December 4, 1938, p. 3.

Chapter Eleven

The Legacy of Benjamin Hardin Irwin

> As to Irwin's final legacy, one must conclude that his "third blessing" teaching eventually became the cornerstone of the modern Pentecostal movement. The biggest difference was that Irwin's followers testified to the "baptism in the Holy Ghost and fire" while Parham's and Seymour's followers testified to the "baptism in the Holy Ghost and tongues." Therefore, for all his faults and weaknesses, Irwin will henceforth be known as the prime transitional figure between the classical Holiness Movement and the modern Pentecostal Movement.
>
> Vinson Synan

In the long sweep of American Church history, Benjamin H. Irwin is of minor importance, but in the area of Holiness Pentecostal history he is indeed a major figure. He played an important role in the transition from the Holiness movement to the modern Pentecostal movement with his "third blessing" teaching on the baptism in the Holy Ghost and fire. During the years from 1895 to 1900, he was the subject of much controversy in the Holiness press and drew large crowds to his meetings. He was as controversial as he was charismatic. After 1898 his Fire-Baptized Holiness church was the fastest growing force in the American Holiness movement. If not for his fall in 1900, his movement might have developed into a major denomination.

Irwin was in many ways a very gifted man. He was an extremely persuasive preacher and enough of an original theologian to attract a large number of very capable followers. His organizational skills helped him to cobble together an international denomination that was held together by nothing more than his dominating personality. Physically he was described as "a fine looking man of large frame possessing an unusually strong voice and very interesting to listen to."[1] Looking back many years later, Joseph H. King described Irwin as: "A man of brilliant intellectual powers, a magnetic personality, an ardent nature, a bold, fearless soul, and a disposition which made it natural and for him to throw himself wholeheartedly into any task he might choose to undertake."[2]

He also was ever a scholar in all his different lives, mastering the study of law on his own, delving deeply into Wesleyan literature as a "John Wesley Methodist," and finally mastering the sparse literature of the Two-Seed-in-the-Spirit Predestinarian Baptist Church. His habit was to visit bookstores wherever he went and to devour books on the long train journeys that he endured as a travelling evangelist.

Irwin's Other Gifts

Irwin was also a gifted writer and poet. His colorful reports of meetings in the many holiness periodicals of the time marked him as a powerful and descriptive writer. Throughout his career, he published poems that bared his inner soul. He was also gifted as the editor of *Live Coals of Fire*. His many articles and sermons constitute his theological legacy as a man who was not afraid to teach many things that were extremely unorthodox and even outside the pale of the Bible. That he was able to convince scholarly leaders such as Joseph H. King to accept his fantastic "baptisms" of dynamite, lyddite, oxidite, and selenite is a testimony to his overwhelmingly persuasive personality.

Remarkably, Irwin stood against the Jim Crow racism of his times when he organized his national movement in Anderson, South Carolina, in 1898. Joining the church was William Fuller, a black man from South Carolina, who was listed as a "Ruling Elder" and evangelist. [3] In the South, Irwin often preached to mixed congregations as well as in all black churches. For his times, he stood out in welcoming and elevating blacks as leaders in his organization.

Throughout his ministry, Irwin demonstrated a deep sympathy for the alienated in American society. In addition to his kindness towards African-Americans, Irwin showed a remarkable interest in the cause of women in ministry. The large number of women leaders in his movement showed that he was ahead of his times, especially in his early decision to ordain women to the ministry and appointing them to serve as ruling elders and ordained evangelists. His care for the poor was seen in his support for Miss Mallory's orphanage in Bethany, Oklahoma. His care for the poor and vulnerable in society was also seen in his clear opposition to abortion.

Irwin also had a remarkable sense of history. By sending copies of *Live Coals of Fire* to the Library of Congress, he was looking forward to having his place in church history available to future scholars. In many of his articles, he demonstrated a familiarity with Protestant, Wesleyan, and Holiness history. He not only knew about the major works of these traditions, he read them. Among his theological heroes were John Wesley, John Fletcher, whose voluminous *Checks to Antinominianism* greatly influenced him, as well as those whom he named his sons after: Vidalin, Fenelon, and Pember. At the end of his life he became devoted to the works of Daniel Parker, founder of the Two Seeder movement.

Irwin's Character Flaws

Despite these impressive qualities, Irwin was plagued throughout his adult life with character flaws that eventually destroyed his reputation as a leader in the holiness movement and almost destroyed his young church. In forming his church, Irwin was the ultimate autocrat. He not only was named General Overseer for life, he appointed all ruling elders and assigned all pastors. He was not amenable to any board and no one ever questioned his absolute authority. This was one of the fatal flaws of the movement he created. It was his own personal realm to govern as he pleased.

His particular demons seem to have been alcoholism and sexual promiscuity. As a young man, he was already known by his neighbors as a drunkard and a man of loose morals. In his different conversion experiences, he repented of his many sins and made brave attempts at reforming himself. Perhaps one of the attractions of the second blessing sanctification experience was the hope of having his sin nature "cleansed" away so he could overcome his besetting sins. Even his Pentecostal baptism in the Holy Ghost with tongues as evidence may have been the hoped for cure. But nothing ever worked.

At least one historian, Joseph Campbell, suggested that one cause of Irwin's repeated failures might have been exhaustion from his constant travels and preaching appointments. This, he said might have caused him to "grossly neglect his private devotion." He went on to say: "Since he was a man enriched with rich natural gifts and a brilliant, sparkling personality, he perhaps came to rely upon sheer human ability and ceased to depend upon Almighty God for spiritual power." [4] Perhaps an attraction of the Two-Seeder Baptists for Irwin was their tolerance of alcohol. Sometimes known as the "Forty Gallon Baptists," they openly approved of drinking alcohol, even in the pulpit. Perhaps as a five-point Calvinist, Irwin could now preach the Gospel while at the same time being "totally depraved." Also, if he was predestined for heaven, whatever he did, he might not have to worry about the sins of the flesh.

His alcoholism and sexual promiscuity seemed to have doomed his two marriages. It is not known how much his first wife Anna knew about his peccadilloes. It is known, however, that Irwin abandoned both wives after committing bigamy with his marriage to Mary Jordan in 1902. For a time, Irwin settled down in an attempt at a normal marriage with Mary in Salem, Oregon. He seems to have been grief-stricken at the death of his daughter Mary Louise. But even with three sons, Irwin abandoned his wife for a younger woman leaving Mary to raise his sons alone. In the end, all three sons rejected the religion of their parents and turned to lives of crime. All three were in prison at one time or the other. Thus, part of Benjamin Hardin Irwin's legacy is as a total failure as a husband and father.

A Legacy of Immorality?

The one son who rose to prominence was Fenelon who in 1927 changed his name to Robert Irwin in honor of the famous agnostic Robert Ingersoll who had become his hero. This horrified his devoutly Pentecostal mother. This name change represented a total rejection of the Holiness-Pentecostal religion of his mother and father. At times he loudly proclaimed that he was an atheist. As a youth, he showed an interest in sculpture by carving figures in oleomargarine at home. He later studied with the famous sculptor Lorado Taft and later moved to New York City where he hoped to gain prominence there in the thriving artistic community of painters and sculptors. With his magnetic personality and artistic talent, he soon became part of the social scene of New York.

All of this came to a sudden halt when Robert Irwin committed three murders that shocked the nation. Known as the Easter Weekend murders on March 28, 1937, Irwin murdered a well-known New York Model, Mary Gedeon and her daughter Veronica. An innocent boarder, Frank Byrnes, was also murdered. All three were strangled or stabbed to death. After a nationwide search for Irwin, he was arrested and tried for murder. Robert Irwin's trial became front page news across the nation. Called the "Mad Sculptor," Irwin's sordid past was trumpeted in the *New York Daily Mirror* and the *New York Daily News* as well as many other papers. In the end, Robert Irwin was acquitted on the ground of insanity and spent the rest of his life in a New York mental asylum. This sad story is told in Harold Schechter's well-written and researched 2014 book, *The Mad Sculptor: the Maniac, the Model, the Murder that Shook the Nation.* Also a psychological study of Robert Irwin was published by Frederic Wertham in his 1948 book, *The Show of Violence.* In a chapter titled, "Manhattan Tragedy" he shows that Irwin showed signs of eventual violence for most of his life.

Given these sordid chapters in his life, the task of evaluating Irwin's legacy as a Holiness preacher is a difficult one indeed. Was he ever sincere? Was he an opportunist who shamelessly used his spectacular gifts to deceive his followers while leading a double life? Did his followers receive genuine spiritual experiences in spite of the unworthiness of the preacher? These are questions that go back to the early beginnings of Christianity. The supreme case was that of Donatus, a North African bishop who in the Fourth Century led a schism and declared that if a priest was unworthy, all the sacraments he performed were invalid. Thus all baptisms, weddings, penances and eucharists, etc., performed by such a priest were null and void. This led to a major controversy that engulfed and divided the entire church. In the end "Donatism" was ultimately rejected as a heresy but the questionable sacraments were seen to be valid due to the holiness and faith of the Church, and the work of grace in these sacramental acts and not that of the priest who performed them.

A classic statement on the question of unworthy ministers for Protestant churches is found the following statement by Martin Luther in one of his "Table Talks" in 1532 where the topic was the fall of Judas:

One ought to think as follows about ministers. The office does not belong to Judas but to Christ alone. When Christ said to Judas, "Go, baptize," Christ was himself the baptizer and not Judas because the command comes from above even if it passes down through a stinking pipe. Nothing is taken from the office on account of the unworthiness of a minister.[5]

Another important statement for Protestants was placed in the Articles of Religion of the Church of England. Article XXVI which reads as follows:

XXVI. Of the Unworthiness of the Ministers, which hinders not the effect of the Sacraments.

Although in the visible Church the evil be ever mingled with the good, and sometimes the evil have chief authority in the Ministration of the Word and Sacraments, yet forasmuch as they do not the same in their own name, but in Christ's, and do minister by his commission and authority, we may use their Ministry, both in hearing the Word of God, and in receiving the Sacraments. Neither is the effect of Christ's ordinance taken away by their wickedness, nor the grace of God's gifts diminished from such as by faith, and rightly, do receive the Sacraments ministered unto them; which be effectual, because of Christ's institution and promise, although they be ministered by evil men. Nevertheless, it appertaineth to the discipline of the Church, that inquiry be made of evil Ministers, and that they be accused by those that have knowledge of their offences; and finally, being found guilty, by just judgment be deposed.[6]

Most Protestants have adopted the view that the message and not the messenger is what produces spiritual results. Even if the messenger is flawed, unworthy, or even in error, individual followers can receive genuine grace through the mercy of God, the effectual scriptures, and the proclaimed Word. Undoubtedly thousands of Irwin's followers received genuine experiences in spite of the preacher's double life. The fact that Irwin resigned as head of the church when his transgressions were discovered instead of trying to hold on to power was to his credit. Also the fact that he abandoned his false teachings in favor of the new Pentecostal understanding of the "third blessing" evidenced by speaking in tongues was to his credit.

Irwin's Ecclesiastical Heritage

In the long run, the most important legacy left by Irwin was the major denominations he helped to found which have survived into the Twenty-First Century. After becoming a Pentecostal following the Azusa Street revival, two of the churches founded or influenced by Irwin united into one denomination. Since the Fire-Baptized Holiness Church and the Pentecostal Holiness Church accepted speaking in tongues as the "initial evidence" of the Baptism in the Holy Spirit, and because they operated in the same territories, the main remnants of the Fire-Baptized Holiness Church merged with the Pentecostal Holiness Church on January 31, 1911, in the camp meeting village of Falcon, North Carolina.

Although two thirds or more of the churches represented were from the Fire-Baptized Holiness Church, the delegates chose the name of the smaller partner, the Pentecostal Holiness Church. Since that time the denomination has grown to be one of the largest Pentecostal bodies in the United States. By the year 2010 the church numbered some 330,000 members in the United States in 2,000 local churches and about 4,000,000 adherents in the world.

The major church that carried forward the name of the Fire-Baptized Holiness Church was the group led by William E. Fuller. In 1908 Fuller's African-American churches requested a friendly separation from the white churches. The reasons given were the Jim Crow segregation in the South that made it difficult for blacks and whites to convene in southern venues. Furthermore, according to Fuller "because of the growing prejudice that began to arise among the unsaved people, it was mutually agreed that we have separate corporations." Also, it was agreed that black folk could better evangelize their own people. The leaders of the church agreed to approve the separation and to deed all the church properties of these congregations to the new "Colored Fire Baptized Holiness Church" which was organized in Anderson, South Carolina, on May 1, 1908. In later years, the name was changed to the "Fire-Baptized Holiness Church of God of the Americas." By the year 2010 the church counted 25,000 members in over 1,000 local churches in the United States. The story of the separation can be found in Vinson Synan's *Old Time Power: A Centennial History of the Pentecostal Holiness Church* (1998).

Another major outcome of Irwin's ministry in Tennessee was the important revivals in the Shearer Schoolhouse in the late 1890s where it was claimed that some 100 persons spoke in tongues. According to multiple sources, these meetings were sponsored by leaders from the Fire-Baptized Holiness movement. Irwin's only attempt to found a headquarters and Bible School in America was in the village of Beniah, Tennessee, in 1899-1900. After Irwin fell, most of his followers in Tennessee and Western North Carolina, joined forces with A. J. Tomlinson after he founded the Church of God in a convention of four local churches in 1906. The headquarters of the church was located in Cleveland, Tennessee, only nine miles by railroad from Beniah.

The connections between Irwin's movement and the Church of God (Cleveland, TN) have been explored by Harold Hunter in his "Beniah at the Apostolic Crossroads: Little Noticed Crosscurrents of B. H. Irwin, Charles Fox Parham, Frank Sandford, A.J. Tomlinson" (1997) and Dan Woods in his "Daniel Awrey, the Fire-Baptized Movement, the Origins of the Church of God: Towards a Chronology of Confluence and Influence" (2010). Wade Phillips, a more recent historian of the Church of God tradition, has given great weight to Irwin and the Fire-Baptized Holiness influence in the background of the Church. In his book, *Quest to Restore God's House: A Theological History of the Church of God (Cleveland, Tennessee,* 2014) he states: "The fire-baptized movement was destined to have a profound and lasting effect on the Church of God, so much so that it would be impossible to understand the spirit and developments in the church in the early twentieth century without a thorough knowledge of the movement, for the Church of God entered the twentieth century having been transformed by this movement."

He goes even further and makes a case for Irwin's revivals in North Carolina and Tennessee from 1896 to 1900 as the birth place of the modern American Pentecostal Movement. He bases this claim on the reported instances of speaking in tongues at the Schearer School House and also in Beniah, Tennessee, at about the same time. He also refers to Stewart Irwin's statement about tongues in an article in *Live Coals of Fire* "The Breath of Jesus," (June 1, 1900 p. 6): "Then came—and that in rapid order—the dynamite and lyddite, for they spake with other tongues as the Spirit gave them utterance. This utterance of speech was beyond understanding by those who witnessed that awful scene, and they were utterly confounded and amazed."

Since this happened six months before the events of tongues speech in Topeka, Kansas, and Parham's new doctrine of tongues as the "Bible evidence" of the baptism in the Holy Spirit, Phillips argues that the Fire-Baptized movement was not only a transitional stage towards modern Pentecostalism, but the beginning of the movement itself. While this speculation is not the point of this book, it is now quite widely accepted that Irwin's movement was the last major transitional step in the holiness movement towards modern Pentecostalism.

As to the Church of God tradition, it is clear that the Fire-Baptized movement in and around Cleveland in the late 1890s was crucial to what the Church of God became; a Wesleyan-Pentecostal church that taught the five-fold gospel as was preached at Azusa Street: salvation, entire sanctification, baptism in the Holy Spirit with the "initial evidence" of speaking in tongues, divine healing, and the second coming rapture of the church. It was a Pentecostal Holiness preacher from North Carolina, Gaston B. Cashwell, who brought the tongues baptism not only to the Fire-Baptized Holiness Church and the Pentecostal Holiness Church in Dunn, North Carolina, in 1907, but also to the Church of God. This happened when Cashwell was invited by A.J. Tomlinson to preach in the service following General Assembly in January. While Cashwell was preaching, Tomlinson fell off his chair and spoke in several unknown tongues. From that point on, the Church of God became a full-fledged Pentecostal denomination. In summary, B. H. Irwin's Fire-baptized movement played a major role in the formation of both the Pentecostal Holiness Church and the Church of God (Cleveland, TN). By 2015 both churches together numbered some ten million adherents around the world.

As to Irwin's final legacy, one must conclude that his "third blessing" teaching eventually became the cornerstone of the modern Pentecostal movement. The biggest difference was that Irwin's followers testified to the "baptism in the Holy Ghost and fire" while Parham's and Seymour's followers testified to the "baptism in the Holy Ghost and tongues." Therefore, for all his faults and weaknesses, Irwin will henceforth be known as the prime transitional figure between the classical Holiness Movement and the modern Pentecostal Movement.

Irwin's Possible Influence in India and Chile

An example of the continuing Fire-Baptized Holiness legacy of Irwin was the famous revival in Puna, India, led by the world famous Indian Christian woman Pandita Ramabai. In 1905 in her girl's school a revival broke out that had all the earmarks of Irwin's teachings and practices. In the beginning of the revival, the girls experienced what they called a "Baptism of the Holy Ghost and fire." One girl seemed to be engulfed in flames, so much so that another girl got a bucket full of water to pour on her, but the fire did not harm her. Soon most of the hundreds of girls began to confess their sins while crying and praying, some kneeling, others seated, some standing, and many with their hands lifted high."

To explain what was happening, Ramabai preached a sermon on the text "He shall baptize you with the Holy Ghost and fire," (Matt. 3:11) where she affirmed that the baptism of fire was a separate blessing following salvation and sanctification. Two years later some of the girls spoke in tongues with the approval of the Pandita. Working with Ramabai was an American Methodist missionary, Minnie Abrams who in 1906 wrote a widely read booklet titled, *The Baptism of the Holy Ghost and Fire* which described the scenes in Puna. In 1909, Abrams, sent a copy of the booklet to the Methodist leader in Chile, Willis C. Hoover, who quickly reprinted it in the Chilean magazine *Chile Evangelico* in October 1909. This article made no mention of tongues, although they came later in abundance in both India and Chile. The descriptions of the teaching and experiences that came with the baptism of the Holy Ghost and fire, as well as the bodily manifestations in India and Chile, were exactly as those seen in Irwin's earlier meetings.

By September 1909, the Methodist Episcopal Church held a trial and expelled Hoover and 37 of his followers. They then organized the Methodist Pentecostal Church of Chile which eventually grew to over 2,000,000 members in Chile. It is not known if there was a direct connection between Irwin and these events in India and Chile, but it is certain that both Ramabai and Hoover were readers of Holiness magazines that carried accounts of Irwin's meetings. The connections between the revivals in India and Chile are found in the 2016 book by Dean Helland and Alice Rasmussen titled: *God Broke Through: The Story of Chile's Methodist Pentecostals.*

Irwin's Influence on American Life and Literature

As to Irwin's influence in American life and literature, two Oklahomans with roots in the Fire-Baptized Holiness tradition made a deep impression on American life and culture. The first was the Tatham family from the Sallisaw, Oklahoma, Pentecostal Holiness Church which had Fire-Baptized Holiness roots. The Tathams were the subjects of John Steinbecks's 1939 novel, *Grapes of Wrath,* called by some the great American novel. Steinbeck's fictional Joad family was based on the story of Oca Tatham whose family went to California in the dust bowl days of the 1930s. In the book, Ma Joad speaks in tongues and is obviously a Pentecostal. After arriving in California some of the Tathams prospered enough to become automobile dealers and hospital administrators. The Tatham family is featured in Dan Morgan's book, *Rising in the West: The True Story Of An "Okie" Family from the Great Depression Through the Reagan Years* (1992) which documents the Pentecostal Holiness roots of the Tatham family.

Another Oklahoman with roots in Irwin's movement was Oral Roberts who was a minister in the Pentecostal Holiness Church before gaining worldwide fame as a healing evangelist. Roberts was born in Ada, Oklahoma, in 1918 to parents who also were ordained Pentecostal Holiness ministers. The churches in Oklahoma had roots in the Fire-Baptized Holiness Church before the merger in 1911. Oral shocked the world when he joined the United Methodist Church in 1969. Before this he held mass healing crusades in the "tent Cathedral" which held up to 20,000 people. His crusades rivaled those of Billy Graham.

In the latter part of his ministry, Roberts went on prime time television and became a household name to the American public. In 1965, he founded Oral Roberts University which soon grew to over 5,000 students. Perhaps Roberts' most lasting legacy was the Charismatic movement which entered all the mainline Christian denominations after 1960. Roberts' television programs brought Pentecostalism into the nation's living rooms. Many credit these programs with creating the interest in Pentecostal Christianity which became the connection with the Charismatic movement. Robert's life and ministry was the subject of David Harrell's Book, *Oral Roberts: An American Life* (1985).

Far from Oklahoma, another writer with Fire-Baptized Holiness roots was the famous James Baldwin, a Black novelist who first gained fame with his autobiographical novel *Go Tell it on the Mountain* which was published in 1953. Baldwin was raised in a Pentecostal church pastored by Mother Rosa Horn who left her Fire-Baptized Holiness Church in Georgia to found her own denomination, "The Pentecostal Faith Church, Inc." in Harlem. In his books Baldwin acknowledged his attraction to the "visceral" worship in the Fire-Baptized kind of Black "sanctified church." After being baptized in the Holy Spirit and speaking in tongues, he became a Pentecostal preacher for a time. This is explored by Dale Coulter in his "Toward a Pentecostal Theology of Black Consciousness" in the *Journal of Pentecostal Theology.*[7]

The Legacy of Worldwide Pentecostalism

Very few of Irwin's followers and their descendants gained the fame and or notoriety of the previous figures. Mostly they were like the Joad family in the *Grapes of Wrath,* poor and unknown to history. But the massive Pentecostal movement that Irwin helped to birth spread over the world to become the fastest growing Christian movement in the world. Today one out of four Christians in the world are part of the Pentecostal/Charismatic movement which now covers the globe. Some have even predicted that if current growth rates continue, sometime in the Twenty-first century, Pentecostals will number one-half of all the Christians in the world.

By 2017, the combined numbers of all Pentecostals and Charismatics in the world stood at 669,177,000 people according to Todd Johnson, Director of the

Center for the Study of Global Christianity at Gordon-Conwell Theological Seminary. This makes the Pentecostal/Charismatic renewal second only to the Roman Catholic Church in numbers of followers.[5]

To be a prime transitional figure in the beginning of the Pentecostal movement which now covers the globe makes Irwin a prominent American religious figure despite his faults and shortcomings.

Notes

[1] As described by Granny Jones of Franklin Springs, Georgia, who once kept Irwin in her home. See Joseph H. Campbell, *The Pentecostal Holiness Church*, p. 194.

[2] Ibid.

[3] "Application for Charter for the Fire-Baptized Holiness Church, August 23, 1905." The charter was signed by J. H. King, G.O. Gaines, R. B. Hayes, S.D. Page, and W.E. Fuller.

[4] Joseph H. Campbell, *Pentecostal Holiness Church*, p. 201.

[5] Lehmann, Helmut T. and Theodore G. Tappert, eds, *Table Talk*, p. 47.

[6] https://www.churchofengland.org/prayer-worship/worship/book-of-common-prayer/articles-of-religion.aspx Accessed February 16, 2017.

[7] Dale Coulter, "Toward a Pentecostal Theology of Black Consciousness," *Journal of Pentecostal Theology* Vol. 25, No. 1 (2016), pp. 74-75.

[5] Todd M. Johnson, Gina A. Zurlo, Albert W. Hickman, and Peter F. Crossing, "Christianity 2017; Five Hundred Years of Protestant Christianity," *International Bulletin of Mission Research 2017*, Vol. 41, No. 1, January 2017, p. 49.

Bibliography

Archives & Collections

Archives of the Pentecostal Holiness Church. Oklahoma City, OK
Archives of the Church of God, Cleveland, Tennessee
Archives of the Assemblies of God, Springfield, Missouri
The Holy Spirit Collection at Oral Roberts University, Tulsa, Oklahoma

Minutes, Constitutions and Manuals

Application for Charter for the Fire-Baptized Holiness Church, August 23, 1905 in Carnesville, Franklin County, Georgia.
Constitution and General Rules of the Fire-Baptized Holiness Association of America (1900).
Discipline of the Fire Baptized Holiness Church of God of the Americas, 1994.
Manual of the Pentecostal Holiness Church, 2001.
Minutes of the Otter Creek Two Seed Baptist Association in Indiana in 1924 and 1925.
Minutes of the Trinity River Two Seed Baptist Association in Texas in 1923 and 1924.
Staver, Hugh and Geraldine, compilers, *First Baptist Church, Tecumseh, Nebraska 125th; 1868- 1993, Grounded and Growing* (Tecumseh, NE: First Baptist Church of Tecumseh, Nebraska. 1993).

Periodicals

The Anderson Intelligencer, August 3, 1898.
Apostolic Faith (Baxter Springs, Kansas).
Beulah Christian,(Providence, RI).
The Fayetteville Weekly Observer
Live Coals of Fire, (Lincoln, Nebraska, October, 6, 1899-June 15, 1900).
Mound Valley Herald
The New York Daily Mirror
The New York Daily News
Signs of the Times: Devoted to the Old School Baptist Cause (April 15, 1880): pp. 86-89.
The Christian Witness and Advocate of Bible Holiness
Sent of God, Hepzibah Faith Mission Association (Tabor, Iowa).
The Sunday Oregonian, December 4, 1938.
The Visitor, Official Organ of the Brethren in Christ.

The Way of Faith and Neglected Themes
The Wesleyan Methodist Guide to Holiness and Revival Miscellany.

Primary Sources

Arthur, William. *The Tongue of Fire or the True Power of Christianity*. Columbia, SC: L.L. Pickett., n.d.

Baldwin, James. *Go Tell it on the Mountain*. New York, Dell Publishers, 1953.

Bartleman, Frank. *How Pentecost Came to Los Angeles*. Los Angeles, 1925.

Brumback, Carl. *Suddenly... From Heaven*. Springfield, MO: Gospel Press, 1959.

Carradine, Beverly. *The Sanctified Life*. Cincinnati: Office of the Revivalist, 1897.

Fletcher, John. *The Works of the Reverend John Fletcher*. 4 vols. New York: Lane & Scott, 1851.

Godbey, W, B.. *The Autobiography of William Baxter Godbey*. Cincinnati: God's Revivalist Press, 1909.

Hayes, W. M. *Memoirs of Richard Baxter Hayes*. Greer, SC: Dunlap Print, 1945.

Jernigan, C.B., *Pioneer Days of the Holiness Movement in the Southwest*. Kansas City: Pentecostal Church of the Nazarene Publishing House, 1919.

Jones, Charles E. *A Guide to the Study of the Holiness Movement*. Metuchen, NJ: The Scarecrow Press, 1974.

Kendrick, Klaud. *The Promise Fulfilled*. Springfield, Missouri: Gospel Press, 1959.

King, Joseph H., and Blanch Leon, King. *Yet Speaketh: Memoirs of the Late Bishop Joseph H. King*. Franklin Springs, GA: Publishing House of the Pentecostal Holiness Church, 1949)

Lawrence, B. F. *The Apostolic Faith Restored*. St. Louis: The Gospel Publishing House, 1916.

Lehmann, Helmut T. and Theodore G. Tappert, eds. *Luther's Works*. Vol. 54, *Table Talk*. Translated by Theodore G. Tappert. Philadelphia: Fortress Press, 1967.

McDowell, John Hugh. *History of the McDowells and Connection* (Memphis: C. B. Johnston, 1918.

Nichol, John. *Pentecostalism*. New York: Harper and Row, 1966.

Shaw, S.B. *Echoes of the General Holiness Assembly*, Chicago, Illinois; S.B. Shaw Publisher, 1901.

Stephens, C. T., comp. *Blood and Fire Songs*. Oklahoma City: Reprinted by Charles E. Jones, 2004.

Articles

Adley, Tharwat. "Blessed Be Egypt My People": The Neo-CharismaticMovement in Egypt" in Vinson Synan, Amos Yong and Kwabena Asamoah-Gyadu. *Global Renewal Christianity: Spirit-Empowered*

Movements Past, Present, and Future, Volume 3: Africa. Lake Mary, FL: Charisma House, 2016: 93-108.

Bundy, David, "Spiritual Advice to a Seeker: Letters to T. B. Barratt from Azusa Street, 1906,." *Pneuma* 14:2 (Fall 1992): 160-167.

Coulter, Dale. "Toward a Pentecostal Theology of Black Consciousness." *Journal of Pentecostal Theology* 25:1 (2016).

Hughes, George. "Baptism of Fire," *Guide to Holiness and Revival Miscellany.* New York: n.p. (February, 1879): 20.

Hunter, Harold. "Beniah at the Apostolic Crossroads; Little Noticed Crosscurrents of B. H. Irwin, Charles Fox Parham, Frank Sandford, A.J. Tomlinson. *"Cyberjournal.HTML (*January 1997). http://www.pctii.org/arc/beniah.html

Irwin, B. H. "The Baptism of Fire Experience." *The Way of Faith and Neglected Themes* (Nov. 13, 1895): 2.

Irwin, B.H. "In the Upper Room, Salem, Oregon, Nov. 24." *Apostolic Faith* (December,1906): 4.

Irwin, B. H., "My Pentecostal Baptism—A Christmas Gift." *Triumphs of Faith* (May 1907): 114-117.

Irwin, B. H. "The Pentecostal Church." *Live Coals* (June 1, 1900): p. 2.

Irwin, B. H. "Pyrophobia." *Way of Faith* (October, 28, 1896): 2.

Irwin, B. H. "Some Facts, Dates, Etc. In Our Family History" in John Hugh McDowell. *History of the McDowells and Connection.* Memphis: C. B. Johnston (1918): 562-564.

Jones, Charles Edwin. *Guide to the Study of the Holiness Movement.* Metuchen, NJ: Scarecrow, 1974.

Jones, Charles Edwin. "Miss Mallory's Children: The Oklahoma Orphanage and the Founding of Bethany" *Chronicles of Oklahoma,* Vol 71 No. 4 (Winter, 1993-94): 392-421.

Johnson, Todd. M. Gina A. Zurlo, Albert W. Hickman, and Peter F. Crossing, "Christianity 2017; Five Hundred Years of Protestant Christianity," *International Bulletin of Mission Research 2017,* Vol. 41, No. 1,January 2017, p. 49.

King, Joseph H. "History of the Fire Baptized Holiness Church" *The Pentecostal Holiness Advocate* (March, 24, 1921): 4-5.

Lowrey, Asbury. "Is the Baptism of the Holy Ghost a Third Blessing?" *Divine Life and International Expositor of Scriptural Holiness*, (September, 1879): 46-47.

Morrison, H. C. "A Sad Duty," *The Pentecostal Herald,* XII, June 20, 1900.

Nabb, Tim. "B. H. Irwin: The Fire Baptized Revolt, 1895-1911." *Pentecostal History.* http://www.seeking4truth.com/bh_irwin.htm

Packard, J. F. "The Baptism of Fire," *The Wesleyan Methodist Guide to Holiness and Revival Miscellany* (July, 15, 1896): 6.

Pike, J.M. "The Baptism of Fire." *Way of Faith* (Nov. 13, 1895): 2-4.

Robinson, A. E. "My Friend: Joseph Hillery King" in *The Apologist* (June 1946).

Schrag, Martin H. "The Spiritual Pilgrimage of the Reverend Benjamin Hardin Irwin." *Brethren in Christ History and life* Volume IV, Number 1 (June, 1983): 7.
Taylor, G.F. *The Pentecostal Holiness Advocate* (May 2, 1930): 8.
Troy, J.C. "Religious Department." *The Charlotte Daily Observer,* March 27, 1898.
Woods, Daniel. "Daniel Awrey, The Fire-Baptized Movement, and the Origins of the Church of God: Toward a Chronology of Confluence and Influence." *Cyberjournal for Pentecostal-Charismatic Research* No. 19. http://www.pctii.org/cyberj/cyberj19/woods.html
Wynn-Brown, Bertram. "The Antimission Movement in the Jacksonian South: A Study in Regional Folk Culture." *Journal of Southern History* Vol 36, No 4 (Nov., 1970): 501- 529.

Unpublished Manuscripts

Fankhauser, Craig. "The Heritage of Faith: An Historical Evaluation of the Holiness Movement in America." Unpublished M.A. Thesis, Pittsburg State University, Pittsburg, Kansas, 1983.
Fugate, Nicholas. "The Ring of Fire, Church of God and the Fire Baptized Holiness Movement." (NP. ND.).
Irwin, B. H. *Live Coals of Fire,* June 1, 1900.
Kerwin, Jim. "Isaiah Reid (1836-1911): His Life, Leadership, and Influence in the American Holiness Movement." Unpublished MA thesis, Regent University, 2006.
Phoebus, Samuel J. "The Fire Baptized Holiness Church: Its History and Practices" Unpublished A. B. Thesis, Biblical Seminary in New York, 1949.
Purinton, William T. "'Red Hot Holiness,' B.H. Irwin and the Fire-Baptized Holiness Tradition," unpublished paper.

Secondary Sources

Caldwell, Wayne Ed., *Reformers and Revivalists: The History of the Wesleyan Methodist Church* (Indianapolis, IN: Wesley Press, 1992).
Campbell, Joseph H. *The Pentecostal Holiness Church, 1898-1948* (Franklin Springs, GA: The Publishing House of the Pentecostal Holiness Church, 1951.
Clark, Elmer. *The Small Sects in America.* Nashville, TN: Cokesbury Press, 1937.
Croswell, Laurence and Mark Croswell. *Lift Up a Standard: The Life and Legacy of Ralph C. Horner.* Indianapolis, IN: Wesleyan Publication House, 2012.
Conn, Charles W., *Like a Mighty Army Moves the Church of God* (Cleveland, Tenn.: Church of God Publishing House, 1955).

Conn, Charles W. *Like a Mighty Army: The History of the Church of God 1886-1996, Definitive Edition*. Cleveland, TN: Pathway Press, 1996.

Crowley, John G. *Primitive Baptists of the Wiregrass South: 1815 to the Present*. Gainesville: University of Florida Press, 1998.

Davidson, William F. *The Free Will Baptists in History*. 2nd edition. Albany, GA: Randall House, February 20, 2001.

Dayton, Donald. *Theological Roots of Pentecostalism*. Grand Rapids, MI, Francis Asbury Press, 1987.

Dieter, Melvin. *The Holiness Revival of the Nineteenth Century*. Metuchen, NJ: Scarecrow Press, 1980.

Dorgan, Howard. *Giving Glory to God in Appalachia: Worship Practices of Six Baptist Subdenominations*. Knoxville, TN: University of Tennessee Press, 1987.

Douglas, Annie. *A Mother in Israel: The Life Story of Mrs. Annie Douglas*. Oklahoma City: Charles Jones reprint, 2002.

Haines, Lee M. "The Grander, Nobler Work; Wesleyan Methodism's Transition, 1867-1901" in Wayne E Caldwell, Editor, *Reformers and Revivalists: The History of the Wesleyan Church* (Indianapolis: Wesley Press, 1992).

Kaufman, Elder A. H. *Fanaticism Explained*. Grand Rapids, MI: Self published, 1904.

Keen, John S. *Memoir of F.W. Henke with Notes and Comments*. Highway, KY: Bible Advocate Printers, 1899.

Knight, Henry H. *From Aldersgate to Azusa Street: Wesleyan, Holiness, and Pentecostal Visions of the New Creation*. Eugene, Oregon: Pickwick Publications, 2010.

Moon, Tony. *From Plowboy to Bishop: The Life of Bishop Joseph H. King*. Wilmore, KY: Emeth Publishers, 2017.

Morgan, Dan. *Rising in the West: The True Story of An "Okie" Family from the Great Depression Through the Reagan Years*. New York, Knopf, 1992.

Phillips, Wade. *Quest to Restore God's House: A Theological History of the Church of God. (Cleveland, Tennessee)*. Cleveland, TN: CPT Press, 2014.

Schechter, Harold. *The Mad Sculptor: The Maniac, the Model, and the Murder that Shook the Nation*. New York: New Harvest Haughton Mifflin Harcourt, 2014.

Stephens, Randall. *The Fire Spreads: Holiness and Pentecostalism in the American South*. Cambridge, MA: Harvard University Press, 2008.

Stephenson, Herbert F. *Keswick's Authentic Voice*. Grand Rapids, MI., 1959.

Steinbeck, John. *Grapes of Wrath*. New York: Viking Press, 1939.

Synan, Vinson. *The Holiness-Pentecostal Movement in the United States*. Grand Rapids MI: Wm. E. Eerdmans, 1971.

Synan, Vinson. *The Holiness Pentecostal Tradition*. Grand Rapids: Eerdmans Publishing Co., 1971, 1978.

Synan, Vinson. *The Old Time Power, A Centennial History of the Pentecostal Holiness Church*. Franklin Springs, GA: Lifesprings Resources, 1973, 1998.

Synan, Vinson. *Under His Banner: History of the Full Gospel Business Men International*. Costa Mesa, CA: Gift Publications, 1992.

Synan, Vinson, *Voices of Pentecost: Testimonies of Lives Touched by the Holy Spirit.* Ann Arbor, 1.1ichigan, Servant Publications, 2003.

United States. *Fifteenth Census of the United States.* Los Angeles, CA: United States, 1940.

Wertham, Frederic. *The Show of Violence* N.Y. Greenwood Press, Publishers, 1948-1949.

Section Two

A Selected Irwin Reader

by Daniel Woods

A Note on Sources

Outside of the years from 1893 to 1900, few primary sources bearing Benjamin Hardin Irwin's own words exist. This paucity makes scholarly treatment of his entire life and ministry a great challenge. One exception for Irwin's early life is his recently-discovered conversion narrative published in 1880 by a Baptist paper in Indiana (Document 1). Another exception is a fourteen-month period from November 1906 to December 1907 when Irwin embraced the emerging Pentecostal Revival. During the height of the of the Azusa Revival in Los Angeles, Irwin left two descriptions of his quest to be baptized in the Holy Spirit with the initial evidence of speaking in tongues, along with two short letters concerning his inchoate Pentecostal ministry (Documents 47-50). In addition, a few poems have survived from his youth and his last years. All the rest of the documents that allow us to hear Irwin's voice date to an eight year between late 1893 and early 1900.

Beginning in 1893, Irwin began to send regular evangelistic reports and occasional sermons to holiness papers. He developed a habit of writing his reports on Mondays. And though Irwin's name can be found in a several periodicals during the 1890s, he preferred to send his reports primarily to one paper. For 1893-1895 that paper was William McDonald's *Christian Witness and Advocate of Bible Holiness* (Boston and Chicago). Following Irwin's fire baptism in October 1895, he added J. M. Pike's *Way of Faith and N eglected Themes* (Columbia, South Carolina). Both of these weeklies placed heavy emphasis on sanctified living, but Pike additionally highlighted the more controversial doctrines of divine healing and the imminent return of Christ. Pike's paper proved far more receptive to Irwin's testimonies to the experience of a fiery baptism so by the early spring of 1896 he was writing almost exclusively to the *Way of Faith*. Scholars currently have access to a complete run of the *Christian Witness* from 1893-1895 and to the majority of copies of *Way of Faith* between the fall of 1895, when Irwin first appeared in its pages, through the end of 1896 (a total of 48 extant issues out of 60 published during a fourteen-month period). Only a smattering of copies of *Way of Faith* have survived from the rest of the decade, making a close study of Irwin's words and movements difficult for 1897 and 1898, years critical in the development of the Fire-Baptized movement.

Irwin's voice returns in 1899. In April of that year the Fire-Baptized Holiness Association, which he had organized in the summer of 1898, decided to issue its own newspaper to be called *Live Coals of Fire*. According to J. H. King, "In the year 1899 Irwin raised a sufficient sum of money to purchase a printing press and outfit with which to issue a periodical in the interest of the F. B. H. Association. This plant was placed upon the premises of Irwin's residence in the city of Lincoln, Nebraska, and the first issue of the periodical was sent forth in October, 1899, bearing the name of *Live Coals of Fire*. Irwin was the editor of the paper which was declared to be the official organ of the Association," and this was "the first paper in the United States that taught the Baptism of the Holy Ghost and fire was subsequent to sanctification" ("History of the Fire-Baptized Holiness Church: Chapter II," *Pentecostal Holiness Advocate* [March 31, 1921], 11). Although *Live*

Coals of Fire was issued for only nine months before Irwin's resignation (from October 1899 to June 1900), the paper is a vital resource for understanding both the man and his movement. It contains invaluable sermons delivered by Irwin during the preceding year—most of them preached between April and August 1899, and recorded in shorthand by A. E. Robinson, his young traveling companion who would soon move from Toronto to Lincoln to work in the *Live Coals of Fire* office as a printer. This paper also features Irwin's "Editor's Correspondence" (reporting on his evangelistic work and the state of the inchoate church across North America) and his "Editorial Articles" (addressing the doctrinal and organizational bases of the movement's unity), all written between September 1899 and April 1900.

Editor's Note

The primary sources selected for this reader are presented, with only a few exceptions, in chronological order by date of composition. Document 1 is Irwin's 1880 conversion narrative published in *Signs of the Times: Devoted to the Old School Baptist Cause*. The next 45 primary sources cover the years 1893 to 1900. Documents 2-8 and 10-13 come from *Christian Witness* and cover late 1893 to early 1896, Documents 9 and 14-32 come from *Way of Faith* and cover October 1895 to October 1897, Document 33 comes from King's 1921 history and covers events during 1898, and Documents 34-46 come from *Live Coals of Fire* and cover April 1899 to April 1900. Documents 47-50 demonstrate Irwin's embrace of the Azusa Revival and the new Pentecostal message in 1906-1907. Lastly, Documents 51-52 allow us to hear the faint voices of B. H. Irwin and his long-abandoned second wife Mary Jordan Irwin from the mid-1920s.

All documents were written by Benjamin H. Irwin unless otherwise indicated. Editorial comments are restricted to introductions and footnotes—with the exception of occasional clarifications and elisions indicated in brackets. First names have also been provided in brackets when known. Obvious typographical errors have been silently corrected, but eccentricities and inconsistencies in spelling, capitalization, and punctuation have been reproduced faithfully. All uses of italics and bold print are found in the original documents.

Part One

Before the Fire

Conversion

Introduction

Composed when Irwin was in his mid-20s, this lengthy conversion narrative opens a window on the Predestinarian Baptist faith of his upbringing, the intellectual nature of his conversion struggle, and the stirring of an evangelist zeal as part of his born-again temperament. The only other substantive extant testimony to Irwin's life before 1890 is found in his 1899 sermon "Repentance and Confession" which appears later in the collection as Document 35. In this sermon Irwin discusses a five-year period of backsliding, perhaps in the early 1880s (which would date it after this conversion narrative).

Document 1 – "The Sword of the Lord and of Gideon," *Signs of the Times: Devoted to the Old School Baptist Cause* **(April 15, 1880), 86-89.**

Dear Sister Lina – As I am alone this afternoon, I shall endeavor to give you some account of my wanderings in this dreary and desolate world, and how I hope the good Lord has led me about and instructed me in the way of truth. This life has been to me a veritable valley of Achor—a place of trouble and tribulation; with now and then a faint glimmer of light breaking through the dark. But we should not be moved by these afflictions, for God in his wisdom has appointed us thereunto. Paul, when in the city of Athens, preaching Christ and the resurrection, sent Timothy, a minister of God, and his fellow laborer in the gospel of Christ, to the church at Thessalonica to comfort them concerning their faith, favoring told them that they should suffer tribulation. The people of God are chosen in the furnace of affliction and if they suffer for righteousness' sake happy are they. If they suffer as Christians, they should not be ashamed, but should glorify God on that account. There is much contained in the apostle's charge to Timothy, and we ought all to bear it in mind at all times, *endure affliction*. My years have been years of sadness, and my path has been one of thorns; yet I feel that God, in the midst of his wrath against me, has remembered mercy. I trust that he has not forsaken me altogether, nor entirely removed the covenant of his peace. I knew that he has promised to be a God unto his people, and I know, too, that the Strength of Israel cannot lie. O if we could only realize the length and breadth and height of the meaning of the word, GOD! Methinks it contains everything that is desirable to the Christian, not only in this world, but also in the eternal world. What more could we desire than to know that He is unto us a God? If God be for us, who can be against us? The thought that He has promised to be unto me a God, is the sweetest and most endearing of all thoughts, inexpressible and full of glory. But has He taken away my stony heart and given me a heart of flesh? Has He written His law upon the fleshy tablets of my heart, and is He merciful to unrighteousness, remembering my sins and iniquities against me no more? Sometimes I hope I have had a glimpse of the heavenly countenance, and that my eyes have seen the King in His beauty. O how healing is that divine light that gives us a knowledge of the glory of God as it shines in its uneclipsed effulgence in the face of Jesus Christ! But when I contemplate the depravity and the corruption of my heart, and the wickedness of my thoughts, I am made to doubt and tremble and fear.

I do not remember the time when I had no regard for the Old Baptists; for my parents and grandparents were Baptists. From my earliest recollection, I have been associated with Baptist people. I always delighted to go with father and mother to meeting, and I looked upon the solemn worship of God with feelings of reverence and awe. I remembered the preachers who used to come to our house when we lived in northern Missouri, especially Elders Whitely, Guyman, Rogers, Blakely, Wright, Sidwell, Willoughby, and Wortman. Elder Whitely was a very tender preacher; his voice was rich and full of melody, and I always wept under his preaching. My dear mother was faithful member of the church from her youth until her death, and a very spiritual minded person. I shall never forget with what perfect liberty she told her remarkable experience but a few hours before God took her away from us. If I felt as certain of my salvation as I do of hers, I could have no fears at all. Her place on earth is vacant, and we all miss her; yet I would not, if I could, call her back to this gloomy world. She passed the dark river in hope of the glory of God, and with strong consolation. My father is still living, and has always been a faithful attendant on the Baptist meetings. He is a firm believer in the doctrine and practice of the Predestinarian Baptists, and has an experience dating back over fifty years. For half a century he has attended Baptist meetings and associations, but has neglected his duty, and still remains out of the church. But if he never unites with the church militant, I hope that he may reach the city of the living God, the heavenly Jerusalem, the general assembly and church of the first born.

But it was in February, 1871, when I was made to feel and know I was a sinner. It seemed to me that I was the vilest wretch on earth. My sins against God rose up before me in fearful magnitude and number; they bore me down and crushed me under that awful weight. I was then living with my father, three miles south of Tecumseh, Nebraska. Brother George and I had been to that place, and were going to a dance that night, about two miles east of father's. We came down the valley of the Nemaha, and as we walked upon the creaking snow, and beneath the myriad stars that shone in splendor above us, we conversed about many things; about the constellations and bright stars that could be seen that night, my dear brother pointing them out to me; about the sad and happy death of little Nell, as delineated by the powerful pen of Dickens; and about bride of Abydos, so classically written by Byron. I remember so distinctly of talking with him about this last piece, and of listening with such deep interest to his recitations from it. Byron's writings were the delight of my boyhood, and I have spent hours together in reading the poetry of that wretched man. But as we were walking along in the stillness of the night, beneath the white stars that looked so coldly down upon the frozen earth, and I was worshipping at the shrine of an infidel author, the mighty God appeared to me in his character of Justice. God who commanded the light to shine out of darkness, shined in my heart, and then for the first time I saw the awful depth of my wicked heart, and learned that I was ten thousand talents in debt, with not a farthing to pay. O the vast length that I had gone in sin and transgression! I was made to feel in that hour that my heart was desperately wicked and deceitful above all things. Who could know it? None but God, who knoweth the thoughts and the intents of the heart. He showed then what I was by nature—a child of wrath. I saw myself a vile, wicked, corrupt, loathsome, condemned worm of the dust. I had been stricken down upon the road of sin. The whole head was sick, and the whole heart was faint. There was no soundness in me, but wounds and bruises and putrefying sores; they had not been closed, neither bound up, neither mollified with ointment—Isaiah 1. I sought a balm in Gilead, I sought a physician there; but my wound was incurable; I could not find a cure in medicine. I told my brother that I could not go to the party, but was going home. He asked me why, and I told him I was not feeling well. We separated there on the lonesome prairie, and I went home. It was not a home any more. I could find no rest nor comfort; there was no peace for my weary, heavy-laden soul. The stars no longer shone for me. I wanted to be away from everybody and everything. I felt like I wanted to be buried in the heart of the earth, where no one could ever see me. I went home with a bruised and bleeding heart. I saw myself under the awful sentence of a righteous law, which I had violated, and I saw no way in which I could escape the ire and wrath of God. But I called on God to be merciful to me, a sinner. The prayer of my heart was that he might save me from an impending death; but O! my very prayers were sinful. How could one so wicked and impure dare to offer a supplication before so pure and holy a being as God? It seemed that I could not utter a word, there hung over me such a weight of guilt. If God should consign my soul and body to everlasting punishment, justice could no more than met. Then how could I supplicate the Just One to rescue me at the expense of divine justice? I looked upon God as an unchangeable being, and that justice was one of his attributes. It is a fearful thing to fall into the hands of the living God. There is an awful terror in the frown of offended Deity. Nevertheless, like David, the sweet psalmist, "Let me fall into the hand of the Lord; *for his mercies are great*." But then, when under conviction, I could see none of the beauty, none of the sublime splendor and glory of the doctrine of justification by faith and the imputed righteousness of Jesus

Christ, which I hope I have seen in later years. I could not then trust the doctrine of imputed righteousness, which I trust has since been revealed to me by the Spirit, which searcheth all things, yea, the deep things of God. I have sinned since then as I had not sinned before. I thought everybody looked upon me as a vile and sinful wretch, and I was such a miracle of sin and wickedness that nothing was too bad for me to do. It was so open, out breaking, that I expelled, though even it that I had no superior; but was it was in another and a worse direction that I engaged with all my power and ability. I returned to the poisoned cynical writings of Byron, Moore, and Shelley, and sought to bury my whole being in their infidelity. *I determined to become an infidel.* I pledged myself that I would prove the bible a fabrication and a religious myth. I determined to confute the idea that there is a hereafter or a God! O the profound mystery of godliness! See how far he will allow his children to wander from him—how far he will permit them to go in sin and blasphemy. Even when my experience had taught me that there was a God of infinite justice, I was so presumptuous as to attempt to deny his being. I feel sometimes yet that sin will never be forgiven me. This, the darkest and the blackest of sins against God, could not be forgiven me, were it not for the mediation of Jesus Christ, as a Daysman, making reconciliation for the sins of the people. And how efficacious must be the blood that can cleanse from such sin! But John says, that Jesus' blood cleanseth us from all sin. If I am his, the efficacy of his blood is sufficient for me. I abandoned the society of Christian people, and to a great extent even that of my wife. I formed associations of friendship with the leading infidels of the country, spent all the time I could with them, and eagerly listened to their arguments. I collected and read all the infidel writings I could find—John S. Mill, Herbert Spencer, Darwin, House, Paine, and many others. I seldom read the bible, and derived no satisfaction from reading religious works. At the instance of an atheistical associate I read, "Paley's Evidences of Christianity," and pronounced it a failure. For several years I devoted most of my time to the study of law, and was admitted to the bar. But the law was always dry and uninteresting to me, although I tried to the utmost to become attached to it and to make it a life work. Nothing was so irksome to me as the dull pages of Blackstone; so I determined in my own mind that I would not practice in that profession. I then determined to master the mathematics, and began study of some of the higher branches; but I made little or no progress in that direction. I was poor, and had to work for a living, and could not devote much time to studying, and I was now in a critical place. I had quit going to our meetings for more than a year, and I had spent all of my substance in the vain pursuit of evidence to overthrow the truth. In all that incongruous mass of testimony which I had been so long and so assiduously collecting, there was no was consistency, no harmony, no truth. It was incompetent, insufficient. It gave no relief to the uneasiness of my mind; it yielded no balm for my aching heart. I was yet in the gall of bitterness and the bond of iniquity. Every thing was bitter to me. I was drinking from the bitter waters of Marah, and there was no tree that I could throw in to make them sweet. O! there was a dreadful darkness as could be felt, like that which hung over the land of Egypt for three days and nights. But this darkness, this awful gloom, was the precursor of a glorious day to me. I look back to that time and feel that the time of the Father had come. The long years of conviction and bondage had all expired. The first born smitten, and the angel of God's presence was there. The blood of the Pascal lamb, that taketh away the sins of the world that had been sprinkled on the lintel and the door posts of the door, and the destroying angel had passed over! It is with rapture that I speak of this. I called to God in my affliction and he answered me. "He brought me to his banqueting house, and his banner over me was love. I sat down under his shadow with great delight, and his fruit was sweet to my taste." It was on Friday the 21 of April, 1879. It was riding alone on the wide prairie, meditating on the power and justice of God, and mourning on account of my sins against the light and knowledge. Oh the anguish of my soul! The heavy burden that I then bore pressed me down to the earth, and I implored the heavenly master to have mercy on me. And there, where no ear could hear and no eye could see, save the Almighty one, the holy spirit of truth came to me, and removed the dark cloud and the heavy burden that had hung over me so long, and carried my burden into a land not inhabited—into the wilderness of forgetfulness. When I return in mind to these moments of rapture, I can but recall the words of poor Cowper,

"What peaceful hours I then enjoyed?
How sweet their memory still?"

How I rejoiced then in hope of the glory of God. I had heard of joy before, but I had never experienced it. It was then that the Spirit spake comfortably to me; it was then I was made to believe that my sins were forgiven, and that my iniquities were pardoned. Then I beheld for the first time, in the person of Jesus Christ, an all-sufficient Savior, the Deliverer who had come out of Zion, and who turned away ungodliness from Jacob, the lot of his inheritance. I saw him then as the vilest sinner's advocate with the Father. I had read before of his coming out of Edom, with dried garments from Bozrah, glorious in his apparel, traveling in the greatness of his strength; but not until then could I realize that he was God manifest in the flesh, speaking in righteousness, mighty to save. For eight long years I had been doubting, fearing, despairing, and sinning against his holy name. But God, who is rich in mercy, will not cast away his people whom he foreknew. His mercy endureth forever. Had it been otherwise, I had been forever lost. An apostle says, "According to his abundant mercy he hath begotten us again unto a lively hope by the resurrection of Jesus Christ from the dead." It is this hope which maketh not ashamed, and which is an anchor for the soul, both sure and steadfast, that is worth more to the poor soul that it sick of sin than everything else together. It reaches to that within the veil—to that inheritance which is incorruptible and undefiled, and that fadeth not away; and it is this that makes it so dear to the believer. When the love of God is shed abroad in the heart, we can then rejoice in this hope of the glory of God. O how rich I was when O could call Jesus, who was anointed with the oil of gladness above his fellows, that he might comfort them that mourn in Zion, that he might give them beauty for ashes, oil of joy for mourning, and the garments of praise for the spirit of heaviness—how infinitely rich I was when I could call him my Elder Brother, and view him as the Mediator between God and men. What a glorious relationship is this! I could then, I thought, understand why he laid aside his glory, and came out from His Father, and became incarnate; why he took not on him the nature of angels, but the seed of Abraham; why he was made in fashion as a man, and assumed the form of a servant; why he was made of a woman, made under the law, which has been violated; why

> "Aside the Prince of glory threw
> His most divine array,
> and wrap'd his Godhead in a veil
> of our inferior clay."

It was because of the love he had for his church, ["]which is his body, the fullness of him that filleth all in all." And that love was predicated on the oneness of Jesus Christ and his bride. And is bone of his bones, and flesh of his flesh; and no man ever yet hated his own flesh, but nourisheth it and cherisheth it, *even as the Lord the church*. Thus the apostle shows the mysterious union and relationship of Christ and his people. They being involved in sin and transgression, and under the curse of the law, when the fullness of the time came God sent forth his beloved Son to redeem them from under that curse, that they may receive the adoption of sons. He is the Head, the Husband, the Shepherd, and as such is responsible for the offenses of his people. It is this relationship that enables me to understand why it is that God can be just and the justifier of the unjust; why it is that our heavenly Master bore our griefs and carried our sorrows; why he was wounded for our transgressions and bruised for our iniquities; why the chastisement of our peace was upon him, and why it is that we are healed by his stripes. When God was pleased to reveal his own beloved Son in me, I beheld him as one that was near of kin, as a gracious friend, in whom I could trust implicitly. O how delightful it was in that golden hour of deliverance to lean upon him as my beloved Savior! It seemed to me that all my sorrow was gone, and that I could never see any more trouble. I thought that my enemies, which so lately had threatened to destroy me, were that day broken in pieces by the glorious Captain of my salvation, and that I would see them no more forever. True, that burden of sin and guilt was taken away when the heavenly smile of my blessed Savior broke in upon me through the dark cloud of God's wrath, and since then I have been relieved from its awful weight; still there is a cruel thorn in the flesh, and this old corrupt nature is all the time warring against the spirit, so that I cannot do the things I would. There is a constant warfare going on within, "as it were the company of two armies."

I went home that night, but did not sleep much. I was relieved from a great burden, and felt like one who had been liberated from a long imprisonment. Everything seemed to smile approbation upon me. I was a new creature; old things had passed away, and all things had become new. Joy inexpressible was mine. No language can ever express that sweet salvation and ease of mind that I then enjoyed. But I told no one; I only intimated to my wife "that another great burden was removed," but she understood it to have reference to the past week of school. This peace of mind remained for several days, and it was worth more to me than all my life had been. There is more enjoyment in one hour of that serene tranquility of mind, than there is in a life of half a century of revel and debauchery. O the sweetness of those days of rest! Nothing was as irksome then; all was delight, and rapture, and joy, and love. Then I hope that I loved my God, who had loved me even when I was dead in sin. I loved him because he first loved me. I then looked upon Jesus as my Savior, who had delivered me from the fear of death, and from the wrath to come. He had come to me in the extremity of my weakness, when I had lost all confidence in self and in an arm of flesh. He had taken me up out of a horrible pit, and had placed my feet upon the Rock, and had put a new song into my mouth, even praise to his matchless and adorable name. It was then that my prayers went out on the wings of the wind toward all of the children of God everywhere. Never before had I felt such love for the chosen of God, for those whom the Savior had forever perfected by the sacrifice of himself. I could see a beauty to holiness then which I had never seen before, and I wanted to be with the poor and afflicted people of God, and to tell them what great things the Lord had done for my soul, whereof I was glad. I was so anxious to hear a gospel sermon, and see the kind faces of the brethren, that I could scarcely wait until the time of the next meeting. On the eighth of March I went down to my uncle's, who was the pastor of Union Church, and remained over night with him. It was a lovely night, and I took uncle into the starlight, and inquired about the standing of the church and her articles of faith, and then told him about some of the Lord's dealings with me, and asked him for his advice. He told me to do my duty, and spoke very encouragingly to me. He was greatly affected and delighted when I spoke of coming to the church. I shall never forget that conversation; it was tearful, yet full of inward rapture. The next morning my uncle was sick, and unable to go to meeting; but Elder Wood, an old father in Israel, whom I dearly love, and who is loved by all for his Christian character and virtue, was there that day, and preached a most profound sermon. It was Sunday, and after the preaching Elder Wood gave an invitation, and I went forward and tried to talk, but could not find expression for my feelings except in tears and sobs, for which I was ashamed, and felt as though I had ruined myself and disgraced the cause of Christ. Yet I was received, and it was agreed that I should be baptized at the next meeting. Union Church consisted of but five members when I came to it, and that day only two of them were present. Therefore, Brother Brittain, who also is my uncle, requested me to relate my experience again at the April meeting, which I had a desire to do. At this meeting all the brethren were present, and I was received from this church without being questioned, on Saturday before the second Sunday in April, 1879, and the following day I was baptized by the pastor of the church, Elder Isaac A. Irwin. It was a lovely morning, and a large crowd of people were gathered at the water. It was to me a most delightful scene. I how beautiful everything was. In the deep blue waters of the lovely Nemaha, around which hung so many sacred reminiscences, I was about to follow my heavenly Master into the liquid grave. And as uncle took me by the arm, and said to me, in his gentle tone, "Now we'll go down into the water," I was filled with feelings and emotions I had never had before. With what rapture I went down into the beautiful blue stream. There are no words with which I can tell of my feelings then. I felt that I was going where Jesus had been, and then the thought of my unworthiness filled me, and a secret sorrow. I often think of that day, with its events, and I fear that I was not a fit subject for that solemn ordinance. Then my doubts and fears began to return, yet

I know that it ought to be the answer of a good conscience toward God. I was afraid that I deceived my brethren and myself, and I was troubled about it.

> "And now there is an aching void.
> The world can never fill."

But these doubts and fears and tremblings are a part of the inheritance of the saints. However, during the short time I remained there, I had a great deal of enjoyment with the brethren. Our meetings were pleasant, and I hope they were seasons of refreshing from the Lord. But it was not for me to stay with them long—"God moves in a mysterious way." I lost my health, and concluded to travel in quest of it. So, in July, I left my home and my church, and started on my way in company with my youngest brother. We traveled through parts of Missouri, Iowa, Illinois, and Indiana. I am happy to say that my health has greatly improved since I left home. For this I am thankful to God. Since I have left my home beyond the Missouri, I have had some very delightful seasons with some brethren I have met. I can never forget them for their kindness and hospitality toward me. I attended five associations—the Morgan, Sangamon, Sandy Creek, Big Springs, and Wabash District, have been with about twenty churches, and have formed the acquaintance of a great many brethren and sisters in Missouri, Iowa, Illinois, and Indiana. I shall name a few of the ministers whom I have met, most of whom I have heard preach; Claybaugh, Guymon, Stout, Blakely, Vanmeter, W. A. Thompson, Williford, King, Murray, Gillet, McCay, Dark, Curtis, G.Y. Stipp, Vancleave, Jones, Southard, Tabor, Whitlock, and Ludwick. I must express my sincere thanks to all those precious brethren and sisters for their unmerited kindness toward me while among them. Surely, when I was there, the lines were fallen unto me in pleasant places, and I had a goodly heritage with them. And this remark is equally applicable to the dear brethren and sisters and friends in Crawfordville, with whom I am now staying.

If this poorly written account of my journeying in this world of sin and sorrow is of any comfort to you, I am amply paid for my trouble.

Yours in tribulation, B. H. IRWIN

Holiness Preacher

Introduction

About two years after Irwin began preaching holiness, his reports and sermons begin to appear in some periodicals in 1893. The selections in this section sample the topics and tenor of his early holiness ministry. First, a sermon and several letters sent to *Christian Witness* in late 1893 and early 1894 establish a baseline for his holiness ministry (both content and style) before he claimed to be baptized in fire. These documents also illustrate Irwin's tendency to travel and preach until so exhausted in body and mind that he had to pull away for a period of rest before resuming his itinerancy. Two additional letters written to the same periodical in the Fall of the following year illustrate Irwin's activities and priorities just before he experienced the fire on October 23-25, 1895.

Document 2 – "The Friendship of the World," *Christian Witness and Advocate of Bible Holiness* **(January 11, 1894), 2-3.**

"The friendship of the world is enmity with God." James 4:4.

The carnal mind always seeks the friendship of the world. This is why half-hearted Christians are ever entangled with the affairs of the world, and are constantly forming alliances with men of this world. The carnal mind, still remaining in the hearts of those who are not wholly sanctified, hates God, and hates holiness, and hates the true disciples of Jesus, and is essentially and eternally antagonistic to everything that is good, and true, and right. It is not a subject of law. God never made any law for it. There never was any law made for the carnal mind. Law always contemplates the good of the subject; but the carnal mind is essentially and unalterably and necessarily evil and devilish; is not subject to the law of God, neither, indeed, can be, but it is enmity against God—necessarily, unalterable, essentially. Therefore the one way in which God proposes to deal with it is to destroy it.

That passage in Rom. 8:7 is fatal to the theory of repression. It can never be educated, cultured, or intimidated up to the point of acquiescence, much less to love, the divine will. It hates God's law and God's will, and God's Word, and can *never* be changed. This fundamental truth lies at the very basis of the doctrine of entire sanctification.

Why, then, do men professing to be Christians, covet the friendship of the world when God says, "Whosoever, therefore, will be a friend of the world is the enemy of God?" Men unite themselves with confessedly Christian institutions of darkness, attend the county fair, the theater, the horse race, play cards, visit and converse for hours on worldly topics on the Sabbath, read Sunday newspapers, smoke cigars and attend church fairs and sociables, and still claim to be Christians. The Word says they are the enemies of God. Is it not time we were drawing the line where God draws it [?] But the answer to the question above is simple and plain. Out of these things come wars and fightings among you. And men indulge in these things that "they may consume them upon their pleasures." But God has declared in his blessed Word that "Whatever therefore ye eat or drink, and whatever ye do, do all to the glory of God." (1 Cor. 10:31.) Hundreds of thousands went to the World's Fair this year solely for the pleasure they hoped to get out of it; very few, I imagine, went there *for the glory of God*. One minister united with a secret order that he might increase his congregation; another played cards that he might win the unsaved; another attended the theatre that he might better be qualified to describe the pleasures of sin, and all were bitterly opposed to holiness. Where are we drifting?

But some are inquiring for "the old landmarks," blessed be his name! John says, "If any man love the world the love of the Father is not in him." (1 John 2:15). And Paul says, "For if I yet pleased men I should not be the servant of Christ." (Gal. 1:10.) Take these infallible witnesses, James, John, Paul. Their testimony ought to alarm the worldly professor.

No man can be on friendly terms with this wicked world, no matter what his ostensible purpose or object may be, without being an enemy of God. No man can love the world or the things that are in the world, and have the love of God in his heart; no man can please the world and be a faithful servant of Christ. As Christians we must be completely separated from evil and from evil associates and entirely devoted to God.

And if we do this is it will inevitably bring down upon us the enmity and hatred of the world, and if we live godly in Christ Jesus we will suffer persecution as surely as the promises of God are true. (2 Tim. 3:2.) And if we "preach the word" "with the Holy Ghost sent down from heaven," and testify definitely to the experience of entire sanctification, even though we do it in the meek and lowly, and gentle, tender and loving spirit of the man of sorrows, and walk before God with a perfect heart, the world will still hate us, misrepresent us and misinterpret us our motives, and go about to "kill" us as they did our Saviour; and many of our "own familiar friends" will "murmur at it," and go back and walk no more with us (John 6:61, 66) even as they did when Jesus was here on earth.

For my own part, "I glory in the cross of our Lord and Savior Jesus Christ, by whom the world is crucified unto me, and I unto the world." (Gal. 6:14). And I rejoice that the world hates me, for I am not of the world, glory to his name! I covet the hatred of the world. I do not want the religion that will please the world. It would not be the religion of my Saviour. This may seem a rough way of putting it but it is my way of speaking and I shall not try to speak smooth things. I love the truth of God better than I do the applause of men, or the friendship of this world, or even the good will of the people of God. Give me pure love, though it wear a rugged exterior rather than a sickly, simpering, sentimentalism.

There is all the difference in the world between sweetness and sweetishness. Lord, give us a honey comb experience, six-sided, every inch occupied and filled to bursting, with pure love, sweeter than the dews of Hermon or the honey of Hymettus! Give us the honey in the comb, with the solid walls of truth, and loyalty to God, an uncompromising in courage, and holy boldness to do his will without tempering or toning down, or adjusting things to suit the carnal mind. I will take the diamond in the rough rather than cut or polished glass; I would prefer gold in the nugget to smooth burnished brass! I want the pure gold purged to its last analysis, "pure as transparent glass."

Document 3 – "Kansas," *Christian Witness and Advocate of Bible Holiness* **(January 25, 1894), 13.**

Smith Centre, Kan., Jan. 11, 1894.

Dear Witness: Our meeting here closes to-night. It has been a most glorious meeting. We have had a decisive victory all the way. Many have been converted and many sanctified wholly. The holiness people have organized a Holiness Local Union in conformity with the Western Holiness Union, with a membership of over forty. The M. E. Church has been greatly built up; nearly all the members have been wholly sanctified. The pastor's wife has been sanctified, the pastor greatly blessed, and the members wonderfully strengthened. The entire community for miles around has been stirred on the question of holiness. Some are mad, and many are glad. One aged Campbellite lady was wonderfully sanctified and several of the church members converted. I go from here to Colorado for a few days to rest, and then I shall begin at a small place called Lansing, in Eastern Colorado, and from that place I shall come by easy stages back to Lincoln, where the Nebraska Holiness Union expects to hold its second annual meeting in latter part of February. The blood of Jesus Christ is all my plea, and it sanctifies wholly. B. H. Irwin.

Document 4 – Mrs. S. C. Curry, "Kansas," *Christian Witness and Advocate of Bible Holiness* **(January 25, 1894), 13.**

Smith Centre, Kan., Jan. 13, 1894.

Dear Witness: On invitation of our pastor, Rev. T. A. Windsor, Rev. B. H. Irwin commenced a meeting here Dec. 6, continuing until Jan. 11. The attendance was good. Bro. Irwin preached holiness with great power, and the Lord owned and blessed His Word from the first. About forty have been wholly sanctified; twenty-five or thirty have professed conversion or reclamation, a great many of whom were in the church. Some had never been converted. There has been a wonderful shaking among the "dry bones." All the surrounding country has been stirred as never before. One dear old lady, a member of the Christian Church, testified that she has asked the Lord a year ago to send one of His "ministering angels" to show her the way into a clearer light. When she saw the notice in the paper that this evangelist had come, He revealed to her by his Spirit in a way that seemed marvelous that this was the man that was to show her what she must do. She is now walking in the light of holiness. Amen. We are looking forward to still greater things from the Lord, because He is leading and we are following and the work seems but [word(s) missing] glory to His name.

We have organized a local union, and intend to have our holiness meetings weekly. Our prayers and blessings follow Bro. Irwin to his new field, especially that his health be preserved to do much for his Lord. We also desire the prayers of Holiness people that the work so graciously begun in Smith Centre may be entirely committed to Lord's own keeping and that we may be kept from building on the foundation already laid anything that must be burned.

We hope to send another list of names to the WITNESS soon. Mrs. S. C. Curry.

Document 5 – "From the Field," *Christian Witness and Advocate of Bible Holiness* **(February 8, 1894), 12.**

Lansing, Col., Jan. 20. —Sanctified wholly, glory to God! The field is white unto the harvest, and the laborers are few and I am unable to carry on the work, being confined to my room this week. Racked with pain, but rejoicing with unspeakable joy. Sick and sorrowful and shut in, but shouting "Glory to God for holiness." Jesus, who is my sanctification is all and in all to me. My God supplies all my needs according to his riches in glory by Christ Jesus (Phil. 4:19). Holiness is sweeter and more precious to my soul now than ever before; and if I ever get up from this sickness I shall preach and teach the doctrines of entire sanctification more definitely and more constantly than I have ever done. Glory! The blood of Jesus Christ is all my plea. It cleanses me now.—B. H. Irwin.

Document 6 – "Nebraska," *Christian Witness and Advocate of Bible Holiness* **(February 8, 1894), 13.**

Oxford, Jan. 29, 1894.

Dear Witness: I came here on the 22d and began on the 23d, with the M.E. pastor, Rev J. F. McKay. The meetings had been in progress for one week, and the altar was full the evening before I came. Bro. McKay is true holiness man—a loyal Methodist, and he preaches holiness without apologizing for it. We have had uniform victory all the way. The walls of sin are tumbling and crumbling, holiness has the right of way, and this "great potential idea of Methodism" and the gospel prevails. Hardened sinners and lukewarm church members are being greatly stirred.

The leading members of the church are coming out clearly into the light or entire sanctification, and some Presbyterians and others are being convicted for a clean heart. Last night the altar was crowded with weeping penitents, and backsliders, and earnest believers seeking holiness. Many have been converted and sanctified already, and the work appears to have just begun. Two little girls came to the altar last night burdened for others. The Holy Spirit is brooding over these troubled waters. I expect to remain here for a week yet, and then I go to Burr Oak, Kansas, to assist Rev. M. L. Custer, the M. E. pastor there. Let all the readers of the WITNESS pray for me that my faith fail not, and that my health may not give way.

"Oh, now by faith I am crucified, and by his blood I am sanctified." Unspeakable glory fills my soul. I am bathing in the warm, tropical, transparent waters of the upper deep, and heaven lies just beyond.

"Oh come with me to the banquet of love,
That's spread for all who are born from above!"

Invested with fire I am all the Lord's. B. H. Irwin.

Document 7 – "From Oklahoma," *Christian Witness and Advocate of Bible Holiness* (October 10, 1895), 12-13.

Mulhall, Okla., Oct. 1895, Dear Witness:—I began here on Wednesday, Sept. 25, and have seen the power of God displayed in a most wonderful manner. It is the first district camp of the central district of Oklahoma. Rev. J. F. Palmer of Guthrie is the presiding elder, and Rev. W. E. Jones is the pastor on this charge. Mulhall is a beautiful little town of six or seven hundred people, situated in a rich and glorious land. My impressions of Oklahoma are very favorable, and I have never found more orderly or intelligent and candid people than I found here.

Much wildfire and rank fanaticism have damaged the cause of true holiness in these parts, but the people are hungry for the Bread of Life and when they hear the truth of God they accept it much more readily than the sin-hardened people in some older settled countries that I have been laboring in of late. Praise the Lord! God's pure truth commends itself to the earnest, honest soul everywhere. The pastor and the presiding elder are true and solid on the question of entire sanctification. Brother Jones was converted under the faithful labors of Sister Tyler. The presiding elder of the West Oklahoma district, Rev. N. M. Engeart was also with us one day, and preached a definite clear-cut holiness sermon. Bro. J. D. M. Buckner, pastor of the First M. E. church, Guthrie, is here, soul and body, and preaches ably and with no uncertain sound, the blessed doctrine of entire sanctification as a second work. He related with great power and telling effect, last night, his own personal experience and the altar was filled with seekers after the great salvation. I knew Brother Buckner when he resided in Nebraska, and was the President of our State Holiness Association, and am glad to find him true and loyal to the doctrine and experience of holiness.

Preacher and their families have come from all over the district—some coming a hundred miles in their buggies. Quite a number of these M. E. preachers have gotten out into the experience and are going back to spread the fire of holiness on their charges. One preacher last night renounced the lodge devil and said to the writer that God had been calling upon him for some time to do this, and that he finally got to the place where he felt the Spirit was about to leave him, and had to give up these Christless institutions of darkness or backslide altogether. One woman was sanctified and fully saved from the tobacco habit. She had been smoking for twenty-three years. My Lord, help us! The writer found an own cousin of his here who says he believes in holiness. Hallelujah! If he gets sanctified (and I am praying that he may) he will be the first one of my kindred who is called by this name. I do not know how many have been sanctified wholly or converted, but I think not less than seventy-five. Old grudges have been cleared up and restitution made, and men and women have confessed and repented to the bottom and got real salvation. The presiding elder said this morning in his prayer that he expects to be true to God on the question of the second blessing, and claimed Oklahoma for God and holiness, "and all the people said Amen." Bless the Lord! This camp meeting will make an eternal impression on the religious character of Oklahoma. There are M. E. preachers in this part of Oklahoma who have been and will be true to God and real, practical, Bible holiness. The outlook for Oklahoma in the direction of holiness, is very auspicious. Brother Burchfield was here part of the time from his work at Purcell, but he, fortunately, was called away to attend a wedding to which he was a party. Brother Gould of the Free Methodist church was here and rendered most excellent service. One tobacco-soaked preacher withdrew in disgust and the meeting went right on all the same. Brother Palmer's son was converted. Bro. A. B. Woods, formerly of Poweshiek county, Iowa, is here one of the committee, and is "diligent in business and fervent in spirit." His wife has been blessedly sanctified and their two daughters converted to God.

My next meeting will be at Holt, Okla., about twenty miles southwest of Enid, on the Rock Island R. R. Then I shall go (D.V.[1]) to Cleburne, Texas, for a siege. Will all the saints pray for me? I need your prayers.

My own experience is richer and sweeter than ever. My heart is hot and I can say from the deepest depths of my soul, that there is no controversy in soul with God. I love holiness for its own sake. My health is improving and I am trusting God for strength to do whatever he would have me do. Glory to Jesus!

Document 8 – "From Holt, Oklahoma," *Christian Witness and Advocate of Bible Holiness* **(October 15, 1895), 12.**

Dear Witness:—From Mulhall the writer came across the country, by the way of Waukomis, in a covered wagon, and, after two and one half days' hard traveling part of the time over hard "gumbo," and part of the time through deep sand and "black jacks." I found myself on the banks of Indian Creek, twenty two miles due west of Enid, in a rich and fertile land. I was delighted to find some old and tried friends living here in true contentment and really happy.

Brother William Hixon and his children have secured themselves permanent homes here, and are comfortably situated already. They take the WITNESS and some of the family to enjoy the blessed experience of entire sanctification, having sought and found the great salvation in the writer's meetings over a year ago in Lane County, Kansas. They are established in holiness and have been true to the cause ever since they came to this territory. On Thursday, evening I attended the prayer meeting, two miles from where I am at this writing, and we had a most blessed meeting. The people desired preaching the following night. The Lord was with us in power and two were blessedly sanctified.

These meetings were held in a log school house 16x20 feet in size, with a sod roof and a dirt floor. It was very primitive, but God was with us in sanctifying power, and as they sang "The Glorious Fountain" I was forcibly reminded of other scenes and other days when the power of God came down in marvelous effect upon the people.

On Sunday, Oct. 18th, a day never to be forgotten, I drove thirteenth miles east to Bro. Baumgartener's and went two miles still farther, and preached to a small but appreciative congregation in an open air arbor, built of stakes set in the ground and covered with brush. Here in the balmy air and the glorious sunshine I preached to these hungry souls and five came forward to the altar and knelt on the prairie grass, as definite seekers for sanctification. It was a melting time, and the pure fire from heaven fell upon the people. They urged me to come back and preach to them again.

Yesterday, being urged by saints and sinner alike to do so, we pitched our tent on a beautiful spot on the right bank of Indian Creek, and began the battle in real earnest last night. We had no lumber for seats: and so the people had to sit on wagon seats, chairs, cotton-wood logs and on the ground. But they came, and we lighted the tabernacle with ordinary lamps and began to sing the songs of Zion. The first service under the tabernacle was a time of heart searching, and four knelt at the altar as seekers and as I commented on Matt. 5:22, 23 the Spirit applied the truth, and three of these seekers made confession and publicly promised the Lord that they would make restitution. Glory! I see more and more the essential necessity of deep and thorough work, and do not intend to allow any shallow skim milk professions to go out from my meetings. Lord, save us from a popular, trashy kind of salvation. Give us the genuine holiness that rejoices and is exceedingly glad when reviled and persecuted and when all manner of evil is spoken against us falsely for Jesus' sake.

It is plain to be seen that nothing short of true, practical, Bible holiness will ever reach these people: and that will and does. Men get hungry for a pure heart here the same as they do in Iowa. The carnal mind is just the same, and we have the very same Jesus here.

We are confidently expecting great things here on the banks on Indian Creek. Pray for the Indian Creek camp. God bless the workers everywhere and the cause of holiness. B. H. Irwin.

Notes

[1] *Deo Volente* ("God willing"). Premillennialists in the 1890s frequently employed this abbreviation to emphasize the imminence of Christ's return.

Part Two

The Fire Falls

Baptized in Fire

Introduction

Two letters when pieced together give Irwin's contemporary day-by-day account of what happened to him in Oklahoma on October 23rd, 24th, & 25th. The first letter, written to J. M. Pike's *Way of Faith* after Irwin returned to Nebraska, discusses the events of October 23rd and 25th; the second, a brief letter sent to the *Christian Witness* while Irwin was still in Oklahoma, fills in the gaps for October 24th. This less familiar letter has the advantage of being the first Irwin wrote after experiencing the fire. A third letter, written to *Christian Witness* from Lincoln on November 5th, reveals a less direct presentation of his fire experience.

Document 9 – "The Baptism of Fire," *The Way of Faith and Neglected Themes* **(November 18, 1895), 2.**

An Experience

Four years ago, the 16th of last May, about 11 o'clock at night, I was sanctified wholly by faith, and immediately entered into soul-rest. My heart was cleansed for all interior pollution by the precious blood of Jesus Christ. Twelve hours later, while sitting in my own pulpit, and they were singing the last hymn before preaching, I received the witness of the Spirit to my entire sanctification, and suddenly I was filled with the spirit; the conscious baptism with the Holy Ghost.

I was at the time expecting to preach a definite holiness sermon, and my mind was drawn to my text—"Let us go up at once and possess it, for we are well able to overcome it." Num. 13:30—when suddenly I was melted, as it seemed to me in a flood of tears, which continued all through that sermon, and all that afternoon. I had a new Bible and the church had a new preacher. The Holy Ghost in his fullness had come into my soul. The flood gates of heaven were opened wide, and there came into my soul successive waves and mighty inundations of light and love and joy and faith, and power and glory and loyalty to God, and from that moment to this my soul has been kept in a constant stretch for God. Since then Jesus has been a satisfying portion to my soul, and yet I have had seasons of inexpressible longings after the deeper and greater things of God. I have had times of profound thirsting after the living God—to know more of his love and power, and to have a more intimate personal acquaintance with him and a more clearly defined knowledge of his blessed word. For weeks and weeks the Lord had been searching and probing into the inmost recesses of my heart, and as this divine heart searching went on, the Holy Ghost put into my heart unspeakable soul-hunger and thirst, until on October 23, 1895, I found myself in the very furnace of intensest desire, and I was clearly conscious that I was being led every step of the way by the personal Holy Ghost. Intuitively I knew I was approached a great crisis in my experience. Many things had contributed to lead me down to this point. The loss of property, declining health, disappointments, persecution, betrayals, and the slander of many. I living on my knees before and I felt deeply humbled. My heart overflowing with supreme love to God, and an intense desire to know and so his whole will.

I had been reading Upham's "Life of Madame Guyon" and Dr. Watson's "Coalds [Coals] of Fire." I knew that some of my brethren in the ministry, and in the ranks of the laity as well, professed to have an experience of fire which I had never known. Moreover I had been praying for fire all summer in my camp meeting, and had seen the need of it in many places. And as I read the word alone on my knees, the Holy Ghost seemed to direct my mind to those passages where fire is spoken of, and especially to Matthew 3:11—"and with fire." And to that wonderful Scripture in Rev. 15:2, "A sea of glass mingled with fire." And that single word seemed to linger about my soul and in my dreams and deepest meditations, everything seemed to gather about that single word fire, and while I knew and enjoyed the experience of entire sanctification and had the baptism of the Holy Ghost upon my soul, yet I knew that some of my brethren enjoyed any experience of fire to me unknown, and I felt sure to many holiness people whom I believed sanctified, had never experienced this of which I speak. I believe Miller Willis had it, and C. P. Carkuff and Jesse Bathurst and Geo. M. Henson.[1] And if these enjoyed it why not myself? I became convinced and satisfied that there was an experience of fire for me, and that it was my privilege and duty to ask for and receive it.

God had sent Bro. C. P. Carkuff two hundred and fifty miles, all the way from Ness City, Kansas, to tell me his experience, and while he as relating it to me, about 12 o'clock in the night, of the 23rd of October, 1895, as we lay together alone, I saw in the room above a cross of pure, transparent fire. It was all fire. I have been enabled to see that cross in the same place above me every moment from that time to this. No fire that had ever was kindled on earth was half so pure, so beautiful, so divinely transparent as that. In a few moments the whole room where we were lying seemed to be all luminous with a seven fold light (Isa. 30:26), and a little later still the very heavens were all aglow with transparent flame. The very walls of the room seemed to be on fire. But as yet there was no sense of heat connected with it; but until the night of the 25th, when on the train, en route for home from Enid, all at once I became conscious of the fact that I was literally on fire. This expression may seem a strong one, but I cannot express it any other way. Everything about me seemed to be on fire—actually burning, blazing, glowing. I felt that I was in the very midst of a burning fiery presence. At no time in my life have I known or felt such unutterable ecstatic bliss. For five hours I felt that I should certainly be consumed—and there I entered into an infinitely deeper and more wonderful rest than I had ever known before. I rested in the eternal rock, in the measureless depths of an infinite ocean of pure, living fire. Now I know what God means by the sea of glass mingled with fire. Every fiber of my nature seems to be literally on fire; and from every pore of my body seems to issue a stream of living fire. My entire being, spirit, soul, and body seems literally conflagrant. I feel at this moment dashing over my soul, these blissful, burning, leaping love-waves of living fire. It is no cleansing; it is not the witness of the Spirit; it is not the baptism with the Holy Ghost; it is not a dream; it is not a delusion nor a deception; it is none of these. It is the baptism of fire. It is the actual fulfillment of the promise contained in the last clause of the 11th verse of the third verse of Matthew to me. Hallelujah to Jesus.

Lincoln, Neb.

Document 10 – ["Report,"] *Christian Witness and Advocate of Bible Holiness* **(November 7, 1895), 10.**

Dear Witness—My experience this morning is one of fire and glory. I am living beneath a cross of immaculate fire, in the center of an infinite ocean of eternal glowing flame; and dashes and flashes, and great waves of pure fire surround, and overwhelm, and rest upon me! All is holy conflagration. I have the burning bush experience, tongues of fire, waves of fire, vast inundations of living flame—Glory, glory, glory! Holy, holy, holy! Hallelujah!
B. H. Irwin.
Enid, Okla., Oct. 24, 1895.

Document 11 – ["Report,"] *Christian Witness and Advocate of Bible Holiness* **(November 14, 1895), 12.**

Lincoln, Neb., Nov. 5, 1895. For a week past I have not been idle or asleep. There never before was such an awakening in this city on the question of sanctification. My own pastor, Rev. C. L. Lemon, has been preaching the gospel of full salvation until a large per cent of our church are in the experience of holiness, and among these all the leading members. And in nearly every other church in the city there are those who are enquiring the way. Even Lutherans and Presbyterians and Baptists are awakened. One blessed Presbyterian Brother has a regular holiness prayer meeting at his house every Monday night, and there are enquirers at most of the weekly meetings. One the leading pastors of the city is now studying, I am told, Dr. [Daniel] Steeles' Half Hours, and his best members are praying that he may get back into the blessed experience he once enjoyed and preached. The pastor of St. Paul's M. E. church, Dr. C. C. Lasby, by his earnest and unctuous preaching aroused his large church on the subject of entire sanctification, and has a regular Sunday afternoon holiness prayer meeting in his own church. All this seems to be in answer to prayers of faith, which for years, has ascended to God from a few spirit-baptized souls in this city. Oh, that God would send this way a man full of the Holy Ghost and of faith, like Dr. Godbey or Dr. Carradine, to conduct a series of genuine holiness meetings in one of our First churches. The writer believes the way is opening for a mighty revival here on the direct line of holiness in the true Pentecostal order. Oh for fire-baptized men! Let all the saints who have the fire pray that in some way God may come this way this winter in a wonderful sweep of living fire. My own soul is bathing in the sea of God's love, and I never before had such victory and holy triumph in my own soul. I am living within the fire limits. Hallelujah! It is the fire we need—fire—fire!

> I'm in the fire—the fire's in me,
> And blessed be his name!
> My soul is absolutely free,
> And I am all aflame!

B. H. Irwin.

First Fire-Baptized Revival Meeting

Introduction

Three additional Irwin letters from late 1895 reveal the dynamic of the first revival meeting he conducted after being baptized with fire. A leading Wesleyan Methodist pastor invited Irwin to Guthrie Center, a town of about 1,000 people located along the railroad just west of Des Moines. The meetings had begun at least by November 17th and closed on December 8th.

Document 12 – "Guthrie Center, Iowa, Nov. 18," *Christian Witness and Advocate of Bible Holiness* **(November 28, 1895), 12.**

I am here in a blessed meeting with the pastor of the Wesleyan Methodist Church, Rev. J. H. Meek. He is also president of the Iowa conference of the Wesleyan connection. Rev. C. P. Sage is also assisting and Brother O. Fluke is here in charge of the music. These brethren are filled with the Holy Ghost and have the divine fire. [2] The outlook is glorious. One brother was sanctified last night and got delivered from the tobacco habit. God is still able to save to the uttermost. Others are seeking the great salvation, and still others are earnestly inquiring about this blessed doctrine of entire sanctification. Several of the M. E. people are in the experience and are coming over to help in the meeting. The fire is kindling in many hearts. Blessed be to God for the living fire! For myself, I am going out on the promises of God as never before, and I find them easy and delightful to claim them now, and not only so, but I am searching for the commandments of God, and I want to know all his will concerning me. I expect to obey God rather than men (Acts 4:19, 20) and walk day and night in eternal sunshine. I hear the music of God's breath in the tops of the maple trees near by, as I write these words; it used to make me nervous, but now it soothes my spirit, and strengthens my faith in God. Deeper and richer, and more unspeakably blessed than this, is the constant and eternal diapason of heaven that is going on in my soul! Hallelujah! Earth has no such harmony as this—the indefinable melody of holiness. Nor can the dull, coarse ear of carnality catch the strains of this heaven born music of the higher regions of God's grace. Neither can the eternal harmony of heaven be broken by the wickedness of man nor the malice of devils. God's blessed Word never was so wonderful to me before. I never before had such a keen relish for its deepest truths, nor found such comfort and strength and peace and restfulness in studying it. The Holy Ghost is unfolding and illuminating it to my heart in a new and marvelous sense. Oh, blessed be His name! The living fire is burning on "the main altar of my heart," and this unspeakable experience of fire is daily increasing on my hands! And it is my prayer that God may send this living, leaping fire into hundreds of purified hearts this winter. May God baptize this holiness people with this fire from heaven. It is this that conserves the experience, and without it we are liable to yield and compromise at many points. "Baptize us with fire we pray." May the Lord save us from the spirit of compromise and worldly conformity; and from dead, powerless, money-loving holiness! For my part, I have no confidence in this careful, cautious, fearful preaching that will not attack sin, and expose the corruption in the church. It is not of God. It is of the devil. I am proving God's words true in many respects. I have tested many of his precious promises and find them solid stepping stones, leading to glory. The past is forever buried beneath the blood and the present is blissful—the triune God reigns supreme in my heart of hearts; and the future lies out before me, an infinite expanse studded with the stars of hope and fragrant with the "exceeding great and precious promise" of my God, and I expect to trust and obey and walk in the light as he is in the light, no matter what the cost may be to myself. B. H. Irwin

Document 13 – "Guthrie Center, Iowa, Nov. 25," ***Christian Witness and Advocate of Bible Holiness*** **(December 5, 1895), 12.**

Hallelujah! I am glad to be able to report progress, victory, sheet lightning, dynamite, and fire! Glory to God! The dear Lord is with us here in gracious, sanctifying power. Yesterday was day of holy conquest. We had three services, and eleven hungry souls knelt at the altar for entire sanctification and professed the blessed experience. Some of these were remarkably clear, other are glowing with the fiery baptism. One man and his wife who have used tobacco all their lives got sanctified wholly and both were completely saved from the appetite; and they took the tobacco they had on hand (a wagon load of "long green" leaf tobacco) and made a bonfire of it! A sister who saw the flames said they were blue like the supposed flames of the pit! Up to the present writing fifteen have professed the experience of entire sanctification, and others are seeking. Sinners are convicted of their sins, and the community has awakened on the subject of the great salvation. The work goes on gloriously. Sin is being uncovered, and sinners of every class located. The writer expects to be here at least one week yet, and possibly longer. Calls are coming in faster than I can fill them, and all for straight, clear-cut definite holiness work. Blessed be his name. B. H. Irwin.

Document 14 – "Another Good Meeting," *The Way of Faith and Neglected Themes* **(December 18, 1895), 1.**

Dear Way of Faith: Our meeting closed here last night in a decisive victory. About twenty-five have been sanctified or converted, and a deep conviction is on the whole community. The devil is stirred and the cause of holiness is established here in Guthrie. This meeting has been one of great depth and power. It has been a time of deep heart-searching, probing and rock-blasting. Baptists, Methodists and others have been greatly blessed. One Baptist sister was sanctified, and several Methodist Episcopals and nearly the entire Wesleyan church have got out into the clear light of entire sanctification. Several have received the fire. Hallelujah! One brother testified that the Holy Ghost has permanently located in his heart, and that his house had been haunted the night before by the Holy Ghost.

Yesterday, the last great day of the feast, was a wonderful day. Two were sanctified during the communion service, and three others seeking the great salvation, and one old man was in great agony of soul, seeking to be reclaimed.

Hypocrites have been located and exposed. One man and his wife got deliverance from the tobacco habit, and burned a wagon load of "long green." One sister got restored in her body, and another whose mind had been so deranged for years claimed to be completely restored. The writer believes she is. Bless the Lord! She was also sanctified during the meetings.

Brother Fluke has been with me during these meetings, conducting the singing. We go next to Tuttle's Grove, near Coon Rapids, Iowa, where we begin for God and holiness to-night.

My own soul is in a blaze of living fire. I am constantly in an atmosphere of delicious fire. The blood cleanses me now, and the very God of peace sanctifies me wholly.

B. H. Irwin
Guthrie Center, Ia., Dec, 9, 1895

Notes

[1] Irwin would have been familiar with the radical holiness preacher Miller Willis through W. C. Dunlap's *Life of Miller Willis: Fire-Baptized Lay Evangelist* (Atlanta: Constitution Publishing Company, 1892). He had crossed paths with the other three preachers while evangelizing in Kansas. Irwin encountered Carkuff as early as the spring of 1895, spent "a few days" resting in Carkuff's Ness City home in May, and ministered together with him in Ransom that summer. See notices in *Christian Witness and Advocate of Bible Holiness* for April 5, June 7, and July 12, 1895, page 12 in each issue. Bathurst and Henson were less apparent in Irwin's 1895 field reports, but both would later join his Fire-Baptized movement for a few years. Bathurst became one of Irwin's most trusted associates, a relationship Irwin honored in 1904 by naming his son Vidalin Bathurst Irwin.

[2] Irwin's remark that Sage and Fluke "have the divine fire" does not mean that they too had experienced a definite "fire baptism" at this point, but rather that the Spirit of God was noticeably anointing their ministries. See page 32, note 23.

Part Three

Spreading the Fire

Letters from Indian Territory

Introduction

Letters from the summer of 1896 illustrate the solidification of Irwin's message and of opposition to it. Irwin's reports disappear from *Christian Witness* by March 1896 and soon thereafter from all other holiness papers with the exception of J. M. Pike's *Way of Faith*. By June *Way of Faith* had become the primary outlet for Irwin's voice, running news of his meetings in nearly every issue. Letters from this summer demonstrate the ways Irwin's meetings could empower individuals, families, and churches, while at the same time disrupting both established and emerging communities. The following four letters document a quick swing through several settlements in the Indian and Oklahoma territories populated primarily by recent migrants.

Document 15 – "Woodward, Okla.," *The Way of Faith and Neglected Themes* **(June 17, 1896), 6.**

Dear Way of Faith: We are having a decisive victory on the old fashioned gospel line. Yesterday was a victorious day for the cause of holiness. In the morning one sister came weeping her way to God for pardon, and several others said they wanted pure hearts; in the afternoon three knelt at the altar for entire sanctification, besides the pastor of the M. E. church with whom I am holding the meeting; and at night one sister was gloriously sanctified. Conviction is spreading and deepening. One of the oldest professional gamblers in the section expressed his desire for a clean heart. The Sunday school superintendent and his wife were at the altar for entire sanctification. The people here say they have never heard the gospel preached on this wise before; but they confess and deny not that it is the Word of God.

The Baptist evangelist, Sid Williams, has lately been here, but much of his work seems to be superficial.[1] For my part I have no confidence in the popular hold up your hand, join the church, be baptized sort of conversions that fail even to wean them from the common dance. May the Lord help me to do work that will stand the tests of temptations and persecutions, as well as the ordeal of the judgment to come. This is a small town on the Panhandle Railroad in western Oklahoma. It has about five hundred inhabitants, fourteen saloons, about one hundred prostitutes, and gamblers and libertines and all other classes of sinners. The congregations are fair, respectful, and rapidly increasing in size. District Court is in session, and prominent lawyers are here from other cities in the Territory. The people are getting interested in the meetings, and the outlook is exceedingly good for genuine revival.

The people here have never been used to the "altar," and the idea of being "saved from sin" is entirely new to them. But the truth is beginning to dawn upon them. I remain here for about a week yet.

B. H. Irwin
May, 1896

Document 16 – "Minco, Indian Territory," *The Way of Faith and Neglected Themes* **(June 17, 1896), 2.**

Dear Bro Pike: My meeting in Washita County, Okla., was held ten miles west of Cloud Chief, the county seat, in a lovely arbor prepared for the purpose. It is about eighty-five miles due west from this place [Purcell, Indian Territory]. It is [text unclear - about one hundred?] miles south of Woodward, and about forty miles north, and in sight of, the Wichita Mountains. The brethren who desired the meeting came to Woodward with team and wagon after me, and when I said to them, "You have come a good ways after me," they replied, "Yes, but we would gladly have gone across the continent to get you, if we could not have secured you in any other way." They came from Iowa to the Territory and have never heard a holiness sermon preached until they heard the writer, and none of them had ever before seen a sanctified person. But one of them had been taking THE WAY OF FAITH for three or four years, and they had intelligent views of what holiness is, and fully believed in it, and were hungering and thirsting after it. I soon found out that none of them professed nor enjoyed the blessed experience. They had read Godbey's books and some of Carradine's and Knapp's, and they wanted the genuine teaching from one who actually enjoyed the blessing.[2]

We were three days from Woodward to Centre Point where the meeting was to be. The first night out, we camped in the open prairie twenty-five miles south of Washita. Before retiring we read Hebrews, the 10th chapter, and had worship, I gave the proper instructions to the two brethren who came after me, and while I prayed they consecrated all to God, appropriated the blessing, and got gloriously and wonderfully sanctified right there on the buffalo grass; and one of them, Bro. Henry Washington Cuffle, jumped up and down and shouted, and praised God till 3 o'clock in the morning. The other was so still and restful—"quietness and assurance"—and there, with the south wind softly whispering to us God's message of tender love, and the far off, silent stars piercing the deep blue sky, which hung above us like an infinite curtain of matchless blue, we rested in the everlasting arms of the eternal God; and from that moment on our journey was one blazing path of seraphic joy.

We reached our destination the third day at 8 P.M. As soon as it was noised about that we had come some of the brethren came in about 9:30 P.M., and two were blessedly sanctified, and two others seeking. The next day we called at another brother's just before dinner, and before we sat down to eat we prayed, and three others were sanctified wholly, and another just after dinner.

That night I preached the first sermon in the arbor, and six more were at the altar; five of them for pardon. The next service eight went forward. Not a single service without some being at the altar. The work was as thorough as I have ever seen, and I am sure the devil will never get over it, nor hear the last of it. I was there only four days, and about a dozen got the clear experience.

The brother who was so wonderfully sanctified in the prairie has since been instantly healed in answer to the prayer of faith, and also received the *baptism of fire*. Hallelujah! Yesterday we traveled sixty miles, and one of the mules got very lame, and we took the case to the Lord in prayer, and he completely healed the faithful dumb brute, also in answer to the prayer of faith. Bless God for the healing power! John Wesley's horse was healed once. Glory to God! Others of these faithful brethren are earnestly seeking the fire, and they will receive it too.

One of the most remarkable cases of entire sanctification that I ever saw occurred the last day. A sister had been fighting holiness and suddenly she became convinced that it was true, and rushed forward after it, and after an agonizing confession and prayer she found it.

Let me call attention to the fact that a single WAY OF FAITH taken in the community has been the means of arousing a score of people to the realization as to their privilege and duty as to entire sanctification, and but for this fact this meeting would never have been held nor these souls sanctified. These people accept the teaching of THE WAY OF FAITH on all the cardinal teachings of sanctification, divine healing, second coming, and the fire.

The day after I arrived there a married daughter of one of the brethren who came after me gave birth to a fine boy; she was sanctified in less than two hours after and named the child BENJAMIN HARDIN IRWIN MOORE.[3] The child is doing well, and will no doubt become a fire baptized holiness preacher.

This is the land of horned toads, centipedes, campbellites, tarantulas, "freegrass" outlaws, poison belladonna, murderous "white caps," and backslidden Baptists who deny that anyone can backslide. A band of eighty "white caps" was recently organized in this community, whose business is to frighten intimidate and murder.[4]

I organized these sanctified brethren into a Wesleyan Methodist church, the first one ever organized in the Territory, I presume. THE WAY OF FAITH is their organ.

The God of fire is now sweeping through my entire being like a mighty forest flame; my spirit is glowing with the pure love of God, and my heart and very flesh are burning with the supernatural fire from the upper furnaces. There is a fiery cyclone of unutterable glory going on in my soul as I write this.

>Oh the fire, the blessed fire!
>How it blazes, burns, and glows,
>Leaping, dashing, rising higher,
>The more severe the north wind blows.

I go to-day to the Kansas State Holiness Camp for a couple of days. Then I return to this, the Indian Territory.

B. H. Irwin

Document 17 – Mrs. A. L. Werhan, "Cloud Chief, O. T.," *The Way of Faith and Neglected Themes* (July 1, 1896), 5.

Dear Way of Faith: For several days I have been impressed to tell you what Jesus has done for me and my family, he has so blessed us. He sent Bro. B. H. Irwin here to preach a full gospel to us, and when he arrived Jesus gloriously sanctified our souls. Praise his holy name! My husband, myself and four daughters, one son-in-law, one daughter-in-law and two neighbors, sisters, were sanctified wholly. We were very sorry that Bro. Irwin could not stay with us longer. I do pray the Father to open the way for us to hear him again soon. The Holy Ghost stirred up the devil to such an extent that he smote Bro. Irwin in the face; but glory to God, that trial proved to us that one of God's anointed stood before us to proclaim the truth. God bless Bro. Irwin and his work. You will doubtless receive a full account of this meeting from the pen of Bro. Irwin. Although he was with us but a few days we learned to love him.

God bless THE WAY OF FAITH and its editor and all of God's holy servants and children.
Your sister in Jesus,
Mrs. A. L. Werhan

Document 18 – "Purcell, Indian Territory," *The Way of Faith* (July 8, 1896), 1.

Dear Bro. Pike: I closed here last night with signal and decisive victory. Saturday night the devil was stirred for miles around, and the faith of God's true saints was strengthened with might by His Holy Spirit, and claimed the victory. Yesterday afternoon we had a Pentecostal service of great power, with thirteen at the altar for entire sanctification, most of whom received the blessing; and another brother, a blessed man of God, whose experience of sanctification everybody admits, sought definitely and found the baptism of fire. Bless the Lord! At night (the closing service) four men were at the altar for entire sanctification, three of whom received the blessing, the other still seeking. The M. E. preacher here, Rev. C. S. Burchfield, is a young man of promise, every fiber of whose being is loyal to God. I have seen but few preachers stand by the fiery truth like he has during this meeting. Some were brought face to face with the question of entire sanctification and have drawn back, to perdition, I fear. But true fiery holiness is established in this place, and I am persuaded the devil will never be able to uproot this work. Every effort has been made to leave a work here that will be permanent, thorough and radical. THE WAY OF FAITH will be the holiness paper for these people from this day forward. These blessedly sanctified people are in for all that God has for them, and do not propose to limit the Holy One of Israel.

During the week's meeting souls have been reclaimed, sanctified wholly, and baptized with fire, and others are seeking. For my own part I am in for war—war to the hilt—a real hand to hand fight with the devil and sin, and I just love it—hallelujah! I have not been on speaking terms with the devil since God sanctified my soul, and do not expect to be again. Last night after service I suddenly found myself in a rich and inexhaustible diamond field of truth. To me it was new. God is unfolding his word to my heart and brain as He never did before. And I am going on in search of still deeper truths. Intense loyalty to God and obedient faith are the keys that unlock the treasure house of Divine revelation. O how I love the fire—this baptism of living flame—which sets the teeth of the devil on edge! Glory to God for the heavenly fire.

B. H. Irwin

Iowa Battle

Introduction

Irwin's meetings were almost always as divisive as they were dynamic. His insistence on identifying publicly both sins and sinners he encountered frequently triggered intense opposition, especially in more established communities. His repeated trips to Coon Rapids, Iowa, in 1896 illustrate the nature of this opposition and the energizing impact it had on Irwin and his followers. These "furnace fires" also exhausted Irwin, forcing him into periods of exile back in Lincoln or in the home of one of his supporters "in the field." During one respite from his battle for the soul of Coon Rapids, Irwin revamped and published a sermon on the Prodigal Son that reveals much about his hermeneutics.

Document 19 – "Coon Rapids, Ia.," *The Way of Faith and Neglected Themes* **(July 22, 1896), 5.**

Dear Bro. Pike: Our tabernacle meeting is sweeping on with blessed results. Yesterday afternoon one aged woman was healed of rheumatism of twenty-two years' standing, and got right up and walked nearly half a quarter of a mile, and said she felt rested over it. She walked back again to the night meeting, and returned after meeting to the house and felt none the worse. She had not ventured to walk without her crutches; except across the room occasionally, for nearly twenty years. She was also delivered from the morphine habit and sanctified wholly. Her case was almost identical with the case of the man mentioned in Acts 3:7. It was indeed wonderful to see her walk up the rough road without her crutches.

At night a young man was powerfully sanctified. He testified that he backslid once by opposing holiness, and by not taking God at his word. God is getting the people where they are willing to "confess their faults one to another," and they are obeying God. Many of the saints are expected tomorrow, and we are expecting a wonderful day. A super natural fear seems to be coming on sinners round about, and "these sayings are being noised abroad throughout all this hill country" Luke 1:65; and the hand of the Lord is with us, "and the power of the Lord is present to heal."

I remain here a week longer, and then go to the Guthrie County Camp, July 21 to 31. After which I go to Woodward, Iowa, to conduct another camp meeting with Bros. Sage, Fluke, and Stevenson. On fire.
B. H. Irwin
July 11, 1896

Document 20 – "Coon Rapids, Iowa," *The Way of Faith and Neglected Themes* **(July 29, 1896), 2.**

Dear Bro. Pike: The devil is enraged again. Last night he cut twelve of our tent ropes down. Tonight he came in an organized (or what seemed to be an organized body of "ungodly sinners,") and while the writer was preaching on Gal. 3:30, and delineating the character of Ishmael, an "ungodly sinner" got mad, came toward the preacher in a rage, made some "hard speeches" and loudly threatened to commit some "ungodly deeds." I said to him as he came near me, "if you lay hands on me, God will strike you dead on the spot," and I believe He would have done it. He was followed by several others who were urging him to go on with his "ungodly" work. They went out and made awful threats and used awful oaths and vile language, and awaited in the dark till the meeting was out, and attempted to do violence again, but the Lord protected us. All the holiness people stood like a wall of fire. The preacher finished his sermon in the regular way, . . . and four came forward, two for the baptism of fire, one for pardon, and one for entire sanctification. It was a remarkable case of regeneration, a sister who had come five miles over a dangerous road.

Thus God set His seal in a most signal manner upon His own precious truth. Adulterers and penitentiary birds do not relish God's searching truth. I feel that my life is in the hands of God, and I am all packed up and ready to go to glory without a minute's warning.

We confidently expect to continue here until the 20th, and then go at once to the Guthrie County camp. I feel the God of fire filling, surrounding, and sheltering me like an infinite fiery presence just now. B. H. Irwin July 15, 1896

Document 21 – "Coon Rapids, Iowa," *The Way of Faith and Neglected Themes* **(August 5, 1896), 3.**

Dear Bro. Pike: Our meeting near Sage's closed last Sunday with wonderful victory. One converted and one sanctified at the last service.

We began here last Tuesday night. The rain has been heavy and continuous ever since and the meeting has scarcely begun. Yet the devil is enraged. Last night it rained so we had no meeting, but the devil came in the dark, as he always does, and cut out tent about forty feet right across the middle. He walked along the altar and cut it as far as he could reach and then across the seats on one side. But the meeting will go right on if the tent is cut.

Bro. Oliver Fluke and sister are here, Bro. McLeun of Des Moines, and also Rev. Albert Johnson, former pastor here.

As for me, I am still blazing my way through the forest of sin and iniquity, and stirring the devil as fast and as far as I can, and telling sinners of Jesus' "mighty love." B. H. Irwin July 23, 1896

Document 22 – W. E. Stephenson, "A Murderous Assault on Evangelist B. H. Irwin," *The Way of Faith and Neglected Themes* **(August 12, 1896), 1.**

Dear Brother Pike: This is the fifth meeting Bro. Irwin has held in this area since last December. He has been used of God in uncovering sin and exposing hypocrisy and fashionable iniquity, as no other man has ever been used in this part of Iowa. As a consequence angry and malicious threats and several murderous attempts have been made upon his person and life. He was notified before he came to this camp that an organized plot of Campbellites, Unitarians and lodge men had been formed against him, and that his life would be in danger if he came. But he knew that God was calling him to take charge of this camp, and so he came. He said he was packed up and ready for glory, or anything else God might call him to do or endure without a moment's notice.

The meeting has been one of marvelous power, surpassing anything I have ever witnessed. Several times, however, I have heard the coarse growl of the enraged tiger; and last night, after God had anointed Bro. Irwin in an unusual manner, and while a powerful altar service was in full blaze, with several souls at the altar for entire sanctification, the baptism of fire, and divine healing, and while all the saints were on their knees in earnest prayer, an unknown number of masked murders rushed under the tabernacle, firing their revolvers into the canvas as they came, and shouting "hands up here." Their purpose was soon manifest, for they all rushed for Bro. Irwin, and made a desperate effort to take him out from under the tent; but they were utterly foiled. The faithful brethren and some of the sisters surrounded Bro. Irwin and clasped him in their arms, declaring they would rather die than allow the murderers to take him. They [the attackers] were soon forced to retreat, and the object of their murderous attack came out of it shouting, "Hallelujah to Jesus for the fire."

Bro. Irwin did not receive a single scratch of a pin, but some of the brethren were badly hurt. Bro. Fluke received a severe blow from a chair over the right eye. Bro. Sage a blow on the head with a revolver, and several in the face. Bro. Hammer was struck in the face. Bro. Smith was knocked senseless, and one sister knocked down. But not a single blow was given by the saints of God. When the murderers found out that they could not get Bro. Irwin, they fired one shot, evidently intended for him, and fled in great confusion. All God's people stood as one man.

The following night at least 500 hundred people came to protect Bro. Irwin, and stand by the meeting. Great indignation was expressed by the citizens that such a cowardly and murderous attack should be made upon a quiet gospel meeting in civilized Iowa, almost under the shadow of the capitol. The white-caps of New Mexico and Texas have more manhood than these Iowa outlaws. The citizens have taken the matter up, and arrangements have been made to prosecute the criminals to the full extent of the law.

It is already known who the criminals are, and their previous threats and assaults are well known. The guilty men are (some of them at least) wealthy church members, and known to be the vilest and most ungodly sinners in all the country. One of them is an ex-penitentiary convict, sent up for bastardy; another sent his wife away from home some years ago, secured a divorce by perjuring himself, and then married the hired girl; who gave birth to an illegitimate child two or three months after they were married. Bro. Irwin had been preaching against this class of sins, and these wicked criminals were brought to judgment, and this is what so thoroughly enraged the unclean devil.

I never heard anyone who could probe, and search, and bring to light, and portray sin in such awful colors as Bro. Irwin can. It is because he has been saved from such depths of sin himself. He speaks as one having authority. Ungodly sinners cannot sit under his preaching without being brought to judgment. The last night of the meeting Bro. Irwin preached again of murderous threats, to a large congregation, when the mob was lying in wait in the grove nearby. But the tent was guarded on every side by armed men who had volunteered to defend Bro. Irwin at the cost of their own lives.

During almost every service during the entire meeting the altar was crowded with souls seeking either salvation, sanctification, divine healing or the fire, and God granted boldness to his saints by stretching forth his hand to heal.

Bro. Irwin declared the happiest moments of his life were when the mob were trying to drag him from the tabernacle. He says he has proved and now claims Acts 12:11, and 2 Tim. 4:17, 18. Bless God for the fire.

W. E. Stephenson, Evangelist
Coon Rapids, Ia., August 4, 1896

Document 23 – "The Spiritual Meaning of Luke 15:22," *The Way of Faith and Neglected Themes* **(August 19, 1896), 2.**

About two o'clock one morning in the spring of 1893, after a sleepless night of agonizing prayer, the blessed Holy Ghost suddenly unfolded this Scripture to my mind and heart. It came to me with the force of a new revelation, and I knew that I had the right key to the correct exposition of this beautiful passage.

There are four leading thoughts in the text. (1) The robe; (2) the ring; (3) the shoes; (4) the feast. What do these things mean? What spiritual significance have they? What did Jesus mean to teach us by the use of these figures? Let us interpret them in the light of God's own word.

I. This robe symbolizes *the experience of heart purity—cleansing from inbred sin*—entire sanctification. Not a theory, not a dogma, but the blessed experience. Properly speaking, this is the negative side of entire sanctification—the destruction or extirpation of the very being of depravity from the heart and life. It leaves us empty vessels, clean and pure, "sanctified and meet for the Master's use." 2 Tim. 2:21. This same thought is expressed in a variety of ways in God's word. In Matthew 22:11, 12, it is represented by the wedding garment; in Rev. 3:4, and elsewhere by the white robe; in Rev. 2:17, it is the white stone; in Psalm 45:13, it is wrought gold and in Psalm 50:2, it is the perfection of beauty. Here we have the fitness for heaven, the qualification necessary for companionship with God and the holy angels, and the blood washed of all ages. These "have washed their robes and made them white in the blood of the Lamb." Rev. 7:14.

II. Next we have the ring, which is *the signet of power from on high*. This is not the power of eloquence, nor of education, nor of wealth, nor of place, nor of personal magnetism, but of the power "which cometh from God only." Jno. 5:44. It is "the power of the Holy Ghost coming upon you." Acts 1:8. This power cannot be bought with money nor retained for selfish or personal ends. Acts 8:20. But it is freely bestowed upon the pure in heart as a gracious gift by him who has all power in heaven and in earth. Acts 28:18. It is never bestowed upon those who hearts are not right with God. He gives this power to those only whom he can trust, to those who will obey his command, and *tarry* until they are in proper condition to receive this heavenly enduement. (Luke 24:49; Acts 1:4). He bestows this unspeakable gift simply for the asking. O brother, receive it, receive it. Receive Him, the author and source of all power, and let Him reign in your heart of hearts, as your comforter, strengthener, teacher, guide. And it is because men will not tarry but run without being sent that they are utterly lacking in spiritual power. Doctors of divinity and great star preachers, and refined, and cultured, and eloquent bishops, are utterly lacking in this indispensable power, which is indispensable in winning souls for Jesus.

Men want this power for base and carnal purposes, as did Simon Magus, or they seek it "not after the due order" (1 Chron. 15:13), and therefore they never receive it. In order to get pentecostal power we must meet pentecostal conditions.[5] In order to receive pentecostal fire we have to be where pentecostal fire falls; and as certainly as we really get in the right place, "everyone shall be salted with fire, and every sacrifice shall be salted with salt." Mark 9:49.

There are two striking Scripture proofs that this is the true signification of the ring in this passage. In the 41st chapter of Genesis, when God would promote Joseph and make him ruler over everything in Egypt except the throne itself, he forced the old king to take off his ring from his hand, and put it upon Joseph's hand, and made him to ride in the second chariot, and the people cried before him,

"Bow the knee," and he ruled all the land of Egypt. And so when you get this power you get this power you will be a prince in Israel, and a ruler in Egypt. Let the reader observe that this power did not come from Pharaoh, as a superficial view of the subject would indicate; but from God. It came from above. So Joseph ruled all the land of Egypt, and taught their senators wisdom. Psalm 105:22.

And again in the 8th chapter of Esther, we have the same truth. When Mordecai was advanced above Haman, "the king took off his ring, which he had taken from Haman, and gave it to Mordecai," "and Mordecai went out from the presence of the king in royal apparel of blue and white, and with a great crown of gold, and with a garment of fine linen and purple. And the city of Sushan rejoiced and was glad, and the Jews had light and gladness and joy and honor, and a feast, and a good day." Esther 8:2, 15-17. Hallelujah!

III. In the third place, we have the beautiful shoes which typify *prompt and willing gladsome obedience to all the will of God*. After we have been cleansed from unrighteousness by the precious blood of Jesus, and filled with the blessed Holy Ghost enduement, then we are ready to "run the way of the commandments." Ps. 119:32. And O, "How beautiful upon the Mountain of Myrrh (Songs 4:6) and upon the mountain of his holiness, (Psa. 48:2) and upon the high mountains of Israel (Ezekiel 34:14), are the feet of him that bringeth good tidings, that publisheth peace, that bringeth good tidings of good, that publisheth salvation, that saith unto Zion, Thy God reigneth." Isa. 52:7.

These are the ones who are called, and qualified, and sent of God, to preach the gospel of peace, and who bring glad tidings of good things. (Rom. 10:15). With their feet shod with the preparation of the gospel of peace (Eph. 6:15), they gladly run on errands of love and mercy and peace; they willingly go at the king's command, through sunshine and storm, winter and summer, through evil as well as evil report. (2 Cor. 6:8). They preach the word of God faithfully. (2 Tim. 4:2; Jer. 23:28), they "reprove, rebuke, exhort, with all longsuffering and doctrine." They "root out, pull down, destroy, throw down the works of the devil,["] and "build and plant" for God. (Jer. 1:10). The gladly suffer the loss of all things for Jesus' sake, and yet they abound in all things that pertain to life and glory. They labor constantly and fervently in prayer, that God's people may stand ["]perfect and complete in all the will of God," (Col. 4:12); as poor yet making many rich, and having nothing, yet possessing all things. (2 Cor. 6:10). "Night and day praying exceedingly that we may see your face, and perfect that which is lacking in your faith." 1 Thess. 3:10.

Salvation saves us from laziness and drowsiness and sets us working for God and the salvation of souls; and this gives us a good appetite for—

IV. The feast, which means *a keen, healthy relish for the truth of God*. How we love God's blessed truth! How we feed and feast upon it! The old appetite for husks, and leeks, and onions, and garlic, and cucumbers, and melons, and fish, and the flesh pots of Egypt is now gone, and how we feed and feast upon the figs, and pomegranates, and grapes of Eschol, and the old corn, and light bread made out of the finest of the wheat, and strained honey, and rich Jersey milk with the cream stirred in, and the fatted calf! What delicious slices of veal! What rich sections of white clover honey! What clusters of grapes! Glory! Hallelujah. Here we have the fullness of the blessing of the gospel of Christ. Rom. 15:29.

This is "the feast, not with old leaven, neither with the leaven of malice and wickedness, but with the unleavened bread of sincerity and truth." 1 Cor. 5:8. This is the marriage feast to which those in the highways and hedges and lanes of this world are now being invited. Here in this delectable mountain God is making "unto all people a feast of fat things, a feast of wine on the less well refined." Isa. 25:6. No spiritual dyspepsia here, no sourness of stomach, but a wholesome relish of all God's deepest, more searching and severest truths. No inward controversy with God, nor with his word, nor with his providences; no opposition to the truth nor with methods which God honors; no limiting the Holy One of Israel; no talking back to the Holy Ghost; no following Jesus afar off; no sleeping on one's post of duty; no lukewarmness; no indifference to Gods work; no quarreling with advanced Christian experiences. But a constant crying aloud and sparing not; a faithful showing God's people their sins; a burning zeal which is according to knowledge; and an earnest loyalty to God in every particular, and a rapid going forward in the line of duty, utterly regardless of innuendo, threat, betrayal, and open opposition. Glory to Jesus.

Thus having a changed heart and the divine enduement, and beautified shoes, and a wholesome appetite for all the truth of God, we go forth in the strength of Israel's God, and do valiant service for him, and he honors our efforts, and our works do follow us. Having these gracious bestowments, we are of "good courage" all the time, and fear not what man threatens to do unto us.

"We will not shrink, Though pressed by every foe.
We will not tremble on the brink Of any earthly woe."[6]

Lincoln, Neb.

Document 24 – "Furnace Fires in Iowa," *The Way of Faith and Neglected Themes* (August 26, 1896), 2.

Dear Bro. Pike: Hallelujah to Jesus for the living fire! The Guthrie County camp is moving forward on the definite fire line, and it will take the fire fighters a long time to put out the glowing furnace fires which have been kindled in the hearts of these saints. Those who have sought the baptism of fire in this meeting are recognized by all as the best holiness people in the community, who have been walking in the light as he is in the light. And obeying God in every particular. They are the deepest saints in the county. These are the ones that everywhere seek the fire. More than twenty of these truly sanctified saints of God have definitely sought and obtained the baptism of fire in this meeting, and their testimony has a blessed unction and power in it, which strikes conviction in the hearts of sinners as it never did before. Sunday was a day of marvelous power, the altar being crowded at every service, and precious souls were healed, sanctified wholly, and baptized with fire. They came believing God, and they found what they came for. The blessed Hoy Ghost put a blessed quietness upon the multitude, and sinners looked on in wonder and amazement. It was old time religion—the pentecostal power and fire.

It was wonderful to witness the manifold demonstrations—the jumping and shouting and falling under the power, and the laughing, and weeping, and to hear the prayers and exhortations, and triumphant songs that went up from purified and spirit and fire baptized hearts!

The camp meeting is wide open on Bible lines; for salvation, divine healing; and the baptism of fire, for anything and everything else that is promised members of all denominations: Methodists, Wesleyans, M. E. S. [Methodist Episcopal, South], Baptists, and even Campbellites kneel at the same altar, and weep, and pray through. One Wesleyan Methodist minister (Albert Johnson) and wife drove 125 miles to attend the meeting and hear and see for themselves. Sister Johnson received the baptism of fire at the second service and is indeed a wonder to many. The meeting is running on Bible lines [more] than any meeting I have ever conducted. The gift of exhortation is present in manifest power.

Bros. Fluke, Stevenson, Sage, and [name unclear] were all at their best. Earnest inquiries are coming from all over the country concerning the fire, asking for meetings on the definite fire line that I am not able to fill. Glory to Jesus! The living fire is spreading in every direction, and the baptism of fire is moving through the land like a mighty conflagration and the foul breath of the devil, which seeks to blow it out, only causes the fire to spread the faster and the farther. It is also noticeable that the preachers who are fighting the fire are backsliding, and their [word unclear] is becoming tame, and powerless and compromising.

The meeting so far is not large in numbers, but the saints are gathering from far ad near, and the God of battles is leading, and there are great searchings of heart in the divisions of the people.

God has graciously touched my own body with renewed strength and I feel more deeply crucified with Christ today than ever before in all my life. For several days my soul has been prostrate at the feet of Jesus in awful agony of spirit, and I have been praying God to cut me loose, absolutely and eternally, from everything in this universe but Himself, and that He might use me in the future as he has never done in the past. I am willing to be known or unknown, and I count it a joy to be despised and rejected of men. I never loved Jesus with such intense, burning, passionate love as I do to-day. I feel literally on fire as I write this, and heaven is bursting in living flame all about me.

The fire that I received in Oklahoma nine months ago is burning with a sevenfold intensity to-day, I am living in the region of active volcanoes, and all the earth and heavens are lit up with the light that emanates from God's interior furnace fires.

B. H. Irwin
Coon Rapids, Ia., August 28, 1896.

Document 25 – [J. M. Pike,] "Rev. B. H. Irwin," *The Way of Faith and Neglected Themes* **(September 16, 1896), 4.**

A note from this dear brother informs us that, through overwork, he has been utterly prostrate for ten days, and unable to read letters of attend to his correspondence. He is, however, slowly convalescing, and will soon be ready for the fray again. He is disappointed on not getting to the Olmitz Camp Meeting.[7] Our brother is passing through trying financial times, and help is needed. If any feel moved to give assistance, send to Rev. B. H. Irwin, Lincoln, Nebraska.

Pyrophobia

Introduction

By the Fall of 1896 Irwin faced not only opposition in person from local toughs, but also in print from articulate holiness preachers who condemned his emphasis on a distinct baptism of fire, a position that by October Irwin had dubbed "Pyrophobia." The following month Pike published "Pyrophobia" as a tract, with the subtitle "A Morbid Dread of Fire." This article illustrates Irwin's knowledge of Methodist history, his ability to construct a logical argument, and his emerging self-awareness as the true voice of the holiness movement.

Document 26 – "Pyrophobia," *The Way of Faith and Neglected Themes* **(October 28, 1896), 2.**

In November 1895, there appeared in THE WAY OF FAITH a brief account of a remarkable experience of the baptism with fire. That account was written under a powerful anointing of the Holy Ghost, and was immediately sent to an evangelist of world-wide reputation, who sent it once to the paper for publication.[8] This is how it came time to get into print. Since that time certain editors, and several evangelists, have greatly exercised over the matter, and have taken it upon themselves to steady the ark; and much has been written and spoken against the baptism of fire as a definite experience. They have condemned it as wildfire, fanaticism, a third work, a third experience, and so on to the end of the chapter; but still the fire burns.

In all candor, I would inquire, who gave these dear brethren the right to sit in severe judgment upon the experiences of others? If one's faith definitely lays hold of God for the baptism of fire, claiming the Scripture promise, "He shall baptize you with fire," who shall hinder? Would these brethren limit the Holy One of Israel and set boundaries to the possibilities of grace, when God has promised to do for us "exceedingly above all we can ask or think?" These dear brethren appear to have been suddenly and violently attacked by a hitherto unknown spiritual malady, which I have named *Pyrophobia*, (if I may be permitted to coin a new word with which to designate this novel disease.) They seem to have become greatly frightened at the idea, and the mere mention of *fire*, and especially the *baptism of fire*, although a scriptural term, throws them into a horrible convulsions; and instead of exposing and condemning SIN in all of its manifold practical forms, such as vain-glory, pride, secrecy, worldliness, and formality, they advocate a smooth, popular holiness, and devote much of their time fighting the fire, and criticizing the experiences of their brethren who have gone on beyond them. One would think, from the vigor and persistency with which they wage this warfare against the baptism of fire, that they were determined to demolish this Bible term, and relegate it from the phraseology of the holiness people. But the fire will still continue to burn. Two years ago a noted evangelist prayed in a great camp-meeting for ten or fifteen minutes for the fire to fall from heaven upon the camp. Now he is fighting the fire. A few months ago, another great evangelist closed an article with the expression, "O for fire! Fire! Fire!" Now he is denouncing this experience as fanaticism! About five years ago a sanctified man received the baptism of fire in his pulpit while preaching the Word. Some months afterwards he stayed one night with another advocate of holiness, who urged to preach this experience of fire. Now this "advocate of holiness" is bitter and malevolent in his opposition to baptism of fire! But the fire continues to burn!

What is the matter with these brethren? Have they "faced about"? Or were they insincere when they prayed for fire and wanted it preached? Just before I was sanctified an old German brother used to pray, "Lord, purify our hearts." When I got the experience, and I began to preach holiness, he objected to the doctrine. I told him he ought to cease praying for purity if he did not mean it. This spoiled the old man's prayer. Will these brethren please not pray for fire any more until they are sure they mean what they say?

In National, State, and local camps, many of these brethren have exerted all of their influence against the experience. But still the fire continues to glow and earnest, hungry souls far and near are receiving it. They see it in the Word, and in the simplicity of the faith, they just accept it. They do not know any better, poor souls! While popular evangelists and teachers of tame holiness are suffering from repeated attacks of Pyrophobia!

On the other hand, some blessed editors, many evangelists and pastors and missionaries, and laymen by the hundreds, have sought and found and still enjoy, and others are seeking the baptism of fire. And whenever it is sought by faith as a definite experience among the sanctified wholly and filled with the Holy Ghost, it is obtained; and so long as it is faithfully testified to, it is retained. Those who have the best experience among the sanctified are always the first to seek it. For these want all that God has for them. I could name hundreds of this class who have received the fire.

The position of the *Christian Witness* in January, 1894, was impregnable when it said, "Experience is the test," and in April, 1891, when it declared "Experience is not to be controverted." In an article with the above title, referring to a brother who had testified to full salvation, the editor said: "He knew what he was talking about by experience. This is the final test. Let people deny it who do not know it. But experimental ignorance proves nothing. Experience brushes away all the sophistries and theories of cold hearted churchmen." This is true, and one of the most remarkable things I have met with is the fact that some of the brethren who are so exercised over this question of fire admit that we who testify to this experience have what we testify to.

A letter reaches me just now from one of the leading (if not *the* leading) opposers of this experience, in which he says concerning the writer's testimony to the baptism of fire, "I do not doubt but that he received what he says he did." Now God is no respecter of persons, and it being conceded that one of God's saints received the baptism of fire as a definite experience, then it follows that all may have it who will, and that all we contend for, Oh, the infinite possibilities of grace!

Besides, inquiries are coming in almost daily from nearly every part of our own country and from other lands concerning the fire; and just now a long and interesting letter in West Africa requesting the writer to pray earnestly that he and his fellow-missionaries may receive the baptism of fire. Noted authors and deeply spiritual pastors and humble saints are praying for and receiving the holy fire. While proud, vain glorious, self-important, advocates of holiness, living on their reputations, are striving to circumscribe, regulate, and monopolize the holiness movement and shut out the real fire. Are all these saints who are seeking and testifying to the baptism of fire deceived? Mistaken? Backslidden? Or are they all hypocrites? It cannot be.

At a great camp-meeting last summer the most deeply spiritual minister on the ground was earnestly seeking the baptism of fire and declared that he would never rest until he found it. At the same moment the leader of the camp-meeting was preaching against it.

And holiness editors who have ceased to trust the Word of God on the dress question and on the wearing of gold and on secrecy, who no longer teach practical Bible holiness, cannot keep such men as the minister above referred to from receiving the baptism of fire.

And though met now and then by a chilly gust from the north, still the fire continues to burn with increasing power and to spread with amazing rapidity.

Nearly a quarter of a century ago it was said by a great holiness leader concerning the great camp at Cedar Rapids, Ia: "The work was thorough. There was a going down to the foundations. Conviction was pungent, entwining into the soul's deepest recesses. * * * The light is shining, and people learning that gold ornaments and costly array cannot be allowed in connection with a true Christian profession."

Thus they taught in the days of power; and thus they teach to-day, if they have the genuine experience.

But now we hear great leaders of State camps declare, "I am glad there has been nothing said on the dress question in this meeting so far, and I hope there will not be."

Of course there was nothing said on the subject after that.

Style and fashion and worldly conformity are as conspicuous in many of our camp-meetings to-day as they are in our theatres or popular churches; and the leaders do not and will not preach against these sins.

In opposing the baptism of fire these advocates of popular holiness resort to the same old arguments which have always been used against sanctification itself: "I got the baptism of fire when I got the Holy Ghost."

You did? Why have you not been testifying to it, then? No one has ever heard you testify to baptism of fire.

"It drives people from the meetings."

The *Christian Standard* said in 1894: "No doubt many are driven away by genuine holiness preaching—yes, even by the best holiness preaching—even by the clearest, safest, most faithful, and most Christ-like holiness preaching."

Brother, read the 6th chapter of John.

"It produces confusion."

I have heard that argument against holiness ever since I began to preach it.

"It divides the holiness people."

Well, glory hallelujah! It does separate the proud, the formal, the vain-glorious; the popular, the fashionable, and the sectarian professors of holiness from the deeply spiritual and the humble who are really sanctified to God.

So does all genuine holiness preaching. The preaching of the living, powerful Word of God always does this. (See Hebrews 4:13.) The Word cuts, probes, sifts.

These arguments are all safe and without weight. The truth is that some of these brethren have nestled down and rested so long in the "second blessing" that they have become fossilized at this point, and it seems impossible for them to extricate themselves. They seem to forget that sanctification is not the end, but a fundamental experience lying almost at the base of the Christian character. "All the higher ranges of faith and love and courage and power lie above the line of entire sanctification." ("White Robes."[9]) They act as though they believed that a few burning testimonies to the baptism of fire, as a definite experience from their meetings, and the fact that some of God's holiest saints are seeking and finding it, will ruin the cause of holiness; and so they shut out all testimony to this experience from their meetings, and, as a result, their meetings fall flat to the earth and are powerless. Would it not be well for these dear brethren to take the advice of Gamaliel (Acts 3:38, 39). Or can it be possible that the craft of some of these holiness preachers is in danger? May God help us to be charitable and yet true to God!

Nothing destroys a tame, formal, and fashionable holiness like the fire. Besides, I had always thought that the church of God, and especially holiness, was founded upon a rock, and that the gates of hell could not prevail against it. God said to Moses, "Behold, there is a place by me, and thou shalt stand upon a rock." Let the rains descend, and the floods come, and the winds blow, and beat against this unshakeable structure, and still it will not fall, "for it is founded upon a rock." Bless the Lord!

For one I am a constant seeker for more of God, and for more of God, and for more of his rich blessings. As I read his wondrous promise in Ephesians 3:20 I am amazed at its fathomless depths. I am determined to experience all there is in this marvelous promise. It will take me to all eternity to do it; but I am going to keep delving into its measureless depths until I reach the bottom. And when I find anyone who has a richer, better experience than I have, I shall redouble my efforts, and seek the more earnestly, not for his experience, but for one as deep and blessed.

In the *Christian Witness* of December 26, 1895, was published the remarkable experience of Frederick Walters. I quote a few sentences from it: "In January, 1881, just ten years after my justification, the Lord graciously *restored* me. . . . Shortly after this I entered into a *crucified state*. . . . Some days after this my wife and I received the *baptism of the Holy Ghost*. The next morning we spoke with new tongues. The Lord still continued very gracious to me, and while I was testifying in a prayer-meeting at Morris Chapel, three miles from Frankfort, I distinctly felt that the *blood of Jesus* was sprinkled over me. These were precious times. But the most wonderful of all occurred a few days later. It was just before midnight on Thursday, February 24, 1881, I received the *baptism of fire*. Neither tongue nor pen can begin to tell these gracious operations of the Holy Ghost upon my being. In fact, one of these would be unlawful for me to tell anyone how it is done unless they have received the same blessing. It is the only state of grace in which we can find Christ as a consuming fire."

Comment on this experience seems unnecessary, unless it be to call attention to the definite distinct steps.

I call attention also to the testimony of William Bramwell: "The truth, the depth, the promises, quite swallowed me up." . . . "Justification is great; to be cleansed is great; but what is justification, or being cleansed, when compared with this being taken into Himself." "To be cleansed from sin is great indeed; but to receive the inward glory in its full influence, this is the salvation."

These utterances would startle and alarm these dear brethren who are so troubled with *Pyrophobia*, and the old saint, if alive and on earth, would find these self-appointed guardians of modern holiness separating him from their company and casting out his name as evil, and calling his utterances heretical wildfire and fanaticism. His biographer says of him that he allowed "no sudden alarm, no picturesque scenery, no political news, no worldly conversation, to interrupt for one moment his union with God." Only two years before his triumphant death, this saintly man, who enjoyed "salvation into all the gospel glory," and who says himself that he had "never had more pleasant walks by faith in the heavenly country," wrote to his friend, using this plain and wonderful language: "I am giving myself to God, to receive a much deeper baptism, which I feel is my liberty in this world. I cannot rest in sins forgiven, or in being cleansed from all unrighteousness. I see the glory which belongs to me in our blessed Lord, is for himself to dwell fully in my soul."

Let all the readers of THE WAY OF FAITH and especially those who are frightened at the thought of the baptism of fire, ponder deeply and prayerfully these words of Bramwell. They ought to be written in letters of fire upon the hearts of all of God's people. To say that we get this "much deeper baptism," this "inward glory," when we receive cleansing, is to beg the question, and to assume the very thing in issue. Bramwell had received forgiveness and cleansing long years before. This is the testimony of a Methodist indeed, a Methodist in the days when Methodists were Methodists; and yet in these mischievous times on which we have fallen we are told that the baptism of fire as a definite experience is a delusion and that is inimical to the cause of holiness to seek for one's self or to teach others to seek anything beyond entire sanctification. These same brethren carefully exclude from their meetings all teaching and preaching on the subject of the Lord's coming and on the subject of divine healing, even forbidding the praying for a sick person in a private tent. They put a Chinese wall around the "second blessing," and cautiously exclude everybody who has the presumption to a take a step in advance.

The baptism of fire has never been called a third work by any of its advocates. We call it what God calls it in his Word—"the baptism of fire"—though there is nothing in the Word of God, nor in the teachings of Methodism, forbidding the use of the expression, "third experience." We prefer, however, the scriptural term. In this connection I refer the reader to THE WAY OF FAITH of May 20th, 1896, where the editor, who is a member of the National Holiness Association, uses these words: "We are, however, fully in sympathy with Brother Irwin and believe he is on the right track. In all that has reached us from his pen he never refers to his richer experience as the third blessing," neither does it cause him to deprecate the 'second blessing.' [. . .] Even if he called it a third or a fourth or fifth blessing, it would be neither un-Methodistic or unscriptural."[10]

So far as the sin question is concerned, it is forever settled in the two works of grace—forgiveness and cleansing. The baptism with the Holy Ghost and with fire, special anointings, undergirdings, and deep inner illuminatings, are subsequent. These are positive (not negative) operations, and lie out beyond the limit of the utter extirpation of all sin. The fire has no cleansing efficacy—that is not its office. It is the blood that cleanseth. This Holy Ghost and fire baptism illuminates, penetrates, empowers, emboldens, unfolds, gives the tongue of flame. This is Christ's baptism, and is two-fold in its nature, including the baptism "with the Holy Ghost and with fire." It is Elisha's double portion. It is equally as scriptural to speak of the baptism of fire as it is to speak of the baptism of the Holy Ghost. It is the "much deeper baptism" of Bramwell, the "inward glory" of which he speaks. It is "Himself dwelling fully in my soul."

This blessed baptism deepens and intensifies our love toward God, makes us more intensely loyal to God, more humble, more Christlike; gives us a clearer insight into the nature of the adorable Trinity, gives us a greater abhorrence of sin, and a more agonizing passion for souls. It gives us a deeper and keener spiritual perception of truth; and widens our spiritual vision in every way. It gives us a broader and more comprehensive view of revelation, and enables us to know God more intimately then ever before.

Brethren, this baptism is your inheritance. Enter upon your inheritance by faith. "Behold, now is the accepted time; behold, now is the day of salvation." Amen and amen.

Beyond the Midwest

Introduction

J. M. Pike's *Way of Faith* played a critical role in generating interest in Irwin's emerging movement beyond the central plains. During the last four months of

1896, Irwin carried the Fire-Baptized message as far as north as Manitoba and as far east as South Carolina. The following year Irwin journeyed to Texas, Pennsylvania, and Ontario, as the excitement over the fire continued to spread. People wrote to *Way of Faith* from places Irwin had never been to testify to the truth of his message. As Irwin traveled to new and exotic places, he observantly noted regional cultural differences but emphasized that the people "screamed and praised God for the baptism of fire" in South Carolina "just like they do in Canada and Kansas." For Irwin, the Fire could burn away differences in region, ethnicity, gender, and class.

Document 27 – [J. M. Pike,] "Tracts! Tracts!" *The Way of Faith and Neglected Themes* (August 26, 1896), 4.

We are now publishing two tracts by B. H. Irwin, the fire-baptized evangelist of Lincoln, Nebraska, and we have seen nothing more striking for some time. One is titled "The New Man," a tract of eight pages and hews to the line as fully as John Wesley's "Character of a Methodist." The title of the other is "The Old Man," and contains sixteen pages. It is original, unique, radical, and merciless in its exposure of wrong being and wrong doing. We still have a good supply of "The Baptism of Fire," giving the experience of Brother Irwin. . . .

Document 28 – W. J. D., "All Hail! From Minnesota," *The Way of Faith and Neglected Themes* (August 26, 1896), 2.

Dear Bro. Pike: I have been a reader of your paper for some time. I read a large number of the leading full salvation papers and magazines. In my humble opinion your paper, THE WAY OF FAITH, although smaller than some others, is *far* in *advance* of any. I read on the leading subjects of the day, *i.e.*, sanctification of the believer, divine healing, second coming of our Lord and King. . . .

I thank God for the help received by reading THE WAY OF FAITH, especially for the deep, sweet, humble, yet powerful and sublimely profound writings of Bro. [G. D.] Watson. And the living, glowing, flaming, consuming words of Bro. B. H. Irwin, who contribute to your columns. Bless God forever for such holy, fearless, fire-baptized men, who cater to nothing but the will of God, who can be found preaching the gospel of full salvation to all people under all circumstances—in the crowded halls, churches, tabernacles; in little school houses, homes, or in the slum districts; on the streets to poor fallen men and women of every color, and the inebriate and criminal in jail, or the poor soul by the wayside. Hallelujah to Jesus. And do so without any guarantee from anybody but God. That sounds irreverent, as if God's guarantee was not better than any other. "Lord increase our faith." These words cut me like the finest Damascus blade, either in print or when I hear them; their words put steel in my backbone, until sometimes I feel I could dare anything for Jesus' sake and for the salvation of sinners. The work of such preaching will abide; the judgment fires will go out, when they come up to these fire-baptized, blood-washed. Blessed be God forever.

We need not be afraid of preaching all the word declares, but let us be careful lest a promise being left us we come short of it.

Oh that God's people will be guided by the word, that all our love of power's ease, and all hobbies will be utterly destroyed by the fires of God's love sent down from heaven to the end that sinners be saved, believers sanctified, both soul and body healed, and kept by almighty power, unto the glorious appearing of our Lord and Saviour Jesus Christ.

Saved and sanctified up to date,
W. J. D.
Spring Valley, Minn.

Document 29 – [J. M. Pike,] "Rev. B. H. Irwin," *The Way of Faith and Neglected Themes* **(November 25, 1896), 4.**

The name of this consecrated worker has become familiar to the readers of THE WAY OF FAITH, and he needs no introduction. He is at present conducting a meeting in Winnipeg, Manitoba, Canada.

He is coming to South Carolina, and will conduct meetings at Piedmont, in the Wesleyan Methodist church, commencing December 19th.

He will also conduct a meeting at Marion, commencing January 1st, 1897. He intends spending some time in the South filling engagements already made, and working as the Lord directs.

Bro. Irwin is a local elder in the Wesleyan Methodist Church, is thoroughly Wesleyan in his view of entire sanctification as a work of the Holy Spirit subsequent to regeneration and received instantaneously after complete consecration and faith. He also believes that the Holy Spirit will lead the soul that is loyal to His teachings on to a fuller, richer, deeper baptism of the holy fire that will be illuminating, energizing, empowering, and filling the being with flaming zeal for God.

Give him a patient, prayerful, unprejudiced hearing. If he uncovers new truth from the divine word and reveals privileges of a deeper union with God, than you have seen before, grasp the truth, and let it spur you to action. Let not Satan cheat you out of the feast, by diverting your attention to the manner in which it is served. The easiest and most useless business in the world is to find fault. Go in for the richest blessings, even though they may be brought by methods which you may not always approve. God bless Bro. Irwin, and may his visit to South Carolina be one of lasting benefit.

Document 30 – "South Carolina," *The Way of Faith* **(December 30, 1896), 5.**

PIEDMONT: I began here in the 19th, and have held three services. At the first service there were seven at the altar for entire sanctification, at the second service twelve, and last night there were eighteen in all.; some for entire sanctification and some for the fire.

Bro. [Andrew Knox] Willis, the pastor, is in full line with the work, and sees clearly the need of the fire among his people. One woman came eighteen miles against the wishes of her unsaved children expressly to get the fire, and she received it in a most remarkable manner. She jumped and shouted and screamed and praised God for the baptism of fire just like they do in Canada and Kansas. Real blood and fire salvation has exactly the same effect in South Carolina that it has in the far North and along the banks of the Neosho [River in Kansas].

The outlook here for a good meeting is extremely good, and there seems to be no serious opposition to the fire. People are coming from far and near, and the gospel plow is going down.

The Wesleyans here are not strong nor rich, but they are true and teachable. We are praying for the fire from heaven to fall in devil-stirring power along the banks of the broad Saluda here. One man got such conviction on account of his backslidings that he became ill and went to bed and sent for the writer and Bro. Willis. When I arrived at his house he was praying aloud and confessing to God his evil doings! Hallelujah! Let the good work go on!

I expect to continue here until 30th inst., and then go on to Marion, S. C. The fire is falling and the blessed Holy Ghost is moving among the people. Pray for us here that a real breaking up time may come.

B. H. Irwin.

Notes

[1] Texas Baptist evangelist Sid Williams (1863-1936).

[2] These "brethren" were Charles Werhan (born 1843 as Christian Carl Werhaus in Hanover, Germany) and his son-in-law Henry Washington Cuffle (born 1850 in Iowa). They had moved their families to Minco from Iowa by 1893. Charles's wife Araminta (or Armanda) Fosdick Werhan (born 1849 in Wisconsin) appears to have been the one disseminating holiness literature in the family and community. See *Twelfth Census of the United States*, 1900, Washita County, Oklahoma Territory. At least ten people, including eight in the Werhan family, would be "sanctified wholly" during Irwin's visit to Minco (see Document 17).

[3] Irwin Moore, the grandchild of the Werhans, was born on May 25, 1896. He grew up to own an electrical appliance store in Inglewood, California. See *Fifteenth Census of the United States*, 1940, Los Angeles, California.

[4] According to Richard Maxwell Brown, extra-legal groups like the White Cappers attempted to enforce "moral regulation of the poor and ne'er-do-wells," especially in communities of high geographic mobility ("Historical Patterns of Violence," in Ted Robert Gurr, ed., *Violence in America: Protest, Rebellion, Reform*, Volume 2 [Newberry, California: Sage Publications, 1989], 39).

[5] This section of Irwin's sermon seems indebted to a letter that C. P. Carkuff had published the previous month in the same paper. Carkuff wrote of people having "sought and found the pentecostal fire," and added, "When we pay pentecostal prices we get pentecostal goods and pentecostal power" ("Holt, O. T.," *The Way of Faith and Neglected Themes* [July 8, 1896], 5.). This paragraph suggests that Irwin sent an updated version of this sermon, rather than the exact one he "suddenly" received on that "sleepless night" in 1893.

⁶ The first verse from the 1831 hymn by William H. Bathurst, *Oh, for a Faith That Will Not Shrink.*

⁷ Irwin did recover sufficiently to attend the Olmitz Camp Meeting, and even felt sufficiently recovered to preach the last two nights. See Oliver Fluke, "Iowa," *The Way of Faith and Neglected Themes* (October 21, 1896), 5. The first Fire-Baptized Association was formed at the annual Olmitz Camp Meeting either in 1896 or 1897. Irwin's late arrival and weakened condition at the 1896 meeting suggest that 1897 is the more likely date.

⁸ The identity unknown of this "evangelist of world-wide reputation" remains a mystery.

⁹ One of G. D. Watson's earliest books, published privately in Cincinnati in 1883.

¹⁰ Here Irwin accurately quotes the most significant paragraph in J. M. Pike's lengthy editorial defense of Irwin, though he elides an interesting statement from his own testimony to the fire experience that Pike included in that paragraph: "It keeps me closer to the great central truth of entire holiness than anything I have ever experienced. Fanaticism causes one to go off on side issues, but this draws me to the center. I love holiness today as never before, and I see it as a second, definite work of grace more clearly than ever before." Pike had published this now-lost Irwin testimony in the April 1, 1896, issue of *Way of Faith* and also issued it as a tract (also lost). In Pike's May 20th editorial defense of "The Baptism of Fire," he contends that a sanctified Christian "may receive frequent manifestations of the Spirit, and each one imparting a richer unction, clearer spiritual vision, and fuller enduement of power, without in the least degree detracting from the value of the 'second blessing properly so called.'" Pike concludes his editorial with this encouragement to Irwin: "It would give us great satisfaction to hear of a general awakening among the saints of God, on the subject of frequent baptisms of the Holy Ghost and fire. We are fully convinced that it would greatly help and not hinder the cause of holiness" (J. M. Pike, "The Baptism of Fire," *Way of Faith* [May 20, 1896], 4).

Part Four

Organizing the Fire

A Glimpse of 1897

Introduction

J. M. Pike's *Way of Faith* had become the primary periodical reporting on Irwin's Fire Baptized movement, but only a few scattered copies published after 1896 are currently available to scholars. The surviving October 20, 1897 issue gives us a suggestive look at what the movement was becoming. Controversy over his teachings appears to be fueling the organization of regional and state "associations." And there are suggestions that the alienation Irwin experienced bred an increasing empathy for alienated segments of American society—for example, the transient poor, Indians, black southerners, and isolated mountain residents. Late 1897 witnessed a flurry of organizing "Fire-Baptized State Associations."

Document 31 – John M. Pike, "Our Contributors," *Way of Faith and Neglected Themes* **(October 20, 1897), 4.**

The number of prominent Christian writers who are becoming interested in the subjects being treated in our paper is continually increasing. We have contributors now, in England, in Canada, and in various sections of this country, and every issue of THE WAY OF FAITH contains original articles, not surpassed by those of any paper that reaches our office.[1]

    These writers are persons of deep religious experience and close students of the Bible. In their supreme love and consecration to Jesus, and their ardent desire for the promotion of holiness, they are one. But they differ in some of the less important religious doctrines, and in the interpretation of some passages of Scripture. We cannot expect the human mind, as present constituted, to think alike. We do not, therefore, hold ourselves responsible for the opinions of our contributors, but we cannot allow extended controversy on any subject. We have a large number of articles on hand concerning "The baptism of fire"—*pro* and *con*. We want to keep the holy fire burning, brighter and brighter; but controversy as to its meaning will not assist in kindling the holy flame into a brighter glow. Brethren, let us get the fire, the real, Holy Ghost fire, which will make us a living flame for God.

Document 32 – "Brother Irwin's Letter," *Way of Faith and Neglected Themes* **(October 20, 1897), 2.**

This is the second annual camp-meeting which the writer has held for these Neosho Valley [Kansas] brethren. Last year it was held at Chetopa, this year at Mound Valley. The meeting this year was a great and decisive victory from first to last, without actual count it was estimated by the brethren that there were at least thirty radical blue sky conversions, fifty cases of sanctification, more than as many cases of divine healing and twenty five or thirty cases of the baptism of fire. Besides, there was a great sifting among the saints, and a permanent settling down with many into the deep things of God. Everything was located. Prejudice was removed to a large extent, the best and most thinking element in the community were convinced, and had to admit that the radical, fiery holiness "which we preach" is of God. Unable to find anyone who knew of a single conversion in any of the "churches" of Mound Valley during the present year, the writer called the attention of the people to the fact, and reminded them of the wonderful conversions during this meeting. Facts are stubborn things, and they are hard to get rid of, especially when wrought before the eyes of the multitude.

One case especially requires special notice. A destitute family of movers trying to make their way to Missouri was passing through the country from the Indian Territory. The mother had been sick and unable to walk, or even turn herself in the wagon a good part of the time, with six small children. A sanctified woman near Coffeeville heard of their destitution and sickness and at once became interested in them. Through her kindness they were cared for; and she induced them to stay and attend the camp-meeting at Mound Valley. They did so, and drove in the camp on Saturday, September, 25th, the poor woman still sick, and unable to walk, or turn herself in bed. She was also unsaved. Some of the "holy women" went to the wagon, and insisted upon having her carried to the meeting. She did not want to come, but they persisted. Four strong men lifted her from the wagon, and placed her upon a cot, and, like the case in the Bible, "brought her to Jesus." We prayed for her, and the writer preached, and then anointed her with oil in the name of the Lord. The brethren laid their hands upon her and she was not only converted right there but instantly healed of all her diseases. The writer took her by the hand, and said, "In the name of Jesus Christ, rise up and walk," and she did so, running back and forth *across* the platform, and testifying of what God had done for her soul. She testified then and there, "The

Lord has healed me, both soul and body." Afterwards (toward the close of the service) she walked, unassisted, to the wagon seventy-five or a hundred yards away. The next day she was sanctified wholly and the same night received the experience of the baptism of fire as a separate and definite experience. During all of the rest of the meeting she was present, and testified with marvelous power to regeneration, divine healing, entire sanctification, and the baptism of fire, as definite and separate distinct experiences. Financial aid was given them, and THE WAY OF FAITH was sent to her by kind friends, and your readers will probably hear more concerning this case, especially with reference to her experience of fire. The Lord instantly healed her sick child also in prayer of faith.

One brother came from Cartersville, Mo., seeking the baptism of fire. He found his true latitude and longitude and got sanctified. He is now seeking the fire.

Another brother, a minister who received the baptism of fire in our meeting in Oklahoma City last spring, came twenty miles to attend the meeting. God used him mightily in digging out deceived souls.

Another M. E. minister came over two hundred miles from Concord, Okla., to get the baptism of fire and went away praising God for the experience of fire.

Thus while men reason and philosophize and speculate and say, "There is nothing in it," people are coming from far and near seeking the experience of the baptism of fire.

Just now a letter reached me from a distinguished preacher, lecturer, and author, in England, stating that he is ardently longing and praying for the baptism of fire. Hallelujah! And pressing calls are coming in from all over the country for meetings on this blood and fire line.

Brethren, come down off the shelf, and, instead of theologizing, get saved and sanctified and baptized with fire. Get the white fire badge on your souls, and live awhile under the focalized-electric light of this uttermost and innermost salvation, and you will never have anything more to say against fire. Get the experience!

Prejudice was so broken down and God so signally set his seal upon the fire gospel that the best people of Mound Valley and surrounding country insisted upon the meeting continuing after the time set for it to close. Bro. Fluke and I had to go to our next appointment, but the meeting goes right on.

About the only one who had anything unkind to say about us was the beer drinking Methodist editor of an illegitimate local sheet which the best citizens of the community will not allow to come into their houses on account of its vileness.

The last night of the meeting we had a mammoth street meeting, which surpassed anything of the kind I ever witnessed. The saints marched around singing the songs of Zion, and formed a circle in which they testified and shouted and sang and prayed; and there, surrounded by three thousand people, beneath the pale light of the moon and stars, and by the light of a dozen torches, the writer preached to the multitude. God sealed the truth to their hearts.

During the street meeting we were called to go to the bedside of an aged saint to pray for her healing. We found her with a raging fever. We complied with

God's word, and God took the fever instantly away. The best physician in the town was present and pronounced the fever gone.

These Brethren at their business meeting adopted the constitution and the basis of union of the Fire-Baptized Holiness Association of Southern Iowa. There must be at least one hundred members of this fire baptized association. This is the second holiness association organized on the definite fire line, and God has marvelously set his seal upon them. Others are already in process of formation, and I pray God the whole country may become a vast conflagration for God. It is already spreading, and will continue to spread to the uttermost parts of the earth. Men may quarantine the yellow fever, and stop the progress of tame holiness by threats and conference resolutions, but the fire cannot be shut up within the narrow limits of heathen temples nor spurious holiness. It will burst through all obstructions, overlap all human barriers, and defy all man-made limitations.

El Reno, Okla. Ter., October 5, 1897.

A Reflection on 1898

Introduction

Virtually no contemporary sources are currently extant for this crucial year of organization. Even though the exposure of Irwin's moral failure in 1900 deeply impacted J. H. King's life, by 1921 the man who followed Irwin as the 2nd General Overseer was ready to attempt in print a winnowing of the good from the bad in Irwin's ministry. King's memories help to fill a void in the primary documents during this crucial year in the institutionalization of the Fire-Baptized movement. Note: Ellipses provided by the editor.

Document 33 – J. H. King, "History of the Fire-Baptized Holiness Church: Chapter II," *Pentecostal Holiness Advocate* **(March 31, 1921), 10-11.**

In January, 1898, Benjamin H. Irwin conducted a series of meetings at Royston, Ga., in the old school building, a small frame structure, located near the Baptist Church. This meeting was more of a convention than a series of revival services, though it was not conducted as such. It continued for ten days of longer. The following preachers were present: S. J. McElroy, A. K. Willis, R. B. Hayes, W. B. Harris, A. C. Craft, I. A. Manley, Thomas Putnam and others. I was serving as pastor of a charge not a great distance from Royston, and attended a few services of the meeting. Just eight months previous to this date I had graduated from the U. S. Grant University School of Theology, Chattanooga, Tenn., and perhaps had the appearance of a Theologue to those ardent brethren of the fiery baptism.[2] At the evening service one of the most zealous ministers present, being appointed to preach felt led of the Spirit to deliver a severe denunciation against ministers of other churches that were quite popular in the world. As I was the only one present his remarks were aimed at me. He strained his voice to the utmost extent, put forth the greatest physical effort to hold this class to shame and profound contempt. I was quite sure that his severe denunciations had absolutely no effect upon me whatsoever. It was amusing rather than convicting in effect. It was an effort utterly without fruit.

Here the Fire-Baptized Holiness Association of Georgia was formed. R. B. Hayes was elected President. Quite a strong membership was enrolled.

The year 1898 was one of the most remarkable years in the way of success in revival work that was ever witnessed in North East Georgia. In January Hayes, McElroy, and Willis conducted a series of meetings at Jones' Chapel, a Methodist church near Danielsville, with gracious results. The next meeting conducted by these brethren was at Pennington Chapel Methodist church, seven miles west of Royston. This proved to be one of the greatest revivals ever witnessed in this country. The power of God swept the surrounding country like a tornado. Demonstrations almost surpassing description characterized most of the services. Multitudes were converted, sanctified, and baptized with fire as it was called at that time. The truth of divine healing and the premillennial coming of Jesus were clearly taught and forcibly stressed. Physicians and drugs were severely denounced, and many abandoned their use and service for the remainder of life. In all the revival services conducted by these men these neglected truths were powerfully emphasized, as well as those that are regarded as more fundamental in faith.

Great crowds attended the meetings [conducted by R. B. Hayes], and marvelous power fell upon the audiences in almost every service. The power seemed irresistible. Shouting, dancing, and praising God with loud voices was a feature manifested in almost every service. Many fell in trances and reported indescribable scenes of the world unseen.

[King then relates his own agonizing experience of entire sanctification during these meetings before returning to his attention to the movements of Irwin.]

From Royston, B. H. Irwin went to Williston, Fla., and conducted a series of meetings. The Florida Fire-Baptized Holiness Association was organized at this time. This was January, 1898. Shortly after this B. H. Irwin held a meeting at Abbottsburg, N. C., and as a result the Fire-Baptized Holiness Association of North Carolina and Virginia was organized.

The work of B. H. Irwin as a kind of apostle of the fire-baptized movement from 1895 to 1898 resulted in State Associations, being organized in the States of Iowa, Kansas, Oklahoma, Texas, Georgia, Florida, South Carolina, and North Carolina. He also introduced the work in the provinces of Ontario and Manitoba, Canada. But each was independent of the other, there was no organic bond that bound them to the other. Irwin desired to centralize them into one national organization, and so he submitted the proposition to the State Associations. The State Organizations voted to centralize the associations into one, and a call was sent out by Irwin to all concerned to meet at Anderson, South Carolina, July 28-Aug. 8, 1898 for this purpose. The various State Associations were consolidated into one general organization, and named the Fire-Baptized Holiness Association. B. H. Irwin was elected General Overseer for life.

A Discipline had been drawn up and published by Irwin, and was accepted by the body thus constituted. Each state association was to be reorganized in conformity to the new discipline. The office of president, vice-president and secretary was abolished. The office of the one that was to be over the State Associations was designated as that of Ruling Elder. He was to be appointed to this position by the General Overseer. The duties of the Ruling Elder given by the discipline were limited and indefinite. The government of the organization was invested solely and entirely in the General Overseer. He alone had authority to make any and all kinds of appointments, to receive and ordain all candidates for the ministry, to deprive of credentials, and expel from the State Associations all that he disliked or disapproved of their work. No one thought that it was contrary to wisdom to delegate such power to the chief officer of the organization, but seem[ed] to regard it as quite appropriate and fitting.

This assembly was termed the First General Council of the Fire-Baptized Holiness Association. This council was to meet solely at the call of the General Overseer. The Ruling Elder could convene the State Association at such time and place that he deemed proper by consent of the General Overseer.

The next General Council was held in Royston, Ga. April 1-16, 1899. B. H. Irwin was present and presided over its sessions. Many changes were made in the discipline relative to doctrine and policy, but nothing was done that limited the authority of the General Overseer. I was a member of the council proper and took part in the business sessions daily. No minutes were kept of these General Councils or State Associations for years. Why such were not made and published is strange and inexcusable. How interesting and instructive it would be today to have such published minutes to read and think over concerning those gatherings of more than twenty years ago.

Notes

[1] The paper's list of "Special Contributors" included such Holiness luminaries as G. D. Watson, E. M. Murrill, C. C. Cary, James Fohl, D. H. Tuttle, Beverly Carradine, J. A. Porter, and Lucius Hawkins—in addition to B. H. Irwin (*Way of Faith* [October 20, 1897], 4).

[2] At the time King pastored in the Methodist Episcopal Church (North). For a more personal account of these events, see J. H. King and Blanche King, *Yet Speaketh* (Franklin Springs, Georgia: Pentecostal Holiness Publishing House, 1946), 78-87.

Part Five

Live Coals of Fire

Pentecostal Expectancy

Introduction

This sermon illustrates Irwin's hunger for end-time Holy Ghost power. Irwin always saw himself as a preacher of true holiness, but increasingly his quest for the endtime restoration of a "Pentecostal Church" occupied his creative energies. As early as 1896 Irwin and some of the Kansas evangelists he credits with being "fire-baptized" before his October 1895 experience began to anticipate a revival of Pentecostal power. See Document 23 and letters to *Way of Faith* by C. P. Carkuff (July 29, 1896, 5) and George Henson (December 30, 1896, 5). In 1899-1900, several of Irwin's Fire-Baptized colleagues used Pentecostal language in the pages of his *Live Coals of Fire*. E.g., see J. H. King's claim that the "modern fire-baptized movement" has sent "flaming evangelists and prophets . . . traversing the earth with lightening rapidity preaching the Pentecostal gospel" ("Matthew 3:11" [October 13, 1899], 5). Clearly Irwin understood his Fire-Baptized movement from the beginning as "Pentecostal" as well as "Holiness." This sermon also includes Irwin's first published identification of abortion as a hidden sin that the fire can flush out into the open.

Document 34 – "Sermon by the Editor: The Pentecostal Church," *Live Coals of Fire* **(June 1, 1900), 2-3.**

Preached at Royston, Georgia, April 5, 1899.

"Run ye to and fro through the streets of Jerusalem, and see now, and know, and seek in the broad places thereof, if ye can find a man, if there be any that executeth judgment, that seeketh the truth; and I will pardon it."

Thank God, judgment has been going on here, and some have been seeking the truth.

"O Lord, are not thine eyes upon the truth?"

That is, God is looking for truth.

"Thou hast stricken them, but they have not grieved; thou hast consumed them, but they have refused to receive correction: they have made their faces harder than a rock; they have refused to return. Therefore, I said, Surely these are poor; they are foolish: for they know not the way of the Lord, nor the judgment of their God. I will get me unto the great men, and will speak unto them; for they have known the way of the Lord, and the judgment of their God: but these have altogether broken the yoke, and burst the bonds. Wherefore a lion out of the forest shall slay them, and a wolf of the evenings shall spoil them, a leopard shall watch over their cities: every one that goeth out thence shall be torn in pieces: because their transgressions are many, and their backslidings are increased. How shall I pardon thee for this? thy children have forsaken me, and sworn by them that are no gods: when I had fed them to the full, they then committed adultery, and assembled themselves by troops in the harlots' houses. They were as fed horses in the morning: every one neighed after his neighbor's wife. Shall I not visit for these things? saith the Lord: and shall not my soul be avenged on such a nation as this? Go ye up upon her walls, and destroy; but make not a full end: take away her battlements; for they are not the Lord's. For the house of Israel and the house of Judah have dealt very treacherously against me, saith the Lord. They have belied the Lord, and said, It is not he; neither shall evil come upon us; neither shall we see sword nor famine: And the prophets shall become wind, and the word is not in them: thus shall it be done unto them. Wherefore thus saith the Lord God of hosts, Because ye speak this word, behold, I will make my words in thy mouth fire, and this people wood, and it shall devour them" (Jer. 5:14).

In the first chapter of Jeremiah we read: "Then the Lord put forth his hand, and touched my mouth. And the Lord said unto me, Behold, I have put my words in thy mouth" (Jer. 1:9).

I call your attention to the fact that is not hellfire: it is heavenly fire. The Lord will come with fire. The Lord will come with fire, and with his chariots like Elijah went up in, to render his anger with fury, and His rebuke with flames of fire. One man said to me: "What does the fire do?" You read the 15th and 16th verses of the last chapter of Isaiah, and you will find out what it does. It unearths the works of the devil to preach the fire. It locates and dislocates hypocrites and false professors. It undeceives people. You can go into these tame holiness meetings and profess justification and sanctification, and go right through without being touched at all. A sister out in Oklahoma attended a meeting that I held about two years ago this spring, and God located her, wonderfully uncovered her sin and the sin of her heart, and the confessions that that woman made were startling. She had been professing to be a Christian for over twenty years, and the summer before she had gone through a big holiness meeting and had not been touched at all. In this meeting, which only lasted a few days in a dirty little hall, God unearthed her, and she got up one day and said she has a confession to make. I had been preaching on confession, restitution, and inbred sin. She said: "I know this confession will ruin me in this town." I said, "That is what you need." She went on to tell that for eighteen years she had been practicing child-murder, and involved her husband,

and a physician or two. Her confession stirred the whole community. Another woman in Lancaster, Pa., said to be the best Christian in that city of four thousand people and having every appearance of being a Christian, had been at the altar seeking the baptism of fire, and the last night of the meeting she got up and made a similar confession. A dentist and his wife in that city were so worked up about it that they could not sleep, and he said: "If that is the case, there is not a saved soul in the city."

The Bible is a tremendously searching book, and the baptism of fire gives a man a spirit of discernment, and enables him to preach the gospel so as to unearth the works of the devil. Blessed be God for the sifting and searching that fire does. You take people who profess the fire when they received the Holy Ghost, and they would not allow you to preach in their meetings. I tell you, you are not sanctified, or you would want this experience in God's order.

I am going to call your attention to some of the characteristics of the Apostolic Church—some of the distinguishing marks. Let me turn first to Ephesians 5:25-27: "Husbands, love your wives, even as Christ also loved the church, and gave himself for it: That he might sanctify and cleanse it with washing of water by the word, That he might present it to himself a glorious church, not having spot, or wrinkle, or any such thing: but that it should be holy and without blemish."

I want to say that the baptism of fire, if you dig down deep enough, lies couched in that word "glorious." You may not be able to see it, but I do, and if you get desperately in earnest for the experience, God will show you. The word "glorious," in its deep etymological sense, contains the thought and the idea of the perfect light. The Psalmist says in speaking of the Bride that she is "glorious within," and without pursuing that thought any farther I simply want to say that this is the highest point, the very apex, of Jesus' intercessory prayer in John 17, that we may have the glory He had with the Father before the world was. That is the apex of this whole subject, and if you take the whole prayer of Solomon, you will find in 2 Chron. 7:1 that after he had made an end of praying the fire fell from heaven, and that was not hellfire. And we are told again in this book that glory of the Lord filled the temple: so I maintain now, and call your attention to it, that the glory that Jesus prayed we might have, and the glory which it is our privilege to have, is an experience that legitimately and properly rises out of the baptism of fire. So you may call it a fourth blessing if you want to. If you were to talk about the fifth, sixth, or seventh blessings you could not frighten me. I am in for all the blessings there for me, no matter how many there may be. It makes me feel good to tell it! Praise God. I have learned the secret of keeping a good feeling in my soul: it is done by keeping the windows open and the shutters off: and the canaries and the red-birds sing, and the sunlight and the air from heaven come in through every part. It is a wonderful thing to have the glory. An older sister in Winnipeg has an experience along this line. She dances, gets reeling drunk every time she dances. One day she was down on the main street, and something seemed to strike her. I said: "Hallelujah!" and she began to stagger, reel and dance. She said afterward that the glory struck her feet. You get get so full of Jesus, and the Holy Ghost, and the divine Father, that the glory is likely to strike you anywhere—in the hands, feet, or head. Glory to God for the fire—the real fire. It makes me love people, and yet hate their sins as never before. It makes me true to the souls of people as nothing else ever did. You think you are true, and I hope you are; but I will tell you when you get real true with your family and others, you will find out long before that there are a lot of things not right, and you will have war all the time.

Paul said to Timothy: "Endure hardness." The Christian life is a warfare; a daily, constant, unending battle with the devil. That is why we are soldiers; and God does not send out soldiers just to muster and parade. He sends out soldiers with the whole armor on, with the burning sword and the trumpet; and they are to kill, and smash up, and tear up the works of the devil. Glory to Jesus, that is what God has commissioned me to do.

In the latter part of the very first chapter of Jeremiah, I call your attention to the statement God makes concerning His people—His ministers. God spoke to the prophet and said:

> "Thou therefore gird up thy loins, and arise, and speak unto them all that I command thee: be not dismayed at their faces, lest I confound thee before them. For, behold, I have made thee this day a defenced city."

God had a fence around Job, and the devil knew it; and God has a hedge of fire around me, and the devil knows it.

"An iron pillar, and brazen walls against the whole land, against the kings of Judah, against the princes thereof, against the priests thereof, and against the people of the land. And they shall fight: but they shall not prevail against thee: for I am with thee, saith the Lord, to deliver thee."

Now look over here another place in the same chapter, in which He says: "See, I have this day set thee over the nations and over the kingdoms, to root out, and to pull down, and to destroy, and to throw down, to build, and to plant."

So you see, God's true prophets, and God's true ministers, are set in this battle to pull down, root out, tear down, destroy, and then to build up and to plant. The Lord help us to see the order of things as He has given them to us in His Word. It is an easy thing to get people forward seeking the fullness of the Spirit, and the other blessings on the hallelujah side of salvation: and if it were not for the siftings and the probings we are having, everyone would be right in line with us, and would seem to have as good a time, but you have to go through this negative side first. Get converted and regenerated first, and then sanctified—get the real nature of sin and depravity, the very inbeing of sin, taken out. This must be done before you have this holy shout that nothing can disturb.

I remember a woman in one of my meetings, backslidden; and she was considered on the finest woman in the city. She made a wonderful confession. We prayed with her, and God mightily blessed her and saved her. That night in the meeting the pastor kneeled beside me, and that woman began to shout. It is a wonderful thing to get saved of God; and these nice, respectable Christians, who are to go to do anything, and too nice to go anywhere except to meeting, need to get really saved of God, need to confess down, through and out, so God can put the holy shout of victory in their souls. Some of you people profess the fire, and think you received it when you got the Holy Ghost, and you are not within a thousand miles of the Holy Ghost. There is a dear brother out in western Kansas who keeps true, straight forward on the main track, and nothing has been able to switch him off. He sings and shouts, and his neighbors know that he is a man of God. He pays them right up according to promise. Well, that man had to confess and made restitution, and then God so wonderfully saved him. We let various things come between us and God and snap the cord, and the connection is broken. It is a wonderful to be filled with Holy Ghost, but it is a more wonderful thing to be baptized with fire.

I want to read in the last chapter of Luke. I want to show the condition the disciples were in, and the condition people must be in to get the baptism of fire. I have seen people come to seek the baptism of fire, and they looked like they were troubled; they look lean and lanky in their souls. They needed something else before they were ready for the baptism of fire.

"And he led them out them out as far as to Bethany, and he lifted up his hands, and blessed them. And it came to pass, while he blessed them, he was parted from them, and carried up into heaven. And they worshipped him, and returned to Jerusalem with great joy: And were continually in the temple, praising and blessing God."

Now, I read this to show you that in order to baptized with fire, one must be washed in the blood, and delighting to do the whole will of God. David said: "I delight to do thy will, O my God" (Psa. 40:8).

There are many professing Christians who cannot say this. They do not delight to do the will of God, and they do not do it.

They returned with great joy. Beloved, when we get to a place where we and our friends are pulled apart we are usually sad. When we come back from the graveyard, we do not usually come back with great joy; but now, look here, these disciples knew that Jesus had gone away, and they did not expect to see Him again, and they went right back in obedience, worshipping, not discouraged or downcast, but went back with great joy. The point I want to make is this. Entire sanctification puts us in a place where we will do His will joyously. The man that led me into this experience of the baptism of fire [C. P. Carkuff] said to me once that he was looking for the commandments of God. If you are really converted, and sanctified wholly by the blood of Jesus Christ, you will take delight in doing the will of God. In a justified state you will do the will of God, but sometimes it may be a real struggle; but if you are sanctified wholly you will take delight in doing the will of God. I make that point to show you that they were sanctified wholly. Mr. [William] Arthur says in his book "The Tongue of Fire" that they were sanctified sometime during the ten days of waiting, but I put the limit somewhere in the fifty days. Their hearts were cleansed from all sin. When the Pentecost came they were obeying God joyously.

What makes you disobey God? It is inbred sin, the devil on the outside cannot do it. Dr. [George D.] Watson tells of scientists going up into the Alps to get snow and see if it was perfectly clean and pure, and when they took a microscope they discovered iron filings from factories in England. He says these things are in the purest snow that can be gathered on earth, and he calls it devil dust. The devil came along and blew the pestilential breath into Adam's heart, and it has been handed down. It makes you fret, worry, get mad and covetous. It is that devil dust in your heart that makes you do these things. When that has been taken out, there is nothing there that will lead you to disobey God. Once you felt prone to wander, but now you feel prone to obey God; prone to do the will of Jesus, obey him in every little thing, and keep his commandments and ordinances. You want to know to what God's will is concerning you. Now that was the condition of these disciples at the close of the last chapter of Luke. We find them returning with gladness of heart.

Now, let us turn to the first of Acts. Jesus had commanded them to tarry in city of Jerusalem until they were endued with power from on high. Now He says:

"Ye shall receive power, after that the Holy Ghost is come upon you: and ye shall be witnesses unto me both in Jerusalem, and in all of Judea, and in Samaria, and unto the uttermost part of the earth."

I was reading, a few weeks ago, in the life of one of God's missionaries, a scholarly young man who went into Arabia. One day he was surrounded by Mohammedans, and they commanded him to say: "There is one God, and Mohamet is His prophet." He replied: "There is one God, and Jesus Christ is His Son." He was a witness for Jesus. Jesus says: "Ye shall be witnesses unto me."

David Brainerd was a witness, Henry Livingstone was a witness, and Adoniram Judson was a witness. It is no wonder that before the latter died God gave him that whole country. He advised people to read such works as Madam Guyon and Archbishop Fenelon. He was a sanctified Baptist missionary. It is a wonderful thing to be saved of God so you will witness for Jesus and unto Jesus. I call your attention to the fact that the Apostolic Church was a witnessing church—unto Jesus.[1] I want you to get this thought. To be a witness, means to be a martyr, and we get the wrong idea when we think that Polycarp and those other saints who were killed were the only martyrs. John Wesley was a martyr, and Martin Luther was a martyr, and there have been many others through the ages. John says we should lay down our lives for the brethren. I am a martyr for Jesus. Some people say that they have a bid for martyrdom; but I am a martyr now. I have laid down my life for Jesus.

The first mark of an Apostolic church, is that it is a true witness of Jesus. That is what is said of Jesus. Every man who is a real member of the Apostolic Church is a faithful and true witness for Jesus. The word "witness" means martyr; and a martyr is one who lays down his life for Jesus. In Acts 2 we are told:

"When the day of Pentecost was fully come, they were all with one accord in one place."

The second mark of the Apostolic Church is the unity of the Spirit, and the unity of the faith. These people were united. People can come together and never be united. There was existing in this Pentecostal Church what [Thomas] Upham calls "divine union." Their hearts were cleansed and purified by the precious blood of Jesus, and now you will notice that there was a oneness of spirit among them. Glory to God. When I was sanctified I had never taken communion outside of the old hard-shell Baptist church, but soon after I was sanctified the presiding elder come along, and I was gladly allowed to come and administer the Lord's

Supper, and I found out that it was a real Holy Ghost communion. I am going to eat with the family. I will commune with you whether you are black or white, yellow or striped. That is because there is unity of the Spirit and unity of the faith in my heart. God has taken all the bitterness, malice and evil feeling out of my heart, and put sweetness and love, and blessed continual victory in my soul, so that I am willing to take any man by the hand who loves God. We cannot afford to tie ourselves up and shut everybody out because they do not agree with us.

The Lord tells us, and it is clearly seen, that these brethren were of one mind. There may be some minor points on which the fire-baptized saints may differ, but on the great fundamental truths of God's Word there cannot be any difference. Every man who has the love of God in his heart will accept all the teachings of God's Word. These brethren stood on that plank. I come to a man who professes to be a child of God, and professes to be saved from sin, and I preach to him the truth of entire sanctification—the possibility of being cleansed from all sin, and he says that he does not believe it. Right there our fellowship breaks. He will not accept the truth of God's Word. I preach to him the baptism of the Holy Ghost, and the baptism of fire, and divine healing, and he says that there is no such thing. I say: "Brother, what do you know about it? Have you ever been sick and gone to God, and been anointed, and had God's children lay their hands on you? He says: "No." "Well," I say to him, "you are not a competent witness." I testify to the fact that I was sick with nervous prostration, and I had God's children anoint me, and God healed me; and this man says: "I do not believe it." "Well," I say, "bless God, brother, we will take different routes." I would have to sacrifice my convictions and go back on my experience to have to backslide to do it. I was taking a number of holiness papers when I received the baptism of fire, they began to ridicule it, and I said: "I will not take them any longer." I took them back to the post office and told the postmaster to return them, and say that I would take them out of the office. I did not want my children to read the devil's poison. Now, brethren, it is by this course that I have kept the victory in my soul, so bright, and blessed and holy. It took me out of the Baptist Church, and the Methodist Church, and the same thing will take me out of everything else that fights what God has done for my soul. I am going to praise God for it and testify to it.

I have pointed out two marks. First, the witnessing: second, the unity of the spirit, and unity of the faith. They have the same spirit, and see eye to eye. Now, I come to the next thing. The Pentecostal is baptized with the Holy Ghost. It is a sanctified church, and it is baptized with the Holy Ghost, for we read in Acts 2:2: "Suddenly there came a sound from heaven as of a rushing mighty wind, and it filled all of the house where they were sitting."

That is the baptism of the Holy Ghost. Now, I want to emphasize one thing. There is nothing said about entire sanctification here. The filling of the Pentecost is not a destructive work; no cleansing connected with Pentecost. Take that wonderful prayer of Paul's in the Ephesians, and there is not a negative position in it. So in this passage, it is of the filling of the Holy Ghost.

"There appeared unto them cloven tongues like as of fire."

And this is after they were filled with the Holy Ghost. Peter was there, James, John, Thomas, Mary, Martha, the mother of Jesus, and the last one of them had the baptism of the Holy Ghost. Can you say this of your church? Are they all filled the Holy Ghost? Some of them are filled with whiskey and tobacco smoke. I make this statement, that there was not an exception to this rule in the Pentecostal dispensation. It does not say, "It was filled," but "They were all filled." If we could have one hundred and twenty true saved and sanctified witnesses, of one mind and of one heart, having the unity of the Spirit, and the unity of the faith, and all were filled with the Holy Ghost, we would have a wonderful time getting the baptism of fire. You will do well to take heed to what I saying. Am I not telling the truth to you, when I say that the last of these hundred and twenty people were filled with the Holy Ghost? Can you deny it? I am glad that I have a clear proof of this thing.

Now there is one other point I want to make. The Pentecostal church is baptized with fire. I will give you proof of it now.

"And there appeared unto them cloven tongues like as of fire, and it sat upon each of them."

So the Pentecostal church was not only a witnessing church, but it was sanctified, filled with the Holy Ghost and baptized with fire. John prophesied this, and Jesus said of John that "He was a burning and a shining light." John had the baptism of fire. He had the seraphic and cherubic nature, and the Pentecostal church had it. Now, in the fourth verse: "They were all filled with the Holy Ghost, and began to speak with other tongues as the Spirit gave the utterance."

These were tongues of fire. The dialects were another thing. God put mighty power upon these people, and the Holy Ghost enabled them to speak with other tongues. What followed? Just people said that they were drunk. Everybody is looking amazingly at the wonderful works of God today. Living martyrs are going up and down the land today traveling hundreds of miles. That is one of the wonderful works of God.

"And they were all amazed, and were all in doubt, saying to one another. What meaneth this?"

That is true of the people today. They are not only amazed, but astonished and perplexed. Some people do not know what to think of this thing. They see the best living people going into it. The Lord help us to get our eyes open to the fact that these are the wonderful works of God.

I give you one note of warning. I know that among the fire-baptized people there is here and there a spurious dance, and spurious shout, but I am exceedingly particular not to put my hands on anyone else lest I should touch the work of God. I am not seeking to screen anything that is not of God, but I can afford to leave God's work in His hands, and He will sift out the false and the spurious. The warning that I want to give you is that you had better not talk about these wonderful things. God says that the natural man discerneth not spiritual things. If the deepest of God's saints are sometimes mistaken in these things, how much more are you who are not wholly saved of God liable to be mistaken. People said that the disciples were drunk, but Peter stood up and said they were not drunk, as they supposed. That was a case of spiritual intoxication. Then he referred them to the prophecy of Joel, which foretold of these wonders. The purpose of all this wonderful display of God's power is to get men under conviction so deep that they will call on the name of the Lord Jesus Christ.

The Starting Point

Introduction

Irwin not only understood repentance to be the cornerstone of a life pleasing to God; he also believed that confession needed to be made publicly to trigger God's healing forgiveness. This sermon includes a personal testimony by Irwin to a five-year period of backsliding in the 1880s that included times of abusing his family in fits of drunkenness. In addition to alcohol abuse, Irwin also continues to highlight stealing, lying, tobacco use, adultery, and abortion as sins that must be confessed publicly. More than once Irwin's insistence on such confessions occasioned threats of violence from others who might be exposed in the process.

Document 35 – "Sermon by the Editor: Repentance and Confession," *Live Coals of Fire*, **(June 15, 1900), 2-3.**

Preached at Kendalls, New York, May 14, 1899.

"I charge thee therefore before God, and the Lord Jesus Christ, who shall judge the quick and the dead at his appearing and his kingdom; Preach the word; be instant in season, out of season, reprove, rebuke, exhort with all longsuffering and doctrine. For the time when they will not endure sound doctrine; but after their own lusts shall they heap to themselves teachers, having itching ears; And they shall turn away their ears from the truth and shall be turned unto fables" (2 Tim. 4:1-4).

That is what Paul said unto Timothy. I want to call your attention to a part of the first chapter of John, 12th and 13th verses.

"But as many as received him, to them gave he power to become the sons of God, even to them that believe on his name: Which were born, not of blood, nor of the will of the flesh, nor of the will of the flesh, nor of the will of man, but of God."

Now I want to call your attention to be subject of repentance, and what it takes to constitute a Scriptural justification, or regeneration. In the first place there must be a godly sorrow for sin; without that nobody gets saved. It takes the Holy Ghost to do that. There may be such a thing as conviction not unto salvation; but the Holy Ghost alone can convict the sinner unto salvation, and I am praying that God will convict sinners here so they will see their sin from God's standpoint, and as He would have them see it.

A brother here said that when uses tobacco he repented every night. That was no repentance. A man gets drunk in the afternoon and goes home in the night with a heavy head, and stomach that will not retain water, and he vomits and reels around the house, and tries to get up in the morning, and feels real sorry on account of his sins. He feels sorry because of the ill effect it has upon him, and vows he will not get that way anymore, but he gets a drink for an appetizer, and before noon is drunk again, and at night is worse. In the morning he feels worse than he did before and promises not to do it anymore. Well, that man has not the first element of repentance.

A man steals a horse and thinks he has made a pretty good haul, but he is overtaken and arrested, and he feels real sorry, but it is simply because he has been caught: there is no repentance in that. Lord help us to get a right conception of true repentance; but before that we must have a right conception of what sin is, and only the Holy Ghost can show us that. When I was convicted of sin, in the first place God showed me, one night as my brother and I were walking along, that I had grieved Him by taking His name in vain, and I felt like I was fit only for hell. Right there I was troubled and inwardly distressed on account of my sins. I had not gone as far as I went afterwards, but God spoke to me about my sins, and that was the particular sin that he touched on in that intimation. I was a sinner. I knew before that swearing was wrong, but the knowledge of sin is not conviction. The knowledge of sin is necessary to conviction, but at the same time this conviction comes from God, a miraculous, supernatural thing, and it takes the direct interposition of the Holy Ghost to convict a man of sin; and it does not matter where a man is, he will not get away from that very sin. A man may come into a meeting, and under eloquent preaching, singing or testimony he may break down and cry, and may, out of human sympathy and considerations of pity, come forward and pretend to be seeking the Lord, and never have a God-given conviction at all. So I say that the first element of real repentance is to be convicted of the sin by the Holy Ghost, and when you get that far in the way to God will feel like David when he said: "Against thee, thee only, have I sinned, and done this evil in thy sight" (Psa. 51:4).

He was looking right to God. He had committed murder, adultery and perjury, and had gone on for about a year in his sin, without being discovered, as he thought. God sent Nathan, and he, a fire-baptized prophet of God, went to the king as he sat upon his throne, and related a little parable with aroused the king against a supposed offender, but he did not realized he was the man the prophet was hunting after; and when he expressed himself severely against the offending party, the prophet in faithfulness to the soul of King David said, "Thou art the man," and the mighty probing of God's Spirit and truth brought him into a condition where he was willing to confess his sin. Before a sinner gets saved he must be convicted of sin—have a godly sorrow, so deep that he will cry to God for salvation. The Scripture says:

"This poor man cried, and the Lord heard him, and saved him out of all his troubles" (Psa. 34:6).

"And it shall come to pass, that whoever shall call on the name of the Lord shall be saved" (Acts 2:21).

So there must be a conviction deep enough to bring forth a cry for pardon, and the sinner who does not cry to God never gets convicted enough to get saved. These stillborn conversions never had it in the world. They are like children born dead, and they never need anything but burial. They come forward in the meetings of backslidden preachers, and they sit like a knot on a log—never cry to God. Hell is full of such people. I would not give much for a professor of Christianity who could not pray, and cry, and shout: "Hallelujah!" Glory to God! I believe in talking the language of the country. We find so many professed Christians who do not know how to say, "Hallelujah," and "Praise the Lord" is something they never think of. The last verse of Psa. 104 says, "Praise the Lord," and the margin says: "Hallelujah!" Some places where we make use of these expressions the people look in amazement; it is so unusual and absolutely unknown to them that they are utterly amazed. The devil has a language, the world has a language, and God has a language, also the language of praise. These are all expressions of praise, but instead of that some of you murmur at the weather—it is always wrong some way. All the grunting, complaining, fault-finding, squealing and bleating that we hear indicates the language of the world. When you preach holiness and someone defends hog, that is a goat bleat; and it is the same with feathers, rag flowers, and jewelry. The Lord help people to go through till they get the language of Canaan, so they can praise God for whatever comes, and for what does not come too.

The first element of a real, Scriptural repentance is a godly sorrow for sin; a sorrow that produces a cry to God for forgiveness, and puts such intense earnestness in your soul that you will call upon God. We read this expression of Saul of Tarsus: "Behold, he prayeth." That is one element, and by no means the least important. Then comes confession. After we have been deeply convicted, and distressed and troubled because we have sinned against God more than man, we call out and plead with God for forgiveness; and nobody ever gets saved without confessing his sins. You can seek, and profess, but you will never get saved until you confess your sins. It means something to confess. When I was reclaimed I had sinned against God in many ways. I had sinned against my family and my neighbors, had cheated and wronged men in many ways, and had quarreled with men. So before I could be saved I had to confess. I used to come home drunk and abuse my wife and children, and I had to ask them to forgive me. Well, I did it, and we had a wonderful time around the family altar. They forgave me, and if I did not know that my wife and family had confidence in me, I would go to the altar and stay there until I knew they did. Then I had to go to men and confess. I went to one man on the street and said, "George, I have wronged, you, and I want you to forgive me," and he turned and cursed me, but I had the victory. I went to other men, and they broke down and wept and forgave me. So I got right with my fellowmen, my family and God. After that I went into the church and confessed all my backslidings, and the congregation broke down and wept. One of the brethren moved that they freely forgive me, and that is a matter of record in the old church today. I confessed to all, took the bottom route and got back to God, and I received as great a blessing from God as when I was justified in the first place. I am glad I cleared up everything. You can go back into that country where I lived for twenty-nine years, and knew almost everybody, and you can talk to those infidels and wicked business men—some of them drunkards and gamblers—and the last one will tell you that God saved me, and that a wonderful change took place in me. I was the most wicked man in all that country. For five years I went where I pleased and no one lifted his hand against me; but I got right with everybody. I had been drunk in many places, and I have been back to those places and held meetings, and souls have been saved; and in those places where I had done wicked things I confessed publicly that I had been drunk on their streets, and God gave me hundreds of souls.[2]

Before you can be born of God, you must confess you sins and restore the things you have cheated men of. I had gone in debt, and after I was reclaimed I paid saloon bills three times to save trouble, and when I came out of that country I came out a free man. I was not bound to anybody there. Seven years ago we dedicated the first tabernacle, and God gave us a wonderful victory, in the little town of Summerville, Nebraska. I had been associated with them politically, and God gave me their hearts. We pitched our tent on the lot of some of those men, and scores of souls were saved and sanctified; and afterwards God enabled me to go again, and send another preacher and organize a Methodist church. I had a spirit of murder in my heart against the people who arrested and abused my father in the war, and I went back to that that country where I had gone to school, and I was invited to the church where those men were. I confessed to them that the murder had been taken out of my heart, and that I felt an intense love for them. Blessed be God for this marvelous salvation that takes out the hatred, and puts a man where he loves to obey God, and is on terms with every human being on earth. In my heart there is no hard feeling against anyone in the whole universe. It is indeed wonderful to get saved of God.

Now, the first element is a godly sorrow; the second is confession, and right along that line is restitution. There are some crimes against God and man which it is impossible to make right. For instance, if I kill a man I cannot make it right with him; if I defraud a company or an individual out of an enormous sum I could not make it right; a man ruins a girl, and he could not make that right; but if it is possible to make things right you must do it. I remember a Free Methodist man who would come to meeting and shout, and in every meeting I ever saw him he was at the altar seeking sanctification. I prayed God to unearth that man and bring him to judgment. One day we had a meeting at his house; his family was there, and some of the neighbors came in. God gave me a lesson on confession, and he came to me and said: "I have something I want to tell you. At the close of the war I robbed a man, and I have never made it right." I said: "Is the man alive?" "Yes." "Will you write and confess this thing?" He promised to do it. At that time, he had several hundred bushels of grain, a lot of cattle, a fine farm, and a bank account. But he lied to me and to God, never made the restitution and never got saved. It was not long till he lost all the property he had, and he is now working hard for a living. When you come to real facts, and get down into men's lives, you will find some reason why they do not get saved. In Colby, Kansas, a woman—an influential church member—was seeking sanctification. God led me to pray that night against adultery, child-murder, abortion and such things, and she said afterward she felt like she was dropping into hell. A few days later she confessed the whole thing to me. She was living in adultery with a man to whom she was not married, her husband was living, and she had been away for thirteen years. She said that one time she changed her name and went to Seattle, and when she stepped off the train the first person she met was a man she knew. She was awfully troubled every time a revival came near, and now she said: "I am going to obey God." I said "You must leave that man." She did not obey God, but went off to another state, went into court, and got a lawyer to take care of her case and thought she was free. She came back expecting to marry the man she had been living with, but it came out that he had another wife. She got acquainted with my wife and confessed it all to her. It took her four years to get saved, but she did get saved. Once during that time, I saw her on the street reeling drunk. It is an expensive thing for some people to get saved. It was for me; it was for that woman and many other people, and it is truly a miracle that some of us are not in hell now. We had to clear our past record to get saved of God. A brother was preaching one time on repentance and told a circumstance like this: "I lived in Nebraska a few years ago, and after preaching on this line a banker came to me and said, 'I want to see you,' and he confessed that in order to get saved he would have to pay back all his property, and he said: "Before I will do that, and turn my family out on the world, I will go to hell." It is a wonderful thing for some people to get saved of God.

Out in Kansas I preached confession of sin, and a man came to the brethren and said: "I want to see Brother Irwin privately." He came and made his confession. He had stolen twenty dollars while we were at church; had stolen cattle, sheep, hogs and wheat; had burned barns and houses and got the insurance, and had committed many other crimes. He confessed for two hours, and then did not get through confessing. I said: "It seems to me the Lord is content with this." He had to make restitution, and he got saved and sanctified, and there was such a change in his personal appearance. He made his confession with the understanding that it would send him to the penitentiary.

A physician in Alabama was guilty of child-murder, and fifteen years after, his wife not knowing anything about it, he said: "Wife, I want to make sure and get to the bottom. I want to know that I saved." He told her all about it, and then he said: "I have resolved to go and confess to the governor." She said: "Obey God. It is better for you to spend your life in the penitentiary than to go to hell. You go, and I will pray to God to deliver you, and if they hang you I will pray Him to keep you till the last." He went to the governor and laid the case before him, and the governor broke down and said, "You are a free man." It means a great deal for some people to get saved. Salvation is no trifling thing. It is easy after you have received the fulness of the blessing of the gospel of Christ, but until you commit yourself, and are making things right, it is a hard thing—a terrible thing.

I believe in my soul that the work of God is hindered because of the child-murder and heart murder in the country. People's hearts and hands are stained with the blood of their unborn children, and until they confess it they will never be saved. I know from observation what this thing means, and when a man preaches on this line he arouses the lust devil and the murder devil all through the country. It means something for adulterers, thieves and robbers to get saved of God.

Repentance is a serious thing, and it involves not only godly sorrow, but it will lead a man to make the confession and restitution God requires. I preached one night to the colored people in the Indian Territory on adultery, theft, and such things. The colored people there are not married, and nearly all practice witchcraft. I turned loose on those things, and at the close of the service they said to me, "If what you preach is true, it will break up our families." I said: "You had better go to the penitentiary than to hell."

It not only means restitution and confession, but a forsaking of your sins, and that is where the real battle comes. You have been doing these things, and now have to quit if you want to be saved. I used to lie—seemed to be a born liar. I used to lie to my parents, my brothers and sisters, and everybody. It used to be a habit, but when God saved me He took the lying devil out of me. I used to steal, and God took that that all of out of me when he saved me. I had to confess to one man, with whom I afterward had the pleas[ure] of boarding, and leading him into the experience of entire sanctification. It is a blessed and wonderful thing to be where you are not afraid to meet the face of man. There are many people in the world afraid somebody will come who knows the dark deeds they have committed.

A man in a large city mission had ruined a woman twenty years before, and one night he was having a wonderful meeting—he had hundreds of friends in that country and that meeting - and a woman came and accused him of ruining her. He had never made the confession to her, and the people thought she was a prostitute tryin[g] to ruin him, so they tried to sing her down, but he said: "Keep still; she is telling the truth. I have been looking for her for years." Blessed be God for a man who is saved deep enough to go through with Jesus. You can be so saved that when the worst thing possible is told [about] you, you will admit it. You will not try to hide it, but will say: "It is so, and I am ashamed of it; but I have gone to God and He has forgiven me, and my record is clear."

I now call your attention to these points in reference to the matter of Bible repentance. First, conviction from God that is unto salvation that will cause you to do these things; a godly sorrow toward God, and a recognition of the fact that you have sinned against God in these things. Then, a confession of your sins, without any effort on your part to shield or protect yourself. Then if you have been drunk, smoking, lying, stealing, committing adultery, cheating or committing abortion, you will forsake them, give them up forever, hate them in your heart, and cry to God out of the depths of your soul to have mercy on you, to blot out your transgressions and forgive your sins, like David cried, and everybody else does who gets saved.

Healing

Introduction

Irwin's acceptance of divine healing, explained here in his own words, was even more recent than his embrace of fire baptism—and every bit as radical. Irwin was careful to identify divine healing as Holy Ghost power intended to help preach the Gospel more effectively in the last days. Once he began to advocate the doctrine of healing, Irwin moved quickly to advocate an extreme "no remedies" position.

Taking medicine, he argued, revealed a lack of true faith in God's promised provisions.

Document 36 – "Sermon by the Editor: Divine Healing," *Live Coals of Fire* **(October 13, 1899), 2-3.**

Preached at Knoxville, Iowa, July 27, 1899.

"Unto whom it was revealed, that not unto themselves, but unto us, they did minister, the things which are now reported unto you by them that preached the gospel unto you with the Holy Ghost sent down from heaven; which things the angels desire to look into" (1 Pet. 1:12).

I want particularly to call your attention to the expression: "Unto them that they preached the gospel unto you with the Holy Ghost sent down from heaven." Now the gospel is the revealed, written Word of God, and we have no right to take from it or add to it: we are to accept it as it has been given to us. Every part of it.

I believe in the plenary inspiration of the Scriptures. I detest and despise in my heart this higher criticism, rationalism, and this seeking on the part of ungodly professors to do away to do away with objectionable parts of the Word of God, and as fire-baptized people we stand on the whole Book, hallelujah! and will not go back on it, either. In 2 Tim. 4:1 and 2, you will find this statement: "Preach the word." That is God's command to every preacher whom He calls. There is a number of preachers whom God never called, and in the 23rd of Jeremiah He tells them, "ye have run, but I have not sent you": and He says to that class, "I am against you": and I am against that class, too. The world is full of unconverted and backslidden preachers, infidels denying the Word, and God calls on me to cry out against them.[3]

When a man gets up to preach I want him to preach the gospel with the Holy Ghost sent down from heaven; preach out what God gives him—and I do not care what that is either. Whatever God gives a man is spiritual, and as long as a man sticks to the old Word and preaches the everlasting gospel, I can say: Hallelujah!

I am going to preach now on divine healing. I believe in it with all my heart. God made me a believer in divine healing, so it is no wonder I believe it. When I got sanctified wholly, I did not think of this question. The matter did not come prominently before me at the time, and I fell in with a class of preachers who shut the truth of divine healing out of their ministry and work. Consequently, I never seriously considered the question. I thought they were right, and did not give the matter a serious consideration for several years after I was sanctified. Once, after I had held a meeting for a Methodist minister, I was called back to attend a holiness mass convention, and his wife said: "I want you and some others (naming them) to anoint with oil and lay your hands upon me, according to the Word of God, and pray for me that I may be healed." I have never had such a request, and it struck me like a thunderbolt out of a clear sky. I never saw any such operation carried on, but instantly the Holy Ghost led me to say, "I will go," and I got the victory right there. Men who are sanctified never draw back and fight the truth. I believe justified people will not fight the truth, but it is true emphatically of sanctified people. None of us had ever performed a ceremony like that, or seen such, but one of the brethren took charge, and told the sister to kneel down; and he took oil and anointed her, and called on me to pray. While I was praying she began to shout, and said: "I feel the power of the Holy Ghost going through my entire body." God instantly healed her, and she rose, jumped and shouted, and testified to the experience of divine healing. I was convinced. God knew there was nothing in my heart against that truth, and He arranged that whole matter so as to settle in my heart eternally the question of divine healing. Several months after that I met her, and she said: "I have not had a single symptom of disease or pain since I was anointed. "God healed her, hallelujah!"

In my own case, after I had been down with nervous prostration for five weeks, shut up in a dark room with the doors guarded, God instantly healed me one morning about 1 o'clock, in answer to the prayer of faith, and I felt the disease going from my system, and the strength and health of God coming into my body. Instantly I became hungry, and as soon as God took the shout off of me, I had a hearty meal, and went to sleep and slept till morning, something I had not done for five weeks. Jesus heals me now.[4] He is my health and strength, and when the devil thinks me he has his grip on me God always defeats him, and puts strength in me again. I have no health or strength of my own, but there isn't an ache or a pain in my entire system, and I expect to live for years if Jesus tarries, preaching the mighty truth of the baptism of fire and divine healing, the pre-millennial coming of Jesus and radical, entire sanctification, blessed be God. Now, I have seen hundreds of instances, but I want you to listen to this passage in Deut. 28: "Then if thou wilt not observe to do all the words of this law that are written in this book, that thou mayest fear this glorious and fearful name, THE LORD THY GOD; then the Lord will make thy plagues wonderful." Mark what the Scripture says: If you will not hear to observe and do all these words, then "the Lord will make thy plagues wonderful, and the plague of thy seed, even the great plagues, and of long continuance, and sore sicknesses of long continuance." That is what the Scripture says will come to those who will not hearken to all the words of His law. In Exodus 15 God says: "And he cried unto the Lord; and the Lord showed him a tree, which when he had cast into the waters, the waters were made sweet; there he had made them for a statute and an ordinance, and there he proved them.["] God made a statute for His people. He made an ordinance for His people and proved them, and His statutes and ordinances are just as binding upon us today as they were then. The laws of health, the fundamental principles of health and of divine healing, are not local or temporary. They are founded on the eternal nature of things. God knew our constitution altogether. He knew our constitution and frame altogether, and the nature of the animals he had created, and He knew which would be good for us to eat and which would not; and when He said, Ye shall not eat swine's flesh, and lizards, vultures, etc., He knew that they were not fit to eat. If they were not fit to for the ancient Hebrews, they are not for His people today, so there is no alteration in these eternal laws of health, for God founds them on the eternal truths as He sees them. But someone says: "Those are the Old Testament scriptures." Well, you keep out of the Old Testament if you don't believe it. What authority have you to mutilate the Word of God, and pick out what suits you and what does not? You keep out of the 27th Psalm, Isaiah 35 and 62, etc., if you do not believe in the Old Testament. Let it alone, and put yourselves among the infidels where you belong. For my part, I accept the Old Testament, and the New Testament, too. And He says in the next verse: "If thou wilt diligently hearken to the voice of the Lord thy God." That is the first thing, and if we do not speak according to the Word of God, it is not the voice of God, and we not want you to accept it. But when we preach the gospel with the Holy Ghost sent down from heaven, you are bound at the peril of your life to hearken. If you do not, you will be damned eternally. You can throw it aside and go to hell in spite of the mercy of God! And may God help you realize that the responsibility rests on you. But you say: "The day of miracles is past." Who gave you authority to repeat that lie? Isn't it the gospel to say to a sick man that he can be healed? When the conditions are met, God will perform the work. Just as soon as the hidden, lurking object is removed, God will heal the sick. Jude speaks of hidden rocks in the feasts of charity. There are hidden rocks nearly every place, and God's fire-baptized truth will bring these to judgment. Men whose children are drunkards and harlots are crying out against the baptism of fire, entire sanctification and divine healing. May God help us to raise the standard and press the battle on the definite white fire line for God.

It is God's voice we are to hearken to, and no matter what God's Word is full of it. I want to read some in Psalms and Proverbs. He says: "Attend to my words; incline thine ears unto my sayings." God wants you to attend.to His words. As long as you obey God, do not limit Him; and keep pressing your way on, and you will keep the victory and the glory, and unction will rest upon your soul. "Incline your ear; attend to the words of God," you who are making light remarks about divine healing, and the fire, and pre-millennial coming of Jesus, and entire sanctification, and salvation from all sin. [5] I want to tell you, if you ever get to heaven you must have sinless perfection, which you are crying out against. John Wesley taught it, and the Bible teaches it, and says everywhere, "Go and sin no more." If Jesus cannot save from sin the Bible is a lie, but Jesus does do it, and will do it still. "Incline thine ear unto my sayings; let not depart from thine own eyes, for they are life unto those who find them, and health to all their flesh." The word "health" there is "medicine." The Word of God is medicine, and I have quit taking drugs, and now take medicine. When I get a pain I look to God, and He takes it away. I am glad in my soul that I can take the little pains in my head and lungs and heart, and tell Jesus to bear them all away, and He does it. Right in the face of infidelity and unbelief, hypocrisy and antagonism to the truth of God, in spite of men and devils. He takes them away, and in the hot battle, when the sun is beating down, God gives me strength, and enables to speak boldly as I ought to speak. I am out in this war, and expect to be in it till Jesus comes, and when he comes I expect to go up in a flaming, blazing chariot of fire! O, the medicine of God's Word! Take a dose of God's Word instead of those nostrums. Take the straight medicine of God's Word and He will break the neck of the devil, and He will enable you to shout while devils flee to their corners in the remotest part of hell. The great secret of divine healing is faith in God that dares to go out in God's promise and throw the weight of your being on it, and jump on the rock of God's truth, and realize for once what a solid footing you have. He has taken away the fences and walls and environments, and wants you to realize that you have all heaven in which to jump and shout and praise God with the everlasting Rock, Christ Jesus beneath your feet.

"If thou wilt hearken diligently to the voice of the Lord thy God, and will do that which is right in his sight, and wilt give ear to his commandments, and keep his statutes, I will put none of these diseases among you which I have brought upon the Egyptians, for I am the Lord that healeth thee." Do you know that God put right in front of His house in ancient times: "I am the Lord that healeth thee. I am the Lord that taketh away thy diseases, that guardeth thee against the diseases and the sicknesses and the sore attacks that come upon the Egyptians, and I will keep you"? We may fall short in some instances, through ignorances and hidden rocks in our feasts of charity which we have not been able to discover, but where the conditions are met God will keep His word; and I would say to every man and woman: it is safe to trust God; to throw yourself on the promises of God, and nothing short of that is safe. I want to say that divine healing is in the atonement. I am going to prove it by the Word of God. Everything that pertains to the salvation of men from that time that the Holy Spirit awakens a dead sinner until we reach streets of the New Jerusalem, was provided for in the atonement. I do not believe in this limited, restricted theory that cuts the vitality and heart out of the atonement of Jesus Christ. Men are going around making political speeches and organizing clubs and writing books against divine healing, but God delivers me from that, and from all doubt and distrust, and I have not turned back nor limited the Holy One of Israel.

Look at this Scripture: "Now unto him that is able to do exceedingly abundantly above all that we ask or think." The difficulty with most people is that they stop short of the best things that God has for them. People start out to pray, and the Holy Ghost brings them right up against something in the way of the blessing. If they would pray right through, not around or over it, but right through, they would get the victory which their souls are crying out after, but the trouble is, they stop short. Backslidden preachers don't want their people converted. We had an illustration of this in a meeting we held in New York last spring. A preacher sent for us, and said he wanted the baptism of fire, and when we got there we found out that he was not sanctified and later on that he was not justified. His daughter came to the altar quaking and trembling under the mighty convicting power of the Holy Ghost, and wanted to make a confession, and he stood beside her and guarded her, and kept her from making the confession; and I believed, and still believe, that something covered up in his own life was the cause, and a confession from that girl would have involved him, exposed him, and brought him to judgment. In one of my meetings a man got wonderfully saved. He had stolen some money from his employer, and he confessed to the man he had robbed; and I said: "Don't you believe you should make a public confession? Don't you think it glorify God and help others?" He said: "It would involve this country in a civil war." The secret of it was, his wife was possessed of the devil, and it would have involved her and a large number of people. In another place a woman got under conviction; and yet she would not make the confession God wanted her to make.

When a brother insisted that she should confess out and get saved, she said that different women had met her on the street and said: "Are you going to confess in that meeting?" implying that it would involve them, and result in a tremendous commotion. I have no doubt if she had made a confession they would have mobbed us, because they thought we were at the bottom of it. Down in southern Oklahoma a woman confessed one day to a series of crimes that she had been practicing habitually for eighteen years. She had been a child murderer and abortionist (this woman in North Carolina [mentioned above] was the same). This woman confessed and involved her husband and a physician. I received a letter saying, "It was good for you that you got away when you did; they would have murdered you." And in many places where I have been they would done so had not God's hand held them back. I want to tell you, all the murderers are not drunkards and gamblers; but some of them dress in silks and satins, and wear jewelry, wives of preachers, as well as other people in the church. These people habitually kill their unborn children.

Now we read in Isa. 53: "Surely He hath borne our griefs, and carried our sorrows." The literal rendering of the scripture is "Surely he hath borne our sicknesses, and carried our pains." Now, no one attempts to deny this, except those infidels and critics who are trying to get this chapter out of the prophecy of Isaiah. Infidels in the church, infidel preachers, commentators and German rationalists, and higher critics, have tried to get this prophecy out of the prophecy of Isaiah, but it stands, notwithstanding all of their criticism. They hate God's Word, the dynamite, and the miracle-working power of God. They hate to see God display His power and manifest Himself, and they have done everything in their power to eliminate this passage and that other one in Mark 16, from God's Word, but have not succeeded. Jesus has borne our sicknesses and carried our pains. Some backslidden preacher has said: "We do not believe that God heals every ache, every time, every child of his asks for healing." I would as lieve [gladly] sear as say that. That is blasphemy. Jesus says: "He is able to save to the uttermost all that come unto God by Him." Do you know where the uttermost is? Again the Scripture says: "Him that cometh unto me, I will in no wise cast out." Think of it. Will you point me to a place in the New Testament where anybody came to Jesus for healing and did not get it? I can show you where they came for salvation and did not get it. Jesus and John said of a very large class of people: "Ye brood of vipers, who hath warned you to flee from the wrath to come?" They did not get salvation, and John insisted that should bring forth fruits meet for repentance before he would baptize them. Every individual who ever come to Jesus for divine healing as far as recorded, was healed. The Bible says the multitudes came, and He healed all that were oppressed of the devil. We read in another place that he healed all sicknesses and diseases among the people. So Jesus carried all of our pains and bore away our sicknesses, just in the same sense in which he carried our sins, hallelujah! They tell you divine healing does not rest on the same basis with salvation, but it does. The basis of salvation is the cleansing blood of Jesus Christ, which is to be accepted on the terms of the gospel, and if a man accepts divine healing on the terms of the gospel, he will get healed just as he gets saved after he accepts salvation on the terms of the gospel. So I defiantly throw out this challenge to the opposers of divine healing; that it rests on exactly the same basis as salvation from sin, and every human being who will meet the conditions can have it.

Now I will give you the New Testament interpretation of this passage: Matt. 8:16, 17: "When the even was come, they brought unto him many that were possessed with devils: and he cast out the spirits with his word, and healed all who were sick: that it might be fulfilled what was spoken by Isaiah the prophet, Himself took out infirmities and bare our sicknesses." Now you see why the devil wants to get that out of the Bible. Jesus taught and practice divine healing, and so did Peter. In Acts 3 the scene at the Beautiful Gate of the temple shows that; and the last of Acts shows that Paul practiced it—he prayed and God healed people. So Peter and Paul taught and practiced divine healing; and Gibbon, the historian, and others, tell us that this gospel of divine healing was practiced in the early church for the first three hundred years, and it was at the end of that time that the church backslid and lost her power. The reason churches today are not practicing divine healing is because they are spiritual adulteresses, committing fornication with the world.

I will close with the last utterance God has given us in His Word on this subject (Jas. 5:14-16): "Is any sick among you? Let them call for the elders of the church; and let them pray over him, anointing him with oil in the name of the Lord; and the prayer of faith shall save the sick, and the Lord will raise him up; and if he has committed sins they shall be forgiven him. Confess you faults one to another, and pray for one another, that ye may be healed. The effectual fervent prayer of a righteous man availeth much."

Fire and Dynamite

Introduction

This sermon provides a good opportunity to consider the logic that propelled Irwin to move beyond a Baptism of Fire to multiple subsequent baptisms—each more explosive in its power than the last. Together they form an ever fuller presentation of what Pentecostals would come to understand in the 20th century as Holy Ghost Baptism (with the Dynamite especially important because of it brings supernatural power to witness). By the time Irwin began publication of his *Live Coals of Fire* in October 1899, he was fully committed to an experience of Dynamite separate from—and subsequent to—the experience of Fire Baptism. In this sermon Irwin lauds the power of the Dynamite to expose hidden sin and explode resistance to salvation. [6] This power complemented the Fire's effect of causing a Christian "to cry out in horror at all manner of sin" ("John Dull's Letter," *Live Coals of Fire* [October 6, 1899], 2). Within six months of preaching this sermon, Irwin would also point out that the "Dynamite has awakened a distinctively missionary spirit" in the Fire-Baptized Holiness Association, leading several to make plans to leave as soon as possible for Cuba, South Africa, and other distant lands ("Editorial Correspondence," *Live Coals of Fire* [January 26, 1900], 1). Late in the paper's short run, reports of other definite experiences began to appear—first lyddite in the February 23 issue, followed by the even more mysterious baptisms of oxidite and selenite.[7]

Document 37 – "Sermon by the Editor: The Dynamite," *Live Coals of Fire* **(November 10, 1899), 2-3.**

Preached at Moonlight, Kan., August 18, 1899.

"But ye shall receive power after the Holy Ghost is come upon you; and ye shall be witnesses unto me both in Jerusalem and in al Judea, and in Samaria, and unto the uttermost part of the earth" (Acts 1:8).

This is the last word that Jesus spoke before He ascended up to Heaven. In the fifth verse there is the command He gave His disciples to tarry in Jerusalem until they received the promise of the Father; and you will notice in the verse, Jesus says: "Tarry ye in the city of Jerusalem until ye be endued with power from on high."

Now I see brethren nearly every place I go, and especially among preachers, with a subtle, delusive spirit of compromise. I listened to a preacher a few weeks ago, and he preached in a sweet, loving way—preached holiness—steered clear of any offensive language. Well, he had a big collection to take up, and there was a reason for it. He spent three-quarters of an hour in taking up the collection and raised the money he said he needed, and went out of the meeting denouncing the fire.

Lord help us to get to a place where we will detect the subtle spirit of compromise. I am not in much danger from my enemies, but I am in danger from my friends. I love them so well they may lead me into bypaths, sometime, without my knowing it, but God has been opening my eyes.

I bless God for spiritual discernment, and for deliverance from all that subtle spirit of compromise which seeks to destroy the highest peace of God's deepest saints. We need help along this line.

When men begin to compromise they first begin to cry out in a quiet, nice way, perhaps privately, against severe preaching, and do not like to have a man tear up their churches by the roots and show the rottenness in them. Lord give us a spirit that will enable us to preach the gospel from the standpoint of a spiritual surgeon with the sweetness of heaven and the loyalty of Jesus in our souls.

I was reading Fletcher's portraiture of St. Paul, and I was struck by the awful things he says against backslidden preachers and professors, and yet he had the sweetness of heaven in his soul; and the same Spirit that inspired those wonderful scriptures that we use when we speak of charity and gentleness, inspired Matthew 23, Jeremiah 23, and Ezekiel 34 and all those hell-shaking chapters that get under people and make them realize that they have no salvation in their souls.

God has shown me in my commission (Jeremiah 1:17-19) that He has not only set me in defense of the gospel of Jesus Christ, but against false preachers and churches, and against false professors and compromisers, and I have declared war against all of these in the name of Jesus Christ, and that is what the dynamite of heaven does for me.

In these days of compromise and apostasy, when I see the people going back and finding them toning down, I am strengthened with more dynamite than I ever was before, and more determined to press the battle to the gate keep the war at white heat until men and devils will recognize the fact that I am for war against sin and the devil, shams and frauds, compromising, toning down, and everything else that is wrong and tends to hinder the work of the Holy Ghost and drag the people down from the height to which they have been led by the Holy Ghost. Lord help us not to oppose in our spirits anything that God has promised or commanded in His Word. I am out eternally on this dynamite line for God.

I am standing just where I have stood ever since God sanctified my soul, and as added light comes I walk in it; as God shows me new truths I am going to walk out in the light and power of these things which He reveals to me, and I keep the victory in my soul in doing this, and I shall keep it unless I compromise or lose my experience. People have compromised and toned down and made terms with the backslidden church, or with husband, or wife, or family, and some here are backslidden without any power because they have been deceived by the devil on this line.

God says here: "Ye shall receive power after that the Holy Ghost is come upon you." The word "power" in every one of these passages is "dynamite." Jesus used the word dynamite. Paul used the same word. It is the strongest word in any language. It means the irresistible might of the omnipotent God; the strength, energy and power that we need in order to live up to all the light that God may give us that we may testify up to the high water mark of our experiences and shout the walls down in spite of men and devils. He wants us to have and keep the victory.

Jesus said: "Ye shall receive dynamite." O, the Lord help you if you have any opposition in your spirit to the dynamite. You need to be sanctified wholly. Entire sanctification takes out of you all opposition to everything that is of God, and the dynamite is of God, the Scripture says so. I am in for the dynamite.[8]

The apex—the acme, of this Pentecostal experience is the mighty dynamite of God. Jesus did not tell them to tarry till they got the Holy Ghost and fire, but the dynamite is mentioned. You go in recklessly for all that God has for you.

Dynamite is a dangerous thing to handle. Get it and let the Holy Ghost handle you. You get sanctified, get all compromise and shrink out of you, and all worldliness and church notions out of your heart, and let God put the mighty dynamite in you and He will blow things up just as He wills.

In Toronto I preached on the fire, and a few divinity students came along and began to ply me with questions, and never said a word against the fire or me, but the Holy Ghost showed me that they were possessed of devils and God raised me off the floor with a shout such as I never had given before, and they turned pale and were utterly confounded at the mighty dynamite of God. Another time God put the dynamite on me in a private house and shook hell, and without any preliminaries I said, "I am going," and I left the ungodly company.

I want to tell you, God has a few that have the real dynamite—only a few—but I will not discourage you in seeking the dynamite and when you testify and say you want it, I am not going to throw a wet blanket over you and get you discouraged from you seeking it. I want you to get it, and if you do not get down and get the right kind and the full measure you will find it out when you come in contact with those who have the hell disturbing, earth-quaking dynamite.

Jesus says, "Ye shall receive dynamite after that the Holy Ghost is come upon you." He wants us to have it. We need it to preach the gospel in such a way that sinners and hypocrites will never get over it.

But He goes on to say: "And ye shall be witnesses unto me." God wants to make a martyr out of you. People [word unclear] to the word dynamite because it is Greek. Well, hallelujah! I have that much Greek and the fire also, and the consciousness that the blood cleanses me from all sin, and I am in line with everything that God does for you, whether it be Greek, English, or Filipino. God does not care how many profess. He wants a few that have the real fire and the real dynamite in whom He can put confidence. God wants that kind of men.

The word "witness" is in the original "martyr." It means a man who will not only lay down his life for the cause of Christ, but who has and actually does lay down his life for the cause of Christ. It is not only to be willing to do it—we must actually lay down our lives. In the deepest spiritual sense I have laid down my life in this cause; have committed myself, soul, spirit, and body, family, reputation, everything to the cause of the baptism of fire, and the eternal gospel of Jesus Christ, which is the "dynamite of God unto salvation to everyone that believeth." The gospel is the dynamite of God—the mighty shaking power—the disturbing power of God. It tears things up. A brother one said to me: "What does the dynamite do?" I said among other things that it tears up the works of the devil. It makes people feel that they never had any religion at all, as if their bones were out of joint and broken. It makes people restless and uneasy about their salvation until they get to God and get saved. In communities where the people are sin-hardened, having fought the truth of God and the work of the Holy Ghost, as in this community, and where many have committed the unpardonable sin, the power of God will shake them in the last day, and they will find out the fire-baptized and dynamited gospel of Jesus Christ has in it just what the Bible says it has.

I get letters from all over the country. I have one from a party who is out in the work in Pennsylvania, preaching the eternal fire and getting people saved from, and in that letter there was this request: "Pray for my father and mother; they are fighting God and the work of the Holy Ghost; they are bitter against the truth as it is in Jesus Christ." [9] The Lord God help you fathers and mothers who are standing in the way of your children, fighting the work of God in them, and standing in the way of your children, fighting the work of God in them, and seeking to cause them to compromise and backslide and go down to hell. You that never speak to your neighbors about salvation or seek to get people saved, would rather have somebody join your church than to get saved from sin. God's eternal dynamite will blow you hellward unless you get right with God and confess out the awful deeds and words you have committed against the fire-baptized saints. God wants us to be so saved to Him and so filled with His Spirit and baptized with fire, and dynamited with all dynamite from heaven, that you will go up and down the country as living martyrs for God.

"Ye shall receive dynamite after that the Holy Ghost is come upon you," and without this dynamite you will not have the martyr spirit in one and keep it there. Then men will witness for God, testify unto Jesus with their lives and testimony, at the sacrifice of their homes and friends, and at the time cost of their lives. There are some who have counted the cost and paid the price, and they are not permitted to live in their homes, of, if they are, they have no peace or fellowship with anybody there, and it all happens from the fact that God has made them martyrs to Jesus.

"Ye shall be martyrs unto me both in Jerusalem"—that is in your church—community and religious centre—"and in Judea"—that means all the borders of the church, and if you keep true to God it will cost your church membership. If we keep true to God we will find ourselves cast out of every church in the land. God says you are to testify and be witnesses unto Him in Jerusalem and in all Judea. Among your own brethren—"and in Samaria"—that means respectable professors. God wants you to be true to Him in your church, family, and then true in the whole border of your church, and then true in regard to the other churches, and when all these churches and all your own friends and family kick you out, then you go to the heathen and keep true to the fire and the dynamite and your experience and testimony there. That is what the dynamite means, and you need the dynamite of God, the mighty energizing power of God, in order to keep true to Jesus.

I am glad that Jesus has left this word on record, and without ignoring any experience, either justification, entire sanctification or the baptism of the Holy Ghost and fire, the culminating point of your testimony is the mighty dynamite of God. I believe that the holiness people as a body backslid entirely because they never went on and received the fullness of the Spirit, and I have reason to believe that there was a large class of people that not only taught and received the experience of entire sanctification but also taught and received the baptism of the Holy Ghost, and when the mighty fire of God began to be preached in its fullness as a definite experience these people backslid because they said they got it all when they got sanctified.

All that kind of argument has been given again and again against this marvelous statement of Jesus Christ that we should tarry until we were endued with power from on high and against this statement that we should receive power from on high after that the Holy Spirit has come upon us and I believe that the thing that keep the unity of the faith and the unity of the Spirit among the fire-baptized people and cause this movement to prosper and prevail and expand itself all over the earth is that the fire-baptized saints of God press their way on into still greater depths of experience and power with God and actually get this definite experience of the divine dynamite. The Lord wants to teach us something along this line. We have the utmost limit of the Christian life but God wants to keep us on our knees and faces before Him. That is the way we prevail with God and men.

It is not so much the preaching of the gospel or the singing that bring down the ranks of sin and sweeps souls into the cleansing fountain, and gets them baptized with the baptism of Jesus, as it is the mighty prevailing prayers of God's deepest saints. The Lord wants to teach us along these line. I know a little child of God, wonderfully filled with the power of God, and yet that person is seeking more and more of God. I received letter from her in which she says: "We need more of the mighty dynamite of God. There is not enough power among the fire-baptized people of God, and unless they seek the fullness of the mighty dynamite of God the people who have banded themselves together as fire-baptized people will divide and backslide and separate, and the work will come to the naught;" but let me tell you that the deep saints of God that see the need of it. It is the ones that have the brightest experiences of the fire that seek for the dynamite. I do not know but what this principle will hold good forever in this life and in the next.

I believe that the bright shining angels in heaven are seeking to know more and more of God, and I want to declare to you that I am a constant seeker of grace, and yet I am not casting away my confidence, I am not neglecting to testify to what God has done for my soul, but I see depths and divine experiences out beyond the fire line, and away out beyond entire sanctification; and I am going out for them I am keeping true to the fire, and sanctification, and justification, and divine healing, and premillennial coming of the Lord, and everything else He has wrought in me.

As long as we are on our faces before God we will never have any discord, and devils will tremble and sinners will flee from the mighty presence of God.

I am glad this dynamite locates the devil and tears up his works in the hearts and consciences of people, and causes them to stick forth their claws. You can pick people out with a devil grin on their faces, you can see the children of hell that are exposed by the mighty dynamite of God. May God give you spiritual courage, and fire and dynamite to go through on this dynamite line for God.

I want to ask you who believe in sanctification and the fire, and profess it, and say you believe in the dynamite, if you have any objections, in the face of this scripture, to anyone coming to the altar and seeking it? Well, if you have not any objections, forever hold your peace and do not try to discourage people seeking it. I am glad that God has put an eternal quietus on that point in my soul. He has saved me so completely that I that I am in line with every word that He has spoken.

It is necessary for us to tell the truth, and God says in His Word, "Lie not to one another," so if you have no objections to the dynamite. I want you to go in for it. Encourage those that are in for it, and when they get it do not have a long face, but shout and tell them you are glad they have the dynamite. I have the real fire tonight; the kind that Ezekiel speaks of when he says; "Out of the fire went forth lightning."

There is a type of fire that never produces lightning that comes in sheets, but there is a kind of fire that is real hot and burns people that are not walking in the light and makes men and women tremble and turn pale. That is the kind of fire that God wants us to have; not the lurid fire of hell, but the white, living eternal fire of God, and out of this fire comes forth the jagged, zigzag lightning that strikes and kills us tears up the works of the devil, and smashed things up generally.

I want to see the people of God get where they are willing to have the Holy Ghost and the holy fire, and the holy lightning and the divine dynamite strike and explode and tear up things all around them. The fire and dynamite do that kind of thing, and when you get them you will be a terror to the community.

God wants to put a measure of dynamite upon you that will blow the devil and the compromising spirit right into hell. That is the direction in which these things go when the mighty dynamite of God strikes them.

It is one thing to get saved up to a standard that men have fixed, and another to get saved up to the standard of Paul, and Daniel, and Jesus.

It is one thing to profess the dynamite and the fire and entire sanctification and loyalty to God and so on, and it is another thing to have the real experience that does what God wants done in a community.

But you say: "If you have what you say you have, why don't sinners get saved?" Let me tell you. God is simply bringing the people to judgment in these last days. There are comparatively but few going to be saved from now till Jesus comes. The people have settled it forever that they are going to hell, and thousands of people who belong to church, and many of them preachers, have committed the unpardonable sin. [10] Men say of these manifestations that they are of the devil. A preacher said to me concerning the holy dance, that it was of the devil. Every speech of that kind is an eternal damnation to your soul. You sit in judgment upon the work of the Holy Ghost and attribute it to the devil, and you commit the unpardonable sin, and then you can treat with indifference the truth of God and go down to hell at last. There are thousands of people in the land who are as effectually damned as they will be when they have been in hell ten thousand years. I held a meeting in the eastern part of this state two years ago, and the people were threatening, and smoking, and swearing; and God was saving the people and healing the sick right along; over fifty souls have been saved and many healed, and the devil's followers acted like they were going to tear the meeting up. I prayed that afternoon in my tent, and God gave me a message on the sin against the Holy Ghost and I preached it; and God showed me as I preached that sermon that the sin against the Holy Ghost was directed particularly against divine healing and the manifestations that the Spirit of God brings on the people. It occurred in the case of casting out devils and divine healing and the manifestations that the Spirit of God brings on the people. It occurred in the case of casting our devils and divine healing, and I applied the truth, and the people were actually scared; and whereas on previous nights they had gone away swearing and yelling, that night they went away frightened, and were afraid to say anything against the truth of God lest they should commit the unpardonable sin. And I warn you who are talking against the manifestations of the Spirit of God, and ridiculing the fire, and dancing and shouting that you will go down to a hell that is never-ending if you do not repent. At the peril of your souls I warn you not to lift your voice nor think a thought in your hearts against anything theses saints do in the spirit of God. You may be mistaken about it. It is not the devil; it is the Holy Ghost, and the safe thing for you is to say nothing about it. May God help you to let Him have His way.

Region, Race, Class, & Fire

Introduction

These examples of Irwin's "Editorial Correspondence" show Irwin at the height of his influence sweeping back across the South—from the mostly-white high mountain communities of southeastern Tennessee to the heavily-black towns of lower South Carolina. These letters, written in October 1899 first from the mountains of Tennessee, then from the towns of Abbeville and Marion in South Carolina, and finally from the steps of the Capitol in Washington DC, provide some of the richest descriptions of the ways Irwin's fiery ministry burned across regional, racial, and class barriers.

Document 38 – "Editorial Correspondence," *Live Coals of Fire* **(October 27, 1899), 1, 3.**

Sunday, October 15th, was a glorious day at Beniah, Tenn.[11] The altar was crowded in the morning service, and one man received the definite experience of the dynamite. He is one of the most prominent and reliable of the holiness people of this section, and is (or was at the commencement of the meeting) a member of the Methodist Church. He had been for a long time bound by the opinions of a few Methodist preachers, but in this meeting he was delivered from his preacher. His preacher had written him "warning" him against wild-fire and fanaticism, and actually wrote to him that, should he go off with the fire-baptized people, he would be sorry he ever led him into the experience of sanctification! It is amazing, the attitude assumed by these preachers who are fighting the fire. Backslidden themselves, they would rather others would backslide and be lost than to see them go on and receive the heavenly fire. They are "afraid by the reason of the fire." The fire and the dynamite seem to give them a great deal of trouble. May the Lord give to His people experiences deep enough so that they will not be moved by these "warnings," and cries of "Be careful," "Look out for snags," and so on. Hallelujah to Jesus! The fire will burn its way through everything, and the eternal dynamite will blow up these "snags."

We had some remarkable testimonies in this meeting. One sister declared that when she received the baptism with fire, the Holy Ghost built a "nest of white glory" in her soul. Another, finding herself bound in some way, cried out in the desperation of faith, and in the spirit of Patrick Henry, "Give me liberty or give me death," at the same time assuming the attitude of holy defiance, and Andrew Jackson's determination. Let it be remembered that we are in the land of "Old Hickory," Andrew Johnson, Peter Cartwright, David Crocket, and Parson Brownlow.

Brother Newberry and his wife, and Mrs. Lucius Hawkins, came down from Mount Eagle, Tenn., to attend this meeting.[12] They seemed to enter right into the spirit of the meeting. They seemed to enter right into the spirit of the meeting. Sister Newberry sought definitely and received the heavenly dynamite, while Sister Hawkins received the definite experience of the fire. They came into the meeting with hearts open to receive the light, and were eager and willing to walk in it. About a year ago they withdrew from the Methodist Church, South, on account of the corruption therein. And since that time they have been working for the Lord independently of the "church," and God has been blessing their efforts. Praise the Lord for a few young men with enough spiritual backbone and holy courage to act on their convictions and obey God rather than man. A score of such men filled with the Holy Ghost and baptized with fire and "dynamited with all dynamite" would spread the fire and dynamite throughout the entire state and Tennessee, and give great trouble to the backslidden preachers and the apostate churches. We are praying God to raise up men and women enough to carry this glorious gospel of fire and dynamite into every county and precinct of this beautiful state. Already there are several truly fire-baptized workers in this state, upon whom we are persuaded the Lord can depend. They are, W. B. Martin, Frank Porter, Dollie Lawson, Emma DeFriece,[13] and some others who are not ordained, but are as true to the fire and the eternal dynamite as the needle is to the north star. There are in this region several young persons who are evidently led of the Lord and called with a divine call into the Master's vineyard, and from these we shall doubtless hear in the near future.

Others are being called definitely into the foreign field, and before many months will be on their way to Africa. Of this I shall speak more particularly in a subsequent letter, but suffice it to say here that these will go under the auspices of the Fire-Baptized Holiness Association of America, the first missionaries sent by the Association to the heathen lands. They expect to go to Africa and establish a fire-baptized mission in the Dark Continent; and we are praying to make that mission the Centre of fire-baptized holiness in Africa, from which shall radiate the divine fire and glory and power into every part of the Dark Continent. We entreat the earnest prayers of all the fire-baptized people who may read this, in behalf of this contemplated African mission. We praise the Lord that, in answer to prayer, He is calling some the fire-baptized saints into distant lands. We confidently expect to go to Africa ourselves in the not distant future, and hold camp meetings on the blood and fire and dynamite lines; indeed we have had a divine conviction that God would open up the way for this, and we feel more deeply assured of it now than ever. The great railroad now being built from the Cape to Cairo, it seems to us, is providential. The Lord is evidently undergirding that great enterprise, and thus opening up the way for the fire-baptized missionaries to carry the fire and the dynamite throughout the entire length of that immense continent. That great railroad, carried through by the indomitable energy of such men as Cecil Rhodes, Lord Cromer, and others, with its immense arms stretching out to the east and to the west, is evidently intended to facilitate the travel of God's true missionaries into that land of darkness and superstition.[14]

Some of our fire-baptized preachers and workers are being called to South America, and others to India, Japan, and China. But, brethren, be sure that your call is from God, and then go; but before you go "tarry" for the enduement of the dynamite from above.

We have been asking the Lord for nearly two years now, to send forth fire-baptized missionaries into every part of the earth, and plant the standard of the white fire in every continent, and on every island of the sea; and we have the assurance that He will do it. "And when this gospel of the kingdom" (which is the dynamite of God unto salvation to every one that believeth) is preached "in all the world as a witness unto all nations," then Jesus will come in the clouds of heaven and set up His kingdom upon the earth, and we shall reign with His Glory, glory, glory! This dynamited gospel has not yet been preached in all the earth; it is the mission of the fire-baptized movement to deliver the nations, peoples, and kindreds, and tongues, of the earth, this glorious, manifold gospel. Who has a commission from God, and a message from the Throne, for the most degraded and benighted inhabitants of darkest Africa? and who is not only willing but burning with an irresistible desire to carry "this gospel of the kingdom" to them? Beniah, Tenn.

* * *

The meeting at Beniah increased in power from the beginning. Some were sanctified wholly, and several received the baptism of fire and the heavenly dynamite. There were remarkable cases of divine healing, and some very clear cases of conversion. One Swiss lady, living in the Home, after hearing a sermon definitely on the dynamite on the dynamite, said to the writer "There was dynamite in dat sermon last night and it did good; without dat dynamite I would not have gotten converted." Hallelujah to Jesus for the dynamite. This was a remarkable case, and a clear case of regeneration. This sister, we understand, came from Boston, Mass., to Beniah, and for several months has been fighting off conviction. She was bitterly opposed to the meeting, and declared she would not attend; but God got hold of her, and with His almighty dynamite unearthed her, smashed up her resolutions, and actually saved her. After her conversion her face shone, "as if it had been the face of an angel." Brother Newberry and wife, and Mrs. Hawkins from Mount Eagle sought definitely for the eternal dynamite, and testified unequivocally to the experience. Several renounced the apostate church, and united with the Fire-Baptized Holiness Association. The Lord put the holy dance upon a number of the saints in this meeting for the first time. Such jumping, and screaming, and shouting, and dancing before the Lord, we have seldom seen. The utmost harmony prevailed among the workers, and the glory of the Lord rested upon His people and filled the tabernacle, throughout the entire meeting.

We found one brother in this meeting, a contributor to one of the leading holiness papers, in a completely backslidden condition. He came to the altar meek, humble, and teachable, "seeking salvation," and determined to go on until he receives the definite baptism with fire. He confessed that he had lost ground, in fact, backslidden, by opposing the manifestations of the saints. He had been afraid of wild fire and fanaticism, and had counseled with, and harkened to, the "warnings" and "cautions" of those who denounce as false fire and wild fire, the wonderful displays of God's power in some of His deepest saints. "Afraid by reason of the fire." Everywhere where the real fire is accompanied by something of this kind. Sometimes it is the holy dance, sometimes the holy scream, and sometimes the holy laugh; some leap and jump, while others fall prostrate under the power of God. Some have the "jerks," while others have sudden and long continued attacks of the "hot chills." Glory to God for the diverse manifestations of the spirit.

It is plain to be seen that the work which Brothers Martin and Porter have done in this section of the country is solid and thorough. Their work abides. May the Lord help all our workers to do work that will **abide**. We want work that will abide the test of the Judgment, and of temptation, and of persecution, and of every form and degree of opposition.

This was our first meeting in Tennessee, and it has been the means of endearing these blessed Tennesseans to us. The fresh air, the pure water, the glorious weather, the autumn foliage flaming out its dying glories, the delicious persimmons, and the kindness and hospitality of its simplehearted inhabitants, completely captivated us, and carried us away in the Spirit. It was both interesting and amusing to observe the frequency and the regularity with which John E. Dull visited that fine persimmon tree down near the spring![15]

In company with John E. Dull, we left Beniah on the 19th, and drove to Cleveland, the county seat of Bradley county, Tenn., and took the evening train for Abbeville, S.C. We arrived in Atlanta, Georgia, about 11 o'clock the same night, and remained there until noon the next day. Here we purchased a very rare old book entitled, "The Experience of Several Eminent Methodist Preachers in a Series of Letters Written by Themselves to John Wesley, A. M.," and published in 1812. This book contains sketches of twenty-one early Methodist preachers. It is a real treasure, and we expect to gather out of it much that will encourage and edify.

At noon on the 20th of October we boarded the Seaboard Air Line for Abbeville, S.C., where we arrived about 5 o'clock p.m. We found Brother and Sister Harris shouting and praising God for the baptism of fire. The children were sent out and the people notified, and about 7:30 we had a fine little congregation, to whom John E. Dull preached. It was a blessed service. About a dozen were at the altar seeking the Lord, some for pardon, and some for the fire, and some for entire sanctification. The people seemed hungry for the truth, and willing to walk in the light.

We came here on invitation from W. E. Fuller, ruling elder for the Colored Fire-Baptized Holiness Association of South Carolina, and our meeting here will be held mainly for the colored people; although we expect to preach part of the time for the whites.

There is no man in the fire-baptized holiness movement who is truer to the cause, or who has a clearer experience of the baptism of fire, than W. E. Fuller. He is doing a wonderful work among his own people, and has the confidence of both white and black in the community in which he lives. He is the man who came forty miles to the Anderson to see the writer. He has been true to the fire from the beginning, and he is wise, energetic, and sweet-spirited.

He came to Abbeville last spring and organized a little band (*ecclesia*) of four; now there are thirty-six, all of whom (except two) we are told, enjoy the experience of the fire.[16]

Brothers Hayes and Starr were here a few weeks ago, holding meetings for the colored people, and God greatly blessed their work. [17] The saints got happy and shouted "Fire, fire, fire," with such jubilant victory in their souls that the fire department became alarmed, and rushed out with their engines and entire force, thinking that the town was on fire, and in danger of being destroyed! The authorities took advantage of this and ordered the meeting closed, we are informed. It is a pity that the ungodly, wicked men of this world cannot distinguish between the shout of victory and the signal of distress—the distressful cry of alarm.

It was here that Stephen Olin, sometime during the second decade of this century, if we remember correctly, took charge of a Methodist college. We have inquired diligently, but, so far, we have not found any one who seems to know anything about it. No one seems to know if an institution ever existed here. There is no trace of it now, at least as far as we have been able to discover. Methodism in this country is as dead as a stone, and as cold and inanimate. The spirit and genius of good old Stephen Olin appear to be as foreign to this place as they could well be.[18]

No wonder! The Methodist Church in this state has committed itself against the true gospel, and is walking arm in arm with infidels, and with the world, and with impenitent sinners. Its preachers smoke and chew, and belong to the lodge, and fight, not only the fire, but holiness and divine healing, and the coming of the Lord. No wonder Stephen Olin and the Methodist college at Abbeville are forgotten, and no trace of them can be found.

But, glory be to His name, Jesus is appearing in these last days "in another form." This time it is in the form of the Fire-Baptized Holiness Movement; and the old gospel of full salvation is coming back. The true gospel, which is the power of God unto salvation to every one that believeth, is returning to the "land of the wreck and the tomb," and these glorious pine forests, which stand like sentinels in this grand old historic Southland, shall again resound with the triumphant jubilant shout of victory, and the sweet songs of Zion should again be sung "with the spirit and with the understanding..."

Abbeville, South Carolina

Document 39 – "Editorial Correspondence," *Live Coals of Fire* **(November 3, 1899), 1.**

We remained three days in Abbeville, and held meetings separately, for the white people and for the colored. Our meetings for the whites were held in private houses, and for the factory people. The congregations were so large, and the houses were so crowded, that we could hardly find room to stand, much less to jump and dance; and the interest was so great that the people wanted us to continue for a week or two, but our engagements were such that we felt compelled to go on. Some were saved and sanctified, and others were seeking. We find that Brother and Sister Harris have been at work here among the factory hands, and many of them are enquiring the way, and several have lately been converted and sanctified, and others have received the baptism with fire.

It appears that there is a great work for our fire-baptized evangelists and workers to do in this southern country among these great cotton mills. Thousands of men and women are constantly at work here, and their religious privileges are exceedingly poor. The big, proud, worldly church, and the unsaved preachers, fighting holiness, and chewing tobacco, have no real interest in them, and do not want them in their "heathen temples." These poor and needy people are hungry for the pure gospel, and it is a part of the fire-baptized mission to carry to them the everlasting gospel. We are delighted to know that several of our southern evangelists have already felt the call, and have gone forth with the true missionary spirit to these destitute and neglected places.[19] One sister was gloriously sanctified, and her face fairly shone with the radiance of the divine presence. Another was so pleased with the faithful preaching of the simple truth, that she told the preacher that she would like to sit all night and listen to such a sermon. Sometimes the truth, unmixed and unvarnished, literally fascinates, hallelujah!

Our meetings for the colored people were in a little despised, out-of-the way, back alley building called "Zion:" but God was with us in marvelous power in every service. Such singing, such shouting, such dancing, such praying, it has never been before been our privilege to hear. Many of these poor colored people (rich in faith and perfect in love) have the real baptism of fire, and hell-shaking dynamite. They are among are the most respectable and well-to-do of the colored people of Abbeville. They are among the very best people in the town. They are not only saved from the use of tobacco and from swine's flesh, but they are also delivered from the proud, backslidden church. Some of the best members in the big St. James colored church came out while we were there, and united with the Fire-Baptized band. One man, a prominent, influential member, whose wife and mother-in-law had been fasting and praying for him a week, testified that an "angel from glory" came down and told him to leave St. James and unite himself with "Zion." To him, that was authority enough to join the fire-baptized band, which so accordingly he did. Another prominent member came in with us in the last service, giving during his testimony, a very striking illustration, which convinced everybody that he had taken the right course. The services lasted till nearly midnight, and there was the most perfect freedom that I ever saw. The colored people dance before the Lord differently than our white people, and this feature of the meetings amongst them was peculiarly fascinating to Bro. Dull. He declared that it was his opinion that the Sunday night service (in which he was the only white person present) was the most remarkable meeting ever held, and that he didn't expect to witness anything like it again.

One colored sister in testifying to sanctification and the baptism with fire, said that she felt like there was a magnolia flower right in her heart. She certainly testified to more than she understood; for the magnolia is one the loveliest flowers we have ever seen—so white, so beautiful, so exquisitely fragrant.

Some of the colored people fight the fire as bitterly as do some of the whites; and as they persecute their own brethren who preach and testify to the fire, as wickedly as some of the whites do us. In this country the proud, supercilious, ungodly whites look upon with scorn and contempt because we hold the meetings for the colored people, and preach the gospel to their former slaves; and some of them look at us as though they would like to burn us at the stake, for carrying the "unsearchable riches of Christ" to the hungry blacks. Be expect to be "obedient to the heavenly vision," regardless of consequences.

On the other hand, the unholy, hypocritical negroes persecuted the sanctified ones amongst them because they allow white men to come and preach for them occasionally, and accuse them of "drinking out of white-mouthed bottles." Carnality is the same in all ages, and in all nations, and peoples. Everywhere it hates God and the truth; and it is always hates and persecutes all who will live godly in Christ Jesus.

Bros. Hayes and Star held a tent meeting here six weeks ago, and the people got so happy one night that they shouted, "fire, fire, fire," so loudly and so earnestly that the fire department came rushing out, thinking the town was on fire! And the meeting so disturbed some of the carnal white people that they compelled the brethren to take the tent down and close the meeting. The mayor's son was seen helping cut the tent down, we were informed, and the police refused to do their duty in stopping the mob but stood by and encouraged it. A merchant near by spoke bitter words against the meeting and said it ought to be stopped; while a woman living close to the tent swore about it and said it ought to be torn down. In less than a week a big fire broke out, and burned the mayor's house to the ground, and also the woman's, and in a few hours that merchant's store was in ashes!

People will learn after a while, that is a dangerous thing to speak wickedly against the fire-baptized preachers, or interfere with a fire-baptized meeting. It is dangerous to undertake to stop the slant lightning, or for the uninitiated to regulate the eternal dynamite. Better keep hands off the ark and let the kine run!

From Abbeville we went to Marion, S.C. and spent one day with Bro. Foxworth. It was indeed pleasant to get back once more to the scene of my illness, and to the spot where the Lord so wonderfully healed me, on the 14th of February, 1897. Here we met Sister Bryant again, and found her unwavering in her loyalty to the cause of the white fire, and without one word to say against the heavenly dynamite. Here we also met Bro. Avant a true and tried prophet of the Lord, and Bro. Looney came in unexpectedly to us on his way to the Kingstree meeting. There is no truer man in the movement than Bro. Looney. He is one of the few men whom we feel that we can absolutely depend.
Marion, S.C.[20]

***

We remained in Marion one day, and then hastened on to Kingstree, S.C. on the 27th. We were met at the depot by Brother James Epps, and carried to his hospitable home two miles in the country, where we entertained in a most royal way. It is not often our privilege to sojourn in such a home, or with a family as Brother Epps. His is a typical southern home, a genuine old time plantation. He has a large three-story house with high ceilings, long, wide halls, lovely piazzas, and deep cherry fire-places with a large library, and books in every room. The house was built in ante-bellum days. It stands in the midst of a grove of large and stately oak, sycamore, long-leaved pine, hickory, and live oak.

The plantation is a large one, extending several miles in length, and there are a good many cabins upon it for the colored tenants and servants. Six or eight families live on the plantation and till the soil. They have the utmost confidence in Brother Epps and love him very much. He is good to them, and treats them as becometh a man professing godliness. He attends their prayer meetings and thinks it not beneath his dignity to worship God with his colored servants.

We shall never forget while life and memory endure the kindness and consideration we received in Brother Epps' home. Everyone—even the very youngest of the family, which consists of fourteen children—seemed solicitous for our welfare and comfort. We felt unworthy and did not deserve such kindness.

During the meeting, Sister Epps received very clearly the experience of the baptism with fire. Brother Epps himself was sanctified years ago under the teachings of John S. Inskip. Later on he received the experience of the fire, and has been a faithful witness "unto Jesus" ever since.[21]

We were invited to Kingstree to hold a meeting for the colored people by Isaac Gamble, one of our colored fire-baptized evangelists who lives at this place. But the brethren agreed to have the meeting conjointly for the colored and white people. The colored brethren occupied one part of the tent, and the whites the other part. One part of the altar was for the whites and the other for the colored. Everything went on harmoniously. Everybody in this community has the utmost confidence in Brother Epps, and also in Brother Gamble. Bro. Gamble was born and raised in this place and his life has been a standing proof of reality of the doctrine and experience of entire sanctification. Everyone concedes that he is a sanctified man and that for thirty years he has lived a holy life; and the same is true of Brother Epps.[22]

One man—a travelling man living in Charleston—informed us that no truer or more consistent Christian than Isaac Gamble could be found anywhere in South Carolina; and he has known him for many years.

The Kingstree meeting was a wonderful meeting. In some respects, it surpassed any meeting we have ever held. The Holy Ghost had the right of way throughout. The results of this meeting will never be known, except they are revealed in the light of the judgment. Some confessions were made in this meeting which were utterly astounding; but the writer has had similar confessions in almost every meeting he has held since he received the experience of the baptism with fire. Everybody seemed to be pressing on into the deeper and richer experiences; there was no turning back, or limiting the Holy One of Israel.

In this meeting Sarah M. Payne,[23] Brother and Sister [May] Looney, Brother [F. M.] Britton, W. E. Fuller, and others sought definitely and received the heavenly dynamite, while others were clearly converted, healed, sanctified and baptized with the Holy Ghost and with fire. We remained in the meeting but four days; but during that time there was a profound interest manifested among the people, both white and colored, and a real Holy Ghost awakening. We came away on Monday evening leaving the meeting in charge of John E. Dull. We found it impossible to do the work of three men—our physical system could not stand.

The interests of LIVE COALS OF FIRE require one man's entire time; so we decided to return to our sanctum sanctorum and devote our entire time for some months at least to the paper. Brother Dull will fill his appointments in the South before his departure for Cuba.

The following saints were present at this meeting, viz., John E. Dull, our co-laborer, W. S. Foxworth and wife, and sister, Brother and Sister Bostick, Brother and Sister Looney, Sisters Payne, [Nora] Arnold, and Gaines, Brother [R. W.] Gregg, Brothers Britton, white; and Wesley Barr, Isaac Gamble, Uncle Powell [Woodbury] and son, W. E. Fuller, and others, colored.[24]

Brother Foxworth's sermon Sunday afternoon on the "Dynamite" was a terrible explosion, and had a convincing effect on everybody who heard it; at least upon everyone who is not prejudiced against the truth, while Brother Dull's sermon Sunday night on the "False Christs" shook the kingdoms of darkness as they have never been shaken before in this section of country.

Brother Foxworth contributed $50 toward the liquidation of the $250 which stands against our property in Tennessee.

All hell is in a rage because what God hath wrought, and because what He is still going to do; and myriads of devils and wicked men are counselling together, and flying from one part of the earth to another in the vain attempt to thwart the work of the Holy Ghost and put a stop to this invincible fire-baptized holiness movement. But the irresistible nitro-glycerin of the eternal Trinity can neither be destroyed nor controlled by men or devils.

I writing this letter on the steps of the Capitol of the United States, in full view of the magnificent statue of John Marshall, the most illustrious of American jurists, and my soul is basking in the sunshine of that liberty which comes, not by constitutional provisions, nor by legislative enactment, nor judicial interpretation, but the knowledge of the truth as it is in Jesus Christ, who said: "If ye continue in my word, then ye are my disciples indeed; and you shall know the truth, and the truth shall set you free." Hallelujah!

Washington, D.C., October 31.

Defining the Movement

Introduction

In this editorial Irwin reflects on the coherence and formation of the Fire-Baptized Holiness Association as an organization. This piece is vitally important because of the absence of any contemporary records from the 1898 organization in Anderson, South Carolina (or from any of the state associations formed earlier).

Document 40 – "The Central Idea," *Live Coals of Fire* **(November 10, 1899), 4.**

It has been said that holiness is the central idea of Christianity, and so it is, provided it be true holiness; and we desire to say that the central idea of the Fire Baptized Holiness Movement is that the baptism with fire is a definite experience. Around this burning nucleus, everything which has contributed to make up the Fire-Baptized Holiness Association of America, has been gathered. Here at this central point we have fought all our battles, and won all our victories; and on this glorious battle field we expect to engage the enemy again and again, and win many more magnificent and decisive victories. Here we have stood from the first, ever since we received the unspeakable experience of the baptism with fire, in October, 1895, and here we shall we stand till Jesus comes. Our position is impregnable, supported as it is by Scripture and experience.

We received the experience of the baptism as a definite experience. We have sought it as such. It was the most marvelous revelation of the Holy Trinity. It was the most marvelous experience of our life. It marked an epoch in our personal history, and revolutionized our entire life as nothing else ever did or ever can. It was to us, the beginning of a series of unfoldings of the Word of God, which, while in the flesh, we shall never be able fully to give out to others.

We had known and realized the Morning Star experience before, but now the Sun of Righteousness Himself, in His Threefold splendor and glory was fully risen in our soul, and now we had the conscious personal acquaintance with each of the Eternal Three.

A few days later we felt as if we were inspired; our very fingertips were hot in the celestial fire of God, and our flesh seemed to burn with the manifested Presence of the inworking Deity. We felt constrained to write, and every word of our testimony written at that time was written under the divine "anointing which teacheth us of all things, and is truth, and is no lie, and which abideth." And that testimony went forth in the power of the Spirit, and has been used by Him in bringing hundreds of souls into the definite experience with the baptism of fire.

Later on, while at the Olmitz camp meeting, in an awful agony of prayer for the prosperity of Zion, known only to God and ourselves, we were led out one night into a vast hot ocean of prevailing prayer, and it was clearly opened up to us by the Spirit of God, that the Fire-Baptized saints should unite together in a definite organization, and the name of the Association and the outlines of the constitution all came to me like a divine revelation. The next morning I arose, and, being in my tent alone, wrote out the original Constitution, and submitted it to some of the brethren. It met with their most hearty approval. A few days later it was adopted, and the first Fire-Baptized Holiness Association ever organized was actually in existence; and it has stood true to the cause of the fire from that day to this. Since then many other Fire-Baptized Holiness have been organized in various parts of this country and Canada.

In the Basis of Union, adopted in the organization of the original Association, it was declared that *"we believe in the baptism with fire as a **definite** experience."* This was the pivotal point. Upon this all depended. We were a unit on this point, and whenever we have organized since then we have made this the vital question: and the distinguishing feature of our organization everywhere. For any our evangelists to deny this, or teach otherwise than that the baptism with fire is a definite experience is treasonable to the cause of the fire.

A brother in Virginia writes us, saying: "The holiness preachers here are all fighting the baptism of fire. They say they received it when they received the Holy Ghost." And so it everywhere. Those who are bitterest in their opposition to the baptism with fire, claim they have it, and that they received it when they received the Holy Ghost. This we deny, and here we differ; and it is at this point where the conflict rages, and has from the very first.

Our enemies, those who have fought us so bitterly, and accused us of teaching a third work, and of seeking to destroy the holiness work throughout the country, have uniformly and unitedly made their attacks at this particular point. They all maintain that the baptism with fire is never received as a definite experience but always coetaneous with the baptism with the Holy Ghost.

Here we differ, for this we deny. We teach and maintain that the baptism with fire is a definite experience, and always subsequent to that of the Holy Ghost. Here we plant our guns, and throw up our breastworks, and raise the standard of the white fire; and from this high vantage ground of Scripture and experience we challenge the enemy. So far we have held it against every assault, and we are confidently persuaded that we shall hold it till Jesus comes.

Holiness as a second, definite work of grace was the central idea and the impregnable rock of early Methodism, and "the baptism with fire as a definite experience, obtainable by faith on the part of the Spirit-filled believer," is the central idea and invulnerable stronghold of the Fire-Baptized Holiness Association of America; and if any amongst us cease to believe this teaching they are no longer members of our Association.

The testing time is upon us and we praise God for it. But, nevertheless, we must meet it, and we ought to meet it squarely. We remember that John Wesley at one time expelled four hundred members in the city of London. But we do not expect to have to take part in the doing of anything of the kind. But it may be well to call the attention of our readers to Sections 1 and 3 of Article 14, of our new Constitution, and to the Basis of Union. Let all the members of the Fire-Baptized Holiness Association of America, and especially all the evangelists read these Sections of our Constitution.

There may be those amongst us who are not fully informed as to these important articles of faith, and if there are such, we entreat you to study the Basis of Union and also the Basis of Membership in the Constitution. If you do not and cannot agree with Association you have a perfect right to go elsewhere, and we shall commend for your honesty in so doing.

But if you "affirm and teach" that one may receive the twofold baptism of Jesus with the Holy Ghost and with fire "at one and the same time," then you are no longer in harmony with the Fire-Baptized Holiness Association of America, and, if you are an honest man, you will no longer consider yourself a member of the Association.

The Fire-Baptized Holiness Association is committed for time and for eternity on this question, and all our evangelists, so long as they remain with us, are expected to stress this point, namely, that the baptism with fire is a definite experience, obtainable by faith on the part of the Spirit-filled believer, and if any teach otherwise, they thereby cease at once to be members of the Association.

We trust also that in receiving members into local Associations, and especially in the appointment of local leaders, great care be exercised in that direction. It were better not to receive one than afterwards to be compelled to cut him off. Let us "Keep the munition, watch the way," and stand squarely upon the teachings of the Association as set forth in "Keep the munition, watch the way," and stand squarely upon the teachings of the Association as set forth in the Basis of Union.

We desire to treat every brother with fairness and candor, and in referring to a brother was recently withdrawn from the Fire-Baptized Holiness Association of America, we shall quote his own published words. He says, "I stand rejected by the Fire-Baptized Holiness Association on the charge of unsound teaching," and then proceeds to say: "I affirm and teach, that with a Bible regeneration and sanctification it is the privilege under this Pentecostal gospel to receive the twofold baptism of Jesus, 'with the Holy Ghost and with fire,' in Pentecostal order, i.e. *at the same time,*" The italics are ours. Now we submit to our readers, and appeal to their candor and judgment, if he has not deliberately departed from the faith of the Association by taking common ground with the enemies of the fire. Then he goes on to say that he himself did not receive the experience in Pentecostal order; and closes his article with the statement that his article "is no invitation for controversy."

With this last statement we fully agree. We will not enter into controversy with anyone, nor will we allow ourselves to be drawn into it. We allow our precious brother the perfect right to his views, opinions, and beliefs; but we submit to our readers, that according to his own statements he is no longer in harmony with the Fire-Baptized Holiness Association of America in his teaching on this essential point, and therefore, according to the provisions of the Constitution of the Association and his own published utterances, he "at once ceases to be a member thereof." We commend him for his consistency in withdrawing from the Association.

However, we shall continue to teach, as we have taught for the past four years, that the baptism with fire is a definite experience, and LIVE COALS OF FIRE shall always stand by this Central Idea of the Fire-Baptized Holiness Association of America, and we trust that every evangelist in the Association who is not squarely with us on the teaching that the dynamite is a definite experience for which we are commanded by the Savior Himself to tarry, will return to us at once their certificates of ordination.

Whirlwind from the North: Irwin's Last Recorded Sermon

Introduction

This two-part sermon is the last we have from Irwin (though he lives until 1926). This is also the only recorded Irwin sermon preached in an African-American church, and the only one he preached in a "mainline" church. Both factors make this sermon distinct. Irwin goes to greater length than usual to explain the full dimensions of Fire-Baptized teachings, and he also remarks on the way blacks in the South were currently embracing the movement.

Document 41 – "Sermon by the Editor: A Whirlwind from the North, Part 1," *Live Coals of Fire* **(December 1, 1899), 2-3.**

Preached at the African Methodist Church, Lincoln, Nebraska, November 12, 1899.

I want to call your attention to a portion of the first chapter of Ezekiel. The Lord gave the sermon last night in a dream—the first time since I began to preach that I ever received a sermon in a dream, but God gave it to me and I am going to preach as He gives it to me. I thought I could hear you colored people shouting and praising God for the fire, and I thought that I could see you dancing before the Lord and acting just like the colored people acted three weeks ago tonight in Abbeville, S. C. I preached to a colored congregation in that city three weeks ago tonight, and such manifestations and demonstrations of God's power I never saw, before or since [see Document 39]. There was, I think, only one other white person there, Brother [John] Dull, and they got to dancing all over the house and kept it up more than an hour, while I shouted, and cried and laughed, and jumped, and praised God; and that is the kind of salvation I believe in. I believe in a salvation that makes people happy. I enjoy my religion—actually enjoy it, praise God! at home and away from home and away from home, in the pulpit and out of the pulpit; I really enjoy my religion. Once I heard a Baptist preacher say that he endured religion for fifteen years, but I praise God that I have enjoyed salvation ever since God converted me. I was happy before I got sanctified; conversion made me happy, wonderfully happy. I used to love the prayer meeting and all the meetings where God's people were assembled, and I loved to read the Word of God, and loved secret prayer, and the faces of God's people looked beautiful to me, before I got sanctified, hallelujah! Salvation shines out in the faces, and in actions and manifests itself in the voice and in every way, blessed be God. I love a salvation that shines forth and I am going to read this passage, commencing with the first verse, and bring out some of this from the Scriptures.

"Now it came to pass in the thirteenth year, in the fourth month, in the fifth day of the month"—he is exceedingly definite, is he not? Praise God for definiteness. I believe in getting converted sometime. I have seen people who did not know when they got converted, and hardly knew whether they were converted, but I knew when I was converted. I was there. And then I knew when I got sanctified wholly, if I was a Baptist preacher at that time. It took place about 11 o'clock, one Saturday night, May 16, 1891, and I was there too, hallelujah! God sanctified me wholly. Then I know when God wonderfully and miraculously healed me, and I know when He gave me the mighty baptism of fire, too. He filled me with the Holy Ghost twelve hours after I was sanctified wholly, and four and a half years later He gave me the definite baptism of fire, and I have had it for over four years and it is an abiding experience; and I know where that took place. I was out in Oklahoma in a sod house about 10 or 11 o'clock. Praise God forever and ever for the real experience of the baptism with fire. And I know where I got the dynamite. I had been reading Benjamin Abbott's Journal, and reading about the slaying power that he and the other early Methodists had, and I asked God to give me the dynamite and He gave me the dynamite and gave it to me, and I have it still tonight, and still I am seeking for more. I praise the Lord for these definite epochs in my experience. I praise God that he saved me from limiting the Holy One of Israel, and it makes me feel good when I think that the Spirit has free access to my soul, bless His name forever and ever! Men are drying up, and backsliding, and losing the sweetness, and unction, and fire, and power, out of their souls by stopping short and saying there is nothing more. May God help us to get away from the opinions of men and from the dogmas and doctrines of the "church," and let the Holy Ghost have His way with us. It was the Holy Ghost that led me to seek these things, and it was the Holy Ghost that revealed them to me, and gave me these experiences. I praise God that He has complete right of way through my entire being. I am completely spoiled for this world. It has no use for me and I have no use for it. I am going through with Jesus, and we are having a hallelujah time together.

"In the fifth day of the month as I was among the captives by the river of Chebur"—and we find these captives all over the land and in all the churches, souls captured by the devil, and that is a good place to get a revelation of from God. Some people are bound and have no freedom, and when they get into certain places they cannot open their mouths. The Lord help you to get rid of the old man, and you will be free. I am free in the Lord; free to testify, pray, shout, and preach in eternal truth as it is in Jesus, and I will be free, and I want to say that if you find under certain surroundings you feel tied up, you need to die. Dead people are free. It takes a real death to sin and the old man to set one free, and then you will let God have his way with you and use you as he wants to use you, and you will not have to ask the preacher or the presiding elder what you shall do. That is the way God wants to bless you and set you free, so that when you get among the captives you will get revelations from God. I never got many among the saints, but when I get in a tight space God shows me things to come and gives me the assurance that He is going to keep me all the way, praise His name!

"I was among the captives" then "the heavens were opened, and I saw visions of God." Praise His holy name! "Visions of God." Hallelujah for the visions. I believe in visions and revelations. A sister in the Queen's dominions told me a few months ago that God gave her two visions one night, and she said that they seemed to open into her soul; and blessings came, one after another, as the Lord kept unfolding these things to her heart. And when I looked around and saw that her husband, a beastly, hoggish man was bitter against her, and against the fire, and against divine healing, and how he persecuted her, and compelled her to stay in the kitchen and cook hog meat which God calls filthy, unclean, and abominable, to satisfy his depraved appetite; and when I saw how patient and gentle and uncomplaining she was, and how true she was to the fire, and to all that God had done for her, I felt in my soul that I had found out the secret and the true explanation of these visions and revelations which God was vouchsafing to her. God was calling that woman to work in His vineyard, and He was permitting her to pass through this course of discipline, so that she would be true to Him; and these wonderful visions and revelations from God were given to her to encourage her by the way.

God wants a few people who are true to Him, and He will have them—a few faithful men and women who are faithful men and women whom He can trust, and to whom He can safely entrust these marvelous blessings. One reason who you do not get "visions of God" and revelations from heaven, is because God sees that He cannot trust you with these things. "The heavens were opened," hallelujah to God. When Stephen was preaching that marvelous sermon that shook the earth, and from which it has never ceased shaking, the heavens were opened, and saw Jesus standing on the right hand of God, and the Scripture says he saw the glory of God. One real clear vision of the glory of God will settle forever the love of the world, and the pleasures, and amusements, and friendship, and companionship of the world. One clear view of the glory of God will forever kill you to the world and crucify the world to you. It is a marvelous thing to get a clear view of God, Jesus says: "This is life eternal, that they might know thee, the only true God, and Jesus Christ, whom thou hast sent." Hallelujah for a real knowledge of God.

"In the fifth day of the month, which was the fifth year of King Jehoiachin's captivity, The word of the of the Lord came expressly unto Ezekiel." I just want you to notice that expression—"the word of the Lord came expressly unto Ezekiel." God seemed to make a special case of Ezekiel just gave him personally the Word of the Lord. Do you know what that means? I remember once in starting out to read some scripture I thought I would read five chapters, and I only read three or four verses in the first chapter when I began to taste the sweetness of the Word of God and could not get any farther. It came expressly to me. God began to break it to my heart and unfold it to my very spirit, and I just revealed and delighted myself in that Word. There are not many church members who know what I am speaking of now, and very few preachers know what it is to taste the real honey of the Word of God. When God begins to expressly unfold, and reveal, and illuminate, and expound the blessed Word to you, you will find yourself amazed at the depth of it, at the extent of it, at the power of it, and the wonderfulness of it.

It is no wonder Ezekiel preached the fire, is it? No wonder he preached the dynamite, and the slant lightning. He was a fire-baptized preacher who dealt in slant lightning and eternal, hell shaking dynamite. If you do not know that, read the first ten chapters and you will find the lightning, and the dynamite, and the power, accompanied his word everywhere. In the very commencement of his ministry God gave him a special revelation of His own precious Word. "The word of the Lord came expressly unto Ezekiel the priest, the son of Buzi, in the land of the Chaldeans by the river Chebar; and his hand of the Lord was there upon him." I want to call your attention to that expression. He was away off in the land of captivity. Though in the land of captivity, yet in spirit he was not a captive. Just like Madam Guyon and Bunyan, he was free in spirit. His body was tied down, and he was shut in that sense, but in the deep spiritual sense of the word he was free, the Spirit of God came and spoke to his heart. Do you know that nothing can interfere with liberty of a soul that will obey God? God will keep you, and give you sweet liberty, and enlargement, and revelations and visions of Himself, and unfoldings of His Word, such as the world cannot comprehend. The Scripture says: "The hand of the Lord was there upon him." Right there in the land of captivity. Let me tell you something that occurred in my own experience. About three years ago we were down in South Carolina, and some of the brethren wanted us to lay our hands upon them, and pray that God might qualify them for the work and send them out as efficient workers for Him; and while that service was going on the mighty power of God fell upon the saints assembled there, and I felt it and realized it, and I said, "I want you to lay your hand upon me;" and that was my ordination service, I had been preaching before, but on that occasion, while a sister was leading in prayer, I felt the great hot Hand of God come down on my head and cover me like a helmet of fire, and at that time I had never thought of this scripture, but I know that God's hand was upon me, and I told the brethren and sisters that it was so and what that meant. It meant three things to me. In the first place it meant that God would lead me every step of the way, and He has done it, and I am persuaded He will do it till Jesus comes. In the second place, it meant that God would protect me against all the fiery darts of the wicked, and I have realized that is a most marvelous and wonderful way, and especially during the last year; and in third place, I realized that God would supply every need of my soul: and so, the mighty hand of God resting upon me signified divine guidance, divine protection, and divine support, and I know from experience just what Ezekiel knew twenty-five hundred years ago, when the hand of God rested upon him by the river Chebar. O, it means something to be where you can trust God in all cases. It means something to be conscious that God leads you every step of the way, right in the face of persecutions, and slanders, and threats, and warnings of men, and it means something when things are giving way in an outward sense, to all appearances, to trust God and bring down sacks of flour, and bank checks, and printing presses, and automatic rheostats out of the sky, in answer to prayer! I know what am talking about, and tonight have my feet on the neck of the devil, and my eye fixed on Jesus, with an eternal shout of victory in my soul. Blessed be God for an experience that unfolds the truth of the Word of God. If I did not have an experience along this portion of this chapter, I would not preach it. I do not preach those scriptures that I have not experienced. God gives me for messages such scriptures as I have experienced, and when I deliver such a message it always sticks.

Then he says: "And I looked and, behold, a whirlwind came out of the north." He looked, and Matthew Henry says he looked right up; he wanted to see what was going on. He expected something to take place. These things I have been talking to you about to come down from above. They are from above. It is God, the high and lifted One that supplies them. The blessings of God come down from above. "Every good and every perfect gift is from above."

"I looked, and, behold, a whirlwind came out of the north." I want to say, beloved, that where the true gospel is preached in the might and power of the Spirit, there will be spiritual whirlwinds, dynamic explosions, death-dealing slant lightning, fiery cyclones, and irresistible, destructive tornadoes. A sister up in Canada was so filled with power by the Spirit of the Lord that she jumped about three feet the first time, and about four feet the next time, and still higher the third, and the people screamed and cried out and fell under the power, and an unsanctified preacher was scared and turned pale, and said he expected her the next time to go right out through the roof. She did not do it of herself. It was the fire and dynamite of God which were operating through her.

Do not quench the Spirit. Here is where the trouble so often lies. God wants to break your bones and loosen your joints, and then He can use you. I remember before Brother Willis died, one day after the meeting was out he stood there, and I said something which touched him and God put the dance upon him, making the third time in that one service, and he danced with such power and unction that large robust men wept under it. I said to him: "Why did you dance so many times?" He said: "I do not know, God put it on me." I would to God you would get saved up the dancing point; saved so would send the police around to see what is the matter, and talk about sending you to the asylum. Some people have so much of a reputation to look after, or some wife, or husband, or daughter, or son, or preacher or presiding elder—they stand right before you all the time, and you are afraid to swing out for God. Lord help us.

The whirlwind came from the north. You never undertook to control anything that was as hard to control as a tornado. You will get your eyes blown out, and your hair spoiled, and the feathers blown off your hats. You will get a shock that you never had before. This salvation is a close-cut and close-fitting garment, praise the Lord. It is a real serious thing to get saved. It is not so serious after you get it, but it is serious getting it. The seriousness is mostly gone when you have gotten saved down to the bottom. The devil is not after you very much till you let go everything that is of the world and sin.

Some people professing holiness and the fire are not bothered much by the devil, but I want you to get where the devil will be continually after you. A man is not worth much for God until all the devils in hell and on earth are let loose upon him. I know this, that with the mighty fire of God on my soul, and the eternal, hell-disturbing, divine dynamite, I am more than a match for the devil. This thing of living a sanctified life means a hand-to-hand, ceaseless fight with a personal devil, and you need all the equipment you can get, to win in such a battle. I would not give much for religion that would not stir the devils to the very depths of hell, and I know that the religion of Jesus Christ is enough to keep a man in the very gates of death, and at the mouth of hell, and make him shout and praise God continually. Get this whirlwind out of the north in your souls, get this tornado of fire and dynamite.

Now he goes on: "And I looked, and behold, a whirlwind came out of the north, a great cloud, and a fire enfolding itself, and a brightness was about it, and out of the midst thereof as the color of amber, (or, as burning coal) out of the midst of the fire."

In some of our meetings we have had such whirlwinds of divine power that the police and the city authorities became alarmed and ordered the meetings stopped, but judgment followed. If you do not understand this slant lightning, you had better not undertake to regulate it. I want to tell you that God has taken men out of the world (several of them during the last six months) who have fought the mighty baptism of fire and the dynamite of God which rested upon His fire-baptized saints. Out in Kansas I had warned the people one night along this line, and four young men did within six weeks. May God show us the danger of opposing the work of the Spirit of God.

"A brightness was about it"—a real bright appearance manifesting itself, and let me tell you, the genuine fire of God, the real fire, which comes as a definite experience to the fully sanctified, Spirit-filled soul, will burn and blaze its way wherever it goes. There is a colored fire-baptized brother in South Carolina whose face glows and burns, perfectly surcharged with the blessed fire of the living Trinity, and there are others also of like experience who literally shine, glory be to Jesus, and white people, and black people, and every other kind of people admit, and acknowledge, and testify that these saints have what they profess to have. I praise God for this fire.

Let me call your attention to an error I find nearly everywhere I go. I hear people testifying that the fire cleanses them from sin, but I want to utterly demolish that idea. It is not the fire that cleanses. There is not a single scripture anywhere that teaches that. I am aware of the fact that persons who are not familiar with theological terms will get terms mixed up, and yet their experiences are clear, but God wants you to be instructed on this subject. It is not the fire that cleanses from sin; it is the blood that does this.

"The blood, the blood, is all my plea, Hallelujah, it cleanses me."

The Scripture says, "The blood of Jesus Christ his son cleanseth us from all sin," so there is nothing of a sinful nature left to be cleansed from. The Lord help us to state this vital truth as it is, and not allow anything else to come in and take the glory from the Precious Blood. The blood cleanseth from sin. We go down before God, having had a revelation from God of the inbred sin of our hearts, and having seen the turpitude and vileness of inherent depravity, and realizing that God has promised to wash us in His own blood, and make us whiter than snow, we fall at His blessed burning feet, confessing out the traits and characteristics of the carnal nature, and then believe Him for the blessing, and He sanctifies us wholly, and gives the witness of the Spirit that we are sanctified wholly; we still we have not received the baptism with fire. So you see, it is not the fire that cleanses form sin. It is the blood that does that; nothing in the whole universe can cleanse us from sin, but the precious blood of Jesus Christ.

(Concluded next week.)

Document 42 – "Sermon by the Editor: A Whirlwind from the North, Part 2," *Live Coals of Fire* **(December 8, 1899), 2-3.**

Preached at the African Methodist Episcopal Church, Lincoln, Nebraska, November 12, 1899.

What then, does the fire do for us? It does so many things that I cannot enumerate them all tonight; but I shall mention two or three of the most important.

II.

In the third chapter of Matthew, where John is speaking of Jesus, he says, "Whose fan is his hand, and he will thoroughly purge his floor and gather his wheat into the garner; but he will burn up the chaff with unquenchable fire." Now the word "chaff" is not used here to represent sin at all. Last summer, one day, after I had preached, and proven from Scripture that the blood cleanses from all sin, and that it was not the office of the fire to cleanse from sin, a sister who had listened very attentively, and who was fully convinced that the fire does not cleanse from sin, said to me: "What does that scripture in Matt. 3:12 mean, then? and what does the fire do for us? and what is the 'chaff'?" I stooped down and picked up a head of wheat which had two or three grains of wheat in it, and said to her: "Here is a beautiful illustration. Here we have a head of wheat; some grains are left and some have fallen out. And here you see the 'chaff.' At one stage of the growth of that wheat it was just as necessary as the stalk or the grain itself. But this wheat has reached the stage where the 'chaff' is no longer necessary. Before that wheat can be turned into flour and converted into bread and be of use to us, the 'chaff' must be removed. This 'chaff' in our lives represents those things not depraved, not sinful, not wrong in themselves, but which, as we advance in our religious experiences, and especially after we advance in our religious experiences, and especially after we get entirely sanctified and receive the clear light of the baptism with fire, we find no longer necessary, and which we need to and do not get rid of. And the abiding fire of Christ's baptism burns these out of our lives.

Whereas, before we receive the baptism with fire, though entirely sanctified, and having the abiding witness of the Spirit to that gracious work, yet now there are many things which I cannot do, with this added light, which before that I could do. They were not sinful, not wrong in themselves, and they did not condemn me, but now God shows me in the light of this glorious experience of the fire, that they are not necessary, and I must forego them or lose what I have. For instance, I was taught to believe that one must belong to some 'church' in order to keep saved, but, glory to His name, He has shown me otherwise. I have found out that it is a delusion and a snare of the devil that I must belong to a rotten, corrupt church in order to keep saved. I found this out in the light of the experience with the baptism with fire. God shows me by His Spirit and Word that I ought not to belong to these holiness-hating, sin-loving 'churches,' which will allow the Holy Ghost to manifest Himself as He will in the meetings. God shows me that these backslidden churches and unconverted or apostate preachers are no longer necessary to keep me saved. Again, I used to think I had to stand well with the 'holiness' people or I would not get any 'calls,' and would have nothing to do. But, hallelujah! the Lord shows me I can be used without the least assistance from this source. There are poor hungry children crying for the bread of life in every part of the earth, and I can go to them and break to them the true bread without being 'called' by these heathen 'churches,' or sent out or recommended by these fashionable, unconverted 'holiness' people. I have more calls now than I can fill in two years. In my case, hallelujah to Jesus, the fire has burnt out all this 'chaff' or rubbish. He has "thoroughly purged his floor,' and burnt up this 'chaff' with the unquenchable fire which burns continually like a vast conflagration throughout my whole being. O, this mighty baptism with fire! May the Lord help you to see what it does for us.

Then it reveals us to the different persons of the Trinity; and introduces us, as it were, to each one personally. Nothing, absolutely nothing, but the experience of the baptism with fire can ever give you a knowledge of the Holy Trinity. You may have a nice theory about it, and you may be familiar with all the 'theology' and all the Hebrew and Greek in the world; and yet, without this unspeakable experience of the fire—the definite experience of fire—you will never know God in His wondrous Triune fulness.

Another thing the fire does—it gives you backbone; not stubborn mulishness; not opinionated self-will, but real holy backbone. You will stand for the true and the right against everybody on earth and under the earth, and keep as sweet as heaven while you are doing it. Your dearest friend, not even your closest companion, will be able to swerve you from the 'strait' way. Satan cannot move you, nor men, nor devils, to do what you believe to be wrong.

Again, the baptism of fire gives clearer and deeper spiritual discernment than you will ever knew before. You live on the sublime heights of which the Isaiah speaks, in the midst of the 'munition of rocks,' where the air is pure and transparent. You live up in the rock-buttressed city of magnificent distances, and having the eagle eye, you can see afar, and discover in advance the subtle approaches of foe. God will sometimes permit mysterious things to happen, but He will disclose to you the reason of all His mysterious and permissive providences concerning you. And all the while you will have your feet on the neck the devil, and the heaven-born shout of victory in your soul.

Another thing the fire does—it blows up the works of the devil, defies his utmost ingenuity, and utterly defeats his subtlest and most hidden plans. The fire discloses his secret plotting and brings to light the hidden things of darkness, as nothing else can do. It gets under things and unearths things, it searches and gives trouble to all the agents and emissaries of Satan. It puts fire to the foxes' tails and sends them howling back through the cornfields of the Philistines. It makes the apostate church and the hireling preachers wish you had never come, and pray, like the Gadarenes, that you may depart, and never return.

There is might, and power, and glory, and revelations from God in the baptism of fire, which are not to be found elsewhere.

There are a few of the things which the experience of the fire does for us when we get the genuine article. There are many others but I cannot enumerate them here.

III.

In the third place, the baptism of fire is the enabling act of the gospel. You go up here when the legislature is in session, and they will pass laws, and take them through the process required by law, starting out, "Be it enacted," and closing up with the penalty attached for the violation of that law. There is what is called the Enabling Act, without which it could not be enforced; so God wants to give you the mighty baptism of fire, and put the eternal dynamite in your soul, so you can do what you have to do without compromising, or getting sour or bitter in your spirit. O, may God unfold this truth to us, the absolute necessity of the baptism of fire, to enable us to do what God wants us to do.

Also out of the midst thereof came the likeness of four living creatures. And this was their appearance; they had the likeness of a man.

God showed the prophet this whirlwind, this cyclone of spiritual power, coming out of the north; He showed him the fire infolding itself, and the brightness of this fire, and then right out of the midst of this divine glory and divine manifestation came the four living creatures. These four living creatures represent fire-baptized men and women. They do not represent angels. Matthew Henry says they do, but they do not. George Smith, one of the most learned and profound Bible scholars of modern times, a sanctified English Methodist layman, took up this subject, and examined every passages that speaks of this matter, in his book, "The Doctrine of the Cherubim," and he tells us that these living creatures represent redeemed souls—souls that are washed in the blood of Jesus, and I want to add that these living creatures represent fire-baptized souls only. They had an appearance of a man. The Bible says, "Mark the perfect man;" they had the appearance of that man. Fire-baptized men and women look like Jesus, glory to God forever and ever! They have the likeness of the Christ of the Bible. They have it in preaching, in testimony, in praying, in missionary work, in personal appearance and in every other sense. God looks down into their hearts and sees there the likeness of Jesus. I praise God for the likeness of the Man of Calvary that the mighty baptism of fire brings out in us. You can have a fine statue here in the darkness and you will not see it at all, you cannot tell who it represents or what it is; but you turn the white electric light on and you can tell at once what it is. When this cyclone of spiritual power, this infolding fire of God, with the brightness of heaven and the burning coal appearance, comes into a man's heart and life they bring out the divine image and show Jesus in you, and that is one reason for the absolute necessity of the experience of the baptism with fire.

IV

I thank God for the unspeakable unfoldings and revelations and visions of God which come to the soul that is really given up to God. Ezekiel goes on to say "And every one had four wings." That means that the man or woman that has the baptism of fire sees in every direction at once, hallelujah! God says, "Walk circumspectly," and that word conveys the idea of looking all around you at one and the same time. God wants you to get where you can see the devil in every direction from which he may come. He wants you to get up on this high vantage ground, above the clouds of doubt, and the storms of fear, and enjoy a clear atmosphere and a clear vision to see the devil, for he will come upon you from every side at once. O, the wonderful insight which the fire gives! I want you to get it.

They had four wings. That means they flew in every direction at once. O, the fire-baptized people, you cannot keep track of them. The devil has lost track of them, he cannot bottle them up like Sampson did Cervera, hallelujah! The devil has lost track of these "ignorant and unlearned" fire-baptized saints. He cannot locate them, he cannot hedge them in. He has been trying that for four years to my certain knowledge, but he has utterly failed, and shall continue to fail. This burning whirlwind is more than Satan can manage. He cannot hinder its onward progress. It is the mightiest movement on the face of the earth today, and will increase in power until Jesus comes. God is in it.

Each one had four wings. When get the baptism of fire you will want to leave home and friends right away. God is sending missionaries to Africa—we have three, possibly five, who are to go to South Africa, and they will plant the standard of the fire and spread this everlasting gospel of fire and dynamite throughout the whole of that wonderful continent. God will do it through them. Others are going to Manila, and to Cuba. LIVE COALS OF FIRE is circulating in Manila tonight. Others are going to South America, India, and China, right on this white fire line. I praise God for the way he is blessing His own cause, and causing the fire to spread.

Then he says, "And their feet were straight feet," blessed be God! They did not turn aside and make crooked path, they went straight through with Jesus. God says in His Word: "Make straight paths for your feet." That is what the fire-baptized gospel does. It enables men and women to make straight paths for their feet, and they will go through on that line. Then he goes on and says: "And the sole of their feet was like the sole of a calf's foot." Matthew Henry says that a calf's foot is parted, or cloven, and we know that is the foot of a clean animal. Now God says, "How beautiful upon the mountains are the feet of him and bringeth good tidings"—clean and beautiful—and the closing up of this verse says: "And they sparkled like the color of burnishing brass." That is the beautiful shoes, the preparedness of the gospel. That is the beauty of men who are not only called but qualified and prepared to work God wants them to do. "The preparation"—Paul says in Ephesians their feet are to be "shod with the preparation of the gospel," and the literal reading of that is: "with the preparedness of the gospel." So, brethren, when a man or a woman gets the real experience of the baptism of fire, whether he is educated or not, though he cannot read a word, yet in a spiritual sense he is prepared to go forth, preaching the gospel of Jesus Christ. If it were otherwise those uneducated heathen in India, China or Africa, white, yellow, and black, never could preach the gospel; but the best preaching, and the most effective preaching that is being done in the world today is being done by men and women who have no education. That is the truth of the matter, and I am not saying it in disparagement of a sanctified education. Paul was educated, but Peter and John were ignorant and unlearned, and so were the rest of the apostles; and some of the most efficient workers I know of are men that can scarcely read the Word of God. May the Lord help us get God's idea of what it means to have feet that burn like fine brass, feet that are ready to go on the errands of mercy, that are willing to obey God, that will go promptly, and quickly, and rapidly, in obedience to the commandments of God!

"And they had the hands of a man under their wings on their four sides; and they four had their faces and their wings. Their wings were joined one to another; they turned not when they went; they went every one straight forward. As for the likeness of their faces, they four had the face of a man, and the face of a lion, on the right side; and they four had a face of an ox on the left side; they four also had the face of an eagle." Now here are the four peculiar characteristics of the fire-baptized holiness people. It has been so in all ages of the world. They have had the likeness of Jesus, the courage of the lion, the strength of an ox, and the discernment of the eagle. So brethren, with the likeness of Jesus, the daring courage of the lion, the never-failing, patient endurance of the ox, and the keen, far seeing discernment of the eagle, these living creatures go forth into every quarter of the earth, locating and exposing sin and the devil, and capturing souls for God.

I want to tell you that the strength represented here by the 'ox' is the same strength that Paul speaks of when he says: "I can do all things through Christ which strengtheneth me." That is the likeness of Jesus, the courage of the lion, the strength of the ox, and the eagle eye that sees the approaches of the devil and the snares and pitfalls that beset us. The eagle is said to fix his eye on the sun and soar above the world, out of reach of the fowler's gun and every danger, and soar away on wings that never tire. In like manner, the fire-baptized saint of God fixes his eyes on Jesus; and with the strength of the ox and the courage of the lion, he rises right above the world, its pleasures, its amusements, its honors, its friendship, its temptations, and everything pertaining to it; and keeping his eyes fixed on Jesus, and with no fear of falling from the dizzy height when God requires, he swoops down with perfect safety and takes the prey. Now this is a part of the description of the fire-baptized saints of God. The soul that has the real fire has genuine spiritual discernment. A fire-baptized soul is a perfect enigma to all the world; they do not understand him, but he sees right through them, and so the Scripture says: "He that is spiritual discerneth all things." The man that has got that far discerns all things, and when he hears testimony he can discern the true ring from the false. I am not saying now that one can go around and look into men's hearts and tell them what they are. It is only the Spirit of God that enables us to do these things, and only when and as he will. When danger approaches, and the hidden pitfalls lie concealed all about us, God puts this spiritual discernment, this inner vision into His saints, and when they do have the courage and fortitude to cry out against it and deal with it faithfully as God would have them do.

"Thus we their faces; and their wings were stretched upward; two wings of every one were joined one to another, and two covered their bodies. And they went every one straight forward; whither the Spirit was to go, they went; and they turned not when they went." I call your attention to this verse—they went whither the Spirit was to go, and where the Spirit of God wanted them to go. So many people who once knew the Lord, who once had salvation in a measure, enjoyed religion to some extent, now have drawn back. The Spirit wanted them to go somewhere and they would not do it. The Spirit wanted them to jump, or shout, or dance, and they would not do it, and the result is, they have lost their spirituality, and the unction and power out of their souls, and now they are dry, and empty, and powerless. O, the real fire will lead to go as the Spirit leads. If he calls you to Africa you will go, or to Siberia. You will go and you will not be afraid of the smallpox or diphtheria or yellow fever or any other disease.

V.

Again, when you get the real, definite experience of the baptism with fire will know the Spirit of God; you will know His voice, and the devil will not be able to come in and pretend to be the Holy Spirit and deceive you. He may mimic the Holy Ghost, but he cannot deceive you. It is not possible, the Scripture says, to deceive the very elect. The fire-baptized saints are the very elect. The sanctified people are God's elect, but the fire-baptized people are God's very elect. They occupy the inner circle, stand right up next to the Throne, and have the ear and the audience of Jesus.

I close with those two verses: "As for the likeness of the living creatures, their appearance was like burning coals of fire. That was the appearance of the living creatures, and that is the appearance of the fire-baptized saints of God, like burning coals of fire"—"and like the appearance of lamps;" not only burning coals, but lamps, that give out light as well. You can take a heap of coals, white hot, and they will not give out a great deal of light, but the lamp gives out the light, and so the two thoughts are brought out, that the experience of the baptism with fire puts a bed of burning coals in you that will glow and burn for God and enables you to blaze and shine for God. There is light connected with the fire. It illuminates, and scatters the darkness round about God wants us to be white hot for Him, to have a great bed of burning coals in our hearts, and He wants us to be a flame, a blazing emitting light, throwing it out like a beacon light, illuminating everything around us. Glory to God for the burning white fire that shines! "It went up and down among the living creatures." That was the Spirit, the Spirit of God, the eternal Spirit of burning. The blessed Holy Spirit is going up and down among the fire-baptized saints, and here lies our strength and power. The baptism of fire is the bursting forth of the pent-up Trinity in your heart and mine. The Spirit of God is going up and down through the whole realm of your affections, imagination, reasoning powers, your will, and every part of your nature, giving life, energy, unction, power and glory to your entire being. They he says, "And the fire was bright"—hallelujah!—"and out of the fire went forth lightning." There is a kind of lightning that flashes in the heavens, a kind of pyrotechnics that you can stand off and admire but which can strike anywhere and never kills anything; but the lightning which Ezekiel saw was slant lightning and it struck something, and every time it struck something, and every time it struck it killed. It came out of the fire, and it represented the Word of God preached in the omnipotent power of the eternal God. You let a man come into the community who has the real baptism of fire and the slant lightning of this text, and his preaching will kill your experience if have not the paid the whole price. The brightness of his experience, the power of his testimony and of his prayers, the unction, and fire, and dynamite of his preaching will kill your experience, and you feel like you do not have any salvation at all. That is what the slant lightning which comes out of the fire does.

Then the last words are, "The living creatures ran and returned as the appearance of a flash of lightning," showing the agility, the activity, the quickness and the promptness of the fire-baptized soul. He is sent forth by the omnipotent power of God, and he turns not to the right nor to the left, accomplishing that whereto he is sent. God does not have to talk, and plead, and coax him to do what he wants done; but he waits on God, and delights to do His will. If you have the baptism with fire, one little intimation from God and you will bound right out for God and souls. That is what the fire, and lightning, and dynamite will do for you. "They ran and returned." They ran on the errands of love and of mercy, and came back and reported their doings, awaiting His orders to go on other errands for God. They were ready to go anywhere in the universe on a moment's notice. Amen.

Delimiting the Movement

Introduction

During the last months of Irwin's leadership he took on multiple "doctrines of devils" that he felt were seeping into the Fire-Baptized movement. The following three documents reveal his deepening concerning over issues such as the promotion of "marital purity" (no sex within marriage other than for procreation), an anti-organization spirit, other burgeoning religious movements (like the Jehovah's Witnesses), and the advocacy of even more extreme holiness codes than those preached by Irwin himself.

Document 43 – "Doctrine of Devils," *Live Coals of Fire* (February 9, 1900,) 4.

"Now the Spirit speaketh expressly that in the latter times some shall depart from the faith, giving heed to seducing spirits and doctrines of devils" (I Tim. 4:1).

Evidently we are living "in the latter times," and already some are departing from the faith. Many are "teaching for doctrines the commandments of men," and some are giving heed to these seducing spirits, and many are following their pernicious ways. Others will yet apostatize, and go out in that dark, fierce storm of unbelief and utter rebellion against God from which none have returned. The heavy atmosphere of these last days is pregnant with perfidy, falseness, and infidelity, and innumerable "destructive heresies" and damnable doctrines of devils. False and self-deluded teachers, commissioned and sent by the prince of the power of the air are filling the earth with their abominable doctrines, and deceiving multitudes of people, who are being led "captive of the devil at his will." Satan is diligently employed, and he is marshalling his legions are never before, and bringing into requisition every agency of darkness and of hell to undermine, subvert, and destroy the foundations of the faith of God's elect. He knows that if he can succeed in shaking our faith in God, he has won the victory. Hence his masterly, and subtle, and persistent efforts to induce the true saints of God to believe his lies. But thanks be to God, it is not possible for the devil or his false prophets to "deceive the very elect."

It will be necessary in handling the subject before us to speak very plainly, for we do not intend that a single member of the Fire-Baptized Holiness Association of America shall be deceived on any of these lines. Our Association is committed against these "doctrines of devils," and we do not want any of our members, much less any of our evangelists, to teach any of these unscriptural and heretical delusions. The Bible says we should "hold fast the form of sound words," and that we should "take heed unto the doctrine," and "give attendance" thereto, and the we should "keep that which is committed to our trust," because "some have erred concerning the faith."

The first of the these "doctrines of devils" to which we wish to call attention is the so-called, or rather mis-called marital purity delusion. The very name itself is misleading, and contains in it an implied falsehood. This teaching is being propagated by some of the most corrupt and heretical of the false teachers of our day. Those have a form of godliness but deny the power (dynamite) thereof. They deny the divinity of Jesus Christ, and degrade Him to the level of a mere creature. They teach that we are already living in the millennium, thereby denying the historical, personal coming our Lord Jesus Christ. It is also advocated by a few ranting fire-fighters in St. Louis, Tabor, and Atlanta. This false doctrine is built upon a fallacious and unscriptural assumption. It assumes that all intercourse between husband and wife, except it be for the procreation of children, is lust. This a false assumption, and directly opposed to the plain teachings of God's Word. The Word of God declares that "Marriage is honorable in all, and the bed undefiled; but whoremongers and adulterers God will judge" (Heb. 13:4); and again we read in (1 Cor. 7:3): "Defraud ye not on another, except it be with consent for a time, that ye may give yourselves to fasting and prayer; and come together again, that Satan tempt you not for your incontinency." Yet in the face of these scriptures, the skinny advocates of these scriptures of this fallacious doctrine of devils denounce as lustful that which God in His wisdom has ordained, and in His holy Word allowed. Let the reader consult Adam Clarke in his exposition of this last passage. It will do you good.[25]

This doctrine is an assault upon the institution of marriage itself. They falsely assume that to be lust which God permits, and upon this assumption the advocates of this doctrine proceed to build their unscriptural and pernicious argument against all intercourse between husband and wife, except as above stated. They assume as a fact the very thing in question, which requires to be proven; and because their position cannot be supported by the Word of God, they unhesitatingly denounce as lustful everyone who does not accept and teach their pernicious doctrine.

This doctrine not only strikes a blow at the institution of marriage, but it is a calculated to lead men and women into the promiscuous practice of free love, fornication, and adultery. It produces alienation, unholy discord, and unwarrantable separations in the family, and leads to distrust, deceit, and domestic infelicity. It produces marital infidelity rather than marital purity. It ignores the sacred privileges of the married state, and places men and women on a level with brute creation. It disregards the inherent, God-given laws and propensities of our nature, and fallaciously holds up the abuses of wedded life as conclusive arguments against the rights, privileges, and felicities of marriage itself.[26]

We unhesitatingly denounce this teaching as of the devil, both as to its origin and effects. Its tap root has its source in unbelief and infidelity, and its branches bear the deadly fruits of free love, fornication, adultery, distrust, domestic infidelity, heartless and cruel separations, and a disregard for all the sacred privileges of the holiest of all earthly relations. We shall not tolerate this detestable and damnable doctrine in the ranks of the Fire-Baptized Holiness Association. We have declared it against it in our constitution, and we shall stand for the defense of the declaration of the Royston council.[27]

II.

Another of these "doctrines of devils" is the teaching that one is not born again until he is sanctified wholly. These deceivers talk about "going through the regeneration" and get unsanctified Christians all mixed up and confused in their experience. They teach that converted people are not regenerated until they are sanctified wholly, and go into hairsplitting distinctions between being "begotten" and being "born again," confining the one to conversion, the other to entire sanctification.

"This persuasion cometh not of him that calleth us," but of him who would cause us to seek something we already possess, and thus cast away our confidence, and deny what He hath already done for us. It is a subtle device of the devil to entangle us in doubt and unbelief, and thereby destroy our usefulness.

The distinction above referred to is one without a difference, a mere mental distinction, fine spun theory, and entirely without foundation in Christian experience, and wholly unsustained by the Word of God. It is unmethodistic and unscriptural, and contrary to Christian experience.

We are acquainted with three sisters, who once had blessed experiences, and were eminently useful in the Lord's work until they embraced this fatal delusion of Satan, but from that time until the present they have been blocks and hindrances to the work of the Lord, and have had no power for good, either with God or man.

III.

Another of Satan's delusions is the anti-ordinance and anti-organization heresy of rank comeoutism. This is the natural result of the cold formality of a dry, spiritless ecclesiasticism. These two, namely, a dead, tyrannical sectarianism and a raving, insubordinate come-outism, constitute the antipodes of the devil's religion. They are the Arctic and Antarctic poles of the axis upon which the religion of this world revolves. If the devil cannot get us to settle down in the dead, spiritless churches and become satisfied with an empty "form of godliness" without having the power thereof, then he will do everything he can to drive us to the other farthest extreme, and inject into our minds and hearts the spirit of insubordination, anarchy, and rebellion to all authority, divine, as well as human and Satanic.

Let it be remembered that government is of God, and so also is organization. But because government has been abused by the backslidden and apostate church, and because law has been made the instrument of cruelty and oppression, despotism and destructiveness in the hands of ecclesiastical tyrants, these poor deluded souls would do away altogether with organization and with all government and utterly reject and disregard all authority. Thus they would place themselves without the pale of all authority, and beyond the reach of all discipline.

This violent, unteachable spirit of rank come-outism is the quintessence of religious insubordination. It is self-willed, intractable and iconoclastic, and when it finds that you will not follow it, it becomes sour, bitter, and uncharitable in the Scripture sense of the word. Because Judas carried the bag and habitually stole from the Lord's treasury, it would do away entirely with the treasury portfolio. These rank come-outers overlook entirely the fact that there was and is a divine organization called the ecclesia, and that it consisted of numerous local organizations. It was of this divine organization that Jesus spoke when He said: "The gates of hell shall not prevail against it."

The Apostle Paul himself held revival meetings such as the fire baptized evangelists are now holding, and undoubtedly organized the brethren into local ecclesia, just like the fire-baptized evangelists are doing today. And Apollos and other of the apostles did the same. They undoubtedly shouted and danced, and leaped with joy then exactly as the saints do today, and got sanctified, and filled with the Holy Ghost, and baptized with fire, and dynamited with all dynamite, and healed, and had visions, and dreams, and wonderful manifestations of the Spirit.

Paul established ecclesias in Asia Minor, and in Crete, and appointed Timothy bishop over the Ephicene ecclesia, and Titus bishop over those in the island of Crete. He also gave them authority under God, to ordain elders in every city and in every place where elders were needed; and himself laid down in his letters to those bishops the qualifications of those who should be ordained by them to the work of the ministry.

Here, in the apostolic ecclesia, we find organization, and government, and discipline, which things are right and scriptural in themselves. They are never wrong in themselves: it is the abuse of them that is wrong.

One brother wrote to the Editor and told them it was worse than drunkenness and robbery to organize the Fire-Baptized Holiness Association of America, and yet the same brother wanted his articles and tracts published in the LIVE COALS OF FIRE which is the organ of said Association! Some of these come-outers have embraced the damnable and detestable doctrine of spiritual marriage, and others have gone so far that they totally disregard the Lord's day, and think it no harm to hunt and fish on Sunday. One sister writes to us that she was glorified in her body and had no further use for the Bible! In Toronto there is a class of blasphemous fanatics who utterly reject the Word of God, and speak of the blood of Jesus as a putrid thing! A narrow, sectarian, apostate Wesleyan preacher in South Carolina made practically the same statement, if we have been correctly informed! In Oklahoma City and elsewhere in that Territory, there are some of these rank come-outers, heartless fanatics, who teach that it is a sin to weep over the loss of their own children and denounce everybody as carnal who sheds a tear on the grave of their departed loved ones.

These are a few of the fruits of this spirit of rank come-outism of which we have spoken. We trust that none of our evangelists or people will ever become tainted with this abominable "doctrine of devils." Beloved, let us keep our Association forever free from this detestable delusion. If it should appear anywhere within our borders, let us as one man lift up our voices against it and instantly expel it.

Document 44 – W. S. Foxworth, "Bondage or Legalism" (with editorial remarks by B. H. Irwin following), *Live Coals of Fire* **(March 23, 1900), 4.**

It is possible for good people to get under bondage to their own ideas, whims and vows. For instance, I know a lady who will not eat anything that is cooked on Sunday. If she happens to be at a place where there is nothing prepared for Sunday she will fast until Monday rather than break the vow she has made in her heart not to eat anything that is not cooked on that day. I know another who will not eat any breakfast, thereby burdening herself with this bodily affliction through life, without once considering that all we do independent of the Word or the leadings of the Holy Ghost, whether fasting or otherwise, is acting in fleshly energy, and must inevitably be useless. I know of others who will not eat fish, beef, chicken, bread, vegetables, or anything where bacon or lard is used in the cooking, thereby making themselves an offence by asking questions at the table, and insulting the courtesy of the people who are kind enough to entertain them. I know of an evangelist who when he goes into a new place to hold a meeting, announces from the pulpit what he does not eat, and I have been along with him when it was very difficult for the ladies in the country to prepare a meal for that brother.

Such people as these make themselves burdensome, and they really hurt the cause of fire-baptized holiness. One brother denounces another for blacking his shoes, forgetting that this as well as shaving and brushing his hair, is part of his toilet. One sister denounces another for wearing a corset or artificial teeth, yet at the same time it would be dire neglect for the sister to discontinue to use of either. There may be instances where one cannot wear a corset to the glory of God, but there may instances where they can. One concluded that he would never trim his beard. Finally, when it had gotten into a very unsightly condition, he was prevailed upon by some of the saints to give up this idea. [28] You find others who are in bondage to some rash vow that they made weeks, months and years ago, ignoring the fact that it would be much better to confess their mistake and repent of it, than to go on under the galling yoke which they have made for themselves.

Now I want it understood that I am not defending the hog. I do not own one in the world, neither do we use hog meat or lard in our home, but I do think it is time to cry aloud against these delusions that some of our people have fallen into for there are some sections where the people are charging the fire-baptized holiness movement with these teachings.
Marion, S.C.

[We heartily endorse the spirit and wisdom of Brother Foxworth's article. It is timely. We would rather be burnt at the stake than to compromise with sin, or the world, or the fallen church, or found endorsing anything which is questionable; but there is a gospel liberty which is larger and more blessed than any human definition. There are measureless depths in the salvation of Jesus, beyond the shallows and the shoals, and the hidden rocks. May God save our people for all self-imposed bondage to unscriptural vows, and from mere external and legal observances. The devil would like to bind us and foot, and cripple or destroy our influence for God and for true holiness; and if he can hamper us in this way and entangle us in the externalities and outward observances of religion, he will have accomplished his purpose. Ed.][29]

Document 45 – "Editorial Correspondence," *Live Coals of Fire* (April 20, 1900), 1.

We left Mercer [Missouri] on Monday, March 12th, for Eddyville, Iowa. We were detained about two hours in Ottumwa, one of the most wicked, ungodly towns in the country. Arriving in Eddyville about 11'oclock at night, about the first thing we heard was the solemn hooting of a DesMoines river owl. It represented pretty well the false and apostate churches of these degenerate last days. The reader will find a graphic account of this state of things in Isaiah 34. These birds of darkness and of prey cannot stand in the light of day "for everyone that doeth evil hateth the light, neither cometh to the light, lest his deeds should be discovered" (Marginal reading).

We remained two days in Eddyville, preaching in the Fire-Baptized Holiness Mission. It had been thirty-five years since we were in Eddyville. Then we were a small boy, emigrating with mother, sister and brothers to the Territory of Nebraska. Things have changed since then, but not for the better, so far as we see. Increase of knowledge, and labor saving machinery, may not mean improvement morally or religiously. Knowledge has increased amazingly since that time, and wonderful inventions, discoveries, and mechanical machinery: and with these crime, and infidelity, and every manner of sin.

From Eddyville we came to Chariton, Iowa, where we met W. E. Stevenson and others whose names are in the book of life. Charles LesCault, John Nelson, Sarah Clark, John E. Dull and E. D. Wells, and wife were all there; and on Friday, the 16th, we all drove out to the Mason schoolhouse, twelve miles northeast from Chariton. It was the coldest day of the season, and the trip was a severe one, but the Lord kept the fire at such a white heat in our souls that we scarcely felt it. Brother Dull preached at night, and on Saturday afternoon, Brother Wells. Sunday morning the Lord gave us a message, and the lines were sharply drawn. All hell was in an uproar. Here we saw the fatal and awful consequences of false teaching. The "Flying Roll" was represented by a long-haired deceiver, and those who had lately "departed from the faith," and taken up with the compromising teaching of others, were entertaining him and "bidding him God speed."[30] Here we found the abominable teaching that "Jesus has come" in full blast, and the other false and unscriptural teaching that "the devil is bound" and the "world has come to an end." Also the unscriptural notion that we should not "resist" anything, but just let Satan have full sway no matter when he may do. For our part we believe in "resisting" the devil, and in protecting our neighbors, if it can be done without violence and in the spirit of Jesus. It is better to "resist the devil" than it is to resist the truth and the work of the Holy Spirit. The Lord save us from this fanatical non-resistance delusion of the devil. We heard nothing of this amongst our brethren until "certain" who had backslid and toned down in their testimony and preaching made it a pretext for opposing some of God's truest and most loyal followers.

Sunday, after the morning service, we drove back to Chariton in company with John E. Dull, John Nelson and Charles LesCault. We spent the night with W. E. Stevenson and his estimable wife. We were a little crowded, some of us having to sleep on the floor; but then we were welcome, and had a hallelujah time. There were two unoccupied Methodist beds in the other part of the house, but we were forbidden to enter that part of the house; that is, John E. Dull and B. H. Irwin. It is a great luxury to us to realize that the gruff old nicotine mad Methodist devil cannot endure our religion. When the truth is told about the adulterous, apostate, holiness-hating church, as well as when God's little ones, filled with the Holy Ghost and baptized with fire, leap and dance and shout, it always stirs the devil and brings out the "old man" from his deceitful, religious hiding place.

The next morning, we shook hands with our friends, and shook the vile Methodist dust from our feet, and boarded the train for Lincoln. We remained at home for three days, as busy as a bee, in our library and in the office of LIVE COALS OF FIRE.

On Friday, the 23rd, we went to Hamlin, Kansas, in answer to a pressing call from N. G. Pulliam and W.E. Stevenson, who were pushing the battle vigorously at that place. We found them plowing deep and patiently drilling. Indeed, some heavy blasting had already taken place. A few had been saved, some had received the fire and the dynamite, and one or more had been healed. But there was a "hidden rock" in the way here. It was the leaven of false doctrine which had already worked corruption in the lives of some.

It was the doctrine of so-called "marital purity. One man teaching this damnable delusion of the devil, and loudly professing that he was "delivered," had induced his wife to accept the same delusion. At the same time, he carried the hired girl all over the country by day and by night until she became infatuated with him, lost her salvation, and committed adultery with him in her heart. She got under awful conviction and was going to confess all, but this same man and his wife used all their influence to keep her from doing so. Finally, the truth came out, and the devils of lust and of "marital purity" were completely exposed and brought to judgment. Yet when confronted with the facts of the case, and openly charged with the appearance of evil if nothing more, he declared, but evidently with the mouth only, that he had the "victory." Later on, and after we had come away, he confessed, we are informed, to having had lust in his heart toward the same young woman.

This case demonstrated the awful danger of this miscalled teaching of Satan and his deluded followers, commonly called, for purposes of deception: **"marital purity."** We do not want this detestable doctrine of the devil taught in our Association and by, the help of God, it shall not be. If any of our evangelists are teaching it, we request of them to send us their credentials at once, and leave the Association.[31]

We remained at Hamlin four days, long enough to see this doctrine of devils blown to atoms, and its advocates brought to judgment, and then Brother Pulliam carried us ten miles to Falls City, Nebraska, where we took the old "Atchison and Nebraska" train for Lincoln again.

We remained at home sixteen days, reading, writing and working in the office and about the house, and preparing to start on our Eastern trip. Lincoln, Neb., April 12

Departure

Introduction

In Irwin's last correspondence to *Live Coals of Fire* he assesses the impact of his ministry as he announces his need to take a sabbatical in some "quiet resting place," either in a large library in one of the "large cities of the East" or in "the mountainous districts of Pennsylvania or New York." Within two months Irwin's drunkenness and sexual immorality would be exposed. At that time he was in Omaha, leaving us to wonder whether or not he ever traveled east for his time of rest.

Document 46 – "A Desert Place Apart," *Live Coals of Fire* (April 20, 1900), 4.

The Lord has graciously opened up the way, supplied the necessary means, and enabled us to go apart, for four or five months into some "quiet resting place," where we can take a much needed rest from all active evangelistic work. But we shall not be idle. We expect to be closely and constantly occupied in other directions. All our engagements for the future have been or will be provided for, and the work will continue the same as heretofore. Brother J. H. King, who for nearly a year has had charge of our work in Toronto, Canada, has kindly consented to assist on paper during our absence. He is already in Lincoln, and at his post of duty. He knows something of the wiles of the devil, has the **definite** experiences we teach and can be trusted in the day of battle. We shall continue to write the leading editorial for each issue, and exercise the general oversight of LIVE COALS OF FIRE as well as of the work elsewhere.

For nearly nine years we have been almost incessantly engaged in active evangelistic work. We have preached the gospel in twenty-three states, territories and provinces to our own people, to negroes and to North American Indians. We have preached the preaching the Lord bade us to preach without fear or favor. We have never sought for easy places or lucrative calls, nor have we shunned to declare the whole counsel of God. We have never compromised the truth, nor toned down in our testimony, and we have this witness that during our evangelistic work we have pleased God. No man's blood is upon our hands. Hallelujah!

During our absence and retirement, we expect to spend our time in the large cities of the East, where we can have access to the large libraries of our country. A portion of our time, however, we hope to spend in the mountainous districts of Pennsylvania and New York.

Any of our friends who feel that the Lord would have them write to us during the summer, can do so by addressing their letters to Lincoln, Nebraska; but none of our correspondents need look for an answer before September. All matters relating to the fire-baptized work will be promptly attended to by Joseph H. King or others at the office of LIVE COALS OF FIRE.

We feel that this blessed opportunity which the Lord has so graciously opened up for us, will be the realization of the most delightful of the most delightful waking dreams of our youth. We have long desired the privilege of going apart, from the noise and clatter of the world, into the deep, quiet solitudes where the wicked throng never go, and there spend a whole summer, shut in with God. We need to get alone with God, where can without interruption read the Bible and a few other holy books, and meditate, and pray, and sink deeper and deeper into God. The inspirational mood seizes our soul oft as we contemplate the glorious outlook.

We expect to be occupied day and night during these months of golden opportunity; and we hope to be enabled to accomplish more during our retirement and seclusion than we could possibly accomplish in the active, public work. And we expect to come forth with a deeper and richer experience than we have known hitherto.

We have our work, both editorial and evangelistic, in capable and trustworthy hands, and we shall rest in the assurance that it will be carried forward with glorious success. With more than one hundred and twenty-five active fire- baptized workers in the field, men and women who "count not their lives dear unto themselves;" and with a fire-baptized paper every issue of which is a volley of devil-disturbing lyddite shells, and which is absolutely untrammeled by an ungodly official board, we feel consciously assured that nothing on earth, or under the earth, can stop the onward progress of this chariot of fire.

We earnestly entreat each and every reader of LIVE COALS OF FIRE to pray, earnestly and constantly, every morning and evening during the absence of the Editor, that God will not only endue him greater power than ever before, and make him a real, living flame of white fire, but also that He will give him wisdom from above, clearness of thought and of expression, and fully equip him to do the special work for which he feels called apart.

Notes

[1] Irwin here uses the term "Apostolic Church" as a synonym for "Pentecostal Church." Throughout *Live Coals of Fire* he presented his vision of an "Apostolic Church" as the antithesis of what he identified as the "Apostate Church," which is "honey-combed with secrecy worldliness, and is utterly destitute of spiritual power. It sides with the devil on nearly every question that arises. It opposes the Word of God on divine healing, and on the premillennial coming of Jesus; it rejects the glorious doctrine and experience of entire sanctification, and teaches people that it is impossible to live in this world without committing a sin. It professes to know It professes to know God, but in works it denies him, being abominable, and disobedient, and unto every good work reprobate." This is a "False Church" that "dreams like the world, walks arm in arm with ungodly men, votes with the saloon keepers, and belongs with the Christ-less lodge. It defends and justifies sin, and practices what it preaches. It ridicules holiness, eats hog, and grunts and complains about the weather and hard times" (*Live Coals of Fire* [November 3, 1899], 8).

[2] While the events in this paragraph may have occurred prior to Irwin's 1879 conversion, his lengthy 1880 testimony (see Document 1) makes no mention of drunkenness, cheating in business, or abusing his family. Benjamin and Anna Irwin's children Maud and Stewart were very young at the time of his conversion, having been born between 1876 and 1879 (*Nebraska State Census*, Johnson County, 1860-1885). Therefore, it seems likely that the five year period Irwin describes here took place in the early to mid-1880s.

[3] Here Irwin hearkens back to the First Great Awakening and Gilbert Tennent's 1740 sermon "The Dangers of an Unconverted Ministry."

[4] Irwin experienced a protracted illness followed by an instantaneous healing in the Marion, South Carolina, home of W. S. Foxworth during the first six weeks of 1897 (see Document 38). Irwin's periodic bouts with physical exhaustion and "nervous prostration" fit the characteristics of what Dr. George Miller Beard identified in 1869 as Neurasthenia (or "nervous exhaustion") This malady afflicted many educated Americans in late 19th century. See T. J. Jackson Lears, *No Place of Grace: Antimodernism and the Transformation of American Culture*, 1880–1920 (University of Chicago Press, 1981).

⁵ Here we see the origins of what the Pentecostal Holiness Church would later identify as their "Five Cardinal Doctrines": Salvation, Sanctification, Holy Spirit Baptism, Divine Healing, and the Imminent Return of Christ. Justification by faith is assumed here, but later in this sermon Irwin will articulate it as well when capsulizing his core doctrines. When Irwin began his association with *The Way of Faith and Neglected Themes* in late 1895, editor J. M. Pike was emphasizing all these doctrines except Fire Baptism. Sanctification, and especially divine healing and the pre-millennial return of Christ, were the "neglected themes." Over time Irwin made "the fire" an equal part of the formula. By the time Irwin began publishing *Live Coals of Fire* in 1899, he frequently substituted "the dynamite" for "the fire" as the fifth essential doctrine (as both contained the potential in make believers more radically effective witnesses for Christ). On at least one occasion Irwin referred to these core commitments collectively as "the full gospel" ("Danger of Compromise," *Live Coals of Fire* [October 20, 1899], 3).

⁶ While there is insufficient evidence to establish exactly when Irwin began to advocate an experience of dynamite beyond receiving the Fire, a date of late 1898 seems likely. *E.g.*, in a letter written in November 1899, Fire-Baptized evangelist E. D. Wells testified, "One year ago I sought for this experience and received it, and I have had it ever since. It put within my soul and life a power for which I had hungered" ("The Dynamite," *Live Coals of Fire* [December 1, 1899], 7).

⁷ Wade H. Phillips makes a valiant effort to distinguish the perceived nature and intended purpose of each of these later baptisms in his *Quest to Restore God's House: A Theological History of the Church of God (Cleveland, Tennessee): Volume 1, 1886–1923* (Cleveland, Tennessee: CPT Press, 2014), 125*ff*.

⁸ Irwin draws on W. B. Godbey's recent discussion of "dynamite," just as he drew on G. D. Watson's 1894 book *Live Coals of Fire* in his initial 1895 testimony about experiencing the Baptism of Fire. See W. B. Godbey, *Commentary on the New Testament. Volume V. Acts-Romans: Paul the Champion Theologian* (Cincinnati: M. W. Knapp, Revivalist Office, 1899), 11–13. Godbey renders Acts 1:8 as follows: "You shall receive dynamite of the Holy Ghost having come on you," and adds "if you will receive the Holy Ghost as a personal, indwelling Sanctifier and abiding Comforter, he will supply you with all the dynamite you need to blow all the sin out of you and to qualify you to blow up the Devil's kingdom wherever you go, and enjoy an everlasting victory in your heart and life" (12–13).

⁹ This was either Ezra and Lea Sheets or Harry and Anna Sollenberger, young couples who had left the River Brethren settlement in Moonlight, Kansas, to bring Irwin's message of fire and dynamite to their extended families in the Cumberland Valley of Pennsylvania. (Lea Sheets and Anna Sollenberger were sisters.) After much opposition from local authorities, the Sheets and Sollenbergers eventually opened a Fire-Baptized mission in a working-class Philadelphia neighborhood. See H. E. Sollenberger, "Peaceable Habitation" *Live Coals of Fire* (November 10, 1899), 7; "Official List of the Fire-Baptized Holiness Association of America," *Live Coals of Fire* (June 15, 1900), 8.

¹⁰ Protestantism traditionally identified the "unpardonable sin" as refusing Jesus Christ, primarily by rejecting the conviction of the Holy Spirit. Irwin extended this fatal sin to include resisting the Holy Spirit empowered endtime ministry of the Fire-Baptized saints.

¹¹ In late 1899 Irwin was planning to open a School of the Prophets for training Fire-Baptized evangelists and missionaries at this rural southeastern Tennessee crossroads due to a generous donation of land by a local holiness leader named Dollie Lawson. Several Fire-Baptized leaders relocated their families to the community in anticipation. Most dispersed following the exposure of Irwin's moral failure in 1900. For more on Beniah, see Harold D.

Hunter, "Beniah at the Apostolic Crossroads: Little Noticed Crosscurrents of B.H. Irwin, Charles Fox Parham, Frank Sandford, A.J. Tomlinson," *Cyberjournal for Pentecostal-Charismatic Research*, Vol. 1 (January 1997) <www.pctii.org/cyberg/>; Daniel Woods, "Daniel Awrey, the Fire-Baptized Movement, and the Origins of the Church of God: Toward a Chronology of Confluence and Influence," *Cyberjournal for Pentecostal-Charismatic Research*, Vol. 12 (January 2003) <www.pctii.org/cyberg/>; and, Phillips, *Quest to Restore God's House*, 119ff.

[12] William Wisdom Newberry, a Methodist minister, was a graduate of Roanoke College and Vanderbilt University. Later he became a Christian & Missionary Alliance pastor and the author of the provocatively titled book *Untangling Live Wires* (New York: Christian Alliance Publishing Company, 1914). Newberry wrote the volume "with the express purpose of helping earnest Christians who have become entangled with side issues" and "fanaticism" (*The Alliance Weekly* [January 2, 1915], 221). Though Newberry does not mention his brief commitment to Irwin's Baptism of Fire, his book can be read as a reflection on his time at Beniah. "Mrs. Lucius Hawkins" was Newberry's mother-in-law, the mother of Ethel May Anderson Newberry. She published widely under the name "Mrs. Mary Hawkins" and then later "Mrs. Mary M. Anderson" and "Mrs. Mabette Anderson." Her husband Lucious Hawkins was a regular contributor to *Christian Witness* and other holiness papers during the 1890s. She would also later join the C&MA. Her *The Latter Rain and Its Counterfeit* (Columbia, SC: J. M. Pike, 1907) was one of the earlier books critical of the Azusa Revival (see *John Sawin File Project: The Life and Times of A. B. Simpson* [Regina, Saskatchewan: Archibald Foundation Library, n.d.], 111–112). Mary Anderson Hawkins does not appear to have joined the Fire-Baptized Holiness Association, but W. W. Newberry appeared in the list of "Ordained Evangelists" in the *Live Coals of Fire* beginning with the January 26, 1900 issue. His name last appeared in the paper's penultimate issue (June 1, 1900). The Federal Census located the Newberrys and their two small children boarding in the home of one of the Fire-Baptized families in Beniah on June 6, 1900 (*Twelfth Census of the United States*, 1900, Bradley County, Tennessee). Newberry had left the Fire-Baptized Holiness Association by this time, and he would soon move his family from Beniah as well.

[13] Frank Porter was a Fire-Baptized Evangelist [hereafter FBOE]. The Church of God (Cleveland, Tennessee) views Porter and his frequent evangelistic partner William "Billy" Martin as vital to the foundation of their denomination. See Charles W. Conn, *Like a Mighty Army: A History of the Church of God*, Definitive Edition (Cleveland, Tennessee: Pathway Press, 1996), 22*ff*. FBOE Emma DeFriece lived in nearby Birchwood, Tennessee. FBOE Dollie Currie Lawson, who had donated the land for the building of the proposed School of the Prophets, had deep family roots in the holiness movement, and her late brother-in-law W. E. ("Holy") Henck founded the East Tennessee Holiness Association in 1888. See Woods, "Daniel Awrey, the Fire-Baptized Movement, and the Origins of the Church of God."

[14] The rapid railroad expansion of the 1890s accelerated both the movement of radical holiness evangelists and their hope for a rapid evangelization of the world before Christ's imminent return. See Daniel Woods, "'Spiritual Railroading': Trains as Metaphor and Reality in the Holiness and Pentecostal Movements, 1880s to 1920s," paper presented to the Joint Session of the Society for Pentecostal Studies and the Wesleyan Theological Society, Lexington, Kentucky, March 2003.

[15] FBOE John E. Dull of Albia, Iowa, was a former member of the Friends Church known in Fire-Baptized circles as the "Earth Quaker." Dull often ministered in the South and contributed regularly to *Live Coals of Fire*. Like many of Irwin's lieutenants, Dull was still in his 20s at this time (*Iowa State Marriage Records*, Monroe County, 1888).

[16] This church planting activity by William E. Fuller (FBOE Mountsville, South Carolina) is verified by Patrick L. Frazier, Jr. in *Introducing the Fire Baptized Holiness Church of God of the Americas: A Study Manual* (N.p., 1990), 14. By 1900 Fuller had set two Fire-Baptized churches in order there, Zion in the countryside and New Zion in town.

[17] FBOE R. B. Hayes (Royston, Georgia); FBOE Jonah A. Starr, Jr. (Royston, Georgia).

[18] Steven Olin (1797–1851) was a Methodist minister and educator whose questioning of slave ownership by Bishop James Andrew precipitated the 1844 schism of American Methodism into separate Northern and Southern churches. See Julia M. Olin, ed., *The Life and Letters of Steven Olin* (New York: Harper & Brothers, 1853). Irwin identified with Olin's radical commitment to revival, religious education, and racial outreach.

[19] Historian David Carleton confirms Irwin's observation about the religious "neglect" of the white migrants in many of these company-run communities. See his *Mill and Town in South Carolina, 1880–1920* (Baton Rouge and London: Louisiana State University Press, 1982), 103–106.

[20] FBOE and South Carolina Ruling Elder W. S. Foxworth (Marion, South Carolina); FBOE Mary G. Bryant (Marion, South Carolina); future FBOE W. W. Avant (Abbottsburg, North Carolina); FBOE W. B. T. Looney (Royston, Georgia).

[21] James Epps played an important role in establishing the holiness movement in lower South Carolina, both among whites and blacks. See Randall J. Stephens, *The Fire Spreads: Holiness and Pentecostalism in the American South* (Cambridge and London: Harvard University Press, 2008), 84, 310 n79. Epps was impressed that Fire-Baptized ministers had greater joy than other traveling preachers and showed far more interest his family's spiritual condition: "One part of their work was to talk to each member of the family often and seriously about their personal salvation. The result was that before they left, four of my children, not clear in their justification, were cleared up and sanctified, and two more little boys claimed pardon" ("James Epps' Letter," *Live Coals of Fire* [December 1, 1899], 5). After receiving the fire, Epps served as the Local Elder of the newly-organized Fire-Baptized Kingstree band ("John Dull's Letter," *Live Coals of Fire* [January 29, 1900], 3).

[22] For many years FBOE Isaac Gamble (Kingstree, South Carolina) was James Epps's closest associate in ministry. Just months after the end of the Civil War, Gamble's father arranged for his nine-year-old son to work on Epps's plantation. Epps led Gamble into salvation that year and into the experience of sanctification around 1882. See "Memoir of Isaac Gamble, Colored Evangelist, Chapter One," *Live Coals of Fire* (June 1, 1900), 5; and, "Memoir of Isaac Gamble, Colored Evangelist, Chapter Two," *Live Coals of Fire* (June 15, 1900), 4. Epps seems to have left the Fire-Baptized movement soon after 1900, but Gamble continued to serve as a Fire-Baptized evangelist for at least another five years ("Official List of the Fire-Baptized Holiness Church," *Live Coals* [January 11, 1905], 3). Yet the two continued to do noble work together in the community. *E.g.*, in 1907 Epps and Gamble collaborated to build a school in Kingstree that became the public high school for blacks in Williamsburg County until it was closed during integration in 1970. There are two accounts in local tradition. One has Epps donating the land, with Epps and Gamble jointly building a six room L-shaped schoolhouse. The other has Gamble donating the land and a house for the two-year-old school (which had started in 1905 in the Old Mt. Zion AME Church). See Cassandra Williams Rush, "Tomlinson Oh Tomlinson," *Kingstree News*, February 16, 2015, 1.

[23] FBOE Sarah Minerva Payne (Chadbourn, North Carolina) was a former school teacher who moved to Lincoln, Nebraska, in December 1899 to help Irwin edit his paper and to serve as the Local Elder of the Lincoln Fire-Baptized Band. See [B. H. Irwin,] "Sarah M. Payne," *Live Coals of Fire* (December 15, 1899), 4.

24 Everyone in this list was either currently a Fire-Baptized Ordained Evangelist or soon would be. "Sister Gaines" could have been either Estelle or Ina, Wesleyan sisters from Central, South Carolina. Estelle also served as Ruling Elder of South Carolina and as General Secretary and Treasurer of the Fire-Baptized Holiness Association. Both women left the organization in November 1899 for reasons that are not clear. Irwin did not appoint another General Secretary and Treasurer after Estelle Gaines's departure.

25 From Adam Clarke's 1831 *Commentary on the Bible*: "'Let the husband render unto the wife due benevolence.' Though our version is no translation of the original, yet few persons are at a loss for the meaning, and the context is sufficiently plain. Some have rendered the words, not unaptly, the matrimonial debt, or conjugal duty—that which a wife owes to her husband, and the husband to his wife; and which they must take care mutually to render, else alienation of affection will be the infallible consequence, and this in numberless instances has led to adulterous connections. In such cases the wife has to blame herself for the infidelity of her husband, and the husband for that of his wife. What miserable work has been made in the peace of families by a wife or a husband pretending to be wiser than the apostle, and too holy and spiritual to keep the commandments of God!"

26 Some of Irwin's contemporaries referred to "marital purity" as "marital continence." Others, like holiness evangelist and writer A. H. Kauffman, called it "social purity" (not to confused with a broader movement in the late 19th century aimed at ending prostitution). Kauffman delivers a particularly revealing testimony as one who practiced and then was set free from "social purity" in his *Fanaticism Explained: Symptoms, Cause and Cure* (Grand Rapids, Michigan: By the Author, 1904), 82–91. According to C. B. Jernigan, the teaching of marital purity "sprang up" in the holiness movement around 1897–1898 "to the hurt of many once happy homes. . . They taught that a man must live with his wife just as he did with his mother or sister." See his *Pioneers Days of the Holiness Movement in the Southwest* (Kansas, Missouri: Nazarene Publishing House, 1919), 154. The marital purity movement awaits its historian. For now, a good starting point is an unpublished 1987 paper by Nancy J. Hardesty, "Marital Purity: Early Holiness and Pentecostal Teachings on Sexuality" (photocopy in authors' possession).

27 At the Royston General Conference in 1899 Irwin led the Fire-Baptized Holiness Association in adopting a strong, and perhaps unique, statement defending the right to enjoy martial sex apart from efforts to procreate. After Irwin's fall, J. H. King and other remaining Fire-Baptized leaders retained the statement in their "General Rules": "The Lord says, 'Marriage is honorable in all, and the bed undefiled,' and the Fire-Baptized Holiness Church firmly holds that there are certain relations between husband and wife which are strictly private according to the Word of God, and into this sacred privacy no one has any right to inquire (Heb. 13:4; 1 Cor. 7:1–5)" (*Constitution and General Rules of the Fire-Baptized Holiness Church* [Royston, Georgia: Live Coals Press, 1905]). At the 1911 merger of the Fire-Baptized Holiness Church and Pentecostal Holiness Church at Falcon, North Carolina, Irwin's statement survived with only minor editorial changes: "The Lord says, 'Marriage is honorable in all, and the bed undefiled,' and The Pentecostal Holiness Church firmly holds that there are certain relations between husband and wife which are strictly private according to the Word of God, and into this sacred privacy no one has any right to inquire (Heb. 13: 4; 1 Cor. 7:1–5)" (*Constitution and General Rules of The Pentecostal Holiness Church, 1911)*. The Pentecostal Holiness Church kept Irwin's statement as one of its "General Rules" for more than a half century, not removing it from *The Pentecostal Holiness Church Manual* until 1969.

[28] A short notice in the *Fayetteville Observer* suggests that Fire-Baptized preachers—or at least some in North Carolina—condemned men for wearing facial hair: "Our old sanctification friends, Messrs, Brooks, Avant and Page, arrived this morning to join in the Fire-Baptized meeting. . . One of the peculiarities of this new sect is that they preach against the wearing of beards and or moustaches. The preachers are supplied with scissors, and when a convert desires it, will clip his whiskers for him. Thus it is a frequent sight to see young and old men being shorn in public of every remnant of hair on their faces" ("Re-Enforcements," *Fayetteville Observer* [April 20, 1899], 3).

[29] Brackets found in the original. Irwin's editorial remarks on Foxworth's article are noteworthy given his well-deserved reputation for extreme legalism in matters of fashion and food.

[30] The "long-haired deceiver" was probably Benjamin Purnell (1861–1927), who preached across rural America from 1895 to 1902 before founding the House of David commune in Benton Harbor, Michigan. Purnell presented himself as the "Seventh and Final Messenger" of the Visitation Movement begun in the late 18th century by Joanna Southcott, the "First Messenger." See Robert S. Fogarty, *Righteous Remnant: The House of David*, 2nd edition (Kent State University Press, 2014), especially Chapter 2.

[31] This is Irwin's second exposure of "marital purity" (see Document 43). By this time Irwin was almost certainly involved in extra-marital sexual activities, going "from the pulpit to wallow with harlots the rest of the night" (J. H. King, "On Unity," *Pentecostal Holiness Advocate* [August 3, 1922], 5).

Part Six

After the Fire

The Third Blessing Reimagined (1907)

Introduction

After a silence of more than six years, Irwin's voice returns in four documents written in 1906-1907 amid the Azusa Revival. By October 1906, while living in Portland, he embraced William Seymour's teaching that the Baptism of the Holy Spirit would be accompanied by the initial evidence of speaking in tongues, We see Irwin's pursuit of such an experience in Documents 47 and 48. The former is a private letter written in the midst of his quest; the latter a testimony composed for publication nearly a year after receiving his "personal Pentecost."[1] Documents 49 and 50 are reports sent to Seymour's *Apostolic Faith* in the early months of 1907. Though brief, they hint at the nature of Irwin's ministry after he had spoken in tongues. These four documents comprise his extant writings as a proponent of the Azusa Revival.

Document 47 – Letter from Benjamin Hardin Irwin to Thomas Ball Barrett, November 28, 1906.[2]

194—12th St.
Salem, Oregon

November 28, 1906

Dear Bro. Barrett:

    I have just read your letter of the 13th to the saints at Los Angeles and it thrilled me through and through. I received my personal Pentecost last Saturday night and such glory as God manifested in my soul no words can describe. But I did not speak in tongues until the next evening, and then but one sentence in Portuguese. Afterwards I spoke a single sentence in three other tongues. Now I am praying for a fuller and more copious manifestation of the languages. Your letter encouraged me greatly. Will you pray for me that I may speak fluently and preach in other tongues? While I was at the altar gathering my Pentecost the Lord gave me a wonderful vision of the glory of God and gave me a rapid but vivid survey of the work in many countries.[3] He showed me Iceland, Norway, and Sweden—I could see the multitudes of souls weeping their way to Jesus in those countries; He showed me West Africa on the Gold Coast and the Congo country where hundreds of thousands of souls were crying for this glorious gospel I could see large cities in West Africa where thousands of black faces were turned toward God eagerly drinking in the blessed truth; then he took me to Brazil on South America, all I could see multitudes of souls weeping their way to the cross then the West Coast of South America came before me I should know [the faces?] of the people I saw in Brazil and in Sweden and Iceland. The he showed me the devil worship [ ] in South India and the poor souls in China accepting the full gospel. In Japan I saw three large cities all of which I'm sure I would recognize should I ever see them. Oh it was wonderful! Amazing! Pray for me and write me if you can. Pray for the work here. Great opposition here.

In His name,
B. H. Irwin

Document 48 – "My Pentecostal Baptism—A Christmas Gift," *Triumphs of Faith* **(December 1907), 114-117.**

"Thou hast men to ride over his heads;
We went through fire and through water;
But thou broughtest us out into a wealthy place."
Ps. LXVI:12

I received my personal Pentecost on Christmas eve, 1906. I had been seeking for over two months. About the middle of October, just after the death of our little Lois, I began in real earnestness to seek the Lord. Every theological difficulty had been settled, completely and forever, in my mind, before I began to seek at all. I started out with the settled determination to continue seeking with all my heart until I should realize in my own soul the fullness of Acts ii:4: *"And they were all filled with the Holy Ghost and began to speak with other tongues as the Spirit gave them utterance."* My conception of the Pentecostal baptism not only implied the experience of justification and entire sanctification as essential prerequisites, but the baptism itself includes the fullness of the Spirit AND speaking in tongues. The speaking in tongues is not simply a sign or evidence of the baptism, but a part of the divine baptism itself. I must get justified and sanctified before I could obtain the baptism itself. I must get justified and sanctified before I could obtain the baptism of the Holy Ghost. I repented in sackcloth and ashes, confessed backslidings, and made the restitution required of me in the Word of God. I found of peace with God through Jesus Christ, my Lord.

Then I asked God to search my heart to the bottom, and to reveal to me the very ground thereof. He did so, and the deep inner heart revealing which He vouchsafed to me amazed me. It was about two o'clock in the morning, and it continued till nearly five o'clock. I was alone with God. Everything about me was silent, but God was working in the depths of my soul. I was made to feel and know that every hidden trait and characteristic of my innermost nature had been searched out. He showed me every streak of carnality in my inner heart life, and I confessed it all out to God, to my wife, and publicly in the meetings. He discovered to me what the experience of entire sanctification must be. It meant perfect sincerity and truth in the inward parts, and perfect whiteness and purity in the deepest regions of the soul, such as will stand the scrutiny of the searching eye of God.

This was in the Pentecostal Mission in Salem, Oregon. The next day I went out to our lonely little home in the fir woods by the Hanchinkee and spent two nights and one day alone with God. Mrs. Irwin and Vidalin remained in the mission. No one came to see me. It was raining, and the weather was dark and dismal. All day I was busy packing books and burning old manuscripts.[4] It was a time of unspeakable interior crucifixion with me. No one but God and myself will ever know that depth of that crucifixion. I was led, step by step, through Romans v:3-5. My Bibles were all locked up, and I had nothing but the Epistles of Paul in Coneybeare's translation.[5] I was greatly blessed in reading the fourth chapter of Romans and the third chapter of Colossians. I consciously felt my spirit being "strengthened with the might of faith," and praises to God involuntarily flowed forth from my heart and lips. Yet I was suffering deeply in the depths of my soul. By the grace of God, I was enabled to rejoice in these and to endure steadfastly, and this gave me the "proof of soundness." I had within me this divine proof that my faith, and love, and hope, and inward experience were sound. I had the witness of the blessed Holy Spirit that I was sanctified wholly. I was crucified "with Christ," and from that moment to this it has been "no longer I, but Christ that liveth in me."

I began at once to "tarry" for the "enduement of power from on high." I was hungry for "the fullness of the blessing of Christ." I went to the altar every time an invitation was given. The devil fought me every inch of the way, and the nearer I came to the blessing, the harder he fought me. Day and night, in the meetings and out of the meetings, for several weeks, I continued to seek and to "wait for the promise of the Father." I tried to fix my mind, and heart, and eyes on "Jesus only." It was here that the devil gave me the hardest fight. He tried to get me to look at the thieves on either side, to see the fear-stricken disciples, the mother of Jesus, the howling, persecuting mob, and even the bare rock of Calvary! But somehow I was enabled to fasten my eyes and keep them fastened on the Crucified One. I looked intently into that suffering face. I could see the nail prints in his hands and feet, and the crown of thorns, and precious blood issuing forth from the five bleeding wounds. I resolved not to read anything but the Bible, not to go down town, and not to talk to any one opposed to the speaking in tongues.

Just before the meeting opened, I went alone into the dining room. After reading a few verses in John, I turned down the light and knelt by a chair near the door. The spirit of prayer came on me, and the power of God. I fell over on the floor and began to pray more earnestly. I could pray for nothing but the baptism of the Holy Ghost. I resolved to remain there until I should find it. I was definitely led to pray to the Father in Jesus' name, and to plead the blood and the promise of Jesus: "Behold, I send the promise of My Father upon you." I felt my faith increasing. Intuitively I knew that the blessing was near. Again and again I prayed the Father not allow me to be deceived, not to let me speak from myself, and not to permit Satan or any demon from the pit to speak through me.

A supernatural tranquility and unearthly sweetness, a divine assurance that the Holy Ghost, the promised Comforter, had come into my soul *to abide forever*, was then and there vouchsafed to me. I knew that I was filled with the Holy Spirit. Then it was that soul "waited in silence for God only." (Ps. lxii:1.) I waited for God, the Holy Spirit, to speak through me. Then I felt my lips and tongue and lower jaw being used as they had never been used before. My vocal organs were in the hands and under the control of another, and that Other was the Divine Paraclete within me. He was beginning to speak through me in other tongues. He caused me to use words which I have never heard or conceived of before. I was enabled to speak with greater fluency than I had spoken my native English. I tried to remember or to retain some of the words, but could not, and I cannot to this day recall a single word.

I arose about midnight and went into the auditorium, where Mrs. Irwin, Sister Crawford, and one or two others still lingered, and testified to the baptism of the Holy Ghost and fire. But I did not speak in tongues to them. I could not do it of myself. I have never put forth the least effort to speak in unknown tongues. I can speak only "as the Spirit gives me the utterance."

Since that I have been used of God in speaking many times in Chinese, Hindoostani, Beengali, Arabic, and other languages unknown to me.

There are many wonderful things connected with this glorious baptism which the Lord will not permit me to tell out; not yet at least. It is enough for me to say that it is the very thing my poor, crushed heart had been crying out for during all these weary, wasted years. It humbles me. It keeps me. It satisfies me. It enables me to faithfully witness everywhere and at all times to the mighty saving power of the Christ of Sinai, Calvary and Pentecost.

Document 49 – [Untitled Correspondence,] *Apostolic Faith* **(February-March 1907), 1.**

Sister Rees from Oakland visited Azusa Mission recently. She brought a report from the saints in Oakland that a leader was needed there in the work, one called and prepared of the Lord. We prayed for God to call someone. Bro. Irwin received the call and went with his wife. His report comes just as the paper is going to press: Oakland, Cal., March 21.—"God is undertaking for us here. Two received their Pentecost last night with Bible evidence. Others are seeking pardon, sanctification, the promise of the Father."—B. H. Irwin.

Document 50 – "Pentecost in San Francisco," *Apostolic Faith* **(April 1907), 4.**

In San Francisco, there have been some striking cases both of conversion and sanctification; and some remarkably clear cases of the divine baptism. Five were converted one night. On another night a Hawaiian brother was gloriously converted, and the next night a Filipino lady was beautifully saved. She said: "Me no speak English much, but me know God—Jesus he got my heart." The Hawaiian could not speak for some minutes after he arose to his feet, the power of God was upon him to such an extent.

In another service a Catholic was clearly saved. He went to his seat, and turning to a companion, exhorted him to come to God and get saved, testifying definitely that God had saved him from his sins.

One Baptist preacher came to the meeting, confessed his backslidings, and cried mightily to God for forgiveness. He gave up his tobacco, and seemed wonderfully happy in the Lord.

One poor crippled German lady was brought to the meetings by kind friends, and received the baptism of the Holy Ghost and fire in a remarkable way.

Another sister about forty years of age, and who had never made a profession of religion, came to the meetings, and evidently was much interested. On Thursday afternoon, she came to the meeting and was clearly converted. The power of God shook her so mightily that an elderly lady friend, who had accompanied her to the meetings, was greatly agitated and excited about it; she declared the sister was having a fit, and said something ought to be done to relieve her. When told that it was the power of God, and that the sister would come out all right, she looked incredulous, and flew around in great excitement. Evidently she had not seen it on this wise before. The sister did not return to the meetings until Saturday night. In the meantime she had been sanctified wholly, without the help of preachers or any one of the saints. God had sanctified. She came Saturday night for the baptism of the Holy Ghost. The writer preached that night on the "Ten Virgins." The sister was again shaken by the mighty power of God. Her husband was sitting by her side, and was evidently amazed; yet he recognized it as the power of God, though not saved himself, he did not resist the power of God, nor try to hinder his wife. When his wife went to the altar, still shaking under the mighty power of God, he sat quietly in his seat, deeply moved by what was going on. She prayed with awful earnestness for the baptism of the Holy Ghost and fire. We instructed her not to pray for the "tongues," but for the baptism of the Holy Ghost and fire. God baptized her with the Holy Ghost and fire, and she "began to speak in other tongues as the Spirit gave her utterance." She spoke in three languages very distinctly. I have not seen a clearer case. When she arose to her feet her husband came up to where she was, evidently deeply moved. She grasped his hand and began to speak (pray) in an unknown tongue. It was wonderful. Everyone present was convinced that it was the work of the living God. All opposition was confounded and put to silence. It was the old-time Pentecostal power.

Brother Seymour came in unexpectedly and preached one blessed sermon for us. All were greatly pleased with the simplicity and power of his discourse. It was all inspiration to me to see his beaming face and to hear him open up the scriptures to our hungry hearts.—B.H. Irwin.

Voices from the 1920s

Introduction

Irwin's later years are no better documented than his early years, although a few primary sources from the 1920s have surfaced recently. While the evidence is scant, in the selections that follow we can faintly see Irwin returning to the Predestinarian Baptist faith of his upbringing—first in Georgia and then in Texas—and his long-abandoned second wife Mary struggling to raise their troubled and fatherless sons in Oregon. Irwin's last statement in this anthology, one of his Two-Seed-in-the-Spirit poems composed around 1925, shows a confrontational attitude toward Primitive Baptists reminiscent of his attacks on Methodist opponents of the Holiness Revival in the 1890s and his identification of those who rejected his teaching on Fire Baptism later in the decade as "tame holiness devils." While Irwin is once more staking out an extremist position within the religious movement he has joined, an impoverished Mary Jordan Irwin is writing desperate letters to the Superintendent of the Oregon State Training School for Boys in the hope that at least one of her sons can be saved from a life of crime and alienation from God. Perhaps the jarring juxtaposition of these two voices provides a fitting conclusion to a consideration of the many lives and works of B. H. Irwin.

Document 51 – Ben Hardin Irwin, "The Two-Seed Doctrine."[6]

I searched the scriptures with an honest mind
And prayed to God that I the truth might find
To guide my thoughts, unfold to me His word,
Prepare me for the conflict, under-gird
My soul with humble courage to proclaim
The hated truth, without fear or shame
And now I feel assured that He has shown
To me the truth directly from the throne.

In every age the serpent and his seed,
A blasphemous and disbelieving breed,
Against the truth of God have always stood,
In opposition to what'ever is good,
The saving truth they heartily despise,
And love instead their father's damning lies.
To darken counsel, and the truth becloud,
Lean on tradition, and profess aloud
To be God's children, and to love his ways,

With hearts estranged, their lips would speak His praise.

He who was born in lowly Bethlehem
For them died not, nor came to ransom them,
He came to ransom and redeem His own,
The woman's seed, the elect of God alone.
There are two seeds; the one from Satan came;
The other own in truth the Savior's name
The one beloved of God, a chosen race,
Born to be saved by God's abounding Grace.
The other filled with bitter enmity,
Doomed to be damned to all eternity.

But this true doctrine is a sore offence The
shallow Primitives, devoid of sense, Full of
all prejudice, traditionalized, asleep The
cannot see truth that lieth deep;
And when confounded by the holy word,
Turn to tradition, which is much preferred
By all whose false historic faith is built
On man's opinions; and herein lies their guilt.

Some say 'tis true, but still it is to[o] deep
To[o] strong and solid for the tender sheep
'tis too mysterious and too profound—
We cannot bear to hear the hateful sound!
Feed them on milk, and food designed for lambs
Skimmed milk is good enough for ewes and rams
A little sweetened water now and then,
Will soothe the aged women and men;
Throw in a spoonful of arminianism,
Build up the cause, and save the church from schism!

Document 52 – Excerpts from Mary Jordan Irwin's letters to L. M. Gilbert, Superintendent of the Oregon State Training School, 1923-1925. Reproduced by Harriette Hammond in "Bob Irwin's Secret Life," *New York Daily Mirror* (April 17, 1937), 6; "Bob Irwin's Secret Life, Chapter IV," *New York Daily Mirror* (April 20, 1937), 6; and, "Bob Irwin's Secret Life, Chapter VI," *New York Daily Mirror* (April 22, 1937), 14. All elisions appear in these published versions of the letters.

September 5, 1923

Dear Sir: I notice that Fenelon has had a letter from Pember. I do not think it wise for these boys to correspond. . . Fenelon is my child and has some good qualities. But his is brimful of poison . . . just the thing that would upset and destroy all the things that you people have done for Pember. Pember is in a good state of mind now. But just a little association with Fenelon will ruin him forever. I wish that you would never let Pember see the letters. Pember will just about run away after 15 minutes if Fenelon should come up to see Pember. I do not wish either boy to know this address. Fenelon has written at times for very pernicious literature. It goes with my mail to this address (360 E. Davis St., Portland) and I can save him from dipping into things that will destroy him. Fenelon is not a Christian, but he is an atheist and well-versed in that literature. You might require Fenelon when he comes to go back to Portland and get permission from Judge Kanzler and communicate with Judge Kanzler and tell him not to grant it.

April 4, 1924

[Dear Mr. Gilbert,]
I have told Pember to ask if you objected to Fenelon writing to Pember. Please tell him for me that you do not object. Fenelon is quite changed for the better on some lines—but not all—Resp'f'ly, Mrs. Mary L. Irwin [170 N. E. 3rd St, Portland]

PS: Please never tell Pember of my thoughts in the past. I am sure you would not.—Mrs. M. L. I.

Junes 22, 1925

Mr. Gilbert, Dear Sir: I am writing to you in the greatest haste. Yet I have some matter[s] to communicate that are of the utmost importance to Pember. I would very much like to have Pember home for his birthday. But I will be out on camp and things at home are in such a condition that I don't think I can return home after camp. Fenelon is in a terrible mental state. He is just ready to kill those of his home who do not come under his will. I don't think I can stay home myself. I believe Mr. Keyser and all the officers there ought to know it and not encourage Pember in any way to come home. But encourage him to go on with his course. I am moving out to the Camp Ground. I do not think it wise to tell Pember the facts about Fenelon. But by tact and wisdom to hold him there. Maybe there will be a turn in things that he can come home. If you communicate with me at all, please send it to 5505 63rd Ave., S.E. That is out in Woodstock, 2 blocks from the Camp Ground. I believe you will do all you can to hold Pember and encourage him and keep his mind pleasantly employed. Fenelon says he is coming down to see Pember the 1st pay day. He will likely come on the first or sometime after. If you could have Pember out of the way on Sunday awhile, it might save endless trouble. This is all I know at present. Will keep you posted as to the conditions here as far as possible. Be sure and talk this over with all officers now, because I believe if everyone encourages him to stay that he will be contented to stay. I thank you for all your interest in Pember. Very sincerely, Mrs. Mary L. Irwin. Please see that Pember's next letter is addressed to my new address.

Notes

[1] A note on the timing of Irwin's Spirit Baptism: In Document 47, a private letter to Thomas Ball Barrett dated November 28, 1906, Irwin claimed to have sought and received his "personal Pentecost" just before Thanksgiving, as evidenced by speaking "one sentence in Portuguese" and "a single sentence in three other tongues." Irwin solicited Barrett's prayers "for a fuller and more copious manifestation of the languages... that I may speak fluently and preach in other tongues." This account appears at first glance to contradict Irwin's fuller testimony to Spirit Baptism in Document 48, which he composed for publication in late 1907. Irwin opened this more considered account with the words, "I received my personal Pentecost on Christmas eve, 1906." He did not mention here the halting sentences he had spoken in November, but instead emphasized his need for greater doctrinal clarity and a fuller surrender to God before he was finally "enabled to speak [in other languages] with greater fluency than I had spoken my native English." Rather than conflicting, Documents 47 and 48 taken together underscore the excitement mingled with uncertainty as Irwin reimagined and then experienced the promised "Third Blessing" he had touted for over a decade.

[2] David Bundy discovered this private letter in T. B. Barrett's papers housed at the University of Oslo in Norway and published it as part of "Spiritual Advice to a Seeker: Letters to T. B. Barrett from Azusa Street, 1906," *Pneuma: The Journal for the Study of Pentecostal Studies* (Fall 1992): 159–170. Bracketed insertions by David Bundy indicate unclear portions of the manuscript. Barrett, who would soon become known as the "Father of Pentecostalism in Europe," had written several letters to the leaders of the Azusa Revival in Los Angeles from New York City, where a lack of funds kept him from heading west. In one letter Barrett described a definite Spirit Baptism on October 7th and said that he was now waiting on the full evidence of tongues speech. It appears that someone in Los Angeles forwarded a copy of Barrett's letter to Irwin in Oregon. Perhaps at the suggestion of an Azusa leader, Irwin then wrote to Barrett and shared his own experience seeking the Baptism of the Holy Spirit. Although Barrett experienced the outbreak of evidentiary tongues he had been seeking on November 15, nearly two weeks before Irwin wrote, he chose to keep the letter for the rest of his life. See David Bundy, "Thomas Ball Barrett: From Methodist to Pentecostal," *EPTA Bulletin: Journal of the European Pentecostal Theological Association* (1984): 19–49.

[3] Irwin's vision of a rapid worldwide expansion of Christianity flowing from the Azusa Revival matches up remarkably well with subsequent history. And it probably resonated with Barrett at the time. In his memoir, Barrett reflected on realizing as he sought the Baptism of the Holy Spirit that "God could send me, now, wherever He liked, to the smallest congregation in the country or to the largest! To China, Africa, Iceland, anywhere." See his *When the Fire Fell and Outline of My Life* [Oslo, Norway: T. B. Barrett, 1927], 110–111.

[4] What a fuller book this might have been had Irwin not thrown his manuscripts into the fire.

[5] *The Life and Epistles of Paul* by W. J. Conybeare and J. S. Howson was first published in the United States by Charles Scribner in 1854. During the 1890s at least three American publishers reissued the two-volume set.

[6] The authors wish to thank historian John Gordon Crowley for providing a copy of this unpublished typescript.

Index

Abortion, 167
Africa, 68, 194
African Methodist Church, 205, 211
Anderson Intelligencer, 47
Anderson, South Carolina, 47
Anti-Ordinance, 55
Apostolic Faith, 86
Arthur, William, 25
Awrey, Daniel, 47, 50, 54, 65
Azusa Street Revival, 84

Baldwin, James, 103
Baptism of Fire, 213-214
Baptism of the Holy Ghost, 174
Barratt, Thomas Ball, 85, 233-234
Bathhurst, Jesse, 21, 50, 84
Beniah, Tennessee, 65-71, 193
Blood and Fire Songs, 48
Brainerd, David, 172
Brethren in Christ, 42
Bricktown, Georgia, 92

Campbell, Joseph, 4
Cane Ridge, 69
Carey, Thurmond, 47, 51
Carkuff, C. P., 26, 132, 171
Carradine, Beverly, 43, 134
Cartwright, Peter, 193
Cashwell, Gaston B., 101
Christian Witness, 18, 25, 26, 36, 48, 79, 123, 125, 129, 133
Church of God, 69, 100, 101
Cleveland, Tennessee, 65, 69
Coon Rapids, Iowa, 143-145
Craft, A. C., 44, 164
Crawford, Florence, 87
Crumpler, Abner B., 56
Cuba, 68

Culbreth, Julius A., 56
Curry, W. T., 42

Dayton, Donald, 24
De Friece, Emma, 67, 194
Dietary Rules, 50
Dieter, Melvin, 4
Divine Healing, 23, 41, 42
Doctrine of Devils, 217-221
Donatism, 98
Douglas, Annie, 39, 50, 54
Dowie, Alexander, 49
Dull, John E., 56, 68, 196, 223
Dynamite, 53, 59, 67, 71, 187-192

Eisenhower, A. L., 42
Epps, James, 199-200
Eradication, 49
Evangelical Visitor, 42

Falcon Camp meeting, 56, 99
Fire Baptized Holiness Association, 48
Fire Baptized Holiness Association Constitution, 48, 165-166
Fire Baptized Holiness Association of Southern Iowa, 43, 164
Fire Baptized Holiness Doctrinal Statement, 49
Fletcher, John, 16
Fluke, Oliver, 21, 28, 134, 145
Fourth and Fifth Blessings, 59-61
Foxworth, W. S., 47, 199-201, 21
Fuller, William E., 47, 50, 54, 81, 100, 196, 200

Gaines, Estelle, 50
Gamble, Isaac, 200
Gedeon, Mary, 98

George, A. L., 50
Godbey, W. B., 55, 56, 134
Guyon, Madame, 25, 172

Hall, A. W., 36
Haney, M. L., 36
Harris, Brother and Sister, 197
Hayes, Richard B., 40, 47, 55, 164-165, 199
Hawkins, Mrs. Lucius, 193
Healing, 180-186
Henke, F. W., 65
Henson, G. B., 44, 47
Hepzibah Faith Mission, 36
Hills, A. M., 60
Hodges, A. R., 44, 47, 50
Holiness Movement Church, 31
Holy Dance, 40, 195
Hoover, Willis C., 102
Horner, Ralph Cecil, 31
Hunter, Harold, 100

Irwin, Benjamin Hardin
  Early Life, 5
  Primitive Baptists, 7, 8, 9
  Conversion, 9, 115-122
  Ordination, 10
  Sanctified, 105, 16
  Fire Baptism Experience, 25, 26, 131-134
  Fire Baptized Theology, 26, 27, 28
  Rejection, 36, 37
  Violence Against, 37, 38
  General Overseer, 48
  Missionary Vision, 68, 69
  Interracial Services, 70
  In Canada, 71
  Irwin Falls, 77-82
  Irwin Speaks in Tongues, 84, 85, 86
  Rejects Dynamite, Lyddite, Oxidite, 86
  Irwin Falls Again, 87
  As a Two-Seed-in-the-Spirit-Predestenarian Baptist, 91, 92
  ordained, 92
  Death in Palestine, Texas, 93
  Gifted Man, 93
  Character Flaws, 97, 98
  Infidel, 118
  Isaac (uncle), 121
  Holiness Preacher, 123-129
  Pentecostal Baptism, 233-236
  Tracts, 157
  Theology 201-204
Irwin, Anna, 79
Irwin, Fenlon [Robert], 80, 82, 98, 240
Irwin, Vidalin, 82
Irwin, Pember, 82, 240
Irwin, Mary Louise Jordan, 83, 84, 87, 239-240
Irwin, Victor, 83
Irwin, Stewart Toombs, 68
Indian Territory, 139-143
Intoxicants, 49

Jernigan, C. B., 42
Jordan, Mary Louise, 82, 83
Judson, Adoniram, 172

Kelly, Edward, 50, 67
Kendrick, Klaud, 4
Kennedy, W. H., 24
Keswick Movement, 23
King, Joseph H., 4, 44, 47, 48, 53, 54, 71, 72, 78, 164-166, 225
King, Joseph H., Elected General Overseer, 81-82
Knapp, Martin Wells, 30
Knight, Henry H., 4

Lawson, Dolly Curry, 67, 194
Legalism, 221
Lemon, C. L., 133
Live Coals of Fire – 50, 57, 58, 59, 74, 96, 167-180, 224-226
Livingstone, Henry, 172
Lowcock, Belle, 50
Lyddite, 53, 59, 60, 71
Lydie, Hattie, 50

McElroy, Samuel L., 40, 44, 50, 164

McNeil, Alice, 50
Mad Sculptor, 98
Manila, 68
Manley, I. A., 164
Marital Purity, 50, 72, 73, 224
Martin, William, 67, 194
Methodist Episcopal Church, 19-20
Methodist Pentecostal Church of Chile, 102
Morrison, H. C., 79
Murrill, E. M., 55

Neosho Valley, 43, 162-164
Newberry, W. W., 55

Oath Bound Societies, 49
Ogle, I. W., 47, 50
Olin, Stephen, 197
Ornamentation, 50
Oxidite, 53
Ozman, Agnes, 84

Packard, J. F., 29
Page, Samuel D., 47, 55, 56
Palestine, Texas, 93
Parham, Charles Fox, 84
Payne, Sarah M., 200
Populism, 55
Pennington Chapel Methodist Church, 165
Pentecostal Herald, 79
Pentecostal Holiness Church, 56, 99, 101
The Pentecostal Church, 167-175
Pentecostal Language, 24
Pentecostalism Worldwide, 103
Pember, G. H., 84
Phillips, Wade, 100
Piedmont, South Carolina Revival, 40
Pike, J. M., 29, 30, 150
Porter, Robert, 67, 194
Pulliam, N. G., 44, 56, 223
Putnam, Thomas, 164
Pyrophobia, 39, 40, 151-156

Quakers, 56

Ramabai, Pandita, 102
Randall, Herbert Edward, 31
Repentance, 175-180
Ritter, Mattie, 50
River Brethren, 17, 42
Roberts, Oral, 103
Robinson, Albert E., 77
Royston, Georgia, 56, 70

Sage, C. P., 21, 28, 146
Sanctification, 174, 210
San Francisco, 236-238
Schearer School House Revival, 66
School of the Prophets, 67, 68
Second Coming, 23
Seymour, William Joseph, 84, 86, 237
Smith, Sarah H., 65, 66
Speaking in Tongues, 66, 174
Steele, Daniel, 134
Steinbeck, John, 102
Stephens, Randall, 5
Stevens, C. T., 48, 50
Stevenson, W. E., 21, 28, 143, 223
Stombaugh, Olive, 50
Synan, Vinson, 100

Tatham Family, 102, 103
Taylor, George Floyd, 4, 35, 60
Third Blessing, 31, 223
Third Blessing Heresy 39
Tipton, Joe, 67
Tobacco, 49
Tomlinson, A. J., 49
Triumphs of Faith, 234-236
Two Seed Doctrine, 238-239
Two-Seed-in-the-Spirit-Predestinarian-Baptist Church, 91, 92, 93

Upham Thomas, 25

Vineland Camp meeting, 30
Violence, 145

Watson, George D., 25, 157, 171
Way of Faith, 29, 36, 131, 136, 140, 141

Werhan, .Mrs. A L., 142
Wesleyan Methodist Church, 20, 29,
    37, 70, 158-159
White, Alma, 30
Willis, Andrew K., 40, 158, 164
Willis Chapel, 61

Wine, John H., 47
Wolford, J. F., 47
Women in Ministry, 49
Woods, Dan, 100

Young, Benjamin, 28, 29

www.ingramcontent.com/pod-product-compliance
Lightning Source LLC
Chambersburg PA
CBHW061438300426
44114CB00014B/1739